THE PACIFIC WAR

The Pacific War
Clash of Empires in World War II

Douglas Ford

continuum

Continuum International Publishing Group
The Tower Building   80 Maiden Lane
11 York Road   Suite 704
London SE1 7NX   New York, NY 10038

ISBN: HB: 978-1-8472-5237-1

Typeset by Fakenham Prepress Solutions, Fakenham, Norfolk NR21 8NN
Printed in the U.S.A.

Book Club Edition

Contents

List of Maps

Abbreviations

ATIS	Allied Interpretation and Interrogation Service
CBI	China–Burma–India theater of operations
CCS	Allied Combined Chiefs of Staff
CINCPAC	Commander-in-Chief, US Pacific Fleet
COS	British Chiefs of Staff
CVL	light aircraft carrier
IGHQ	Imperial General Headquarters
IJA	Imperial Japanese Army
IJN	Imperial Japanese Navy
JCS	US Joint Chiefs of Staff
MID	Military Intelligence Division
ONI	Office of Naval Intelligence
RAF	Royal Air Force
SCAP	Supreme Commander, Allied Powers
SEAC	Southeast Asia Command
SWPA	Southwest Pacific Area
USAAF	United States Army Air Forces
USMC	United States Marine Corps
USSBS	United States Strategic Bombing Survey

Introduction

More than 60 years have passed since the Pacific war ended with Japan surrendering to the US and the Allied nations, and the conduct of the conflict continues to attract attention from a wide audience. Enthusiasts have had access to an enormous range of books, as well as award-winning television documentary programs, that chronicle the major battles. Among professional scholars and casual readers alike, the war conjures some familiar images. One thinks of the Japanese firing the first shots with their surprise attack against Pearl Harbor on 7 December 1941, and setting off gargantuan fires onboard a number of US battleships, including the *Arizona*. Others picture the Japanese and US navies confronting each other with their vast fleets of aircraft carriers in the waters of the Pacific Ocean, and their warplanes dueling in the skies above distant locations such as Midway, Guadalcanal and Saipan. The fighting on the land has also given rise to memorable moments, with the Pulitzer-winning photograph of US marines hoisting their stars-and-stripes banner on the summit of Mt. Suribachi at Iwojima symbolizing the gallantry which troops displayed when fighting their opponents. Finally, the dropping of the atomic bombs in August 1945 (and the iconic image of the mushroom cloud over Hiroshima and Nagasaki) has never failed to raise controversy about the moral justification for using such weapons of mass destruction.

The sustained interest is also due to the distinct features that characterized the conflict. First, the Pacific campaigns saw a number of naval battles that were on an epic scale, owing to the enormity of the ocean. Projecting one's military strength across extended distances, and against enemies with substantial forces, also required navies to invent new weapons and ways of using them. For this reason, both the Japanese and US fleets achieved ground-breaking advances in modern technologies, including the aircraft carrier, maritime aviation and the submarine. The ground battles in the islands of the Pacific Ocean and in Southeast Asia also saw the combatants dealing with challenging conditions, including the mountainous and jungle-covered terrain, coupled with an uncomfortable tropical climate. Troops often found their stamina and endurance put to a formidable test. In the naval, air and land campaigns alike, the Allies prevailed not only because they had the capacity to deploy more weapons than the Japanese. The Western armed forces were also more successful at discovering the correct methods to overcome their opponents, whereas the Imperial forces were less well-prepared.

Secondly, the Pacific war was characterized by a level of brutality not seen in many other conflicts. The indignation which swept the American public in the wake of Pearl Harbor enabled the Roosevelt administration to secure Congressional approval to wage a total war against Japan, whereby hostilities were not to be ceased until the enemy's capacity to resist was completely destroyed. As the conflict progressed, most of the nations within the Allied coalition, including Great Britain and Nationalist China, agreed to conduct the war with a view to securing Japan's unconditional surrender. Likewise, for the Japanese, the war was perceived as a quest to protect Asia from exploitation by the Western powers. Once the tide of the war turned against Japan, the aim was to defend the home islands from foreign conquest. Until the closing stages, the leadership in Tokyo refused to surrender the nation's sovereignty. The determination to continue fighting to the finish, which prevailed on both the Allied and Japanese sides, negated any prospect of a negotiated peace. Indeed, when the Pacific war was terminated, the US and its coalition partners carried out a prolonged occupation of Japan's home territory, to ensure that the nation could never again develop the capacity to wage another war of aggression. Only a few notable armed conflicts throughout the course of human civilization have ended with the victors overhauling the political, social and economic fabric of the vanquished. In order to understand the reasons why the Japanese were compelled to accept such extreme terms, one needs to examine not only the nature of the Pacific war itself but also the underlying tensions which initially fuelled the confrontation.

This work begins by describing the causes and consequences of Japan's emergence as a Great Power. It goes on to explain the factors which propelled Japanese expansion on the Asian continent during the 1930s, as well as the Western Powers' response to the growing crisis, which culminated with the outbreak of war in December 1941. The book will thereafter explore the reasons for Japan's rapid conquest of Southeast Asia and the western Pacific in early 1942, and scrutinize some of the key battles which caused the tide of the war to shift in the Allies' favor by the end of that year, including Midway and Guadalcanal. Attention will then be focused on the military, political, economic and diplomatic features which shaped the conflict between 1943–45, when the armed forces of America and its allies gradually pushed the Japanese out of territory that they had conquered, and eventually established bases within striking range of Japan's homeland. The concluding chapters discuss the reasons why the Pacific war ended with Japan's unconditional surrender, and attempt to resolve the various debates concerning the causes and consequences of the dropping of the atomic bombs on Hiroshima and Nagasaki in August 1945.

While a large amount of literature has been written on the Pacific war, most of it has tended to focus on the US participation alone. The most prominent works by John Costello and Ronald Spector have narrated the course of the conflict, as well as many of the key battles, in considerable detail.[1] However, they have not provided a balanced account of the role played by the other participants, namely Great Britain and Australia. A number of scholars, including Paul Dull and Saburo Hayashi, have documented the Imperial Japanese forces' operations.[2] This book aims to integrate the works on the Japanese conduct of the war with a wider, more multinational version of the conflict, and thereby draw comparisons on the way the opposing sides conducted their campaigns. The bulk of the existing works also emphasize the military aspects of the war. For example, the official histories on US naval, army, air force, and marine corps have provided an exhaustive account of the major operations.[3] This work will put forward a broader overview by focusing not only on the battlefield level. It will add perspectives from within the realms of the military high command, the government, and the public. Most importantly, much of the available literature is over 20 years old, and there are few works which have made use of recently released documents in the US and British archives. This material sheds new light on a number of crucial subjects, including the way in which intelligence activities and knowledge of the enemy played a pivotal role in shaping both the Allied and Japanese war efforts.

Any study of the Pacific war needs to examine a number of key themes and issues. This book first introduces readers to the reasons why the conflict broke out, and examines the interests which the opponents were contesting. As in the European theater of war, the confrontation in the Asia-Pacific region was primarily the product of the Axis powers' moves to acquire new territories at the expense of the established world powers, including the US, British Empire and the Soviet Union. During the decades prior to the war, the Japanese faced a host of economic and political problems that were closely akin to those of their German and Italian counterparts. As an island nation without a large supply of natural resources, Japan was dependent on foreign trade in order to acquire the raw materials that its growing industries required, as well as to provide a reliable market for its finished goods. During the late 1800s and early twentieth century, the Japanese emulated the policies of the world's leading powers, by establishing an overseas empire in Asia.

However, because Japan was a latecomer to the scramble for colonies, its leaders often found their ambitions thwarted by more powerful nations who had already acquired empires, notably Great Britain. The United States had also developed a presence in the Far East by the end of the nineteenth century. Japan could not make significant gains without provoking a reaction from its rivals, and the clash of interests became apparent following the end of the First World War in 1918, when Tokyo explicitly demanded rewards in return for its support of the Western powers' war effort against Germany. During the Washington conference, held 1921–22, the US and Britain persuaded Japan to limit its naval construction and refrain from further territorial acquisition. Although dissatisfied with the outcome, the Japanese government complied with the terms of the Washington treaty, on the grounds that good relations with foreign nations were essential if Japan wished to maintain its trade links with the outside world and thereby keep its economy buoyant. However, the downturn caused by the worldwide recession of 1929–33 led the military to conclude that Japan should establish control over the Asiatic mainland, and gain access to its natural resources, thereby solving its economic probelms. The global conflict during the 1930s was therefore driven by the discontented powers: Germany, Italy and Japan.

Because the United States ended up playing the biggest role in bringing about Japan's defeat, the popular belief is that America was Japan's prime enemy, but the war originated with Japan's clashes with other states whose significance cannot be downplayed.[4] Initially, China was the main antagonist, and in 1931, the Imperial army attempted to redraw the boundaries of East Asia by conquering the northern province of Manchuria. In 1937, following an accidental skirmish in the outskirts of Peking, the Japanese launched a full scale invasion of China. Thereafter, Japan's objective was to subdue Chiang Kai Shek's Nationalist government and secure control over the mainland. When this plan failed, the Imperial forces turned towards Southeast Asia, in an effort to encircle China. Japan was also encouraged by developments taking place in the European theater in mid 1940, when Germany conquered France and Holland, which meant that the latter's colonial territories in the Far East were exposed. Great Britain was in no position to defend the status quo in Asia, since it faced the prospect of a German assault on its home islands. By moving southward, Japan was challenging the interests of the European colonial powers. In the unfolding crisis President Franklin Roosevelt supported America's allies by imposing economic sanctions against Japan. The leadership in Tokyo faced the dilemma of pursuing a lifting of the sanctions by acquiescing to US demands – namely that Japan relinquish a large portion of its conquered territories on the Asiatic mainland – or alternatively securing new sources of raw materials by annexing British Malaya and the Dutch East Indies. The latter move would certainly lead to confrontation with the US, but at the same time, satisfying America's conditions for the resumption of trade was an equally unattractive option, since it amounted to giving in to blackmail. Unwilling to concede, Japan's leaders decided to initiate hostilities with the West. Therefore, rather than arising solely from a dispute between the US and Japan, the origins of the Pacific war can be traced to a multitude of rivalries that were taking place in Asia and beyond.

The fighting in the Pacific theater also needs to be viewed in relation to the parallel conflict that was taking place in Europe. On the Axis side, Japan had an ideological affinity with its German and Italian partners: all three nations wished to redress the global balance of power. In doing so, they ended up confronting common enemies, including the United States and the British Empire. Furthermore, while the Soviet Union did not declare war on Japan until the closing stages of the conflict, eradicating Communism was a key interest which the Axis powers shared. However, cooperation between the leadership in Tokyo and its counterparts in Berlin and Rome remained minimal, even after the signing of the Tripartite Pact in September 1940. The reasons for the Axis coalition's failure to coordinate its strategy, and the consequences for Japan's war effort, will be discussed further in later chapters.

For the Allied powers, Germany was the most menacing enemy. The campaign in the European theaters therefore remained the top priority, with the Pacific most often being treated as a secondary front. For this reason, the conduct of operations against Japan must constantly be viewed within the background of developments taking place in the European theater. Because the US and British Empire could not deploy the same quantity of forces against Japan as they did against Germany, the progress of their operations in the Asia-Pacific region was correspondingly affected.

The second key theme to be addressed is the main reasons for the Allied victory against the Japanese. A number of authors have focused on material factors such as economic and industrial productivity. John Ellis illustrated how America's abundant supply of resources and manufacturing plant enabled it to build an overwhelmingly larger quantity of ships, aircraft and equipment than the Japanese.[5] More recently, scholars such as Richard Overy have argued that the statistics pointing to materiel do not tell the whole story, and contended that one needs to look at equally important features, including the quality of weapons and how they were used on the battlefront.[6] Industrial prowess made the Allied victory in the Second World War possible, but did not render it a foregone conclusion. Economic strength had to be harnessed to construct an effective fighting machine, whose performance was not merely determined by quantitative factors, but a number of intangible aspects, such as the skill and training of combat personnel, along with the decisions made by the high commands.

This book will attempt to reinforce the contention that effective planning and the proper mobilization of materiel were often as equally important as sheer military strength. After all, the conflict was a total war, where success depended on the participants making full use of their economic assets. The US and its allies faced more favorable circumstances because they had a significantly larger supply of raw materials, industrial plant and manpower at their disposal. However, the available resources had to be channeled in order to construct the weapons that were required to vanquish enemy forces. Oftentimes, governments intervened in order to ensure that the war industries manufactured the right types and quantities of hardware. Raw materials and manpower also had to be distributed so that factories could meet their production targets. In this respect, the Allied nations organized their productive capabilities more effectively than their Axis counterparts, including the Japanese. Conversely, Japan's defeat was not only due to the fact that it could not match the economic output of its enemies. An equally debilitating weakness was the government's failure to establish a system where its limited resources could be used in an optimal manner. For this reason, managing one's economic capabilities was as crucial as the mere possession of materiel.

In regard to the actual fighting, success depended on good performance in a number of key areas, including strategy and operations. One of the most significant obstacles to conducting large scale operations in the Asia-Pacific theater was the extended distances which armed forces had to traverse before reaching the battlefront. For example, Japan's home islands and Singapore are separated by over 3,000 miles of water, equivalent to the distance between the British isles and the east coast of America.

A similar expanse separated Japan from the US navy's base at Pearl Harbor. Allied forces faced similar problems. In order to reach their forward bases in Australia, for example, US task forces needed to sail across 10,000 miles of open seas from ports on the west coast, including Long Beach, California and San Francisco. The Western powers and the Japanese both needed to develop sufficient mobility. It was no coincidence that the fighting in the Pacific theaters saw the participants pioneering new ways of deploying their naval and air forces, both of which were crucial for seizing the initiative and eventually achieving victory. Establishing bases also required amphibious forces which could move quickly across the ocean, and neutralize enemy resistance by launching sudden attacks on defended islands. Establishing a logistical network to supply the armed forces operating at far-flung areas such as New Guinea and the islands of the Pacific Ocean was an absolute necessity.

Initially, the Imperial Japanese Navy (IJN) and Imperial Japanese Army (IJA) held a number of advantages, at both the strategic and operational levels. Their success in ousting Allied forces from their strongholds in Southeast Asia and the western Pacific during the opening stages of the conflict was often due to the navy possessing larger numbers of ships and aircraft than its opponents. The army was also well supported by a logistical chain which provided constant

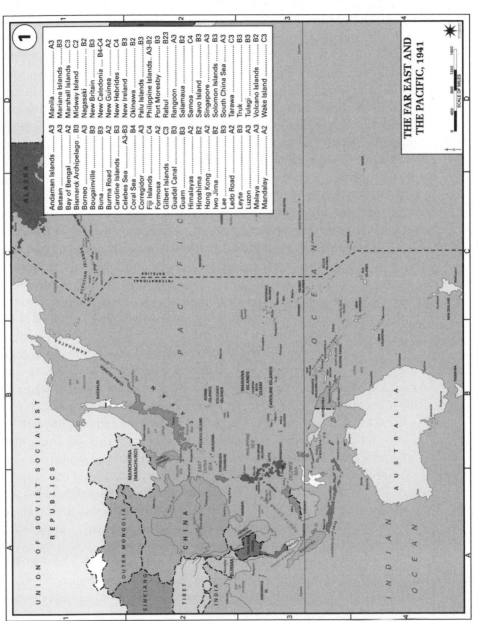

Map 1: The Far East and Pacific Regions

supplies and reinforcements. However, by the middle of 1942, Japan's forces were overstretched to the point where they could not undertake any further territorial conquests. To make matters worse, the high command did not anticipate any full scale counter-offensive against Japan's empire, and subsequently failed to make adequate preparations. The Allies, on the other hand, were not only able to construct larger forces but to keep them properly supplied. Their strategy was to dismantle Japan's hold on its conquered territories and to secure control over Pacific Ocean, eventually preparing positions for an assault against the home islands. The plan proved to be the most effective way of achieving the ultimate objective of the Allied powers, namely to completely destroy Japan's capacity to wage war. Operations were planned with a view to minimizing casualties, and overcoming enemy forces in the most efficient manner. Once again, good planning enabled the US-led coalition to utilize its military strength to attain its stated aims.

The development of proper tactics was also vital. Because geographic factors necessitated the use of naval and air power, the Allied and Japanese forces achieved significant innovations in these areas. In land warfare, the opposing armies had to adapt their combat methods and weapons so that they could operate in the rugged terrain and dense jungles which were common in Southeast Asia and the islands of the Pacific. Again, the Japanese enjoyed a lead during the opening stages of the conflict, but were eventually eclipsed by their opponents. The IJN's capabilities in both surface operations and aerial combat were first rate. Japanese torpedoes had greater range and destructive power than any of their Western counterparts, and wreaked havoc on Allied task forces. The air service developed the Zero fighter, which outclassed its rivals in terms of speed and maneuverability. Pilots were highly skilled at sinking naval vessels and clearing the skies of enemy aircraft. The IJA's successes were equally impressive. Troops were trained to march long distances without relying on motorized transport, and were able to overcome enemy positions through skilful maneuvering, rather than using heavy weapons. Western armies, on the other hand, relied excessively on mechanized forces, whose mobility was severely restricted in areas covered by mountains and wooded country. However, the Japanese could stay on the winning side only as long as they faced weaker opponents. By 1943, the Allies were deploying larger quantities of modern armaments. The Imperial forces, by contrast, failed to achieve any significant advances during the conflict, mainly because their officers held a deep-seated belief that their own techniques and equipment were superior. The shortcomings accelerated the defeat of both the IJN and IJA. By the same token, the Allies understood the methods they needed to develop in order to fight effectively, and this was one of the key factors which enabled them to prevail.

The third, and final, key theme is the contentious issue of race and ideology.

The ethnic divide between the Allies and the Japanese had a profound effect on the belligerents' views of each other, and yet few historians, aside from John Dower, have studied the subject in any great detail.[7] Dower has focused on the views held by the Japanese and American public, as well as the soldiers fighting on the front lines. According to his work, both sides tended to dehumanize their enemy, and the animosity, in turn, gave rise to a level of violence which was not visible in many other conflicts. For the Japanese, the Pacific war was a mission to fulfill their nation's destiny of liberating the people of Asia from Western colonial rule. The idea of *Yamato damashii*, which dictated that the Japanese race had descended from the sun-gods, and proclaimed that they had a preordained right to become the dominant nation of the Far East, was one of the main driving forces behind the decisions made by policymakers and military officials. Furthermore, the fanatical belief that the Japanese were fighting a holy war against the Western imperialists played the key role in motivating soldiers and civilians. The idea provided an instrument for maintaining enthusiasm for the war, both in the battlefield and in the home front, and laid the foundation for the staunch aversion to surrender which the Japanese constantly demonstrated. Likewise for the Americans and their allies, the Pacific war was as a quest to eliminate the so-called "yellow peril." Prior to the war, Westerners tended to view Japan as an underdeveloped nation, which could not possibly achieve the capacity to pose a military challenge. The spectacular victories which the Imperial forces attained during the opening stages of conflict created a mixed feeling of insecurity and contempt. The Japanese were seen as ruthless, barbaric, and not worthy of humane treatment. Dower argues that for policymakers, combat personnel and civilians alike, contempt for the enemy was a key motivating factor in prosecuting the war effort.

This book will reexamine these hypotheses, and illustrate how racial and ideological views were among a myriad of factors which shaped the conduct of the conflict. It will argue that for both soldiers at the battlefront as well as policymakers at the highest tiers of the command structure, decisions were most often influenced by practical matters, including the question as to how enemy forces could be defeated most effectively. For this reason, concerns over military necessities, and a desire to prosecute a successful war, were more decisive in determining the way in which the Pacific war was fought.

The following chapters will enable readers to develop a better understanding of the economic, political and strategic factors which propelled Japan's expansion on the Asian continent during the 1930s, as well as the underlying causes for the outbreak of war between Japan and the Western Powers in December 1941. The book will thereafter explain the reasons for Japan's rapid conquest of Southeast Asia and the western Pacific during the opening stages of the conflict, as well as the complications which the US and its allies faced in their effort to dismantle Japan's hold on its empire. In addition, the following sections will illustrate the strengths and weaknesses of Japan's war effort. Finally, readers will emerge with a better knowledge of why the Pacific war ended with the dropping of the atomic bombs and Japan's unconditional surrender.

1

Japan Emerges as a Great Power, c.1860–1930

Japan's rise as a modern nation during the turn of the twentieth century significantly altered the political and strategic landscape in Asia. It also posed a number of challenges for the powers who had already established a presence in the region, namely Great Britain, Russia and the United States. Until 1900, the three nations between them controlled a large part of the territories in Asia, as well as the routes of access to and from the area. The West's domination remained largely secure, because there were no Far Eastern countries with the military and economic potential to alter the status quo. However, as the Japanese emerged as a Great Power, their geographic proximity to the Asiatic mainland placed them in a favorable position to mobilize their forces and develop an empire in the locality. Fears regarding the dangers exerted by the Empire of the Rising Sun appeared to be confirmed when the leadership in Tokyo started to openly announce its desire to acquire an ascendant position in the Asia-Pacific region. Nevertheless, while the growth of Japanese power did raise apprehensions for the Western nations, none of them, with the exception of Russia, had concrete reasons to anticipate a confrontation until the aftermath of the Great War of 1914–18. Japan's leaders had made it clear that they wished to maintain friendly relations with other countries, and the pursuit of aggressive expansion did not commence in earnest until the 1930s, when the economic effects of the Great Depression led the military to demand that their nation's problems be solved by acquiring new territories, even if the action entailed the risk of alienating foreign powers.

THE RISE OF MODERN JAPAN: CAUSES AND CONSEQUENCES

Until the mid 1800s, the nation with the most extensive empire in Asia was Great Britain. The British had gained control over the Indian subcontinent, and also set up an array of commercial interests in China, while at the same time acquiring a colony on the Malay peninsula and the northern section of Borneo. Russia was another major power in the Far East. The empire of the czars had been steadily expanding beyond the confines of its European territories, and by 1860, Russia acquired a foothold on the Pacific Ocean when it founded the port city of Vladivostok on the Sea of Japan. The Russians also started to seek acquisitions in areas such as China and Korea. Although the United States remained uninvolved in world affairs and followed an isolationist policy, American merchant vessels had been sailing extensively in the waters of the Far East. The US thus had a motive to defend the area against hostile powers.

Japan was in no position to become a leading power, at least until the latter part of the century. It could be best described as a medieval fiefdom, governed by various territorial lords, known as the *daimyo*, and a caste of warriors from the *samurai* ruling class. Without a central government, the nation did not have the political power to pursue imperial expansion. The Japanese had also purposely secluded themselves from external influence and barred foreigners from entering their country since the Tokugawa period of the 1500s. The extended period of isolation was a distinct handicap, since the Japanese denied themselves the scientific and technical know-how which they needed in order to modernize. Indeed, Japan was not even a nation-state.

Yet, in little more than half a century, Japan emerged as a key player in world affairs. Centuries of isolation were forcibly broken in 1854, when the American Commodore Matthew Perry and his "Black Ships" sailed into Tokyo Harbor, and demanded that US whaling ships be granted permission to use fuel and supply facilities in the home islands. A civil war broke out between the factions who wished to open up the nation to foreign trade, against those who wanted to maintain Japan's seclusion. The strife lasted until 1868, when the warlords were overthrown, with the Emperor Meiji appointed as the sovereign ruler. A centralized government was established, and Japan became a unified nation for the first time in its 2,000-year history. The following decades witnessed rapid modernization, and the Japanese made a concerted effort to develop a sound political, economic and military infrastructure. Japan's status as a modern power was confirmed 1894–95, when its armed forces defeated the Chinese, and acquired the island of Formosa. In 1902, Japan gained international recognition of its enhanced standing, when it signed its first formal treaty of alliance with Great Britain. Two years later, in 1904, Japan became involved in a war against Russia, and by the following year, its navy emerged victorious after sinking the Tsar's fleet at the Battle of Tsushima. Japan's armies also crushed their Russian opponents in the plains of Manchuria. The Russo-Japanese war marked the first occasion when a European power was defeated by a non-Western state. Under the Treaty of Portsmouth, brokered by the US President Theodore Roosevelt, Japan gained the Russian-held concession of Port Arthur on the shores of the Yellow Sea, along with the southern portion of Sakhalin island. In 1911, Japan made further territorial conquests when it established a colony on the

Korean peninsula. Japan joined the Great War of 1914–18 on the Allied side. The Imperial forces conquered all German territories in Asia and the south Pacific regions, and emerged from the conflict with the third largest navy in the world following the US and Britain. At the 1919 Paris Peace Conference, Japan's leaders were invited to participate as members of the "Big Five" group of the Allied and Associated powers.

The question arises as to how a small island nation, possessing a meager supply of natural resources, rose to the ranks of the Great Powers in such a short timeframe. The development can be attributed to a number of factors, the first of which was the ruling elite's resolve not to be dominated by the West.[1] Japan's leaders observed how large parts of Southeast Asia had been colonized, as well as the manner in which China was being economically exploited, and concluded that if their country wished to avoid the same fate, radical changes were necessary. In short, economic and military expansion were seen as vital measures to protect Japan's national security. The government painstakingly strove to develop the country along Western standards. Between 1871 and 1873 alone, over 350 citizens were sent overseas to learn about vital aspects of statehood, including government administration, industrialization and military organization.[2] A period of rapid transformation followed. A new constitution and legal code were established, based on the Prussian model. The educational system was expanded, enabling Japan to achieve an exceptionally high literacy rate. Government subsidies were channeled into the industries, and Japan eventually became a leading producer of textiles. The state also encouraged the construction of roads, telegraphs, railways, and shipping lines. In order to help Japan create a strong military force, experts were brought in from the Royal Navy, as well as from the French and German general staffs. The corollary to avoiding domination by the West was to imitate their methods of achieving economic prosperity, namely by establishing overseas colonies and gaining access to raw materials as well as captive markets for finished goods. Although ruling circles saw the push towards reform as a defensive measure, the creation of an empire formed a key component of their strategy.[3] By 1900, although Japan still lagged behind the West in terms of economic advancement, it had acquired the necessary ingredients for conducting an imperialist policy, including a sufficient level of surplus capital and industrial production, coupled with the military power to back up its claims.

Two further factors facilitated Japan's ascendancy, the first of which was morale. The Japanese had a strong sense of cultural uniqueness and their leaders regularly propagated the belief that the people had a special position in the world community. Japan's world view was largely shaped by traditional beliefs that had been passed down through the centuries, which preached the superiority of the *Yamato* race, whose origins purportedly originated from the sun-gods. Mythology therefore played an important part in political life. The traditions of worshipping the emperor, along with the manner in which the education system emphasized discipline and loyalty to the state, ensured a high level of national cohesion and maintenance of a strong work ethic among the populace, thereby enabling the state to optimize its resources. The growth of Japan's military power was similarly augmented by morale. The *samurai* ethos of honor, along with the "way of the warrior" (*bushido*) code, which called upon troops to sacrifice their lives for the emperor and country, were often taken to heart by the rank and file of the armed services, as demonstrated by their performance against China and Russia at the turn of the twentieth century. Morale was undoubtedly an asset which went a long way in bolstering the capabilities of the IJN and IJA, to the point of sometimes compensating for their material and technological shortcomings.

Within the public, the belief of Pan-Asianism, which dictated that the Japanese had a moral obligation to liberate the Far East from Western exploitation, was vigorously promoted. During the reign of Emperor Meiji, the ruling elite, including senior politicians, business magnates, and intellectuals, concocted a national ideology proclaiming that Japan had a preordained right to become Asia's leading power.[4] The aim was to unify the masses behind the push towards modernization and generate mass support for the government. One of the first articulations of this policy for creating a Japanese-dominated Asia appeared in 1890, when a memorandum by Prime Minister Yamagata stated that, in order to become self-reliant and join the ranks of the world's leading powers, Japan needed to define its "line of sovereignty."[5] Specifically, the sphere of influence was defined as the home islands and the areas immediately within their proximity, including Korea, Formosa, and mainland China. The memorandum implied that the Japanese had to act resolutely to secure their empire, even if it entailed excluding foreign powers from the region. Convictions regarding Japan's special role were accepted by a large portion of the populace. Patriotic organizations propagated the view that Asia was being enveloped by Western imperialism, while military circles professed that Japan could not remain secure if it allowed the Far East to remain in the grip of colonialism. In other words, the Japanese perceived themselves as liberators whose duty was to create a new order where they played the dominant role, and help their neighbors onto the path towards development. The swift victories which the Imperial forces achieved against China and Russia confirmed the sense of superiority, and emboldened Japanese leaders to expand their regional influence.

The second additional factor that worked in Japan's favor was geography, and the long distances which separated its homeland, along with its main spheres of influence, from more powerful rivals. The Asiatic mainland consisted of the Chinese empire, which was in a state of decline. Furthermore, while the

Western powers could establish colonies in Asia, the Japanese, by virtue of their proximity, were in a stronger position to exert their influence. Russia learned this lesson, at a great cost during the 1904–5 conflict, as did the British and Americans on the eve of the Pacific war, when they struggled to maintain their far-flung possessions in Malaya, the Philippines and Hong Kong. Geographic factors bestowed a further asset, by placing Japan in a good position to expand its overseas commerce. The home islands commanded the trans-Pacific sea link between North America and Asia. There were also numerous deep-water harbors, such as Tokyo Bay and the Inland Sea, where merchant ships could call at for resupply. The Japanese could thus reap significant benefits from what was becoming one of the most world's most important trade routes.

However, in spite of the advantages which Japan possessed, and the ambitious statements made by its politicians, the pursuit of an expansionist policy faced obstacles, the most important of which was that the nation did not possess sufficient resources to fight a large scale war. Political leaders also realized that Japan's continued growth depended heavily on assistance from the West and the fostering of trade links with the outside world. For this reason, the government wished to maintain cordial relations with the leading powers, including the US and Great Britain. The main aim was to become a respectable member of the international community, and in order to avoid breaches that could threaten national interests, the Japanese acted in what one historian has described as a "cautious and realistic manner."[6]

For the Western nations who had interests in Asia, the rise of Japan entailed a distinct danger. Following its defeat in 1905, Russia temporarily ceased its imperialist activities in the Far East, and began concentrating on areas such as the Balkans, thereby leaving the US and Britain as the remaining counterweights to Japanese expansion. Yet, until the 1920s, neither power had compelling reasons to consider the possibility of a war. From Britain's perspective, the emergence of the Imperial Japanese Navy constituted a challenge that could not be ignored. To complicate matters, the British Empire was already overstretched by 1900, and rivalries with France, Russia and Germany over territories in Asia and Africa raised the possibility of a confrontation with several foreign powers. Statesmen in London believed that Japan needed to be conciliated if Britain wished to reduce the number of its potential enemies. Anglo-Japanese rivalry was thus alleviated by the signing of the alliance between the two powers in 1902. Under the terms, both powers were to refrain from encroachments on the other party's interests, while remaining neutral in the event of a conflict against a third power. The alliance laid the basis for cordial relations until the end of World War One.

The United States also stood to suffer losses as a result of Japanese expansion, and was aware of the potential threat facing its position in the Pacific. America had established a number of important economic ties with China, along with a chain of island bases, including Hawaii, Guam and the Philippines, to protect its sea communications. As early as 1907, naval staffs drew up War Plan *Orange*, which envisaged a confrontation with the Japanese navy. In the event of hostilities, the fleet was to sail to the Philippines in an attempt to contain an invasion, and thereafter conduct a blockade of Japan's home islands in order to curtail its supplies of vital war materials from abroad.[7] However, the significance of the war plan must not be exaggerated. The strategy was drawn up on the principle that the navy needed to prepare for war against the most powerful rival fleets. Animosity was limited to sections of America's populace, particularly those living in the west coast states, which had received a large influx of Japanese immigrants. The rest of the nation was inclined towards peaceful coexistence. The desire for closer relations was reflected in the signing of the 1911 commercial agreement, which guaranteed a certain level of trade to be conducted annually. The Western powers thus viewed Japan as a possible rival, but one that was unlikely to jeopardize the balance of power in Asia. The accepted belief was that, so long as the British and the Americans cooperated, the Japanese would reciprocate.

The situation changed considerably during the First World War. Japan's behavior raised suspicions that it was willing to infringe the interests of other nations. Within months of joining the war in late 1914, Japanese forces conquered all of the German concessions in China, including Tsingtao, as well as the German-held islands in the Pacific which lay north of the Equator. Emboldened by the rapid successes, the government attempted to enhance Japan's regional influence. In May 1915, Foreign Minister Kato issued the Twenty-One Demands to the Chinese, which called for special privileges, including control over the postal system and customs offices, along with a guarantee that Japanese advisors be employed in the civil service. The demands amounted to the granting of extra-territorial rights. China acquiesced, but despite the breakthrough, Japan's reputation was tarnished. As the Great War drew to a close in 1918, the US and Britain became wary of Japanese aspirations for hegemony. The Americans in particular feared the prospect of a naval arms race in the Pacific and the possibility that Japanese activities could upset the balance of power in Asia. British statesmen were equally alarmed. Within the Foreign Office, as well as the cabinet of Prime Minister Lloyd George and his successor governments, questions were raised regarding the wisdom of upholding the Anglo-Japanese alliance. In light of the growing mistrust between the US and Japan, a continuation could possibly alienate America. At the same time, if the treaty was abrogated, Japan could become an enemy, and Britain did not have the strength to fight another conflict after suffering substantial economic and manpower losses as a result of the Great War.

WASHINGTON TREATY ERA, 1922–29

Fearing that a further deterioration in relations with Japan could culminate with a conflict in the Far East, the US President Warren Harding convened an international conference at Washington 1921–22. Attended by officials from the three leading maritime powers, including the United States, Great Britain and Japan, along with a host of European nations, the aim was to set up a treaty that protected the status quo. A number of settlements emerged, among the most important of which were the naval limitation quotas. The US navy, Royal Navy and IJN were to limit their gross tonnage of capital ships to a 5:5:3 ratio, respectively. No new capital ships were to be laid down for a period of ten years, while work on vessels under construction was to be suspended. Japan was effectively forced to abandon its "Eight-Eight Fleet" program which called for the construction of eight new battleships and battle cruisers by the mid 1920s. The US and Britain could thus rest assured that Japan's ability to threaten their interests had been alleviated.

In regard to territorial issues, the Nine-Power Treaty obliged its signatories, including Japan, to refrain from further conquests on the Chinese mainland. Efforts to gain special economic privileges were to be eschewed, with disputes over trade and economic matters resolved by peaceful negotiations with the Chinese, or failing that, via consultation with the Nine Powers. Finally, the Anglo-Japanese alliance, which had elicited considerable US dissatisfaction, was replaced by the Four-Power Treaty, signed between the Americans, British, Japanese and the Chinese.

Although the Washington treaties initially appeared to have created a viable settlement, the danger of encroachments on Western interests did not disappear. For starters, military and naval circles in Tokyo were not satisfied with the agreements.[8] The quotas, which gave the Imperial fleet a considerably lower tonnage than its rivals, along with the nullification of the alliance with Britain, were seen as a plot to diminish Japan's prestige. Throughout the 1920s, a large portion of navy officers, under the leadership of Chief of Naval General Staff Kato Kanji, viewed the revision of the treaty as their main objective. The IJA staff was equally outraged by the terms which forbade Japan from seeking further territorial acquisitions in China. The Western powers were also aware that peaceful relations with Japan could not last indefinitely. In the US, the defense chiefs in particular maintained that war was inevitable. The Joint Board, which provided a forum for army and navy officials to devise a combined strategy, labeled Japan as "the most probable enemy."[9] Likewise, the British viewed the deteriorating state of their relations with Japan as a clear indication that they needed to prepare for eventual hostilities. As early as 1919, the Admiralty, with the support of Jellicoe, the First Sea Lord, along with Lord

Beatty, the Chief of Naval Staff, endorsed a plan to construct an advanced base at Singapore from which the Royal Navy could operate in the event of a war breaking out in the Far East. The Cabinet accepted the proposal in 1921.

To complicate matters, the treaties did not establish a viable means of verifying whether the Japanese were abiding by the arms limitation agreements. This was largely due to American isolationist sentiment. As far as US leaders were concerned, they simply wished to halt the naval race, and had no intention of establishing an organization to prevent its reemergence.[10] Under the circumstances, the prospects of keeping Japan in check during the long run were not favorable.

In strategic terms, the naval treaties contained terms which allowed the Imperial navy to move anywhere western Pacific regions in the event of war, without facing serious opposition. The "non-fortification" clauses forbade the US from developing its bases in Guam and the Philippines, thereby hindering America's ability to uphold a peacetime presence in areas within closer proximity to Japan's home waters.[11] The British were likewise not allowed to fortify any of their bases north of Singapore, including Hong Kong. Financial problems also held back the construction of the base at Singapore throughout the 1920s, and the decade has been aptly labeled as a period during which the British took a lax attitude towards protecting their interests in Asia.[12] By 1941, when the Western powers were faced with the growing prospect of a war against Japan, the adverse consequences of their inability to maintain large naval forces in the Far East became abundantly clear.

Despite the numerous faults which plagued the Washington treaty system, for much of the 1920s, the situation in Asia remained stable. The Japanese government was headed by a civilian leadership which commanded a wide base of popular support, while within the Diet, or parliament, the peace factions held the majority of the seats. The ruling parties advocated a policy of non-aggression, in the same spirit the nation's leaders had done prior to the First World War.[13] The hardliners in the military who called for rapid rearmament and imperial expansion thus could be kept in check. Japan's need to maintain American goodwill was further illustrated during the after-effects of the 1923 Kanto earthquake, when large sections of Tokyo and the neighboring port city of Yokohama suffered extensive damage. The economy was faced with the threat of a downturn which was reversed with generous amounts of American financial and material support. The episode brought home the importance of maintaining friendly relations with the West.

The main threat to Far Eastern security was the civil war that was brewing on the Chinese mainland. The Manchu dynasty had been overthrown in 1911, and Yuan Shikai was appointed as China's first premier. However, the stability of the central government in Peking was undermined because it lacked popularity, and needed to contend with rival factions, the most important of which was the Nationalists, also known as the Kuomintang. The Chinese Communist Party (CCP), under the leadership of Mao Tse-Tung, also became a key player in the power struggle. Both parties wanted to rid China of foreign influence, and opposed Peking's policy of continuing to allow the Western powers to exert their economic and political influence in the country. Peking also had to cope with opposition from various warlords who controlled large swathes of territories. The unrest took a dramatic turn in 1924, when the northern warlord, Chang Tso-Lin and his forces started advancing towards the central Yangtse River valley region. The Kuomintang believed that the situation demanded drastic measures. When Sun Yatsen, the Nationalist leader, died in 1925, Chiang Kai Shek was elected to the party's central executive committee, and he proposed launching the Northern Expedition against the main ports on the eastern coast, including Shanghai. By 1927, the Kuomintang reached the central areas, and in the following year, set up a new base at the city of Nanking.

The developments naturally caused worries for the Japanese, who saw their interests in China being threatened. The Tokyo government took the view that territories not owned by Japan were ultimately under China's control, and the IJA had no right to intervene. The policy was opposed by sections in the government who advocated military action. In particular, they were angered by the army's failure to take countermeasures. When Tanaka Giichi and the *Seiyukai* party rose to power in 1927, Japan began using force to safeguard its interests in China, and decided to dispatch troops to the concession at Shantung. At the same time, Japan's pursuit of a pacifist policy was demonstrated when the army was withdrawn within a few months. Prime Minister Tanaka also issued a written statement which officially recognized the Kuomintang's territorial gains, and endorsed a policy where Japan was to support the moderate parties vying for power in China.

Nevertheless, by the late 1920s, Japanese aggressive expansion had reached an embryonic stage. The Kwangtung Army, which was responsible for protecting Japan's interests in China, began to take increased control over policy. The most violent incident was the assassination of Chang Tso-Lin in June 1928. His train was bombed while he was traveling to Mukden for negotiations with the Japanese. Army officers, under the leadership of General Komoto, calculated that eliminating the warlord would help them enhance their influence in Manchuria. Back in Tokyo, Tanaka's policies of cooperating with the Chinese came under attack from various opposition parties. All that was needed for Japan to embark on a program of territorial conquest was a major crisis which gave rise to widespread demands for such moves.

JAPAN ERUPTS, 1930–33

The political turmoil which swept Japan during the worldwide recession of 1929–33 provided military leaders with the ideal opportunity to pursue a more forward policy. The Great Depression inflicted significant damage on the economy. Silk exports to the US, which provided the main source of national revenue, were cut by 90 percent after Congress imposed tariffs aimed at protecting American producers from foreign competition. The falling demand for consumer goods also led to a downturn in industrial production, and with foreign trade grinding to a halt, the Bank of Japan needed to keep interest rates at an artificially high rate to keep the yen afloat.

The government rapidly lost its credibility for failing to remedy the economic chaos, and subsequently, the navy and army were able to break free from the restraints that had been imposed by the civilian leadership. The opposition voiced against the London naval agreement of 1930, followed by the Manchurian Incident of 1931, marked a dramatic shift in Japanese foreign policy, in two key respects.[14] First, they marked the end of civilian control over government decisions, and signified how the armed services had gained the upper hand. Secondly, Japan no longer viewed international cooperation as the best way to protect its interests in China, and saw military action as the means to achieve national security.

The first step towards dismantling the Washington treaty system was under-taken by the naval general staff. During late 1929, when the London naval conference convened, the foreign ministry (*Gaimusho*) ordered the Japanese delegation to avoid a breach with the US, even if it entailed foregoing the higher 10:7 ratio which navy officials had insisted on. In the following March, after months of wrangling, the Japanese accepted a renewal of the 10:6 ratio that had previously been agreed at Washington. Yet, a large number of naval officers believed that by agreeing to the lower ratio, Japan was curtailing its ability to protect its interests in Asia and thereby jeopardizing its own strategic position. The navy's approval for the London agreement was blocked by a row which developed among factions of the high command. In order to avoid an embarrassing situation whereby Japan was unable to confirm its adherence to the treaty, Prime Minister Hamaguchi obtained permission from Emperor Hirohito to order the delegation at London to sign the agreement. Nevertheless, the treaty caused outrage among naval leaders. The supreme military council officially assured Hirohito that Japan was not to sign any further arms limitations accords once the naval treaties expired in 1936. The unpopularity of the naval agreements was highlighted in November, when Hamaguchi was assassinated by a right-wing nationalist. The vehement opposition to the London treaty laid the grounds for Japanese naval expansion during the 1930s. Officers committed to arms control were purged, and the anti-treaty factions gradually gained the dominant position in the high command. Finally, in 1934, Japan openly announced that it would not sign further agreements unless it was granted parity, thereby bringing an end to the post-Great War era of naval limitations agreements.

The Imperial army's actions played an equally important role in setting Japan on a path towards becoming an aggressor nation. The economic effects of the Great Depression led a large portion of the officer corps to conclude that Japanese interests could no longer be protected by cooperating with the West. The sociological composition of the rank and file was particularly conducive for creating discontent. Most of the middle-ranking officers originated from the agrarian sector, whose livelihood had been severely damaged by the slump in US purchases of luxury goods such as silk. As a result, the army command became reluctant to abide by the government's policy of foregoing further territorial gains. The province of Manchuria was seen as a lucrative prize, since it provided ample supplies of raw materials such as coal and iron ore. The region also produced food crops including wheat and soybeans, while its extensive tracts of open space could enable Japan to establish settlements and thereby partially resolve the problems arising from a rapidly growing population. The Kwangtung Army, under the leadership of Ishiwara Kanji, judged that time was ripe for action. On 5 September 1931, Japanese troops staged a bombing of the trans-Manchurian railway, just outside the city of Mukden, and blamed it on the Chinese in order to establish a pretext for an invasion. Back in Tokyo, the cabinet resigned to the fact that they could not restrain the army. A full-scale invasion was launched, and the action received widespread approval in the Japanese media. Japan was further ostracized from the international community in February 1932, when its forces became involved in further skirmishes at Shanghai. On 1 March, the Japanese announced the creation of the puppet state of Manchukuo. To publicly demonstrate its unwillingness to cooperate with the Western powers, in 1933 Japan withdrew from the League of Nations.

The Manchurian Incident also showed how the terms of the Washington treaties could not be maintained unless its signatories were willing to take punitive measures against the violators. The US and British governments were too preoccupied with their economic troubles at home and not in a position to seriously consider the option of imposing sanctions. They hoped that the civilian leadership in Tokyo could come to terms with the international disapproval that the invasion of Manchuria was causing, and thereby urge restraint on the army. The need for concrete action became apparent when China presented its case to the League of Nations on 22 September 1931. London and Washington requested the League council to work out a settlement. However, because the League's key member states were not prepared to undertake concrete measures to curb Japan, actions were limited to simply issuing verbal condemnations. A commission headed by Lord Lytton of Britain was tasked to undertake a fact-finding mission to the Far East. The commission returned in autumn 1932 with the conclusion that Japanese actions in Manchuria were clearly in violation of the League covenant. The League merely announced that it did not recognize the puppet regime of Manchukuo. World leaders were equally unsympathetic towards Japan, but not ready to take active counter-measures. For example, Henry Stimson, the US Secretary of State, made a public speech which denounced territorial acquisitions by the use of armed force. Yet, unless the major world powers were prepared to punish Japan, either by taking military action or by imposing economic sanctions, international disapproval was unlikely to dissuade its actions.

The Manchurian Incident thus signified how Japan had become one of the key threats to East Asian security. Perhaps more importantly, the occupation of Manchuria set the Japanese onto a series of moves which eventually culminated with the outbreak of the Pacific war in December 1941. Throughout 1930s, the main objective was to achieve economic and political domination over China, and when that failed, the Imperial forces expanded their operations into Southeast Asia. The latter action brought the Japanese into a confrontation with Britain, and later, the US. However, in 1931, Japan was a long way from making any decisions to initiate a war against the Western powers. Therefore, the main purpose of the following two chapters is to explain the process by which the Imperial forces enlarged the scope of their ambitions, from simply securing their interests on the Asian mainland, to undertaking a full-scale conquest of Southeast Asia and the Western Pacific regions, and declaring war on the US in the process.

2

Prelude to the Pacific War: the China Question, 1931–40

By 1933, Japan completed its conquest of Manchuria, and settled into a phase of consolidating its gains. In 1937, however, the army became involved in another confrontation, this time with the aim of achieving hegemony over mainland China. The Sino-Japanese conflict marked the prelude to the Pacific war, in a number of important respects. Strategically, Japan's activities overstretched its armed forces. The army in particular became entangled in a drawn-out war and faced increased difficulties in extending its activities to other regions such as Southeast Asia. At the same time, the failure to subdue China led the military to seek other means of securing its objectives, by occupying parts of French Indochina, in an effort to encircle enemy forces and blockade their supply lines. The move made the Japanese look even more suspicious in the eyes of Great Britain and the United States, both of whom were provoked into imposing economic sanctions that laid the grounds for an eventual showdown. In terms of battle lessons, the Imperial forces enjoyed a good level of success. Yet, the victories against the Chinese led the Japanese to develop a false sense of superiority, and they subsequently failed to prepare for a confrontation against stronger enemies, including the Americans. Likewise, Japan's failure to eliminate enemy resistance led officials in the US and Britain to believe that the Imperial forces were inefficient, and unable to challenge their Western rivals. Japanese military capabilities came to be underestimated, and the miscalculation was to create considerable embarrassment for the Allies during the opening stages of the Pacific war.

CONSOLIDATION, 1933–37

In May 1933, commanders from the Kwangtung army and the Kuomintang signed the Tangku truce, which drew the demarcation line between the two sides' zones of control roughly along the Great Wall, with Peking remaining in Chinese territory.

Although Japan agreed to honor China's boundaries, IJA commanders were determined to prepare for further expansion. Economic necessities, including the need to secure supplies of raw materials and markets for industrial goods, continued to play the central role in shaping Japanese policies. Because foreign policy increasingly came under military control, economic security was achieved by seeking territorial conquests on the Asian continent.

The Japanese also continued to be alarmed by the civil conflict unfolding in China. After the Kuomintang secured control over key cities on the east coast, including Nanking, it attempted to extend its power into the rural areas and gain popular support among the peasants, but their continued policies of imposing high taxes to fund their war effort, along with the failure to introduce any meaningful measures towards land redistribution, made them unpopular. Meanwhile, Mao's Communists, who had set up their headquarters in the province of Jiangxi, began facing constant attacks from the Kuomintang. By the middle of 1934, top Communist leaders agreed that Jiangxi had to be abandoned, owing to the deprivations that the Nationalist blockade had caused. The breakout began in October 1934, and was the first step in what became known as the Long March, which ended with the Communist forces' relocating to the province of Shanxi by the following year. Only one-tenth of the original force survived, and Mao's party had lost control over the southern and eastern regions, but nonetheless, the move succeeded in spreading pro-Communist propaganda in the areas where it had passed through, including a large section of the Yellow River valley. In Japan, the growing power of the Communists raised concerns. Anti-Japanese sentiment also appeared to be highlighted during the Sian incident of December 1936, when Chiang Kai Shek was captured by a former Manchurian warlord.[1] Chiang was released under pressure from Mao, but on the condition that he accepted the Communists' policy of forging a united front against foreign invaders. The development brought home the difficulties which Japan had to contend with in maintaining its interests in China.

In addition to economic and political factors, ideological beliefs started to play an important role in driving forward Japan's imperialist activities. Historians have extensively debated whether the Japanese developed a fascist state, along the lines of their German and Italian counterparts.[2] On one hand, policies were often based on the notion that the Japanese were a superior race, and government statements frequently expressed a desire to achieve domination over its neighbors. Japan's willingness to align itself with the fascist states of Europe was also highlighted by the signing of the Anti-Comintern Pact in 1936. Although the agreement was aimed at containing Soviet subversive activities, it showed how Tokyo was further alienating itself from Britain and the US by pledging its support for the revisionist powers. The army was an outspoken advocate of territorial conquest, and officers were unanimously in favor of achieving autarky by acquiring control over China.

Yet, while Japan's leaders were clearly holding grandiose aspirations, there was never a strong dictator, in the form of Hitler of Mussolini, who could clarify the nation's ultimate objectives. Furthermore, while the military played a significant role in the decision-making process, there were considerable differences of opinion among the services. Whereas the army's national defense policy, which had been drawn up shortly after the Russo-Japanese War, maintained that Japan's aim was to secure the Asiatic mainland and prepare for a showdown with the USSR, the navy on the other hand had its mind set on creating a maritime empire that included the resource-rich islands of the Dutch East Indies. The disagreements prevented the development of a coherent strategy, and the leadership rarely made a careful decision of what Japan's aims were and the means by which they were going to be achieved. Territorial expansion was often carried out to solve immediate problems, without clear thought given to the strategic and economic problems that could arise in the long-term. The declaration of an all-out war against China in 1937 was a key example of this tendency.

POLITICS AND STRATEGY OF THE CHINA WAR, 1937–40

On 7 July 1937, a small detachment of Japanese troops was accidentally fired upon by the Chinese while conducting maneuvers near the Marco Polo bridge in the outskirts of Peking. The Imperial Army responded by launching an invasion of the mainland. Back in Tokyo, the leadership of Prince Konoe Fumimaro fully supported retaliatory action, and decided that the main objective was to coerce the Chinese to cease their encroachment on Japanese interests. One of the main problems with the operation, however, was that the military did not decide on just how much territory was to be seized. The army did set out to occupy the coastal regions of China, and assumed that once this was achieved, the enemy would sue for peace. The success of the operation hinged upon the Chinese accepting large portions of their territory being controlled by foreign forces. If the scenario did not materialize, the Japanese needed to conduct a prolonged campaign. In the latter case, no matter how much territory the army took, it simply did not have the strength to completely eliminate enemy resistance in a country as large as China. Yet, the high command did not comprehend that it did not have the resources to fight the war to a victorious conclusion, and the oversight got the Imperial forces involved in a quagmire from which there were few realistic means of disengagement.[3]

Initially, the army specified that it would not advance south of Peking, since such moves were likely to overstretch the available strengths. However, by August, Japan's forces invaded Shanghai in order to protect trading and commercial interests in the city. In November, the *Gaimusho* issued a statement that demanded a demilitarized zone in northern China to be administered by a pro-Japanese representative. Tokyo also called upon the Kuomintang to cooperate in the fight against Communism. The army, meanwhile, believed that once the Nationalists' capital city of Nanking was occupied, the Chinese would suffer a death blow. Yet when Nanking fell in December, Chiang Kai Shek set up a new capital at the southern city of Hankow. Japan stepped up its demands, and insisted on demilitarized zones in the central regions of China, along with an indemnity and recognition of the puppet regime in Manchukuo. The army command vowed that it would continue the fight until China acquiesced. By October 1938, Japanese operations extended to southern China. Key ports were occupied, while the cities of Canton and Hankow fell. In February 1939, amphibious forces captured the southern island of Hainan, thereby curtailing China's maritime communications with the outside world.

The IJA's relative efficiency over its opponent was highlighted by the fact that China lost a total of 800,000 troops, while Japanese casualties amounted to less than 50,000 during the first 2 years of the conflict. The disparity owed itself largely to superior equipment and tactics. Imperial army troops were skilled at conducting operations in heavily wooded and mountainous country, where poor communications hindered the transport of heavy weapons and motor vehicles. Under the circumstances, the proper deployment of infantry units was of the utmost importance. Amphibious operations against the coastal regions were also conducted efficiently. Landings took place with little warning, and advances against inland targets were launched before the defenders could counterattack. In terms of weapons, the Japanese had a decisive edge in most aspects, including artillery and tanks. The Imperial navy's air arm was also utilized to support the army's operations.[4] Although air units suffered heavy losses during the initial stages, the Japanese developed aircraft with better protection, and provided fighter support for their bomber squadrons. As the conflict progressed, pilots achieved enhanced accuracy, and the air service managed to curtail a significant portion of the traffic on major railways and roads. Attacks against urban areas also laid waste to a significant portion of China's infrastructure.

The Chinese army's shortcomings also laid the grounds for the IJA's rapid advances. While large on paper, with almost 180 divisions and over 2 million soldiers, China's forces consisted largely of small infantry units, most of whom were armed with nothing more than rifles, light machine guns and mortars. Morale was also low. Most troops lived off the land and received minimal pay. Consequently, soldiers had little motivation to fight in areas away from their home regions. In terms of leadership, the army was in disarray because the Nationalists lacked popular support. The Chinese thus found it difficult to create a unified army, and most units deteriorated into disorganized bands of resistance who were unable to coordinate their operations.

Yet, in spite of the progress which the Imperial army managed to achieve, it faced a substantial problem in eliminating resistance. Chiang Kai Shek was under pressure from his own ranks, as well as the Communists, to take all measures necessary to repel the Japanese. The Nationalists refused even to negotiate a settlement unless Japan agreed to withdraw back to the north of the Great Wall. Under the circumstances, a ceasefire agreement was virtually impossible. The Kuomintang received material aid from the Western powers, including Britain and the US, along with other nations that were sympathetic to China, such as Germany and the USSR. Foreign assistance was expected to help the army forestall the invaders. However, the onslaught proved too overwhelming, and the Chinese switched to a strategy of retreating to the hinterland, in an effort to force the Japanese to overstretch their supply lines. Meanwhile, bandits and guerilla units in the forward areas were to harass enemy troops, and disrupt their operations. Chinese peasants were still capable of setting up militia units, and they had enough morale to defend their own villages, even if they could not put up an organized resistance. Furthermore, the partisan forces had the advantage of fighting on their home territory. The Japanese could not completely eliminate all pockets of opposition, nor were they able to conquer a significant portion of territory beyond the coastline. Even in the coastal regions, the IJA often could not pacify localities that were removed from the main cities. In addition to strategic complications, the China venture also imposed a severe drain on Japan's economy. From the onset, the government struggled to raise revenue to support the war effort, while industries found it difficult to produce sufficient quantities of weapons and armaments for the armed forces.

The difficulties which confronted the Japanese stemmed in no small part from the miscalculations that the army command had made, in regard to the nature and magnitude of the opposition its troops were likely to face. The working assumption was that China could be crushed in a single blow, and the assessment signified how the Japanese habitually underestimated their enemies. A cornerstone of Japanese military thinking was an embedded belief that their people were a superior race, and social mores forbade any expression of doubts regarding the strengths of the Imperial armed forces. Strategic assessments were therefore not based on facts, but the notion that Japan would eventually create a new East Asian order where it played the dominant role, and its rivals were to acquiesce in a fait accompli.[5] Consequently, military officials tended to neglect the need to make a calibrated and judicious evaluation of their opponents. The IJA's attitude towards intelligence was summed up by Prince Kan'in, the chief of the general staff during the 1939 Nomonhan border clashes against the Soviets, who remarked, "to rate the foe too highly tends to breed defeatism and cowardice and to erode friendly forces" morale".[6] To ponder over information on enemy strengths was a job more suited to the weak and over-cautious. Neither characteristic befitted a military institution whose traditions demanded a constant show of gallantry.

Military calculations therefore almost invariably reflected an unmasked contempt for foreign armed forces. A Japanese observer in 1932 described the Chinese as "a uniformed rabble ... they are untrained, cowardly, unpatriotic, treacherous, mercenary, and everything else a soldier should not be." Shortly after the outbreak of the China incident, a staff officer at the army ministry in Tokyo reassured his section chief, "the incident will be settled if Japanese vessels loaded with troops merely appear off the Chinese coast."[7] Imperial army commanders did not expect regular troops or guerillas to put up prolonged resistance. Even when the fighting became difficult, the assumption was that by dispatching a few more divisions, the war could be won. Instead, what the Japanese got was a war that did not finish for 8 years. Yet, the complications which the IJA faced on the Asiatic mainland did little to compel its commanders to reconsider their ability to defeat their rivals. Instead, the army focused on its successes, and developed a false sense of confidence. The tendency to denigrate the qualities of foreign armed forces was to prove fatal when the Japanese confronted the Western powers after 1941.

EFFECT ON JAPAN'S FOREIGN RELATIONS

Although Japan was careful not to provoke the Western powers, its actions in China after 1937 did work to further damage its foreign relations. On one hand, the main preoccupation was to defeat the Chinese, and for this reason, neither the government nor military wished to risk a confrontation with third parties. For example, when Japanese pilots accidentally fired upon the American warship *Panay*, along with a number of British vessels, Tokyo swiftly offered a formal apology and extended compensation to the victims' families. Furthermore, Japan needed to avoid moves that could lead Britain and the US into imposing economic sanctions, since such scenarios were most likely to cause significant difficulties for the war effort in China. Fears of Western moves to curtail Japan's imports of raw materials were one of the key factors which led the *Gaimusho* to reject German proposals for converting the Anti-Comintern pact into a formal military alliance during the winter 1939.

Initially, the Western powers' response showed indecisiveness. The Roosevelt administration was tied down by public as well as congressional opposition to American involvement in foreign conflicts, while Britain was unwilling to impose sanctions without guarantees of US support. Nevertheless, the US and Britain could not help but to realize that Japan's aggression in China was threatening their interests, and by 1938, they were undertaking concrete measures to defend their interests against the Japanese. The Americans dispatched a naval mission to London, headed by Captain Ingersoll, in order to discuss the subject of joint action. While isolationist pressure prevented the US delegation from making a firm commitment, the two powers did start working towards stronger cooperation. In July 1939, the US announced that its commercial treaty with Japan would not be renewed after it was due to expire in the following year.

Japan's actions in China therefore made it become even more of a pariah in the international community. This became true especially by 1940, when the government and military started to pursue a more ambitious policy of expanding Japanese influence into Southeast Asia. The moves were part of an attempt to defeat China through prolonged blockade and bombardment. Japanese commanders concluded that the Nationalists were able to keep fighting mainly because they were receiving war supplies via two main arteries, namely the French Indochina railway and the Burma Road, which was used by the British. The Japanese sought to strangulate the supply lines, and the opportunity to execute the strategy arose in the spring, thanks to developments that took place in Europe. Germany conquered France, leaving the latter's Asiatic colonies open to exploitation. Britain faced the prospect of an invasion of its home islands, and by the summer, the Royal Navy needed to protect the transatlantic trade routes to North America against the U-boat campaign. Japan lost little time in manipulating the situation, and in June, the government of Prime Minister Yonai demanded that Britain and France stop sending materiel to China. The European powers did not have the military strength to defend their interests in the Far East, nor could they secure support from the US, who was reluctant to do anything that could provoke Japan. Hence, the British and the French had few choices aside from acquiescing, and agreed to close the supply lines and allow Japanese observers to regulate the flow of traffic through the border regions of Burma and Indochina. Yet, Tokyo was not satisfied with the arrangements, and in the following months, it stepped up its demands by calling for access to air bases in Indochina, so that the Japanese could conduct bombing raids against the central regions of China.

Government policies also started to take an anti-Western tone. When Konoe commenced his second term as prime minister in July, the cabinet included a number of key figures who were to lead Japan on its path towards war, among the most important of whom were the Foreign Minister Matsuoka Yosuke, an outspoken proponent of revising the status quo in Asia, as well as the War Minister Tojo Hideki, who later became the wartime premier. In September,

Japan made further moves to disaffect the US and Great Britain, when its representatives in Berlin signed the Tripartite Pact with Germany and Italy. The terms called for the signatories to aid each other in the event any of them become embroiled in a war against America. Meanwhile, the Western powers carried out measures to strengthen their alliance. Immediately after the fall of France, the Roosevelt administration had pledged to support Britain by all means short of an outright declaration of war on the aggressor states. The destroyers-for-bases deal, where the US navy leased a number of its ships to help the British counter the German submarine fleet, led America to slowly move away of its isolationist stand and become more actively involved in world affairs. Most significantly, in September, the US imposed economic sanctions for the first time, and started sending strong messages which stated that that Japan's aggression would be met with punitive action. Imperial army troops in northern Indochina began clashing with Vichy French forces. Japan's forces overcame French resistance, and Tokyo approved an occupation of the northern portion of Indochina. The move provoked the US into cutting off sales of aviation fuel and grade two scrap iron to Japan. Britain responded by reopening the Burma Road. Therefore, instead of enhancing Japan's international standing, the war in China did irreparable damage to its relations with the West, and significantly increased the likelihood of an armed confrontation.

LESSONS DRAWN FROM THE CHINA CONFLICT

In regard to the development of operational and tactical methods, the Imperial forces' operations in China had a number of adverse effects, both for the Japanese, as well as British and American military officials who observed the developments taking place on the Asian mainland. For Japan's armed forces, their successes created a false sense of superiority, and negated any motivation to improve their combat procedures. Likewise, for the Western forces, the difficulties which the Japanese faced in conquering China reinforced the belief that the Imperial army and navy were not capable of putting up a serious challenge. The misperceptions ended up causing significant embarrassment for both sides during the Pacific war.

The IJA's experiences in China led its officers to believe that their techniques could defeat any opponent they faced. Throughout the interwar years, tactical doctrine emphasized the use of the infantry unit, and relied upon the spiritual bravery of soldiers, or what the Japanese referred to as *seishin*. The victories achieved during the 1904–5 Russo-Japanese war confirmed the primacy of foot soldiers, and unlike their Western counterparts, Japan's forces did not experience the "baptism of firepower" during the Great War.[8] After all, their participation was minimal, and limited to minor operations. Still, the Imperial army emerged from the conflict without clearly understanding the destructive capabilities of modern weapons such as tanks, heavy artillery and machine guns. The problems which the Japanese faced in developing modern weaponry did stem largely from the nation's shortage of industrial resources, which precluded the production of heavy machine guns, artillery pieces, tanks and aircraft, in large quantities. Without access to a large supply of heavy equipment, the Japanese struggled when they attempted to formulate a proper doctrine for their use.

The Imperial army did demonstrate considerable skill in employing its infantry arm. The shortage of mechanized units necessitated a tactical doctrine that relied upon speed and surprise to outflank enemy defenses.[9] Foot soldiers demonstrated a propensity to overcome their opponents with light infantry weapons, and occupy enemy positions by carrying out bayonet charges. In regard to fighting spirit, troops held a high degree of dedication, and demonstrated a willingness to advance even when faced with heavy opposition.

Yet, the advantages were outweighed by the fact that the relatively efficient performance in China gave the Japanese a misplaced sense of reassurance. The IJA continued to rely heavily on tactical skill and spiritual training, leading one US observer to suggest that it showed "a lack of appreciation of modern firepower."[10] A key example of how officers were unable to innovate their tactics was demonstrated after the Nomonhan border clashes against the Red Army in 1939. The Soviets outmaneuvered the Japanese in almost every encounter, and the army high command realized that the reverses were due to the shortage of materiel, coupled with poor tactical skill. An Imperial ordinance was passed, calling for units to be re-equipped with tanks and heavy weapons.[11] However, the army's ineptitude in the use of armor and artillery hampered its efforts to modernize. Consequently, Japanese tactics centered on the infantry for the duration of the Pacific war, and their forces never achieved anything similar to Western levels of sophistication in the employment of mechanized units. Thus, the IJA's experiences in China reinforced a number of flawed practices which were to bring fatal consequences when it encountered the more advanced armies of the Allied powers.

The Japanese navy's air arm also drew a number of mistaken lessons. Although aircrews managed to inflict considerable damage on the Chinese, their successes were largely due to the fact that opposition had been minimal. Commanders failed to acknowledge this fact, and became convinced that they could defeat any opponent, including the Americans, whose air forces possessed vastly superior resources and technology.[12] In a similar manner to the army, the air service followed a concept which called for measures to compensate for Japan's inability to produce the same quantity of weaponry as its Allied opponents, by focusing on quality. The construction of aircraft, along with the training of pilots, was geared to enable the Japanese to overcome their opponents through tactical talent. At the outbreak of war, the navy air arm was superior to the competing maritime powers. Zero fighters ranked among the most advanced combat aircraft of their time. In terms of flying skill, the air service developed a highly dedicated corps of pilots who were able to carry out the navy's main missions, namely to achieve air superiority over areas where Japanese forces operated.

The main failing was that the Japanese did not build their air forces with a view to conducting an extended war effort. Aircraft production targets were modest when compared with the Western powers, while the design of bombers and fighters did not enable them to engage in intensified battles. In particular, planes were fitted with small amounts of armament or armor. The practice was natural, given Japan's shortage of raw materials and productive plant, which in turn prevented industries from assembling large quantities of aircraft. Yet, the deficiency also stemmed from mistaken perceptions which maintained that the Japanese air arm's performance could overcome any material advantages the Allies enjoyed. Operations in China had incurred relatively few losses, and the Japanese developed a belief that their air force was invincible. Planes were therefore not designed to engage in intensified combat operations, and the weakness rendered the naval air service vulnerable to extensive losses when engaging its Western rivals.

While the Japanese drew a number of flawed lessons from their operations in China, for most military authorities in the West, the Imperial forces' performance gave rise to a negative impression regarding their capabilities. Throughout the years prior to the Pacific war, the British and the Americans tended to denigrate Japanese martial qualities.[13] This was partly due to racist opinions which consistently dismissed the fighting potential of non-Western military organizations. However, a more important contributing factor was that neither the Imperial navy nor army had fought a major war since their encounter against Russia in 1904–5. Consequently, there was little hard evidence that could be used to make an informed assessment of the Japanese. To complicate matters, Japan had successfully concealed its rearmament program from foreign observers, thereby negating the prospects of understanding what its military was capable of achieving.

Reports on the IJA's performance tended to confirm the assumption that its performance was second-rate. For example, US observers emphasized how the Japanese had overextended their supply lines, and were not in a position to crush the remnants of the enemy forces that had retreated to the hinterland.[14] Field reports from China demonstrated a misunderstanding of how the Japanese were confronting a number of unique obstacles. The geographical expanse of the Chinese theater meant that the Imperial army was more likely to contend with enemy counterattacks and logistical difficulties than in a battleground as compact as Malaya or the Philippines. Furthermore, because the Chinese were fighting on home territory and could draw upon an endless supply of reserves, they were more capable of effective resistance than a Western army operating thousands of miles from home base. Most importantly, Chinese guerrillas as well as regular troops possessed a significantly higher standard of training than the Allied forces which defended Southeast Asia.

To compound the problem, any successes achieved by the Japanese were qualified by the fact that they were only facing weaker opponents. This was especially true when the British and Americans attempted to gauge the Japanese army's capabilities in amphibious landings and jungle warfare. The misperception largely resulted from the accepted assumption that Western forces would prevail in all circumstances. For example, while combined operations were conducted successfully, the achievement was supposedly made easy because the landings met minimal air and naval opposition. Similar operations against well entrenched forces were therefore deemed likely to face less favorable results. In April 1940, the commanding general of the British forces in Malaya warned that the Japanese could launch a landing on the peninsula, and this made it necessary to improve of the seaward defenses. However, the General Staff at the War Office back in London rebuffed, "regarding the Japanese ability to land on coasts anywhere, this is agreed with ... although [their] ability to maintain forces like this against European troops and aircraft is questionable."[15] Assessments concerning the Imperial army's jungle warfare capabilities were based on similar conjectures. An advance through the Malay peninsula towards Singapore was considered impossible, because the Japanese armies were doomed to face problems in advancing beyond their beachheads. Prime Minister Winston Churchill was a prime supporter of this contention, as was revealed in his minute to his defense chiefs in September 1940, suggesting that the "plight of the invaders, cut off from home base while installing themselves in the swamps and jungle would be all the more forlorn."[16]

The naval air service received equally disparaging remarks. Instead of focusing on the successes achieved at hitting Chinese industrial facilities and lines of communication, Western officials tended to emphasize shortcomings. For example, the British government's joint intelligence committee produced a report on the lessons of air warfare in China, in which the findings were obscured with a dismissive preface, "caution must be exercised in drawing conclusions which may have little or no application to a war between first class powers."[17] When evidence pointing to the Japanese air arm's efficiency did appear, it was not readily accepted. During spring 1941, US aviators received reports on the Zero fighter, which had been observed in action, and the information appeared in a fleet air tactical unit bulletin during the autumn.[18] The plane was described to have a performance "far superior to anything [the Americans] had," in almost every category, including maneuverability and speed. While some aircrews took the information as a telltale sign that they needed to develop adequate counter-tactics, most commanders were inclined to disparage the Japanese. The prevailing opinion was articulated in an article published in the September issue of *Aviation* magazine, which concluded that Japan's aeronautical designs depended entirely on "handouts" provided by Western nations.[19]

In spite of the embarrassing mistakes which the British and Americans made, one needs to take account of the fact that the only source of tangible intelligence was the Imperial forces' operations in China, which often laid the grounds for negative images. Western officials were not fully aware that the Japanese had developed a level of performance needed to establish supremacy in the western Pacific regions. True, the opinions held by the Americans and British were grounded on biases which assumed that their own forces were superior. However, the fact remains that the Imperial forces managed to conceal the majority of their accomplishments from foreign observers, and without solid information on their capacity to wage war, negative views were unlikely to change. Without a direct confrontation which could provide a full picture of what Japan's forces could do, the Allies were unlikely to have a good idea of what they were up against.

THE CHINA VENTURE AND THE ORIGINS OF THE PACIFIC WAR

The China conflict played an important part in laying the grounds for the war that eventually broke out in December 1941 between Japan and the Western powers. From the political point of view, developments on the Asiatic mainland aggravated the suspicions which the United States and Britain held towards the Japanese, and significantly increased the likelihood of a confrontation. In strategic terms, the Imperial army ended up overstretching its strengths, and commitments in China meant that the Japanese were not able to allocate suffi-cient forces to other theaters. Subsequently, when Japan commenced hostilities against the Allied powers, its forces could not provide an adequate defense for the conquered territories in areas such as Southeast Asia and the western Pacific. As the conflict progressed, the shortcoming was one of the key factors which prevented the Japanese from halting the American and British onslaught against their empire. Finally, the successes which the Imperial forces achieved in China gave them an unfounded confidence in their fighting capabilities, which in turn, prevented them from innovating their methods in a way that was suitable for confronting stronger opponents, including the armed forces of the Western powers. Military personnel from Britain and the US also concluded that the failure to achieve a total victory over the Chinese meant that the Japanese were a second-rate foe who were not to be feared. Both sides therefore ended up miscalculating their enemies, and consequently were to face significant surprises once the Pacific war broke out.

3

The Road to Pearl Harbor, 1940–41

While the aggressive actions carried out by the Imperial forces 1931–40 had substantially increased the prospect of a confrontation against the US and Britain, neither the Japanese government nor military high command had a concrete plan for initiating hostilities with the Western powers before the autumn of 1941. Until then, the main objective was to subdue China, with the annexation of the European colonies in Southeast Asia being a secondary goal. However, the sanctions which the administration of President Franklin Roosevelt imposed in July, following the occupation of southern Indochina, cut off Japan's supplies of raw materials. Tokyo was faced with a difficult choice of either securing an end to the embargoes by satisfying US demands that the Japanese army be withdrawn from the Asian mainland, or alternatively, acquiring new supplies by conquering areas such as British Malaya and the Dutch East Indies. The latter action was deemed likely to provoke an armed conflict with other nations who held interests in the region, including America. The decision to go to war therefore was the culmination of Japan's long-standing ambitions, but at the same time, was an act largely driven by opportunism.

Likewise, before the Japanese commenced their attacks on Pearl Harbor and Southeast Asia in December 1941, the United States and Great Britain did not believe that a war in the Pacific regions would materialize. Neither nation was prepared to take military action against Japan, largely because their efforts were focused on containing the growing threat posed by Nazi Germany, and preventing the North Atlantic area from falling under enemy control. Japan was judged unlikely to provoke hostilities, as long as the Western powers made it clear that any infringements on their interests would elicit retaliation. The conclusion was based on the assumption that the Japanese realized they did not have the resources to defeat a coalition of major powers in a protracted conflict, and were therefore inclined to act cautiously.

FATEFUL DECISIONS, SEPTEMBER 1940 TO SUMMER 1941

The months following Japan's signing of the Tripartite Pact with Germany and Italy in September 1940 were a critical period. Although both the Western powers and the Japanese undertook a number of measures which increased the likelihood of hostilities, neither side was willing to make any concrete decisions to go to war.

In Tokyo, the Axis Pact emboldened Japan's leaders to go ahead with their preparations for a possible conflict against America. The navy high command felt assured that in the event of war, Germany would keep the US fleet tied down in the Atlantic, thereby enabling the Imperial forces to carry out their operations in the Pacific without facing substantial interference. At a meeting held by the top cabinet leaders, with Emperor Hirohito present, Foreign Minister Matsuoka stated that the pact was "a military alliance aimed at the United States."[1] Of equal importance, Japan endeavored to make further inroads in Southeast Asia. Following the occupation of northern Indochina, the government forged closer ties with Thailand, and began to mediate in its border disputes with Indochina. In March 1941, a treaty was brokered whereby the Thais gained a significant portion of Cambodia. The move enhanced Japan's influence in the southern regions, and facilitated its effort to secure a base from which it could advance to areas further afield, including Malaya and Burma.

However, while Japan was seeking to undermine the Western powers' position in Asia, its long-term strategy remained undecided.

Officials in Tokyo understood that the annexation of British and Dutch territories in Asia could elicit US intervention, and were circumspect about facing such scenarios. The development of a coherent plan was further hindered by army–navy disagreements. The army command continued to view the USSR as the ultimate enemy, and insisted on preparing for an invasion of Siberia. The border clashes with the Soviets at Nomonhan during late 1939 highlighted the extent to which Russia remained a threat to Japan's northern flank. The non-aggression pact with Moscow, signed in April 1941, did alleviate the possibility of a confrontation. Nevertheless, after Germany launched Operation *Barbarossa* in June, the Imperial army maintained that in the event that the USSR collapsed, Japan needed to be prepared to share the spoils, and for this reason, a large reserve of troops had to be kept in a state of readiness on the Manchukuo-Siberia frontier. Army leaders thus argued that southward expansion be limited to Indochina, and that a conflict against the US and Britain be avoided. The navy, on the other hand, envisaged a complete conquest of the southern regions, and maintained that in carrying out the move, Japan needed to engage in an oceanic war against the Western powers. Yet, as late as the summer of 1941, army opposition prevented the navy from implementing its strategy.[2]

The Associated Powers, including the United States and Great Britain, were equally reluctant to firmly commit themselves to military action in the Asia-Pacific regions. On one hand, both nations were moving towards closer cooperation and started to lay a strong foundation for an anti-Axis coalition. After the US cut off its sales of scrap iron and aviation fuel, in response to Japan's occupation of northern Indochina, Washington took an increasingly interventionist stand in world affairs. Roosevelt's re-election in November assured that the US would continue supporting its allies. The Lend-Lease Act, and the offer of unlimited material aid for the British, as well as any nation whose defense was vital for US national security, signified how the administration was determined to take resolute action against nations who posed a threat to world peace. However, the main aim was to avoid hostilities with Japan. America's desire to make amends was underlined when the Secretary of State, Cordell Hull, accepted approaches from Ambassador Nomura Kichisaburo in Washington for negotiations aimed at ironing out the key points of contention. Hull's position was guided by the four principles he presented to Nomura, which included territorial integrity, non-interference in internal affairs, equal commercial opportunities, and the peaceful alteration of the status quo.[3] Although Hull adhered to his refusal to accept Japan's territorial acquisitions in China, the move reflected how the US was striving to solve the growing crisis in the Far East without resorting to war.

For Western military officials, the main concern was to avert a confrontation with Japan, so that their forces could concentrate on dealing with Germany, which was judged to be the most threatening member of the Axis coalition. For Great Britain, the top priority was to protect the home islands. The second major objective was to safeguard the lifelines in the Atlantic and Mediterranean, as well as its vital Middle Eastern oil supplies. The fixation with the war against Hitler, in turn, severely restricted Britain's ability to contain the Japanese, and subsequently, the defense of Malaya was lowest on the list of priorities. In August 1940, the chiefs of staff explicitly conceded that even in an emergency, Britain could not dispatch a large naval force to protect its Far Eastern stronghold at Singapore.[4]

US strategy in the Pacific was similarly driven by the belief that the Atlantic constituted a more vital theater. The Japanese menace had to be weighed up against the more pressing concerns arising from Germany's conquest of Western Europe, which jeopardized the security of the British Isles. The maintenance of the latter was vital to protect the transatlantic sea lanes and western hemisphere. In June, Roosevelt requested the army and navy planners to draw a strategy based on the assumption that Germany continued to imperil Britain.[5]

Plan Dog, prepared by Admiral Harold Stark, the chief of naval operations in November, stipulated that the collapse of Great Britain held such serious ramifications that the US needed to provide every possible form of assistance, including the eventual dispatch of naval, ground and air forces in order to defeat Hitler.[6]

War plans were thus grounded on the understanding that commitments in the Far East had to be relegated in order to defend the Atlantic. In December, the Joint Board finalized the details of *Plan Dog*, so as to have them ready for presentation to the British during the upcoming Anglo-American staff negotiations to be held at Washington. Between January and March 1941, US and British defense planners aimed to clarify the objectives they were to achieve in the event America entered the war. The British requested that the US fleet be stationed at Manila, so that it could be ready to sail to Singapore. However, Admiral Stark, along with General George Marshall, the army chief of staff, insisted that the Allies needed to concentrate on Germany. The Americans remained reluctant to offer guarantees of military support, and went no further than to promise that they would keep the Pacific Fleet in a state of readiness at Hawaii, and impose economic sanctions if Japan made further moves to threaten the British and Dutch colonies in Southeast Asia. The final plan which emerged from the talks, ABC-1, described Europe as the most decisive theater, and stipulated that the Associated Powers' main effort was to be focused there. For this reason, the US was not to substantially increase its strength in the Far East.

Despite the mounting evidence which suggested that the Western powers faced an ever-worsening position in the Asia-Pacific regions, defense planners did not believe that they needed to prepare for a war against Japan. The lax attitude can be largely explained by the fact that the available intelligence did not provide firm indications that the Japanese intended to initiate hostilities, since their leadership had not formulated such plans. The two main sources of information were diplomats based at the British and US embassies in Tokyo, along with decrypts of Japanese signals communication, neither of which provided firm evidence. To complicate matters, the Imperial government and high command concealed their activities with an exceptional level of success, and the problems of collecting information on Japanese policy became pronounced by 1941. The *Gaimusho* introduced the *Purple* cipher machine in 1939, which used a more complicated code than its *Red* predecessor. The IJN also overhauled its communications system and set up the JN-25a code. Under the circumstances, the British and the Americans could only provide vague assessments of how the situation in the Far East was likely to unfold. To complicate matters, because Japan's leadership had not made any concrete decisions to launch a full scale conquest of Southeast Asia, the available information was, by definition, unlikely to indicate such contingencies. On the contrary, statements made by government and military officials in Tokyo suggested that they were not prepared to confront the Western powers. The armed forces were burdened with a number of strategic complications, the most important of which was the army's commitment of a significantly large force in China. In the light of evidence which suggested that Japan faced difficulties in expanding its military operations, British and US officials were likely to assume that the Imperial forces would move cautiously.

For the purpose of strategic planning, the indications pointing to Japan's hesitancy laid the foundations of a policy that aimed to discourage Tokyo from provoking hostilities. Western defense planners believed that they could compensate for their inadequate strengths by using the threat of Allied opposition as a deterrent. Within the British leadership, the prevailing belief was that if nominal steps were undertaken to improve the land defenses of Malaya, Japan would lose confidence in the chances of conducting a successful invasion. Thus, despite the Royal Navy's inability to send a fleet to Singapore, the reorganization of the ground forces was viewed as a viable panacea. The main hindrance to the development of an adequate plan was not a lack of foresight on the part of British commanders, but the fact that Britain's strengths were tied down in North Africa and Europe.[7] Between late 1940 and early 1941, British officers, under the leadership of Robert Brooke-Popham, the commander-in-chief of the Far Eastern forces, examined how well Singapore could withstand an enemy attack, and concluded that the possible establishment of Japanese bases on the Malay peninsula necessitated a revision of the base's defenses. In April 1941, following months of plea-bargaining, the chiefs of staff in London accepted Brooke-Popham's argument that Singapore's defense perimeter needed to be extended so as to include northern Malaya. The British defense chiefs also approved preparations for a pre-emptive occupation of the Kra isthmus in the event of a Japanese invasion (code-named Operation *Matador*). The plan involved a nominal increase in British strengths from 26 to 32 battalions.

By late 1941, the prevailing belief among local commanders in Malaya was that the British could contain the Japanese. The optimistic view was highlighted at a meeting held at general headquarters Malaya during the autumn. The proceedings were described by B. Ashmore, a senior commander on General Percival's staff, who recalled that the representative from the Far Eastern Combined Bureau, the main British intelligence organization in Asia, "painted a fairly indecisive picture" of the strategic situation. The intelligence officer was unable to clarify whether the recent Japanese occupation of southern Indochina portended further moves into the southern regions.[8] Although the presence of enemy forces within proximity of Malaya raised worries, the upshot was that the Japanese high command would refrain from invading, after realizing that the British beach defenses, along with aircraft based within close range of the landing area, posed complications. In the end, British ground forces proved incapable of withstanding the Japanese, and their weaknesses were exposed when the invasion commenced in December 1941. Numerous historical works, as well as firsthand accounts written by the commanders responsible for planning the defense of Singapore, have debated whether the capitulation was inevitable, and explored the question of how the available forces could have been deployed more effectively.[9] However, the final explanation must follow the postmortem of General Henry Pownall, commander of the British forces in the Far East, who concluded that commitments in Europe and the Middle East took priority, and preoccupations with matters closer to home negated the chances of protecting Britain's empire in Asia.[10] Because Britain was unable to divert its most effective forces to the Far East, Singapore had to be defended with insufficient strength.

US officials held equally ambiguous plans for defending their interests, and their strategy was aimed at convincing the Japanese that any expeditions would meet difficult opposition. In October 1940, in response to arguments put forward by Admiral James Richardson, commander of the US Fleet, that the capital ships based at Pearl Harbor could not physically halt Japanese moves in the western Pacific, President Roosevelt maintained that retaining the fleet at Hawaii was essential to discourage further encroachments.[11] Strategic plans concerning the actions which American forces were to undertake in the event of hostilities also showed a certain tone of over-optimism. After Stark and Marshall approved ABC-1, the Joint Board issued a directive to prepare *Rainbow 5*.[12] The war plan was based on the premise that, while Japan was not expected to be a belligerent, the US and its allies still needed to deal with a possible intervention. American forces in the Far East were to divert enemy strength away from Southeast Asia by conducting raids against the Marshall Islands. The army was also expected to defend the Philippines in cooperation with the navy, while the Asiatic fleet was to "raid Japanese sea communications and destroy Axis forces" while supporting the defense of British and Dutch territories. The ambitious strategy appeared to overlook the fact that American forces were not adequate to hold out against a concerted attack.

The insufficient attention paid towards the lack of military preparedness can be attributed to a growing belief that the mere presence of Allied forces in the Asia-Pacific area could deter Japan, and any operation by the Imperial navy and army would therefore be directed against more weakly defended areas. Defense planners not only became convinced that efforts to discourage Tokyo from provoking hostilities were likely to succeed. More importantly, given the weak state of their forces, the US and Britain needed to shun war by all possible means, at least until their strengths in the Asia-Pacific regions could be sufficiently augmented to cope with the Japanese. Convictions regarding the value of deterrence can be also attributed to the uncertainties which surrounded the course of future events in the Far East. The question as to whether the Imperial navy and army would have the courage to attack British and US bastions at Singapore and the Philippines remained open to doubt. The perception was natural, given the lack of information on Japanese war plans.

As late as summer 1941, the prospect of a war breaking out in the Pacific regions remained uncertain, despite the mounting tensions. In Tokyo, Japan's leaders had not agreed on any definite policies for annexing Southeast Asia. Between late June and early July, top government and military leaders drew up a plan to construct a "Greater East Asia Co-prosperity sphere." Specifically, the Japanese were to concentrate on settling the China war and prepare for southern expansion, while simultaneously staying on guard against the USSR.[13] The first step was to occupy southern Indochina, in order to place Japan's forces in a favorable position to seize the oil resources of the East Indies if the need arose. Further moves were to depend on how the situation transpired. Despite strong warnings from Washington, that territorial conquests of the southern regions would elicit repercussions, Tokyo believed that the US and its allies were unlikely to impose sanctions at least until the Dutch East Indies were seized. Thus, the Imperial forces could afford to bide their time and decide on the next move.

Much to the surprise of the Japanese leadership, within days after the occupation of southern Indochina, the US froze Japan's overseas assets, thereby denying the latter of the funds for purchasing raw materials from abroad. An oil embargo was also imposed, and America's allies, including Britain and the Dutch East Indies, shortly followed suit. As a result, the Imperial forces were denied the resources they needed to prosecute their war effort in China. Policymakers in Tokyo were faced with the choice of either fulfilling America's conditions for lifting the embargo, which was to withdraw the army from the Chinese mainland, or occupying the southern regions in order to secure new sources of raw materials.[14] Even then, the navy and army disagreed over when to commence hostilities. The army believed that it was time to abandon efforts to reconcile differences with the US through diplomatic means, and war had to be declared immediately. Admiral Nagano, the navy chief of staff, along with the civilian leaders, insisted on a last-ditch effort to negotiate a rapprochement.[15]

Meanwhile, Western leaders did not believe that the sanctions would provoke a conflict. On the contrary, the economic repercussions were considered more likely to coerce Japan to reach an accommodation. On one hand, US military officials were wary about punitive actions, on the grounds that such measures might provoke Japan.[16] However, the Imperial forces were deemed incapable of securing new supplies of oil in the southern regions, owing to their lack of available strengths. The War Department's planning division concluded that occupying the islands of Java and Sumatra in the East Indies, while contending with British and Dutch opposition, required a "major operation" that was bound to take considerable time.[17] The IJA could not spare a large number of troops for the expedition, and only a portion of the air force could provide sustained support for the landings.[18] The British were equally confident that Japan could be curbed. The cabinet's joint planning subcommittee concluded that fears over the economic effects of the sanctions were more likely to "make Japan pause and count the cost before taking another step forward."[19]

The political leaders of Britain and the US also hoped that a show of solidarity would discourage Japan from provoking hostilities. In August 1941, President Roosevelt and Prime Minister Churchill held their first face-to-face meeting onboard the battleship HMS *Prince of Wales* off the coast of Newfoundland. One of the key outcomes of the summit was the Atlantic Charter, which pledged that the Allies' ultimate war aim was to rid the world of dictator states. In regard to the Far East, Churchill proposed issuing a joint declaration to Japan. Roosevelt agreed in principle, but believed that time was not ripe to seek a showdown. They agreed that a statement be given to Ambassador Nomura at Washington, warning that "various steps would be taken by the US in retaliation against further Japanese military action." Neither the British nor the Americans foresaw how taking a tough stand was more likely to encourage, rather than dissuade Japan's government and military elite to take a gamble.

THE FINAL CONFRONTATION, AUTUMN 1941

During the early part of September 1941, the ruling elite in Tokyo decided that occupying Southeast Asia was the only viable way for Japan to secure the raw materials which it had been denied by the US-led embargo. Policymakers also judged that, while the action was necessary to prevent the nation's economy from collapsing, it was bound to bring them into a military confrontation against the Western powers. The question no longer centered on whether Japan was to fight America and its allies, but on how long the attempts to negotiate a rapprochement were to continue. Yet, while hostilities in the Asia-Pacific regions had become inevitable, the Associated Powers maintained that they could deter Japanese aggression. US and British leaders had minimal knowledge about the operations which the Imperial forces had planned, and were thus taken by surprise when their positions at Pearl Harbor, the Philippines and Malaya were attacked during the early part of December.

In formulating their strategy, the overriding concern which preoccupied Japan's leaders was to solve the dilemmas caused by the embargoes which had been imposed in July 1941. Stockpiles of oil and essential raw materials could

maintain operations in China for no more than 2 years. Under the circumstances, the only acceptable solution was to annex British Malaya and the
Dutch East Indies in order to acquire alternative sources. Although the move
involved the risk of facing hostilities against the US, the second option, namely
to satisfy Washington's conditions for a lifting of the sanctions, by withdrawing
from Indochina and negotiating an armistice with Nationalist China, was more
unfavorable. Military leaders firmly believed that the latter action entailed a
humiliating loss of pride, since it required Japan to accept an ultimatum and forego
any tangible gains from its ventures on the Asian mainland. By August, the army
and navy general staffs conceded that hostilities were inevitable if Japan failed to
secure a rapprochement.[20] At an Imperial conference held on 6 September, the
cabinet drew up the "Guidelines for Implementing National Policies." The plan
was to eliminate American, British and Dutch influence from Asia, and exploit
the resources of the southern regions to enable Japan to fight a drawn-out war.
Admiral Nagano, the navy chief of staff, explained that if the Imperial forces
took key areas in Southeast Asia and the western Pacific at the onset, they could
prepare for an extended war of attrition. Nevertheless, the navy staffs continued
to hold reservations about their capacity to deal with opposition from US forces,
and proposed that Japan carry on with its efforts to reach a compromise with
America. The army command, on the other hand, proved to be a staunch advocate
of war. General Sugiyama argued that if Japan remained idle, by spring 1942,
Allied military preparations were likely to render their forces more difficult to
defeat. The disagreement was ironed out when the services agreed that preparations for war were to be completed before October, at which time Japan's leaders
could decide whether it was necessary to fight the Western powers.

Although Ambassador Nomura was ordered to continue negotiating with
US officials, his capacity to offer any meaningful concessions was restricted
by the Japanese government's uncompromising stand. The liaison conference
held on 13 September laid out Tokyo's minimum demands. Japan was to retain
its special position in China, along with its territorial gains. Such conditions
were unacceptable to the US, and Secretary of State Hull explicitly stated that
troops had to be withdrawn from the Asiatic mainland if the Japanese wished to
seek an agreement. By mid October, after Tojo Hideki was appointed as prime
minister, the army and navy insisted that Japan had to break out of its encirclement by the ABCD (America–Britain–China–Dutch East Indies) powers at
the earliest opportunity. The final decision to commence hostilities was ratified
at an Imperial liaison conference held on 5 November. The negotiations were
given one last deadline, of 30 November, to pull through, and in the event of
failure, the armed forces were to commence hostilities during the first week of
December. The war plan which the navy and army drew up consisted of several
interlocked components.

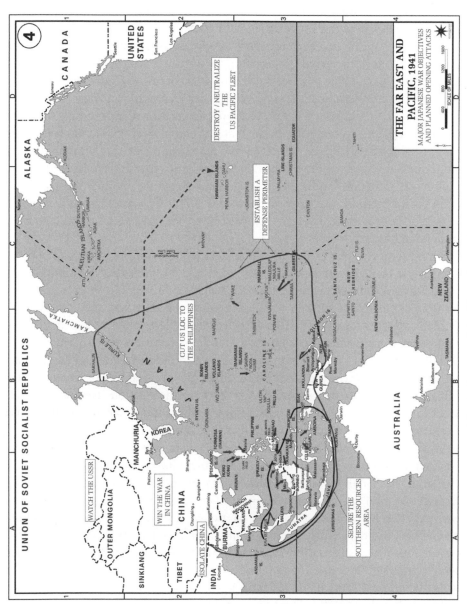

Map 2: Japanese War Plans, December 1941

The main objective was to capture the southern resources region of Malaya and the East Indies. Additional operations were aimed at defending Japan's conquests against an Allied counter-offensive. On the western perimeter, the army was to complete its blockade of China and forestall a British invasion via India, by occupying Burma. On the Pacific front, the navy wrestled with the question of how to defend against American intervention. Capturing the Philippines offered a partial solution, but the Japanese still needed to neutralize the US fleet's capacity to intercept the Imperial forces while they attempted to conquer the southern areas. It was at this point that Admiral Nagano accepted the plan put forward by Yamamoto Isoroku, the commander-in-chief of the Combined Fleet, to conduct a carrier-based air attack on the Pacific Fleet at its main base at Pearl Harbor, before the US navy could mobilize. The final order to prepare for war was issued on 26 November, following the receipt of the Hull Note, which stated that grave consequences would follow if Japan did not accept US demands. The harsh tone was treated as a provocation, and negated whatever hopes which the leadership held on the prospects of achieving an understanding.

The question arises as to why Japan decided to instigate an armed conflict against the United States and its allies, when the latter's industrial and military potential was known to be significantly higher. The main reason was tied to strategic factors. Going to war was seen as the only way to secure Japan's position in Asia against Western interference. The government and military high command became convinced that a confrontation was inevitable, and decided that it was better to initiate it earlier, rather than wait until a later date, when US naval power was likely to be stronger and thereby pose even greater difficulties. Furthermore, if Japan was to procrastinate, its oil and raw materials stocks could only become further depleted. In such scenarios, the navy and army were bound to be placed in a most precarious position.

However, no explanation of Japan's actions in late 1941 can be complete without examining the calculations on which its policymakers based their decisions. Although there was a good awareness of America's economic might, neither the civilian leadership nor military command comprehended how their nation lacked the resources to defeat a coalition of powers which possessed the potential to produce a much greater quantity of weapons. This was mainly because decision-makers preferred not to ponder over evidence which suggested that the Imperial forces might face difficulties. War plans were rarely based on sober calculation, and Japan's leaders engaged in what Michael Barnhart has described as "best case analysis," where they composed a script outlining how they expected the conflict to unfold, and made no allowance for contingencies.[21] Historical precedents played a significant role in laying the grounds for false expectations. The Japanese based their strategic thinking on their experiences during the wars against China and Russia at the turn of the twentieth century, where victory was achieved by dealing a knockout blow at the onset, and thereafter waiting for the enemy to offer peace. However, in both encounters, the Imperial forces were facing opponents who did not have the capacity to stage a substantial counter-attack.

The leadership in Tokyo thus gave little thought to how Japan could fare in a total war, where superiority in armaments production played a decisive role in determining the outcome. By doing so, the Japanese failed to heed one of the cardinal principles expounded by Clausewitz, that statesmen and commanders were "to establish ... the kind of war on which they are embarking," rather than mistaking it for the war they *wanted* to fight'.[22] In September, when the Imperial liaison conflict decided that war would be declared if tensions with the US were not alleviated, the service chiefs provided what turned out to be a sanguine appraisal of how Japan was going to win. The reference document used to answer potential questions, prepared by representatives of the war and navy ministries, opined that, while an American surrender was "well-nigh impossible," Japan could "not exclude the possibility that the war may end because of a change in [US] public opinion, which may result from such factors as the remarkable success of our military operations in the south or the surrender of Great Britain."[23] The Allies were expected to sue for peace after Japan completed its initial conquests. Policymakers also dismissed evidence which pointed to their insecure economic position. In October, shortly after rising to power, Tojo asked the cabinet's planning board to investigate the empire's supply of war materials. Lieutenant-General Suzuki, president of the board, warned that unless shipbuilding was maintained at a sufficient level, Japan could not provide the merchant shipping needed to transport the resources from Southeast Asia and thereby keep its industries afloat.[24] The statement apparently did not raise worries. On the question of funding the war effort, the finance ministry representatives stated that Japan's monetary strength was sufficient, so long as the supply of raw materials was adequate.[25] Neither the service chiefs nor Tojo probed for explanations of what the assessment meant, or what constituted an "adequate supply." The Japanese thus commenced hostilities with a vague idea of how their material requirements were to be sustained.

While Japan's leaders were making their final preparations for war, the US and Britain remained confident that a confrontation was avoidable. In London, Churchill's government maintained that, so long as Britain synchronized its policy with the US, and followed suit in imposing economic restrictions and hinting at further repercussions, the situation in the Far East could be stabilized. Yet, the British began to depend on the US to coerce Japan to behave more amenably. In doing so, they surrendered the initiative of carrying out diplomatic activities and became mere observers of international relations in the Asia. Within the US leadership, most officials were skeptical about the prospects of the Japanese accepting Hull's demands for a withdrawal from China. Yet, neither the White House nor the State Department believed that a failure to reach reconciliation would culminate with hostilities.

In regard to military action, the Associated Powers believed that they could discourage Japanese aggression by undertaking a visible strengthening of their forces. Churchill argued that, with the US Pacific Fleet preparing for mobilization at Pearl Harbor, a British naval force at Singapore would negate whatever optimism the Japanese had in their ability to wage war. In October, the defense committee decided to dispatch Force Z to Singapore, consisting of the modern battleship, *Prince of Wales* and the vintage battle-cruiser *Repulse*.[26] Nobody in the British cabinet nor the Admiralty believed that a token fleet of such obsolescent vessels could resist a Japanese attack on Malaya. The intention was to show that Britain still had a presence in the Far East. London also needed to allay the criticisms which the Pacific dominions of Australia and New Zealand had begun to voice, namely that the British were not doing enough to protect their imperial subjects against the rising tide of Japanese aggression.

US defense officials became equally fixated with the notion that Japan could be deterred by a show of force. This became especially true after the Joint Board approved the plan to dispatch several squadrons of medium-range B-17 bombers to the Philippines. The decision to bolster American strengths in the Far East was made during summer 1941, out of concern that Japan's alignment with the Axis powers necessitated protective measures.[27] In October, Secretary of War Henry Stimson told Roosevelt that the bomber threat "bids fair to stop Japan's march to the south."[28] By reinforcing the Philippines, the Americans could bide their time, and avert hostilities until their military position was strengthened. Large sections of the military leadership also concluded that Allied forces could inflict crippling losses on a Japanese expedition.[29] The belief was based on an underestimation of Japan's military strengths and its determination to eliminate Allied positions in Southeast Asia. The War Department's planning division contended that the Associated Powers should attempt to halt Japan along the "general line of Hong-Kong to the Philippines," the latter of which held the key to maintaining the line.[30] South of this line were "successive positions from which the combined ground, air and naval forces of the Associated Powers could exact a tremendous toll."

The United States thus did not anticipate a war against Japan, and the attack on Pearl Harbor was a genuine surprise. Conspiracy theorists have claimed that President Roosevelt knew about the Japanese plan, but kept the information secret from the public in order to allow the Imperial forces to carry out their operations and thereby give the US a valid pretext for declaring war.[31] However, the theories are based on tenuous evidence. A more credible argument is that the US intelligence community had only vague data on what Japan intended to do. The government and military leadership continued to keep their policies under a tight veil of secrecy. Under the circumstances, the Americans could receive only hazy indications of their adversary's intentions. For example, in March, the naval attaché in Tokyo quoted a statement by a former Japanese admiral to the effect that war against the US would commence with the navy conducting attacks against the Philippines and Hawaii. However, the statement was made long before the navy had finalized its strategy, and appeared more as a boastful announcement.[32]

Intercepts of Japanese communications, which intelligence staffs tended to rely on more extensively, indicated that war was imminent, but did not specify where the Japanese were planning to strike. While American cryptographers had decoded *Purple* by 1941, the information provided by diplomatic signals intelligence was limited to that pertaining to policy objectives, since they were written and sent by foreign ministry officials who did not have a full knowledge of the strategies which their military counterparts were planning.[33] On 15 November, Tokyo instructed its consulate in Honolulu to report regularly on the position of US ships based at Pearl Harbor.[34] Naval intelligence translated the message in early December, and the information suggested that the Japanese were contemplating an attack on Hawaii. Yet the evidence simply indicated that efforts were being made to ascertain the status of the US fleet, without providing concrete details of an impending operation. US intelligence also picked up the foreign ministry's "Winds message" of 19 November, ordering all diplomatic missions to destroy their cipher machines upon receipt of a coded weather report indicating the imminence of war.[35] On 2 December, both army and navy intelligence received word that Japanese missions in Washington, London, Singapore and Manila had been ordered to dispose their telegraphic codes and related documents. Nevertheless, the location of naval units could be determined only by breaking JN-25a and JN-25b, which by all reliable accounts, had not been fully decoded in December 1941.[36] In any case, Japanese operational procedures stipulated that the attacking forces maintain radio silence, in order to achieve surprise.[37] Under the circumstances, information on the Pearl Harbor attack was simply not available.

The miscalculations made by US authorities were thus inevitable, in light of their existing knowledge. Few people believed that the Imperial fleet could mount more than one major operation at a time. The carrier fleet was considered probably to be concentrated in the East Indies and Malaya, which, owing to their oil and mineral resources, constituted much more important objectives.[38] Most importantly, given that war was bound to result in an ultimate defeat for Japan, combined with evidence which suggested that its actions were being limited by apprehension about facing a costly confrontation, the US and its allies were most likely to adhere to their belief that hostilities could be averted. Under the circumstances, it was logical to give minimal consideration to the prospect of having to fight a war in the Pacific. The speed and scale of Japan's victories during the opening stages of the conflict convinced the Allies that their adversary could not be dissuaded.

4

Japan Triumphant, December 1941 to Spring 1942

Between December 1941 and early 1942, while Japan made its lightning conquest of Southeast Asia and the western Pacific, its navy and army appeared invincible to the Allies. Indeed, the Japanese victories owed themselves largely to skilful planning, along with the tactical and technological efficiency of their armed forces. The weak state of the US and British empire also played an important part in facilitating Japan's successes. Yet, as early as March 1942, the high command had to contend with many of the weaknesses which plagued its war machine, the most important of which was that neither the IJN nor IJA had the capacity to defeat the Western powers in a prolonged conflict. The Imperial forces were overstretched, and America had not been knocked out of the war. On the contrary, the US was preparing to strike back, and most importantly, it possessed the industrial resources to build a military force that was far superior to anything the Japanese could deploy. Yet the military leadership failed to comprehend the predicament it faced, and maintained that Japan could deal a crippling blow on its opponents and thereafter secure its conquests against enemy invasions. The misperception led the Japanese to embark on a number of failed ventures in the Indian Ocean and Pacific areas which eventually culminated with the IJN's defeat at Midway in June 1942. The latter encounter was arguably the single battle which turned the tide of the war in the Allies' favor, and emasculated Japan's capacity to conduct further territorial conquests.

The Pacific war commenced 7–8 December, with Japanese forces attacking the US fleet's main base at Pearl Harbor, while simultaneously launching their invasion of British, American and Dutch territories in Southeast Asia. On the morning of 7 December, local Hawaiian time, a task force composed of six aircraft carriers – *Akagi*, *Kaga*, *Hiryu*, *Soryu*, *Shokaku* and *Zuikaku* – reached the vicinity of Oahu, after sailing across 3,000 miles of open sea.[1] The carriers, along with their accompanying battleships and cruisers, had set off from Tankan Bay in the Kurile Islands on 26 November, and took a northerly route across the Pacific. By doing so, the carriers avoided the main shipping lanes and remained undetected. The weather conditions were also conducive for concealing the task force from reconnaissance aircraft, with thick fog interspersed by heavy gale winds. The final order to carry out the operation came on 2 December, when Admiral Nagumo, commander of the task force, received a coded message, "Niitaka yama nobore" (Climb Mount Niitaka). After reaching within 300 miles of Oahu, Nagumo ordered the aircraft to fly off in separate waves, so that they could evade radar detection. By 06:15, all planes from the first wave, led by Commander Mitsuo Fuchida, were on their way. The first bombs started falling on Pearl Harbor at 07:55. The raid lasted a little less than 2 hours, and by the time the Japanese had recovered their planes and the carriers retreated from Hawaiian waters, they destroyed two battleships, including the USS *Arizona* and *Oklahoma*. The battleships, *California*, *Nevada* and *West Virginia*, along with a number of cruisers and destroyers, also suffered extensive damage. Over 100 aircraft were also destroyed, while Japanese losses amounted to a mere 29 planes.

Concurrently with the Pearl Harbor attack, the Imperial forces launched their invasion of the southern regions. The ultimate objective was to secure the East Indies oilfields. In order to achieve this, the army conducted a two-pronged assault. The first column focused on Malaya and the British navy's bastion at Singapore, with the second column taking on American forces in the Philippines. After securing both areas, the invading forces were to converge. The assault on Malaya and the Philippines commenced on 8 December, local time. Unfortunately, the army encountered unexpectedly strong resistance in the Philippines. Although by early January, the bulk of the American forces were confined to their enclave on the Bataan peninsula, the rugged terrain and thick jungle vegetation did not permit easy movement, and the defenders also put up a strong fight. General Homma's conquest of the archipelago was delayed, and the invasion plan for the southern regions was thrown off balance. Yet the high command decided that the East Indies needed to be secured before the Allies could bring in reinforcements. In order to allow the army to commit the larger part of its forces towards its main objective in the Indies, the Imperial high command reduced the size of the Philippines force, and by doing so, incurred a substantial delay in eliminating American forces on the archipelago.

Nevertheless, despite some setbacks, the operations in the southern regions were carried out with considerable efficiency.[2] In Malaya, the forward elements of the Twenty-Fifth Army landed at Kota Baru and Singora on the northeast coast. The British attempted to halt the arrival of reinforcements and dispatched a capital ship force from Singapore, commanded by Admiral Philips, consisting of the *Prince of Wales* and *Repulse*. The aim was to sink Japanese transports in the South China Sea, but on 10 December, naval aircraft operating from bases in southern Indochina sank both vessels, thereby enabling the remaining elements of General Yamashita's forces to land without facing any opposition from the sea. Once ashore, the Japanese advanced rapidly through the jungle, against the weak resistance put up by General Percival's army, and reached the doorstep of

Singapore in less than 2 months. The beleaguered British garrison capitulated on 15 February, with its hold on the supposedly impregnable fortress in ruins.

Allied positions in other parts of Southeast Asia fell with equal rapidity. At Hong Kong, the Twenty-Third Army ousted the British defenders on 25 December. Meanwhile, the Kawaguchi expeditionary detachment struck British Borneo, and captured the oilfields in the vicinity of Miri. On the east coast, Japanese infantry battalions secured Tarakan and Balikpapan by the end of January. A detachment of Allied vessels, consisting of cruisers and destroyers operating under the combined American–British–Dutch–Australian (ABDA) command, which had been established in January and was led by the Dutch Rear-Admiral Karel Doorman, attempted to halt the landing. However, without proper air cover, the ABDA force could not defend itself against enemy planes, and as a result, the cruisers *Marblehead* and *Houston* were hit. With the Imperial forces poised to invade the East Indies, the Dutch were determined at least to save the main island of Java. However, the Japanese onslaught proved too overpowering. On 14 February, paratroopers landed near Palembang in southern Sumatra, and 3 days later, the Thirty-Eighth division captured the oilfields. Doorman's ABDA fleet attempted to intercept the warships and transports heading for Java and the neighboring island of Bali, but could not maintain a concentrated formation against the Japanese fleet's heavy gunfire. The Sixteenth Army thus landed on the east coast of Java without opposition. The final attempt to hold the island was made between 27 February and 1 March. ABDA command received information that several invasion armadas were headed southwards, and Doorman's fleet set sail from the port of Surabaya. During the ensuing battle of the Java Sea, the Japanese managed to sink the majority of the Allied vessels. On 9 March, Dutch forces surrendered the East Indies to the invaders.

In Burma, the IJA attempted to complete the encirclement of China and cut off its remaining supply routes, with the Fifteenth Army assigned to stage the invasion. The bulk of the British and Indian forces near Rangoon were defeated in March, and by May, they retreated across the border into India. In the Philippines, the Japanese overcame the remnants of American resistance around Bataan and Corregidor. Meanwhile, the South Seas Detachment secured the islands of Guam and Wake. By mid 1942, Allied forces were pushed back to their rear bases in the Indian Ocean and Australia, leaving Southeast Asia and the western Pacific regions under complete Japanese control.

REASONS FOR JAPANESE SUCCESSES

The success achieved by the Imperial navy and army in securing control over an area stretching thousands of miles from Burma, all the way through the

East Indies to the islands of the Pacific, in such a short period of time can be attributed to effective strategic and operational planning on the part of the high command, coupled with the fighting skill of the Japanese forces at the battlefront level. In addition, the poor level of preparedness which the Allied defenders demonstrated in areas such as Malaya and the Philippines played a distinct role in helping the invaders.

At the strategic and operational levels, the Japanese succeeded primarily because the navy managed to attain complete command over both the sea and airspace in the areas they intended to conquer. Furthermore, the IJN made good use of its limited strength by concentrating on key positions in the western Pacific. Throughout the period prior to the war, the navy strived to develop a way to optimize its resources.[3] Commanders realized that a numerically inferior fleet had to rely on the element of surprise if it was to have any prospect of defeating its opponents, and focused on commencing wars with a preemptive strike. The idea was to destroy the American fleet before it could threaten Japan's home waters. Indeed, the Pearl Harbor operation was among the most notable examples of how the attacking side could use secrecy and deception to catch the defenders off guard and inflict a devastating blow. With the navy able to achieve supremacy over the Pacific regions, the IJA could be assured that transports were able to carry troops to the areas of operations without facing any significant Allied interference. The army was also supported by a secure supply line which stretched back to the home islands. This meant that once onshore, troops received a steady flow of reinforcements and equipment to sustain their advance.

Japanese operational planning was also helped by an efficient intelligence network. For example, Colonel Tsuji Masanobu, chief of the Twenty-fifth Army's operations staff, recalled how his officers conducted a detailed survey of the landing beaches in Malaya, and meticulously verified the possible routes for the inland advance.[4] Japanese agents also carried out sabotage operations, destroying installations such as air bases, oilfields, and railway lines in a systematic manner. Equally impressive were their subversive activities. Winning the hearts and minds of the indigenous people in Southeast Asia had been a key objective for years. By the time the war broke out, the intelligence services had forged connections with key leaders of the Nationalist movements in most of the European colonies, and extensively spread anti-Western propaganda to the local population. As a result, the invasion received widespread local support. When the Imperial army entered the East Indies and Philippines, the colonial administrations collapsed almost overnight.[5] In Malaya, thousands of Indian troops deserted the British army, and joined forces with the conquerors.

The Imperial forces also successfully devised tactics and weapons which enabled them to out-maneuver their opponents. In particular, the navy demonstrated how it had made a fruitful effort to develop the fighting capacity to secure control over the western Pacific areas. The Japanese sought to circumvent the disadvantages arising from their inability to match Western levels of ship construction, by building vessels with greater firepower and endurance. By the late 1920s, technicians and engineers had developed a number of sophisticated armaments that placed the IJN in a good position to compete with its US and British rivals. Battleships and cruisers were fitted with guns and torpedoes that outranged most of their opponents, as well as larger propulsion systems to increase their velocity and cruising radius.[6] In order to enable gun crews to deliver accurate fire, control towers were constructed with extra elevation so that they could house various pieces of equipment such as range finders, searchlight directors and firing calculators. Officers in the bridge were also able to locate their targets from a longer range. Naval ordnance performed well. The long-lance was the most advanced torpedo to be constructed for the duration of the conflict, and could hit targets up to 10,000 yards away at a speed of 45 knots. Torpedoes were also oxygen-propelled, which meant that they did not produce a wake, thereby rendering them difficult to detect. In the area of tactics, the Imperial fleet developed innovative ways of using modern technologies. Crews were adept at conducting night operations. This was an aspect which most navies, including the British and Americans, had neglected, mainly because maneuvers under the cover of darkness were deemed to be too complicated. Radio silence was also maintained in order to avoid revealing the ships' positions. The Japanese fleet's advantages became fully apparent at the Battle of the Java Sea, when they frequently managed to locate and sink Allied forces before the latter could react.

The IJN also made a painstaking effort to build up its air power. Under the 1937 fleet replenishment program, the 25,000 ton carriers, *Shokaku* and *Zuikaku*, were constructed. In the same year, the navy air staff established the specifications for the Zero fighter, which was designed to fly with greater range, speed, and maneuverability than any rival interceptor.[7] Mitsubishi was commissioned to construct the new fighter, and by September 1940, the first completed machine entered service in China. As a result, the Japanese were able to attain control over the skies in the areas where they conquered, and eliminate their opponents' air forces. Bombardment operations were also carried out effectively. Aircraft manufacturers assembled a number of bomber types which launched torpedo and aerial attacks with a high level of accuracy.[8] Naval pilots in particular were well trained, and demonstrated their capacity to take out enemy vessels both in port as well as in the open sea. The sinking of the British capital ships *Prince of Wales* and *Repulse* off the coast of Malaya demonstrated the skill and accuracy of Japanese bombardment techniques. Aircrews often used several types of maneuvers in conjunction in an effort to overwhelm the defenders. Horizontal bombers initiated the raid, attracting the attention of anti-aircraft crews. Torpedo planes and dive bombers then followed, and were often able to operate without interference. Pilots pressed home their raids, even when they faced opposition. The result was often a highly efficient bombing pattern. The naval air service also provided support for the amphibious operations in the Dutch East Indies and Malaya, with good results. Flying boats conducted reconnaissance missions, while heavy air attacks were launched to take out communications facilities and coastal defense batteries.[9] In order to achieve air superiority over the vicinity of the landing beaches and thus protect the landing parties from aerial opposition, the Japanese undertook to neutralize the nearby aerodromes.

Although the Imperial army was not as technologically advanced as the navy, its tactics nevertheless showed finesse. The most decisive advantage was the maneuverability and fighting skill of Japanese infantry units. In the area of amphibious operations, landing parties rarely faced troubles in securing a foothold on their objectives. The Japanese developed suitable equipment, including landing craft with hinged bows that allowed the quick unloading of troops and supplies. In Malaya, amphibious forces often chose beaches which the defending forces had considered unsuitable for landings, owing to the steep gradient and choppy tidewater. Adverse terrain and weather were not an obstacle, and on the contrary, the Japanese deliberately carried out their operations in such conditions so that they could appear where their opponents least expected an attack. The army also proved adept at conducting overland advances, particularly in the jungle terrain which prevailed in the Far East. Troops did not depend on motorized transport, and could overcome any natural feature, including hills, wooded country, and river crossings. By doing so, the attackers circumvented the main roads, where Allied forces had concentrated their defenses. Within days after the landing at Malaya, the IJA's skilful outflanking moves left British forces with few choices apart from withdrawing and consolidating themselves in more tenable positions at the southern portion of the peninsula. The Japanese also regularly infiltrated their enemy's positions. In the Philippines, small parties often broke through the gaps in the US army's lines, remaining silent, and waited for reinforcements to arrive until a sufficient force was gathered to launch a small assault. Firecrackers and other types of ruses were then set off to confuse the defending troops over the location of the attacking force. Thereafter, the invaders overwhelmed the disoriented American soldiers by launching a full-scale advance. The Imperial army was also aided by the strong morale which prevailed within its rank and file. Troops conducted their advances with little concern for losses, and demonstrated an unquestioned dedication towards their organization. Lieutenant-General Hutton, who commanded the British forces in Burma, noted that the fundamental cause for the Japanese success was the extent to which soldiers had been imbued with an "offensive spirit."[10]

Finally, the Imperial forces were aided because the defending Allied forces were in a weak state. In regard to naval and air forces, the British and Americans not only lacked adequate strengths, but were poorly equipped and inefficiently trained. Part of the problem was that Western personnel held condescending views of the Japanese, and thought that the latter were incapable of putting up a serious contest. A more serious problem stemmed from the fact that the bulk of the Allied navies and air services were committed to the Atlantic theater, which meant the Pacific areas could not be defended with large forces. The most scathing criticisms, however, were directed at the armies. In many cases, the Americans and British outnumbered the Japanese, but lacked the tactical skill to forestall the invaders. Troops were inept at fighting in undeveloped country. In order to ensure that their positions could be defended, soldiers had to adopt more imaginative methods. Many British army officers conceded that their traditional procedures of employing fixed defenses were unlikely to work if the positions could be bypassed and were not held with adequate strength.[11] Defending forces needed to conduct an aggressive patrol of their surroundings, and in situations where difficult terrain restricted the use of motorized transport, the proper deployment of foot soldiers was vital.

Allied commanders also conceded that their failures were due to a prevailing lack of discipline. A US officer who served in the Philippines noted how the morale of troops was unsatisfactory, and insisted that soldiers needed to undergo a "spiritual training" along the lines of the Japanese, in order to develop a more aggressive attitude.[12] Likewise, General Pownall pondered how British troops were overly dependent on creature comforts and held an aversion to strenuous work, both of which gave rise to a situation where training was conducted without preparing troops for battle conditions.[13] Western personnel who lacked the fortitude to fight in the trying conditions which prevailed in the jungles of Southeast Asia and the islands of the western Pacific were simply no match for the efficiently trained Japanese army, whose troops held a high level of stamina.

WEAKNESSES OF JAPAN'S WAR MACHINE

Despite the swift and overwhelming triumphs which Japan achieved during the opening months of the conflict, by March 1942, its forces were stretched to the limit, and did not have the capacity to achieve their ultimate objective of eliminating America's capacity to counter-attack. Yet Japan's leaders prosecuted their war effort without paying due attention to their strategic dilemma. The situation was further complicated because the navy and army disagreed on what the main objectives were, thereby preventing the armed services from developing a coordinated plan.

Strategic planning continued to be hindered by a number of flaws, the most important of which was that the high command did not have a realistic idea of what course of action Japan was going to pursue in order to prevail. Following the completion of the initial operations in Southeast Asia and the western Pacific, the Japanese were faced with a critical decision on whether to consolidate their territories, or pursue further conquests. The liaison conference of 7 March 1942 set out three aims, which were to: (i) "to expand on the military achievements already accomplished," (ii) to secure "long-term political and military indestructibility," and (iii) to take active measures to force Britain's surrender and make America lose the will to fight.[14] However, the order of priority remained muddled, and the paper did not stipulate whether the Imperial forces were to fight a protracted war, or to seek a short and decisive conflict.

To complicate matters, there were no courses of action which held a good promise of defeating the Allies.[15] The first option was to advance towards the Central Pacific and capture the Hawaiian islands, thereby pushing the US navy back to the west coast of America. However, a surprise attack was virtually impossible, because the Pacific Fleet was on full alert after Pearl Harbor, and it also had enough ships to confront the enemy in the event the main base at Hawaii was threatened. The Japanese navy also considered an advance towards the southwest Pacific, in an effort to capture the Solomon Islands and sever the supply line between the US and Australia, thus preventing the latter from being used as a base for Allied counter-attacks against the southern portion of Japan's empire. The operation held equally low prospects of succeeding, since the IJN did not have a sufficient reserve of transports and supply ships that could maintain the army's operations in areas far removed from the home islands.

Efforts to devise a viable war plan were further hindered by inter-service rivalry and the absence of centralized control. Under the terms of the 1889 constitution, the general staffs had direct access to the Emperor, which meant they could push forward their policies without consulting each other. While the navy envisaged an oceanic war against the US and Britain, the army maintained that Japan's ultimate objective was to conclude the war in China and prepare for action in Siberia. A combined Imperial General Headquarters (IGHQ) had been established after the Sino-Japanese conflict broke out in 1937, but the meetings usually saw the service representatives attempting to win Imperial approval for their proposals, rather than working out a compromise. Nor were civilian leaders able to introduce any solutions. Most prime ministers, including Tojo, often did not have the clout to influence military decisions. They often raised important questions concerning strategy, but preferred to allow the service staffs to decide on how to resolve them. In March, Tojo convened an investigation of how Japan could achieve a final victory, but the grand strategy which emerged simply combined the navy and army views.[16] The lack of a strong leadership meant that war plans were usually an amalgamation of the grandiose schemes proposed by the services, and the system did not permit a coordinated deployment of scarce resources. Inter-service rivalry also prevented the Japanese from seizing a number of key opportunities, including an attack on British possessions in the Indian Ocean and a push towards the Middle East.[17] The move would have enabled the Imperial forces to deal a serious blow against Britain by severing its communications to India and the vital Middle Eastern oil supplies. The operation also held immense propaganda value for the Axis powers, since it enabled a link-up with Rommel's *Afrika Korps*. Yet, while the navy supported the plan, the army refused to supply the troops.

In addition to structural faults, war planning was plagued by a number of bad practices. The lightning successes achieved during the opening stages of the conflict reinforced a prevalent tendency in Japanese military thinking, namely to underestimate the challenges facing the Imperial forces. The habit proved particularly detrimental when engaging opponents such as the US and its coalition partners, who not only had a vastly superior economic capability over Japan and the potential to produce a considerably greater quantity of armaments. Of equal importance, the Western powers were determined to fight a total war, where the main objective was to completely destroy the Axis powers' hold on their conquests. Under the circumstances, a series of defeats in the short run was unlikely to halt the Allied effort.

Yet, military calculations continued to be based on the expectation that the conflict would unfold in a manner that was favorable for Japan, and that the IJN and IJA could destroy the Allies' capacity to launch a counter-offensive. Japan's leaders did not consider the contingencies that could arise in the event of failure. On the contrary, they not only became convinced that the armed forces could achieve a decisive victory, but insisted that they had to do so at the earliest opportunity. Any proposals for consolidating, and avoiding further engagements with the enemy, were therefore treated with scorn. Recent works of Japanese wartime strategy have cogently argued that a defensive campaign offered the most sensible means to safeguard the empire. The failed attempts to destroy the US fleet during 1942 at Midway and the Solomon Islands resulted in a needless expenditure of limited strengths, when the navy and its air arm could have been more usefully deployed to reinforce key bastions such as the Marianas and Philippines.[18] Such would have enabled the Japanese to put up a significantly higher level of resistance against the Allied thrust into the western

Pacific, and delayed the establishment of bases within striking range of the home islands.

In addition to leading the Imperial forces to embark on risky ventures, the tendency to overrate Japan's prospects of winning had two adverse effects that proved fatal in the long run. First, the armed services continued to lag when it came to establishing an adequate intelligence network that could properly gauge the fighting capabilities of the Allies. On one hand, the navy and army were proficient at collecting information on matters such as the location and disposition of enemy forces, especially during their early campaigns. However, in carrying out their intelligence activities, neither the navy nor army paid much attention to more important long-term issues, such as the ways in which Japan's opponents could enhance both the numerical strength and combat skills of their armed forces.[19] Because military leaders developed an unquestioned belief that their forces were invincible, they saw no incentive to improve their information-handling apparatus. In fact, some key components of the intelligence machinery were dismantled. For example, when the Imperial army completed its operations in Southeast Asia, the Southern Army headquarters amalgamated its intelligence section with operations, alleging that the former had lost its *raison d'être*.[20] As a result, the Japanese became increasingly misinformed about their foes, and poor knowledge of the enemy played a key role in preventing the military from making wise strategic decisions.

Secondly, the Japanese failed to improve their weapons and fighting methods. The army in particular maintained that, because the British and Americans were unable to hold their positions in Southeast Asia, they were categorically incapable of putting up a serious challenge. In reality, the conquest of areas such as the Philippines and Malaya was quick not only because the Japanese demonstrated a good level of tactical skill. The successes also owed themselves largely to the fact that the IJA only had to face poorly trained and ill-equipped opponents. Yet the rank and file remained imbued with an institutionalized conception that Western forces were unable to achieve the discipline needed to withstand the strains of prolonged combat. The accepted belief was that, in spite of the Imperial army's shortage of modern weapons, its troops could prevail in all circumstances solely by the virtue of their spiritual bravery. The belief that morale and psychological factors could overcome all obstacles was shared by top leaders within the political and military hierarchy. For example, when speaking to a group of reporters in November 1942, General Suzuki Teiichi, the president of the cabinet's planning board, stated, "the key to final victory lies not in the material strength of the nation, but in the spirit which infuses strength in all directions."[21] The lack of concern for technological resources and modern equipment, including tanks, heavy artillery and motorized vehicles, meant that the army did not make any earnest attempts to modify its procedures, and abided by its practice of relying upon the infantry as its primary weapon.

The IJN and its air arm were marginally less blissful than the army, and their combat doctrine demonstrated a degree of understanding that adequate equipment was essential when fighting the Allies. However, neither the fleet nor the air services were constructed with a view to fighting a protracted conflict. Naval policy was geared towards constructing vessels for offensive operations, namely battleships, aircraft carriers and submarines. Little thought was given to safeguarding the oceanic trade routes between Southeast Asia and the home islands, which Japan's war industries relied upon for their supplies of raw materials. At the start of the war, the Imperial navy did not have any ships assigned for convoy tasks, and even when Japan started to construct its fleet of destroyer escorts, the number available was far below the minimum required. Naval traditions had scorned escorting missions as mundane, and not befitting of a fighting force geared for offensive warfare.[22] Because Japanese doctrine focused on the concept of defeating the enemy in a battle fleet action, naval officers paid scant attention to developing the vessels, tactics, and doctrine needed for a successful merchant shipping defense.[23] Consequently, the Japanese were ill-prepared for a situation where the Americans conducted sustained attacks on their transports, and the navy ended up facing severe shortages of oil and other resources needed to support its war effort.

The air services were plagued by a skewed doctrine which stated that the quality of their planes was sufficient to overcome any material advantages which the Allies enjoyed. In fact, Japan could maintain its lead only so long as its forces were facing weaker opponents. Because aircraft and pilots could not be constructed at an equivalent rate to what the Allies could achieve, losses could be afforded only with the greatest difficulty. To make matters worse, the initial successes created a false sense of confidence, and the air services did not try to modernize their equipment.[24] Commanders also failed to grasp the extent to which their successes during the opening months of the conflict owed themselves to Japanese forces having an overwhelming numerical superiority in the air.[25] Instead, the victories were attributed solely to tactical talent, and the significance of statistical factors in determining the outcome of battles was overlooked. As a result, the naval air arm failed to prepare for encounters with stronger opponents.

JAPAN LOSES THE INITIATIVE, MARCH TO JUNE 1942

By March 1942, Japan found itself reacting to Allied moves, rather than dictating its own strategy. The army was scattered across an area stretching thousands of miles across Southeast Asia, and did not have the strength to carry out further conquests. Meanwhile, the IJN's actions reflected its firm belief that a decisive victory was within reach. In the Indian Ocean, the British started to assemble several carriers and battleships at their base in Ceylon, in order to defend the region against incursions. Japanese naval commanders received word on the buildup, and a large section of Admiral Yamamoto's staff believed that the Royal Navy had to be neutralized before the Imperial fleet could confront the Americans. On 26 March, a fleet of five carriers, commanded by Admiral Nagumo Chuichi, sailed westward from Singapore. The objective was to launch a Pearl Harbor-style raid on the British base at Trincomalee. However, Nagumo was unable to repeat the coup achieved against the US Pacific Fleet, because the British and Americans had broken the Imperial navy's JN-25b just a few weeks earlier. On 2 April, as the fleet approached Ceylon, naval signals intelligence provided Admiral James Somerville, commanding the Eastern Fleet, with advanced warning of the attack. The admiral ordered all British vessels to be evacuated to East Africa, so that they could be kept out of harm's reach. The Japanese did manage to sink the carrier *Hermes*, along with the cruiser *Cornwall*. The raid also caused considerable alarm for the British. Back in London, and the chiefs of staff concluded that if the Japanese were to press westward, India would be placed in great danger, with the Middle East and its essential supply lines placed under threat.[26] However, for the amount of naval strength which the Japanese committed, the operation achieved minimal results. The bulk of the Eastern Fleet escaped, thanks to timely warning and skilful maneuvering. Nor did the raid seriously damage the installations at Ceylon, and most of the Royal Air Force's planes emerged unscathed.

Following the Ceylon operation, Nagumo's carriers sailed back to the home islands in order to resupply, and prepare for a showdown with the Americans. The navy command hoped that the fleet could enjoy a rest period during which time it would be able to decide on which course of action to pursue. However, the plan was thrown off balance on 18 April, when the US carrier *Hornet* sailed within 600 miles of Japan, and launched a squadron of medium bombers, headed by Captain Doolittle, to conduct a raid on Tokyo and several other cities. The attacks caused minimal damage, and a large proportion of Doolittle's force either ran out of fuel or were shot down before they could find safety in Chinese Nationalist-held territory. However, the operation dealt a severe psychological blow to the Japanese, who had been presented with visible proof that the home islands were not immune to attack by foreign forces, contrary to what they had previously believed. The naval high command decided that Japan needed to secure its outer perimeter by capturing the island of Midway, along with the Aleutian Islands.

Map 3: Allied and Japanese Areas of Control, Spring 1942

The air arm could then establish advanced bases from which it could intercept any task force that attempted to cross the Pacific and approach the home islands. Perhaps of greatest importance, by threatening areas that lay within striking distance of Pearl Harbor and the US mainland, the Japanese expected to lure the Americans into deploying their remaining carriers and expose them to destruction.

The southern coast of New Guinea was added to the list of objectives when the retreating Allied forces began to build up a large reserve of troops, planes and ships in Australia. The Japanese rightly suspected that General MacArthur, commanding the US army in the Southwest Pacific theater, planned to use the continent as a base for his counter-attack. The army proposed an occupation of Port Moresby, which lay only 300 miles from the north coast of Australia, with a view to sealing Japan's southern perimeter. Although Admiral Yamamoto wished to muster the Combined Fleet's strengths for a decisive engagement against the US navy, he agreed to support the army's expedition, on the grounds that Allied opposition was expected to be minimal. The seaborne assault on New Guinea, (code-named MO), was ordered in late April. A carrier task force sailed from the IJN's forward base at Truk on 1 May, and was joined by a detachment of auxiliary vessels based at Rabaul, on the island of New Britain. However, the US Pacific Fleet was alerted to the attack by signals intelligence, as well as information provided by "coast watchers" stationed across various islands, which reported on the sighting of Japanese ships and communicated with outside world by using high power radio sets. Two of the US navy's carriers, the *Lexington* and *Yorktown*, which were on patrol missions in the southwest Pacific, headed for New Guinea to block the incursion. Japanese commanders were unaware that their moves had been tracked. During the ensuing battle of the Coral Sea, 4–8 May, the Americans lost the *Lexington*, but still emerged with enough carriers to defend their most important outlying position at Midway. Furthermore, the Japanese suffered their share of setbacks when the convoys headed for Port Moresby had to turn back in order to avoid interception by the US task force.

The failure to secure New Guinea made the Midway operation all the more imperative. Admiral Yamamoto wished to occupy the island before early June, and believed that the objective could be accomplished before the US navy could put up a sufficiently strong defense. What the Japanese did not know was that the carriers *Enterprise* and *Hornet* had been rushed back to Pearl Harbor, and put in a state of readiness to counter a Japanese thrust into the Central Pacific. The *Yorktown*, which had suffered damage at Coral Sea, was also repaired within 3 days of returning to Hawaii on 27 May, and ready for action. Yet Yamamoto and his staff presumed that the *Yorktown* had been sunk or at least put out of action, with the remaining carriers still on patrol missions in the southwest Pacific.

The miscalculation of US naval dispositions led the Japanese to embark on a mission which culminated with irreplaceable losses to their fleet. Nor were Imperial navy commanders aware that the Pacific Fleet was picking up information on their movements by reading their radio communications. As early as the third week of May, the Pacific Fleet's combat intelligence unit, code-named HYPO, had intercepted signals which suggested that the Japanese were targeting an objective designated "AF". A growing number of code-breakers based at HYPO surmised that "AF" referred to Midway, and Lieutenant-Commander Joseph Rochefort, the officer in command, came up with a scheme to trick the Japanese into exposing the precise location. The garrison commander at Midway was ordered to make an emergency radio call in plain text, stating that the island's water distillation plant had broken down. A signal was immediately sent back, informing that a water barge was on its way. The ruse was successful, and within 24 hours, a Japanese radio station at Wake Island was heard to be reporting that "AF" was apparently running short of water.

By 21 May, when Nimitz assembled the Pacific Fleet, his intelligence staffs were able to provide him with constant updates on enemy movements. Rear-Admiral Raymond Spruance, who had replaced William Halsey as commander of Task Force Sixteen after the latter temporarily succumbed to a skin illness, was ordered to take the *Enterprise*, *Hornet* and *Yorktown* westward to counter the Japanese. Rear-Admiral Frank Fletcher, based on the flagship *Yorktown*, was in overall charge of the carrier forces while they were at sea. The Americans monitored the enemy's approach by conducting long-range reconnaissance patrols with their bombers based at Midway. On the other hand, Admiral Nagumo, whose task force had set off from Japan on 27 May, was handicapped by two factors. First, he remained unaware that the US navy was preparing to ambush his force as it approached Midway, and held onto his conviction that the American carriers were still in the South Pacific. As a result, Nagumo did not order regular patrol missions that could provide him with timely information on the presence of Spruance's task force. Secondly, Nagumo's underestimation concerning the strength of the enemy carrier force resulted in a failure to provide a sufficient number of planes for the operation.

The first encounter took place on 3 June, when a PBY Catalina reconnaissance plane spotted the Japanese fleet. B-17 Flying Fortresses based at Midway launched an attack, but inflicted little damage. In the early hours of the next morning, Japanese bombers raided the atoll. The defending planes, consisting of obsolete Brewster Buffaloes and Wildcats, were no match for the Zeros. However, the island's anti-aircraft defenses proved fully capable of countering the raid, and the Japanese squadron ended up losing more than half of its planes. The depletion of the attack force enabled the Americans to fight their opponent on more numerically equal terms.

During the subsequent phases of the battle, the Imperial fleet's setbacks were mostly due to misfortune, while the US Navy's successes could be attributed to a number of critical decisions. Shortly after Midway received the first report on the incoming Japanese planes, the Americans raided the carrier *Akagi*, and lost a large number of bombers. Nagumo decided to neutralize the air threat from Midway by launching a second attack, and ordered that his supply of reserve planes, which had been on stand-by to strike the enemy fleet, be re-equipped with bombs suited for ground targets. However, the plan was thrown off balance when a Japanese search plane reported sighting the US carrier force at a position 200 miles to the east. The admiral had to make a difficult decision that could determine the fate of his fleet. Deck crews not only had to carry out yet another refit of the planes to prepare them for anti-shipping raids, but also had to make room for the returning Midway attack force, thereby placing a substantial delay on raiding the American fleet. Meanwhile, Fletcher, who had been informed that the Japanese were within striking distance, ordered the *Enterprise* and *Hornet* to launch their bombers. Most of the torpedo planes either failed to locate their targets, or were shot down by Zero fighters and anti-aircraft flak, but the losses proved to be a worthy sacrifice. Owing to the low altitudes at which torpedo planes conducted their attacks, Japanese defenses were fixed in a position where they were unprepared to counter the US dive-bombers. Planes from the *Enterprise* appeared overhead, and were unopposed as they closed in on the *Akagi* and *Kaga*, whose decks were cluttered with armed aircraft, making them highly flammable. Bombers from the *Yorktown* followed shortly thereafter, and scored three hits on the *Soryu*. The *Hiryu* escaped destruction, and launched its aircraft against the *Yorktown*, which suffered heavy damage. Nevertheless, planes from the *Yorktown* were moved to the *Enterprise*, and squadrons from both carriers joined forces to destroy the *Hiryu*, thereby finishing off the Japanese carrier force. By 5 June, the Japanese lost all prospects of winning their decisive battle. Although the expedition against the Aleutian Islands achieved a higher level of success, with the capture of Kiska, Yamamoto failed to secure the outer perimeter which he had set out to establish. Most importantly, Japan's offensive capabilities were blunted by the loss of four carriers and their accompanying aircraft, along with a large portion of the navy air arm's most skilled pilots. The Imperial forces could achieve further advances against the Allies only with great difficulty.

For Americans, the victory at Midway was due to the excellent use of intelligence, coupled with a number of extremely lucky decisions made by Admiral Fletcher. The Japanese fleet's mistake, of failing to realize that the US navy had broken its communications codes, also laid the grounds for its demise. However, the outcome of the battle still largely owed itself to fortuitous developments. The question thus arises as to whether the Americans could have still won the Pacific war, had they been unlucky enough to lose more of their carriers at Midway. The answer is they were most likely have defeated the Japanese in the long run, mainly because the US had an industrial base that could produce far more ships than its enemies could sink. On the other hand, Japan could not replenish its losses, and its demise was only a matter of time. Defeat had been, arguably, a most likely fate from the moment it declared war on the US. In this sense, Midway affected the course of the conflict, but its role in deciding the outcome was minimal, since the encounter simply speeded up the waning of Japan's supremacy in the Pacific. Equally unfortunate was that Japanese military leaders still did not understand the unfavorable situation they had got themselves into by attacking America. Shortly after the Pearl Harbor attack, Yamamoto remarked to his staff, with a definite air of disdain, "we have awoken a sleeping giant." He understood the magnitude of America's industrial might. What he was unaware of, and what most of the high command did not comprehend, was the manner in which American industrial power made it almost impossible for their nation to win the war. As Japan's strategy during the first 6 months of 1942 showed, its conception of how the war could be fought, and how it would transpire, was flawed from the very beginning. The results of those blunders had become apparent. By the following year, Japan's shortcomings were to lead its forces onto to a series of defeats, which eventually culminated with the complete destruction of its war effort by August 1945.

5

The Allies Turn the Tide, June 1942 to January 1943

During the opening stages of the Pacific war, between December 1941 and spring 1942, the Western powers found themselves following a defensive strategy, but their armed forces were ill-equipped to deal with the Japanese onslaught. The situation improved slightly after June, as a result of two developments. First, the losses which the US navy inflicted on the Imperial fleet at the battle of Midway meant that the Japanese could no longer fight their opponents with the numerical superiority which they initially enjoyed. Secondly, at the global level, the Allies realized that they did not have the capacity to launch a large scale invasion of continental Europe in the immediate future, and Japan turned out to be a stronger foe than originally expected. Subsequently, the Allies decided to divert a greater proportion of their forces to the Asia-Pacific theater, and commenced a series of limited offensives against the periphery of Japan's empire. The operations culminated with the American and Australian forces ejecting the Japanese from their outposts at Guadalcanal and New Guinea by January 1943. Simultaneously, in Southeast Asia, the British made an unsuccessful attempt to weaken Japan's hold on the India-Burma frontier, which nonetheless resulted in considerable casualties for the IJA. Yet, even though the Japanese suffered a significant depletion of strength during this period, the Americans and their coalition partners were not in a position to achieve any decisive victories that could significantly damage the enemy's war effort, nor could they seize the strategic initiative and thereby dictate the tempo of their campaigns. The most which the Allies could hope to achieve was to establish a foothold from which to conduct further advances, and gradually erode Japan's grip on its conquered territories.

DEVELOPMENT OF ALLIED WAR PLANS, DECEMBER 1941 TO SPRING 1942

From the opening stages of the war, the Allied powers established the general principles of their strategy against the Axis Powers, namely to concentrate on fighting Germany, while at the same time staying on guard against Japan. In late December 1941, shortly after the US declared its participation in the global conflict, Prime Minister Churchill traveled to America onboard the battleship *Duke of York* to meet President Franklin Roosevelt. The two leaders held their first wartime summit meeting, code-named *Arcadia*, at Washington. The main agreement to emerge was that Germany constituted the strongest member of the Axis coalition, and for this reason, operations in the European front were to take top priority, with the Pacific to be treated as a secondary theater. The plan amounted to a reaffirmation of the general principle which the Americans and British had set up since late 1940.

Although Allied leaders agreed to the "Germany First" strategy, the plan was not always followed in practice. This was mainly because US defense officials, particularly those belonging to the navy, argued that operations in the Pacific required a much greater commitment of resources than they had originally anticipated. The push for expanding the war effort against Japan created considerable friction with the British, who insisted that neutralizing the German threat was of paramount importance. The Americans could not easily coerce their ally to divert forces away from Europe and dispatch them to the Far East. At *Arcadia*, the British and Americans set up a Combined Chiefs of Staff (CCS). The organization was to be based in Washington, with members of the US Joint Chiefs of Staff (JCS) consulting with their British counterparts, or in the latter's absence, with their designated representatives. The CCS was to recommend the resources which the US and Britain needed to allocate for the various theaters, and help the Allies coordinate their strategy. The setup prevented the US from exercising full control over the conduct of operations against Japan, while at the same time providing a forum to help resolve inter-Allied differences through negotiation. The British had their say over matters related to Allied war planning, and were able to influence decisions on the global distribution of equipment and troops. For this reason, the subject of resource allotments remained a key source of contention within the Allied command for the duration of the conflict. Aside from Britain, the US also had to contend with a number of other nations who were fighting Japan, including Australia and New Zealand. The latter resented not having any control over Allied policy, especially since their homelands were under the threat of a Japanese invasion. American officials needed to avoid moves that threatened to undermine Allied solidarity, and for this reason, there were limits on how much they could dictate war planning.

During the early part of 1942, the immediate concern was to deal with the lightning Japanese advance, which had confronted the Western powers with a situation which they were not prepared for. Whereas pre-war strategy had been based on the assumption that Japan could be deterred from provoking hostilities at least until the Allies could build up sufficient strengths to defend their territories, by January, most commanders acknowledged how they had slim prospects of holding their positions in Southeast Asia and the western Pacific. The most which the Allies could achieve was to mitigate their losses, and subsequently they drew up a plan to delay the Japanese long enough so that the beleaguered forces could be withdrawn to safety. At the request of General George Marshall, a unified organization, designated ABDACOM (American–British–Dutch–Australian Command) was established to manage operations in areas including Burma, the East Indies and the Philippines. As far as the British were concerned, the available forces were simply unable to defend Singapore. When General Alanbrooke, the Chief of Imperial General Staff, decided to dispatch Indian and Australian divisions to the fortress, the move was aimed at buying time so that Allied forces could be evacuated to the East Indies.[1] By mid February, following the failed attempt to intercept the Japanese convoy destined for Java, General Archibald Wavell, who had been appointed commander-in-chief of the Allied forces in the southwest Pacific, along with the chiefs of staff in London, concluded that the archipelago was untenable, and that British Empire forces had few options aside from falling back on rear bases in India and Australia.[2] The Americans meanwhile attempted to divert the Japanese away from Southeast Asia by raiding their outposts in the western Pacific. Between January and February, Task Force Eight, sailing under the command of Admiral William Halsey, launched a series of carrier-based attacks against the Marshall and Gilbert Islands, as well as the island of Rabaul off the eastern coast of New Guinea, which the Japanese were converting into one of their main bases in the South Pacific. Although the operations did little to halt the Imperial forces, they raised the morale of US personnel, while at the same time helping them gain invaluable practice in conducting naval air operations.

Allied officials also faced the stark fact that their forces could not substantially weaken Japan's hold on its territories, nor were they able to halt the Imperial navy and army in the event they launched further offensives. The Japanese conquest of the East Indies, coupled with their elimination of British forces from Malaya and Burma, brought the Japanese within striking range of areas which had previously been considered well beyond their reach, including the Indian Ocean and southwest Pacific areas.

As far as US defense planners were concerned, the most crucial component of their strategy was to protect the oceanic link to Australia, so that the latter could be developed as a base for launching a counter-offensive against the southern regions of Japan's empire. Protecting the lifeline required moves to hold the islands which lay on its flanks, including Hawaii, Fiji, New Caledonia, and Samoa. Japanese advances against the southwest Pacific also had to be halted. However, during the initial stages of the conflict, US commanders conceded that they were bound to remain in a precarious position until they could develop adequate strengths. The development of a coherent strategy was also hindered by differences between the navy and army. Within the JCS, Admiral Ernest King was the chief of naval operations, while General George Marshall was the army chief of staff. In order to resolve inter-service disagreements, the president had a representative, Admiral William Leahy, sit on the JCS. The organization was supported by a network of permanent and ad hoc inter-service committees that were composed of senior planning officers of the army and navy, and had broad responsibility over matters related to strategy, policy and operations.

While the navy wanted to go on the offensive in the Pacific, the army insisted that the US had to abide by its "Germany First" strategy. On 5 March, Roosevelt ordered the JCS to conduct its first strategic review. King advocated forward action, and insisted that US forces develop forward bases in the southwest Pacific, so that they could launch an offensive against Japanese-held islands before the enemy had the chance to fortify them.[3] The navy was heavily influenced by public opinion, which vehemently called for retaliation in response to the Pearl Harbor attack. However, King's army counterparts, including George Marshall, were not happy with the plan, and insisted that resources had to be concentrated in Europe if the Axis powers were ever to be defeated. In Marshall's views, the main objectives were to protect the sea lanes to the British isles, while at the same time maintaining the flow of supplies to the USSR so that the latter could keep its war effort against Germany afloat. For this reason, a large portion of the available ships, including cruisers and destroyers, were needed to escort Allied convoys in the Atlantic. Developing forward naval bases in the Pacific also required a fleet of transports to carry troops and supplies. Again, shipping resources were committed to ferrying war materials to the European theater. Fortunately, the Americans were able to prevent the deadlock from paralyzing their war effort. Defense planners realized that emergency situations required a coherent course of action, and the navy conceded that the German threat had to be neutralized before the Allies could concentrate on other theaters. By April, the army strategists gained the upper hand, when the JCS accepted the plan proposed by Dwight Eisenhower, the director of war plans, for launching a second front in Europe during 1943. Although the British were against the plan because they preferred to conduct a landing in the Mediterranean and North Africa, the build-up was to nevertheless go ahead. In regard to the Pacific, the navy managed to secure the army's approval for sending forces to defend Australia, once the Japanese had established bases within striking distance. In spite of his calls for going on the offensive, King was aware of the difficulties involved in carrying out such measures, as evidenced by his letter to the Secretary of the Navy, in which he wrote, "1942 will be a year of 'build and hold' ".[4] The US navy was inferior to the Japanese in all categories of vessels, and consequently, there were few options aside from awaiting a time when the Pacific Fleet could build up the strength to strike back successfully.

The strategic situation facing the British Empire was even more alarming. Its forces remained preoccupied with protecting the home islands and the Atlantic lifelines from the Germans, while Rommel's *Afrikacorps* threatened to break through Egypt and advance towards the Middle Eastern oilfields, which were a vital source of fuel for the Allies. Under the circumstances, Britain could not devote substantial strengths for its possessions in Asia, and its leaders resigned to the probability that any large scale Japanese expedition would deal a devastating blow. The loss of Singapore severed Britain's links with Australia and New Zealand. In Canberra, Prime Minister Curtin's government started to publicly voice doubts about Britain's willingness to protect the dominions, and proposed that the US extend military support in forestalling an invasion.[5] Roosevelt welcomed the role of protecting Britain's dominions, and on 9 March 1942, Churchill agreed to the US proposal that the dominions be placed under General MacArthur's Southwest Pacific Command. In the Indian Ocean area, the reinforcement of Admiral James Somerville's Eastern Fleet with *R* Class battleships, most of which were relics of the Great War, did not improve the situation.[6] The carriers *Indomitable* and *Formidable* were equipped with limited compliments of aircraft whose performance did not match their Japanese counterparts. Officials within India Command realized that the Eastern Fleet's base at Ceylon could not be properly defended against a Japanese foray until sufficient numbers of carriers and their accompanying planes could be deployed.

The Combined Fleet's sortie into the Bay of Bengal during early April undeniably highlighted the vulnerability of British territories. At the same time, the difficulties involved in strengthening Ceylon's defenses were acknowledged, and Britain's strategy continued to be influenced by its global commitments. While Wavell, who had been appointed as head of India Command, insisted that the defense of the Indian Ocean be treated as a matter of the utmost urgency, the COS and Churchill replied that operations in the Middle East were more important. As the British official history on the war against Japan pointed out, "Wavell's difference of opinion with the COS was natural."[7] Churchill and his staff had to view the problem from the broader angle. The security of the home islands had to take precedence, and India's needs related to those of the Middle East. Nor could the British count on securing military support from their allies. Although requests were made for the US Pacific Fleet to either launch naval offensives on Japan's eastern flank, or send warships to join Somerville's fleet, the Americans were reluctant to commit their limited strengths to defend the British Empire, and made it clear that the proposals were out of the question.[8] The visible indications of Ceylon's vulnerability, and the difficulties involved in bolstering its defenses, gave rise to a strategy of withdrawing major British units from the enemy's striking range and minimizing potential losses. The Eastern Fleet was moved to East Africa on the premise that until adequate capital ships and carriers could be deployed in the Indian Ocean, its presence was more likely to lure further attacks.[9] In reality, Japan had no concrete plans for launching an invasion of British bases in the Indian Ocean. However, only after the IJN's defeats at Coral Sea and Midway had depleted its surplus of naval and air forces, could the British conclude that the enemy was unlikely to muster the strengths needed to support large scale operations.

COUNTER-OFFENSIVES IN THE SOUTH PACIFIC AND BURMA, SUMMER 1942 TO JANUARY 1943

Until the US Navy achieved its first significant victory at Midway in June 1942, the Allies had followed a strategy of reacting to enemy forces wherever they appeared. After the Japanese lost a large portion of their frontline carriers and accompanying aircraft, the Americans were able to fight on more even terms. Even then, the balance of forces in the Pacific theater was not decisively in either side's favor. The Imperial forces still had adequate strengths to threaten key areas in the southwest Pacific, while the Allies could only carry out limited advances against the far reaches of Japan's vast empire. In the words of Ned Willmott, the strategic initiative was like "a gun lying in the middle of the street. It was there for either side to pick up and use."[10] The Japanese remained difficult to defeat, and the victories achieved in areas such as Guadalcanal and New Guinea during the autumn of 1942 came at a high cost for both the Americans and Australians. In Southeast Asia, the British army was stalled when it tried to launch a counter-offensive against the India-Burma frontier. By the early part of 1943, the tide of the conflict had visibly turned in favor of the Allies. The capabilities of Japan's forces were curbed as a result of the defeats which they suffered in the South Pacific and in New Guinea. Although the Americans had incurred their share of losses, their prospect of seizing the initiative was significantly augmented because their industries had begun to produce vast quantities of high performance weapons. The build-up was to eventually enable US forces to launch a counterattack that would bring them within striking range of the Japanese home islands. Of equal importance, the initial attempts to dismantle Japan's hold on its far-flung territories taught the Allies a number of valuable lessons on how to conduct operations in the particular conditions that prevailed in the Pacific theater, as well as the appropriate tactics for overcoming the Japanese.

After the IJN's setback at Midway, the Japanese focused their attention on the southwest Pacific. The main objective was to cut the supply line from the US west coast to Australia, and prevent the Allies from using the region as a base for counter-offensives against the empire. In July, the Japanese attempted to capture the island of Guadalcanal in the Solomons archipelago, with the aim of acquiring a staging point for air and submarine attacks on the trans-Pacific shipping line.

Meanwhile, US defense chiefs planned an operation to seize New Guinea and the smaller islands which lay off its eastern tip, including the Solomons, so as to secure a foothold from which to they could conduct further advances against the inner reaches of the Japanese empire.

On 2 July, the joint chiefs issued a directive to launch a series of attacks against three main areas, namely the Solomon Islands, New Guinea and the IJN air arm's forward base at Rabaul in New Britain. On matters related to grand strategy, Roosevelt and the JCS realized that they were unlikely to secure a British commitment for a landing in northwest Europe at least until 1944, and that the Allies needed to undertake some type of forward action to turn the tide of the war against the Axis powers. The southwest Pacific appeared to offer a favorable theater for achieving this aim, especially after the Australian army, under the command of General Thomas Blamey, halted the Japanese advance against Port Moresby in New Guinea, and started pushing enemy forces back towards the north coast via the Kokoda trail.

The island of Guadalcanal was added to the list of objectives when a US reconnaissance plane observed the Japanese building an airfield on the island. On 7 August, the US navy, along with the First Marine Division, launched Operation *Watchtower*, headed by Vice-Admiral Ghormley, commander of the South Pacific forces. The main goal was to capture Henderson Field, which provided the Japanese with a potentially useful base for interdicting Allied vessels bringing reinforcements to the island. Although the Japanese and US ground forces engaged in a number of ferocious battles, the contest over Guadalcanal was primarily a naval and air engagement. This was mainly because securing control over the surrounding waters and airspace was vital in order to keep the troops adequately supplied.

From the onset, US forces faced a multitude of problems. At the strategic level, the Pacific Fleet had yet to produce sufficient ships and aircraft to achieve a decisive victory. When drawing up the plans for the Solomons operation, Admiral King conceded that the available forces were barely large enough to engage the Imperial navy, and the latter could be expected to put up resistance at any stage.[11] When the Guadalcanal offensive commenced, theater commanders, including Nimitz and Ghormley, doubted whether they had enough vessels to maintain their hold over the South Pacific for a significant length of time.[12] Task forces also needed a large number of destroyers to defend themselves against enemy vessels. However, the navy continued to be burdened with commitments in the Atlantic, where German U-boats were marauding Allied convoys carrying troops and equipment to the British Isles. As late as December, Nimitz concluded that, while the Pacific Fleet had inflicted "disproportionate losses" on its opponent, he did not think that his forces had an edge.[13] Only a further decline in the Japanese navy's strength, coupled with the construction of new US warships, could significantly shift the balance.

Logistical factors also posed obstacles. Keeping the flow of reinforcements and supplies to Guadalcanal was a task which US forces were unprepared to handle. Nobody back in Washington had attempted to methodically calculate the quantity of troops and equipment needed for the campaign, and as a result, battlefield operations had to be carried out much more slowly than originally planned.[14] To provide a few statistical examples, the average marine needed 4½ tons of materiel to maintain himself for a month. The situation was further complicated because the Pacific theaters were largely undeveloped in regard to military bases and transport networks. Facilities had to be built from scratch, thus requiring a large quantity of personnel and equipment to be transported. The only ports that could handle heavy cargo were located in New Zealand and in New Caledonia, both of which lay thousands of miles from the combat zone. Ships sailing from San Francisco were often backlogged for weeks while they awaited to be escorted to Guadalcanal.

In regard to combat performance, while US forces managed to improve their relative efficiency over the Japanese, the Americans were still on a barely equal level. At sea, the Pacific Fleet remained inept at conducting nighttime operations, while the Japanese continued to demonstrate their flair. The differences became apparent during the battle of Savo Island 7–8 August, when the US task force providing cover for the amphibious landing was attacked by Admiral Mikawa's fleet. Although most Japanese vessels were not equipped with radar, their crews made good use of optical equipment such as telescopes to locate their targets. The Americans, on the other hand, over-relied on radar, and paid insufficient attention to other means of detecting enemy forces, including aerial search.[15] US commanders also had not established an effective system for communication, which resulted in a failure to issue timely information once the attackers had been detected.[16] The task force was caught by surprise, and lost nearly all of its participating warships.

In the air, while the US navy and army managed to steadily increase their aircraft strengths during the latter part of 1942, they did not achieve a decisive superiority over the Japanese. As one prominent historian of the air campaigns in the Pacific theater has pointed out, for most of the time between spring 1942 and winter 1943–44, neither side was completely dominant.[17] The bulk of the best American fighter planes were dispatched to Europe and North Africa, and for this reason, the air forces in the Pacific consisted mainly of the navy's F4F Wildcat and army's P-39s, whose maneuverability and range were inferior to the Zero. During the opening stages of the Guadalcanal campaign, aircraft losses ran up to 50 percent on some missions, leading one squadron leader to report that pilots were "anxiously awaiting faster and better fighters."[18] Although Japanese planes were vulnerable, owing to their lack of armor protection, they were difficult to intercept, and their light construction rendered them capable of pursuing their opponents in high speed chases.

The tactical skills of the opposing air arms were also roughly equal. On one hand, the Japanese started to face considerable difficulties in maintaining an adequate pool of trained pilots. The losses incurred during the Midway campaign could not be replaced expeditiously, because the navy's training consisted of a strenuous and highly selective program which required almost 2 years of flight instruction. In order to ensure that frontline units could be supplied with an adequate number of aviators, the navy introduced a streamlined scheme where aviators received considerably less preparation. By late 1942, American personnel frequently reported that enemy airmen were attacking naval targets and planes with less aggressiveness than they had during the opening stages of the conflict. The Japanese also contended with the problems of having to operate at extended distances from their forward bases. After the US marines captured Henderson Field in late August, the navy air arm's closest airfield was at Rabaul. Pilots flying to Guadalcanal had to cover over 2,000 miles, which naturally caused fatigue, and diminished their capacity to engage in pitched battles once they arrived at the battlefront.

At the same time, US personnel had yet to achieve the efficiency needed to properly exploit their opponent's shortcomings, and the Japanese still possessed a good number of talented aircrews. When pursued by fighters, Zero pilots maneuvered their aircraft in evasive action, often carrying out tight turns and loops. American pilots admitted that they had yet to figure out ways to shoot down their opponents. Attacks against naval vessels also continued to be carried out with determination. Reporting on the battle of Santa Cruz, the commander of the *Hornet*, which was sunk during the engagement, noted how Japanese planes approached their targets at sharp degree angles, and made "extremely low pull-outs" after dropping their ordnance at close range.[19] US aircrews were often not sufficiently prepared to deal with the elements they faced. Most of them had trained in obsolescent machines, and did not know how to operate advanced aircraft types. The Pacific Fleet was able to expand its cohort of skilled aircrews by the end of 1942. Nimitz introduced an innovative solution where experienced aviators were periodically sent back to the United States to train student pilots.[20] Carrier replacement air groups were established, consisting of a nucleus of veterans, whose job was to initiate new recruits. As a result, squadrons could be "rotated" for rest and refitting, while carrier groups received fresh crews. The US Army Air Forces (USAAF) undertook similar measures to improve the combat effectiveness of its crews. As early as March 1942, General Hap Arnold, the chief of the USAAF, recommended that a special school be set up in Australia, to indoctrinate pilots on matters such as the tactics to be used against the Japanese.[21] One of the key lessons learned from the Solomons campaign was that in order to defend themselves against enemy interceptors, bomber squadrons needed fly in close formation, with fighter escort pilots ready to take offensive action against approaching Zeros. However, substantial time was required before the Americans could develop a reserve of top-quality aircrews large enough to fight a protracted campaign.

In order to defend its task forces, the US Navy needed a clear superiority, both in terms of weaponry and its methods of using them. Anti-aircraft guns could not always be accurately directed towards their targets because the available radar devices were not built to track the rapid movements which Japanese aircrews carried out. Carrier-borne fighter aircraft thus provided more reliable protection. Yet, US task forces did not possess an adequate system for detecting incoming air raids and directing friendly planes against them. The Americans had developed a doctrine for using radar and radio communications, and acquired many of their ideas regarding fighter control from the British navy, who had pioneered innovations in this area. In October 1941, even before the Pacific war broke out, the US navy established a special program to train fighter direction officers. A year later, the Americans set up a school to instruct personnel on how to operate a combat information center, whose responsibility was to process data on the location of enemy planes, and thereafter disseminate it throughout the task force. However, the available radar devices could not calculate the altitude of enemy aircraft, and as a result, fighters were often not properly positioned. The coordination of fighter movements was further hindered by an inadequate system of communication. Aviators often sent so many transmissions that the result was confusion among their fellow pilots. Fighter directors also issued detailed orders on where to fly, which caused further disorder.

Because the US and Japanese forces in the Guadalcanal area were roughly equal in strength and combat effectiveness, the first 3 months became a protracted struggle in which neither side was able to secure a breakthrough. Between August and November, the opposing fleets played a game of cat and mouse. The Americans interdicted enemy convoys by day, only to surrender control over the waters at night. Meanwhile, the Japanese established a supply line dubbed the "Tokyo Express," where warships and transports delivered a steady flow of reinforcements to the garrison, and the convoys were routed so that they arrived under the cover of darkness. When the US fleet attempted to intercept its opponents, it ended up suffering high losses. In late August, at the battle of Santa Cruz, the carriers *Enterprise* and *Saratoga* suffered heavy damage from air attacks. In September, the carrier *Wasp* was sunk by torpedoes.

By October, the Pacific Fleet began to attain an edge. Task force commanders improved their procedures for using radar to detect enemy forces and communicating the information to ship crews. At the battle of Cape Esperance on 11–12 October, radar-guided fire from the cruisers *Salt Lake City*, *Boise* and *Helena* compelled the Japanese to abandon the engagement. The deadlock was finally broken in mid November, at the battle of Guadalcanal. The Americans enhanced their fire control systems to the point where they managed to destroy over a dozen Japanese transport ships, while inflicting damage on a battleship and two destroyers. The Combined Fleet's losses reached the point where Yamamoto decided to withdraw his vessels from the South Pacific. The Japanese also suffered a further depletion of their air strengths. By December, the Pacific Fleet finally gained control over the waters and skies around Guadalcanal, and was in a much better position to interdict transport ships. The Imperial army's garrison eventually expended its supplies, and by February 1943, the US marines managed to secure the island. General Patch, commanding the ground forces, radioed to Halsey, "Tokyo Express no longer has a terminus at Guadalcanal."

Nevertheless, the opposing navies continued to have roughly equal capabilities. US vessels remained vulnerable to torpedo attacks. At the night action off Tassafaronga on 30 November, not a single shell was reported to have hit any of the ships in Task Force William, while the Japanese lost three destroyers and had a few others damaged. In spite of the loss, during the second phase of the encounter, enemy destroyers launched a devastating raid which resulted in the sinking of the heavy cruiser *Northampton*, and serious damage to three others, including the *Minneapolis*, *New Orleans* and *Pensacola*. American commanders learned that they did not have an edge in terms of experience, skill, or quality of personnel. Admiral Nimitz conceded that the possession of fire control radar was the Pacific Fleet's only significant advantage.[22] Ship crews needed to exploit this asset, while at the same time denying enemy forces the opportunity to use their torpedoes to good effect.

Similarly, while the air war over the Solomons also gradually turned in favor of the Americans, even at the end of 1942, they had not yet achieved a decisive superiority. On the contrary, US personnel remained apprehensive about their ability to counter the moves which enemy pilots carried out. Aircrews flying the F4F Wildcat learned to exploit the weaknesses of the Zero fighter, including its light armor. When the Japanese slowed down to make climbs and turns, they presented a perfect opportunity for interception. One popular maneuver was the "Thach weave," named after Lieutenant-Commander John Thach, a fighter ace from the Midway operation.[23] Fighters flew in pairs, and both pilots kept regular lookouts on each other's tail. When a Zero was seen attacking one of them, the partner plane altered course, bringing his guns onto the enemy. The pilot of the plane being attacked, upon seeing his squadron mate's maneuver, then made a similar turn. Zero pilots, upon discovering that they were simultaneously targeted by two opponents, often broke off the engagement. The Thach weave eventually became a standard procedure among air units. Yet fighting methods were largely defensive, and geared to prevent Zero pilots from utilizing their maneuverability. The US navy's fighter direction systems also continued to show shortcomings. The loss of the cruiser *Chicago* in January 1943 was blamed on the poor handling of protective air groups, which permitted Japanese torpedo planes to attack without being molested.[24]

The campaigns on the ground proved to be an equally arduous learning curve not only for the Americans, but also for their British and Australian counterparts. The Japanese posed a number of challenges, and constructed elaborate defenses that were hard to destroy. Troops proved exceptionally skilled at exploiting the natural features of the jungle. Fortifications were sited on hilltops so as to restrict access, and to give the defenders all-round fields of fire. Jungle vegetation was also used to camouflage positions. Attacking soldiers were sometimes unaware that they were amidst a Japanese position until they were shot at. The Imperial army also built its bunkers in a way that rendered them immune to bombardment, by using heavy wood and earth to bolster protection. The Allies also had to confront an opponent who literally fought to the finish, and tenaciously refused to surrender. Under the conditions, it was of the utmost importance to fight a combined arms battle, where artillery and armor units were used to wear down enemy defenses, and infantry troops followed up to physically occupy the ground.

In their encounters against the IJA during the latter part of 1942, Western armies demonstrated how they did not have adequately skilled troops. Although tactical doctrine emphasized the need to coordinate the movements of all arms, minimal efforts had been made to integrate the idea into a working practice. To complicate matters, Allied troops were not prepared to operate in the jungle, where poor communications and rugged terrain hindered mobility. For example, the US Army's *Basic Field Manual: Jungle Warfare* (FM 31–20) provided practical information on matters such as clearing trails in the undergrowth and crossing rivers, but did not anticipate situations where troops needed to overcome enemy defenses.[25]

During the early phase of the New Guinea campaign, the Thirty-Second Infantry Division proved unprepared for battle. The Australian army was in a slightly better position. Its troops were trained by officers who had fought in the 1914–18 conflict, and had recently gained combat experience in the Middle East campaign. Furthermore, because most units had smaller supplies of heavy equipment than their American counterparts, tactical doctrine tended focus on rapid movement and overcoming enemy forces through skilful maneuvering. In early September, Major-General Clowes' expeditionary force reconquered the island of Milne Bay at the southeastern tip of New Guinea, and the encounter proved that the Japanese could be defeated by well-trained soldiers. Nevertheless, Australian forces did show room for improvement. The fighting skills of the Allied armies were put to test in early November, after the Japanese withdrew back across the Owen Stanley mountain range and consolidated their positions on the north coast. The Americans launched an assault on the stronghold at Buna, while the Australians concentrated on Gona and Sanananda. However, for the first weeks of the campaign, the attacking forces made minimal progress. Troops hesitated to advance unless enemy defenses had been subjected to overwhelming bombardment. To complicate matters, infantry units were initially trained only to carry out frontal assaults.[26] Such tactics frequently made them vulnerable to heavy casualties when the Japanese counter-attacked. For this reason, Allied forces needed to concoct more discreet moves, where they approached enemy positions without being detected. MacArthur became distressed at the way in which the advance had become stalled, and ordered his staff officers to visit the front lines to find out what was going wrong. The main problem cited was General Harding's poor leadership, coupled with a lack of aggressive spirit within the rank and file. Robert Eichelberger replaced Harding as commander of the Thirty-Second division. Eichelberger's first step in enhancing the efficiency of his units was to devise a tactic where patrols were sent out to scout enemy territory, and called in mortar fire upon discovering a bunker.[27] The arrival of tanks and heavy artillery guns in larger numbers also enabled the attackers to take the initiative, and by January, American and Australian forces managed to eliminate the remnants of Japanese opposition.

Nevertheless, the main lesson to emerge from the operations at Buna and Sanananda was that advances could be made only when troops succeeded in neutralizing each enemy bunker individually, by using hand-held weapons such as grenades and mortars. The process most often entailed a slow and tedious task. Soldiers also had to learn how to engage their enemy at close range. General Vasy, commanding the Seventh Australian Division at Sanananda, reported that some of his front line troops were entrenched as little as 20 meters from the Japanese positions.[28]

The Marine Corps faced similar problems. During the initial stages of the Guadalcanal campaign, most marines went into battle having mastered few skills for ground warfare operations, aside from firing a rifle, and they were forced to learn about field maneuvers while in combat. General Vandegrift, commanding the marines at Guadalcanal, reported that the most notable shortcoming among his units was "inadequate physical training."[29] In order to remedy this fault, soldiers had to learn to march long distances through difficult terrain.[30] Thus, by the early part of 1943, the US army and Marine Corps succeeding in taking the initial steps towards applying their doctrine of combined arms operations into practice, and adapting them to meet the challenges posed by the Japanese.

Meanwhile, on the India-Burma front, the British Eastern Army was dealt yet another defeat as it attempted to advance against the border regions. Following the commencement of the Allied counter-offensive in the Pacific, Britain's defense chiefs concluded that it was important to maintain pressure on the Japanese in order to prevent them from developing further threats against India. In an effort to gradually erode the Fifteenth Army's hold on Burma and prepare the ground for making further inroads into Southeast Asia, Wavell drew up a plan to reconquer enemy outposts in the Arakan frontier area.[31] The operation was based on the premise that, by moving swiftly, the British could overcome the enemy's defenses before the latter could bring in reinforcements. Although the chiefs of staff in London warned that substantial air support could not be provided, the general maintained that risks had to be accepted. The prospect of success were further diminished because the British had little experience in conducting operations in undeveloped terrain, and continued to rely on overwhelming firepower to neutralize enemy forces. By January 1943, the offensive was abandoned as the attackers became held up in the face of difficult resistance. Wavell admitted that he miscalculated how numerical superiority and a rapid advance could help his forces attain their objectives.[32] Following the failure of the Arakan offensive, Wavell was replaced by General William Slim, and the command structure of the British army in India was reformed to ensure that troops received proper training. In a similar manner to their coalition partners, the British learned from their initial counter-offensives that improved combat methods were necessary in order to fight their opponent more effectively.

MILITARY BALANCE IN THE PACIFIC THEATER, JANUARY 1943

By the start of 1943, the balance of strength in the Asia-Pacific theater was roughly equal, but the Allies were in a much more favorable position to prevail in the long term. The operations at Guadalcanal, New Guinea and Burma during the latter part of 1942 cost both sides a large number of casualties, which in turn depleted their capacity to launch further offensive operations. However, a crucial factor that prevented Japan from regaining the strategic initiative was its narrow industrial base, which in turn precluded any replacement of its losses.[33] The United States, on the other hand, was able to embark on a massive construction program, and produce an overwhelming quantity of ships, aircraft and weapons. By late 1943, the US and its allies were to achieve a material superiority that was sufficient to launch their counter-offensive in the central Pacific and in Southeast Asia, which culminated with the destruction of Japan's empire in 1945.

Of equal importance, Allied forces had drawn a number of crucial lessons on how to conduct their operations in the Asia-Pacific region. While the Imperial navy and army were not as invincible as they appeared to be during the opening stages of the conflict, they were still acknowledged as a difficult enemy to defeat. The initial counter-offensives against the periphery of Japan's empire highlighted the importance of adequate logistics, and keeping front-line units properly supplied. The Americans and their coalition partners also learned that high-performance weapons were crucial when fighting the Japanese, and subsequently, a larger quantity of top-quality aircraft and ships were allocated to the Pacific theater. Last but not least, the key role played by tactical skill was properly grasped. To provide just a few examples, the US Navy stepped up its pilot training program and placed a greater emphasis on improving its capacity to match the Japanese in its ability to conduct nighttime operations. On land, infantry units were trained to deal with the elements of the jungle, while at the same time conducting an aggressive patrol of their surroundings in order to counter the surprise attacks which the Japanese frequently carried out. The Imperial forces, on the other hand, proved slow at adjusting their combat methods and equipment for a host of reasons, among the most prominent of which was an ingrained belief that Western military capabilities were inferior, coupled with a refusal to acknowledge the shortcomings held by the navy and army. As the campaigns in the Pacific theater were to show, fighting skills were often equally important as numerical strength in achieving a victory. At the start of 1943, the Allies had managed to lay the foundations for developing their superiority over the Japanese in both areas, and were poised to eventually seize the strategic initiative.

6

The Dynamics of War: Strategy and Operations

The previous two chapters have explained how the campaigns in the Asia-Pacific theaters transpired in the first year of the conflict. They have been arranged chronologically, and examined the successes which the Imperial armed forces achieved, as well as the way in which the Allies managed to turn the tide against their opponents during the closing months of 1942. The subsequent chapters will take on a more thematic approach, and illustrate the reasons why the belligerents conducted the Pacific war in the manner that they did, while at the same time comparing the strengths and weaknesses of their war efforts. Chapters 6–9 will deal with the military features, such as strategy, tactics and morale. Chapters 10–12 will examine the so-called "non-military" factors, including economics and diplomacy which, while not directly tied to events on the battlefront, were nonetheless important in shaping the course of the war.

The following pages will focus on strategy and operations. Students of warfare always need to draw a distinction between the various levels of military activities, including strategy, operations and tactics, but are often confused over the meaning of the terms. The simplest explanation is that strategy deals with the broader issue concerning the types of action an armed force needs to carry out in order to achieve its parent nation's political aims. For example, during the Pacific war, the main goal of the Allied coalition was to eliminate Japan's ability to pursue a policy of aggressive territorial expansion. To accomplish this end, the military had to neutralize the Imperial navy and army to the point where they could no longer maintain their hold on their empire. The Allies also sought to establish bases that could be used to strike at Japan's mainland, so as to destroy the political and economic infrastructure which kept the enemy's war effort afloat. However, the Allies faced a number of difficult questions on how to secure their stated objectives, such as which areas they had to occupy in order to prepare the way for an advance towards Japan's home islands. Decisions also needed to be made as to whether the enemy's military machine was going to be destroyed by blockading its oceanic trade routes and bombarding its industrial infrastructure, or whether the home territories had to be physically occupied.

Closely related to strategy is the operational aspect, which deals with issues regarding the timing of military activities, along with the movement of forces within a particular theater, and last but not least, transporting the equipment which front-line units must use in order to defeat their opponents. At this level of warfare, military leaders need to make choices on how to secure their strategic objectives. For both the Allies and Japanese high commands, the aim was to control the expanses of the Pacific Ocean. The enemy's mobility had to be curtailed to the point where it was no longer able to put up effective opposition. Armed forces had to marshal their strengths so that they could inflict maximum damage on their opponents while at the same time minimizing their own casualties. Equally important was to ensure that friendly forces were provided with adequate logistical support so that they could deploy the necessary quantity of armaments.

At the start of 1943, the Allies had achieved only a spate of limited victories in far-flung areas such as Guadalcanal and New Guinea. By the end of 1944, US forces had captured key positions in the western Pacific, including the Mariana Islands and the Philippines, thereby establishing themselves within the inner reaches of Japan's empire. The enemy's supply of raw materials from the southern regions had been severed, while the home islands were exposed to an intensified blockade and air assault. In other areas, the British succeeded in forcing the Imperial forces in Burma onto a retreat, and were poised to reconquer their lost territories in Malaya and Singapore, while Australian forces played a key role in recapturing the island of New Guinea.

A number of factors contributed to the success. Among the most important reasons was that the Western powers managed to produce and deploy a far superior number of ships, aircraft and weapons against the Japanese. The Pacific war was largely a naval conflict, and the balance of forces during some of the main engagements at sea lucidly illustrates the advantages which the Allies enjoyed. By the end of 1943, the US navy had launched eight new large aircraft carriers of the *Essex* class and 35 additional escort carriers, along with dozens of battleships, cruisers and destroyers. The Americans therefore could afford losses, while the Japanese simply could not. In the air, the Imperial forces suffered a similar inferiority. The Japanese had lost over 2,500 planes, while US air units were able to deploy larger quantities of their most advanced machines, including the Hellcat and Corsair fighters which helped them clear the skies of enemy aircraft. During the invasion of Saipan in the Marianas archipelago during June 1944, Task Force Fifty-Eight, operating under Admiral Raymond Spruance, possessed almost 900 planes. Four months later, when the Americans prepared to establish a foothold in the Philippines by capturing the island of Leyte, they deployed 1,400 aircraft against the meager force of just over 100 planes that the Japanese could put up.[1] The Pacific Fleet also possessed a solid base of logistical support, and by the end of the war, it could rely on a service force of over 1,000 ships that transported oil, ammunition and supplies to naval units operating thousands of miles away from their home base.

However, material strength was only one feature which laid the grounds for the Allied victory. Good planning, coupled with an efficient deployment of the available resources, played a crucial role. Likewise, Japan's war effort faltered largely because its leaders often deployed their limited strengths in a careless manner. When assessing the effectiveness of any military organization's strategy, one needs to define a set of criteria. Among the most reliable standards of measurement has been put forward by Allan Millett and Williamson Murray.[2] While defeating the enemy certainly indicates success, at the same time, it is important to judge how well defense officials deal with the challenges facing them. For example, political leaders need to clearly lay out their goals, so that the military can determine what types of war plans it has to develop. Yet, the development of a coherent strategy is often hindered by inter-service disagreements between the various branches, including the navy, army and air force. To avoid a deadlock, leaders must set up a process where the competing services are able to resolve their differences through negotiation. Military organizations also should formulate strategies that are realistic, and ensure that their forces have adequate resources to achieve their missions. An accurate calculation of the parent nation's economic base, along with its capacity to produce weapons and transport them to the battlefront, is thus vital. Strategy must be devised while properly taking into account the enemy's strengths and weaknesses. Based on the above standards, Allied strategy was decisively more effective than its Japanese counterpart.

MAIN OBJECTIVES OF ALLIED AND JAPANESE STRATEGY

The most important strategic task facing the Allied and Japanese high commands was to define their wartime objectives and the means to secure them. In this respect, the US and its coalition partners had a clear goal to work towards, namely to bring about the complete destruction of the Axis powers' capacity to wage war, so that they could not reemerge as a threat to world peace. For the Imperial armed services, the overriding idea was to prolong the conflict to the point where the Allies became weary of fighting and subsequently offered a negotiated peace that allowed Japan to retain some of its conquests. However, the Japanese tended to follow a muddled strategy where they awaited for the situation to turn in their favor, without developing a clear course of action.

At the Casablanca summit of January 1943 (code-named *Symbol*), the US and British leaders outlined the general principles of their global strategy, the first of which was to secure the unconditional surrender of Germany, Japan and Italy. All three nations were to have their home territories occupied, with the Allies undertaking measures to dismantle their militarist governments, war industries and armed forces. The aim was to ensure that the Axis powers could never again wage a war of aggressive expansion. At the Cairo conference of November 1943, President Roosevelt and Prime Minister Churchill, along with the Chinese leader Chiang Kai Shek, announced additional demands from Japan. All territorial gains made since the first Sino-Japanese war of 1894–95, including Formosa, Korea and Sakhalin were to be ceded. Later in the same month, when the British and American leaders met with Premier Josef Stalin at Teheran, the Soviets promised that they would join the Pacific war within 3 months after Germany had been defeated.

The unconditional surrender formula was not a dramatic departure from previous policies pursued by the Allies. The Atlantic Charter, signed in August 1941, even before America entered the war, explicitly stated that the key aim was to establish a post-war order in which military aggression and territorial expansion were outlawed. When Roosevelt declared war on Japan and Germany in December, he publicly proclaimed that the ultimate mission was to rid the world of dictatorial regimes. The declaration at Casablanca simply clarified the post-war settlement which the Allies were to implement, and gave them a concrete objective to work towards.[3] However, the way in which the US and Britain were to achieve the goal remained unanswered. In particular, defense chiefs had not decided whether the Axis powers could be defeated through a strategy of blockade and aerial bombardment, or whether their home territories had to be physically occupied. In regard to the Pacific theater, the question was resolved during the May 1943 Allied summit at Washington (code-named *Trident*). The CCS ratified a strategy that called for a combination of strangulating the oceanic trade routes through which Japan's industries received their supplies of raw materials from abroad, coupled with aerial attacks on its cities and economic infrastructure. In the final phase, the home islands were to be invaded. Yet, neither the Americans nor the British defense chiefs had a definite plan regarding their route of advance.

There were several options, the first of which was to move into the heart of Japan's empire via the Central Pacific. Another strategy under consideration was a campaign via the various islands of the southwest Pacific area (SWPA), including New Guinea, with the aim of eventually securing a base in the Philippines, from which an invasion of Japan could be staged. The final option which received attention was to set up air bases on mainland China, and conduct a sustained bombing attack against Japan. Nevertheless, despite the lack of clarity on which strategy the Allies were going to adopt, the establishment of a clear objective meant that military planners were in a favorable position to identify the actions they needed to undertake.

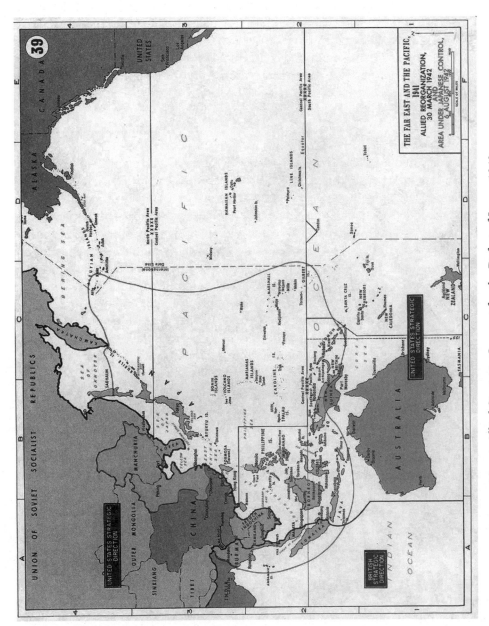

Map 4: Allied Strategic Concept for the Defeat of Japan, 1943

The second feature of Allied strategy following January 1943 was also a follow-up of a previously laid out principle, namely to concentrate on defeating Germany before embarking on major operations against Japan. At *Symbol*, the CCS agreed on a number of objectives for the upcoming year.[4] The landings which had been executed in North Africa during autumn 1942 (code-named *Torch*) committed a large portion of US and British forces to the Mediterranean, and for this reason, the invasion of France and subsequent advance towards the heart of Hitler's Europe had to be postponed until the middle of 1944. Neutralizing the German submarine fleet in the Atlantic was also a top priority, especially since the scale of U-boat attacks against Allied convoys had risen dramatically during the latter part of 1942. The flow of war supplies to the Soviet Union via the Arctic ports of Murmansk and Archangel also had to be maintained in order to ensure that the Red Army remained equipped to fight the *Wehrmacht* on the Eastern Front. In a move aimed to satisfy Stalin's demands that the Western powers divert German forces away from Russia, the Allies decided to stage an invasion of mainland Italy. Finally, Hitler's war effort was to be softened up by intensifying the strategic bombing campaign against continental Europe. The US and British defense chiefs thus understood that, in light of the substantial commitments they faced in their war effort against Germany, they were bound to require a considerable time before they could build up the strength to launch a large scale offensive in the Pacific theater.

At the same time, despite the continued adherence to the "Germany First" strategy, the Allies, or at least the Americans, did endeavor to step up the tempo of operations in the Pacific, with a view to defeating Japan by the most economical means. The Roosevelt administration was aware of the problems that could arise if the war became prolonged, in which case American public support for the war effort was likely to deteriorate. The JCS had already acknowledged how the original plan of staying purely on the defensive in the Pacific was not feasible, since such moves were more likely to give the Japanese the opportunity to reinforce their strongholds and place additional obstacles on Allied operations. The operations in New Guinea and the Solomon islands already proved to be a laborious effort. At Casablanca, Admiral King argued that, while Germany was the prime enemy, the coalition needed to prepare for an attack against Japan's empire after the European war had been won. Therefore, the quota for resource allocations to the Asia-Pacific theaters was to be raised from 15 percent to 30 percent.[5] In regard to territories which the Allies were to reconquer, the Americans stipulated that the Japanese navy's forward air base at Rabaul was to be neutralized, with offensive operations launched against islands which lay at the fringes of Japan's outer perimeter, including the Marshalls and Gilberts archipelagos. The British chiefs of staff agreed to the plan in principle, as long as the move did not jeopardize the war effort against Germany. The prospects of undertaking large scale operations against Japan were further enhanced in June 1943, when the Australian Prime Minister John Curtin secured parliamentary approval for legislation which allowed conscripted troops to be deployed anywhere in the southwest Pacific area.[6]

Aside from the fact that national leaders had a clear perspective of their overall objectives, developing an effective strategy was made possible by the painstaking efforts which US officials had made to draw up a detailed course of action prior to the outbreak of war. Plan *Orange*, originally conceived in 1907, called for the navy to conduct an extended campaign aimed at securing control over the Pacific Ocean. Throughout the decades leading up to the outbreak of hostilities, the Americans consistently endeavored to improvise their plans, and foresaw many of the obstacles they had to confront. Officers at the Naval War College in Newport had carried out annual war games, and the exercises acquainted the players with many of the tasks involved in moving a fleet across long distances, including the establishment of forward bases and maintenance of logistics chains.[7] As a matter of fact, the *Orange* plan has been credited for laying out the fleet's requirements in a manner "so sound that it could easily deal" with a wide variety of contingencies.[8] Once the campaign in the Pacific theater gathered momentum, US strategists were well-placed to identify the measures they needed to carry out. At *Trident*, the JCS presented their strategic plan for the defeat of Japan, which was approved by the inter-allied representatives of the CCS. One of the key objectives was to "maintain and extend unremitting pressure on Japan with the purpose of continually reducing [its] military power."[9] In June, the JCS laid out the specific measures for fulfilling the aim, and stated that, following the capture of Japanese outposts in the Marshall-Gilberts archipelago, the Americans were to reduce the Imperial navy's main base at Truk, while at the same time intensifying attacks on the enemy's shipping lines. The advance was to culminate with the capture of islands within striking distance of mainland Japan. Although the *Orange* plan did not fully envisage the extended timescales needed to attain the stated objectives, it did set out the means to extend US military power into the far reaches of the western Pacific.

The US navy also carried out a sustained submarine attack on Japan's long and vulnerable lines of communication. By early 1944, the Japanese had lost almost half of their transport vessels, and this had two detrimental effects. First, the defense of the outlying garrisons became increasingly complicated, since troop convoys could no longer be dispatched without facing a high risk of getting sunk. More importantly, the flow of raw materials from the southern regions to the home islands became curtailed to the point where Japan's industries struggled to maintain their output of weapons and munitions. US strategy thus became a synergy of the ideas put forward by the naval theorist Alfred Mahan, who contended that destroying the enemy fleet was the key to achieving a victory, as well as Julian Corbett, who argued that prolonged attacks on the enemy's oceanic supply lines provided the most viable way to destroy its war effort. The combination of such moves was, incidentally, the best means to neutralize Japan's hold on its territories and subject its homeland to a large scale attack.

Japan's strategy, by contrast, lacked the clear-sightedness which characterized its Allied counterpart. The high command maintained that its aim was to compel the Western powers to offer a negotiated peace, but never developed a rational plan of action. The problem partly stemmed from a growing realization that the tide of the war was steadily turning against the Imperial forces. In February 1943, the liaison conference conducted a "Review of the World Situation," and General Sugiyama, the army chief of staff, declared that destroying Britain's empire in Asia had become a lost cause. Under the circumstances, the army had few choices aside from attempting to hold its conquests against the impending enemy counter-offensive.[10] As far as the navy command was concerned, the available resources were insufficient to defend Japan's overstretched empire against the ever-growing forces which its enemies were able deploy.[11] By 1944, many leaders, including Prime Minister Tojo, started to doubt whether Japan could survive the war. However, cultural taboos forbade any open expression of such sentiments, and the only strategies likely to be proposed were those that called for a continuation of the fight, in the hope that the Allied powers' will to prosecute the war would dissipate.

Officials within the high command not only refused to acknowledge the possibility of defeat, but they also adhered to their belief that the navy and army could somehow forestall the Allied advance towards the home islands. The main shortcoming with Japanese strategic planning was that the leadership remained unable to comprehend how they were fighting enemies who insisted on waging a total war, and that the Allies were committed continue their effort until they had occupied Japan's home islands, and ensured that its military power was totally destroyed.[12] Navy leaders remained fixated on the idea of preparing for a single decisive battle where the US fleet was to be crushed as it approached the home islands. The accepted belief dictated that all conflicts would replicate the success achieved during the 1904–5 war, when the Russians attempted to relieve Port Arthur, and the Japanese annihilated the armada as it sailed through the Straits of Tsushima. A student at the naval war college in Tokyo once questioned the doctrine, "how will the [Americans] come out into the seas near Japan and stake a decisive battle under conditions obviously unfavorable to them?"[13] Yet, the overwhelming majority of officers did not appear to have seriously thought through the way in which the showdown was to materialize, nor did they grasp the strong possibility of the IJN facing defeat at the hands of the US navy.

The army command held equally confused ideas on how to prosecute the war effort. In September, Imperial General Headquarters in Tokyo ordered the construction an "Absolute National Defence Sphere," comprising the islands of the western Pacific, the East Indies and Burma.[14] The objective was to secure a victory by the start of 1945. In the Pacific areas and in Southeast Asia, the IJA was to destroy enemy forces which attempted to assault any position, and wear out the Allies by inflicting the maximum level of casualties. By early 1944, Japanese strategists realized that more proactive measures were necessary. Imperial headquarters ordered strikes in areas where Allied opposition was believed to be weak. Between March and April, the Fifteenth Army in Burma launched an attack on northeastern India (code-named *Ichigo*). The aim was to force the British to withdraw from their forward bases at Imphal and Kohima, and thereby prevent further advances against Southeast Asia. In June, the army staged an invasion of southern China, to prevent the Allies from establishing air bases that could be used for a bombing campaign against mainland Japan. The Japanese carried out both operations without fully understanding that, in order to protect their empire, they needed to counter the American advance in the Pacific. From the strategic point of view, withdrawing ground units from Asia and deploying them in areas such as the Philippines and Marianas was more likely to delay the establishment of Allied bases within proximity of the home islands. Successes in other theaters, on the other hand, could not alter the course of the conflict. The high command thus lacked a coherent vision on how the armed forces were to achieve their nation's wartime objectives.

CONFLICTS OF INTEREST WITHIN THE ALLIED AND JAPANESE COMMANDS

While defining the nation's war aims and the means to achieve them was the primary task facing military planners, the process of devising a concrete strategy was often complicated by disagreements between the various branches of the armed services, as well as the conflicting policies held by the different nations within the Allied coalition. Again, the Americans and the British proved capable of overcoming the problems. This was mainly because their command structure allowed military officials to openly discuss the full range of options, and decisions were formulated with a view to taking courses of action which brought about the best prospects of success. As a result, inter-service rivalries were placed aside in order to achieve wider objectives. Civilian leaders often facilitated the process either by executing the strategies proposed by the defense chiefs, or in other cases, they attempted to mediate the disputes between the various services. By contrast, Japan's machinery for strategic planning was obstructed by continued army-navy rivalry. The system significantly diminished the Imperial forces' capacity to make good use of their limited resources.

Within the Allied camp, a significant area of contention lay between the United States and Great Britain. Both nations had agreed only so far as they wished to secure Japan's unconditional surrender, but held differing views on how to achieve the aim. The British tended to propose additional objectives, namely the reconquest of their colonial possessions in Southeast Asia, including Malaya and Singapore. Such moves ran contrary to the American policy of working towards the dismantling of European overseas empires, and as a result, the coalition partners often pursued divergent strategies. For example, in the Burma theater, US forces under the command of General Joseph Stilwell focused on securing the northern regions, so that the Allies could expand their supply route to China. The general even claimed that, as more Chinese troops were trained, they could eventually be used to liberate areas as far afield as Hong Kong. American defense planners, including George Marshall, believed that extending aid to Chiang Kai Shek's Nationalists was important for strategic reasons. By carrying on with their resistance against the Imperial army, the Chinese were keeping the bulk of Japan's ground forces committed to the Asiatic mainland, and thus preventing them from being redeployed to counter the Allied advance in the Pacific. The Roosevelt administration also had a political agenda, and expected China to become a key ally in the post-war era. US leaders thus maintained that the Western powers needed to prevent the Nationalist government from collapsing. The British, on the other hand, did not attach the same level of importance to supporting Chiang Kai Shek, on the grounds that his regime was unpopular and had little chance of remaining in power once the war finished. Britain's strategy was fixated on its colonial interests, and called for an advance towards Rangoon, from which it could stage an invasion of Malaya and the East Indies.

Further divisions existed between Churchill and his military advisors. The prime minister, along with influential members of the war cabinet, including Anthony Eden, the foreign secretary, believed that Britain needed to independently reconquer the Malay peninsula if it wished to regain its colonies without having to rely on US arbitration.[15] Admiral Lord Louis Mountbatten, the head of Southeast Asia Command, also advocated the strategy, on the grounds that Britain needed to avenge the humiliation it suffered when Japan conquered Singapore back in 1942. The defense chiefs, including the Chief of the Imperial General Staff, Sir Alanbrooke and First Sea Lord Sir Dudley Pound, maintained that British non-participation alongside America's operations in the Pacific entailed graver consequences. If the US did not receive cooperation from the

British, it could claim that its forces single-handedly defeated Japan, and subsequently dictate the post-war territorial settlement in the Far East. Under the circumstances, the reestablishment of British rule in Southeast Asia depended entirely on American goodwill. The chiefs of staff were also skeptical whether British forces were able to overcome Japanese opposition, especially when they were not able to dispatch a large number of landing craft and warships to the Far East, owing to the demands placed by the war against Germany.[16] Nor did the Malaya strategy win a great deal of favor with the Americans. In January 1944, Mountbatten dispatched the Axiom mission to Washington, the purpose of which was to sell the idea of conducting an amphibious assault against Southeast Asia to the US chiefs of staff, the latter of whom explicitly stated that the operation was more likely to entail a waste of resources, and delay the advance against Japan's home islands.

However, in the end, British policymakers realized that they needed to cooperate with their American ally in order to carry out a successful war effort in the Pacific theater. Furthermore, one of Churchill's notable tendencies was to allow his defense chiefs to make the final decision over strategic matters, and he conceded that the Malaya plan was not feasible. The prime minister's willingness to defer to his advisors saved Britain from suffering an unnecessary setback. In an effort to bring about a greater level of Allied cooperation, after summer 1944, the British took a number of concerted steps to align their strategy with the US. The reorganization of the command structure in the Far Eastern theater, and establishment of Southeast Asia Command, was aimed at enabling Britain to carry out its operations in a more effective manner and demonstrate to the Americans a firm commitment to the war against Japan. Churchill also attempted to secure US acceptance of British participation in the Allied operations against Japan's home islands. At the second Quebec conference of September 1944, the prime minister suggested to Roosevelt that the Royal Navy join forces with the Pacific Fleet. American political leaders strongly believed that in order to remain a respected partner, British forces needed to be fully included in the campaign against Japan.[17] If, on the other hand, Britain's activities were confined to its imperial possessions in Southeast Asia, the US public was likely to accuse their ally of pursuing selfish interests, and the transatlantic coalition could face dangers of collapsing. The American acceptance of the offer committed Britain to a Pacific naval strategy. Thus, the Allied powers managed to overcome their discrepancies, for the sake of formulating a coordinated war plan.

Similar divisions of opinion existed within the US military leadership but again, the various branches, including the navy and army, understood that a unified strategy was necessary in order to achieve the Allies' stated objectives. In contrast to Churchill, who was actively engaged in strategic planning, a key feature which characterized Roosevelt's wartime leadership was that he preferred to leave his military chiefs free to work out their own strategic ideas.[18] Decision-making was therefore largely in the hands of the defense planners, with the president's representative to the JCS, William Leahy, assigned to resolve any disputes that arose. While the navy advocated an oceanic campaign that focused on the central Pacific, the army was more in favor of an island-hopping advance through the New Guinea region that was to culminate with the recapture of the Philippines. The planning for the operations in the southwest Pacific during 1943 reflected the fragmented state of the command structure. In March, General Douglas MacArthur presented his plan for *Elkton*, which envisaged the seizure of islands which lay off the east coast of New Guinea, including New Britain and New Ireland. Navy leaders, including Admiral Nimitz, commanding the Pacific Fleet, and Ernest King, the chief of naval operations, argued that the Americans did not yet have sufficient ships and aircraft to carry out the campaign. In order to prevent a deadlock, the JCS issued a directive which scaled down US objectives in the southwest Pacific to a more manageable level. The Japanese forward base at Rabaul was not to be conquered, but neutralized through prolonged bombardment, with MacArthur focusing on a pincer movement along the north coast of New Guinea (code-named *Cartwheel*).

However, no specific aims were prescribed for the period after late 1943, and the plan reflected how inter-service disagreements obstructed a long-term strategy.[19] In June, when King suggested that the Gilbert Islands be attacked before the end of the year, General Marshall and the army planners replied that the operation required resources to be drawn away from New Guinea. By August, when US forces had advanced up the island's northeast coast, MacArthur presented to the JCS his plan, *Reno II*, which suggested that the Americans needed to focus on a single line of advance towards Japan's home islands, and that the southwest Pacific was to be the main theater of operations. The key aim was to sever Japan's lines of communications with the southern regions by establishing naval and air power in the Philippines. The navy disagreed with the plan, since it committed US forces to a time-consuming campaign that required them to fight a war of attrition as they attempted to capture each individual island.

In spite of the problems, American defense officials did agree that securing control over an area as large as the Pacific Ocean demanded cooperation between the rival services. On one hand, because the US did not suffer resource shortages, and thus could build a vast arsenal, the armed forces were able to follow several strategies simultaneously, with each branch claiming an important role. Yet, war plans demonstrated how the navy and army managed to place their political battles aside in order to focus on their ultimate task of defeating the enemy. In August 1943, following the first Quebec conference (code-named *Quadrant*), the JCS decreed that US strategy in the Pacific was to follow a dual thrust. Priority was given to Nimitz's naval campaign in the central Pacific, which was to be synchronized with MacArthur's operations in New Guinea.

American forces were to converge in the western Pacific, where they could sever the bottleneck of Japan's sea communications. Nimitz's first task was to break the outer perimeter of Japan's defenses, by occupying the Marshall and Gilbert Islands (code-named *Galvanic*). From there, US forces were to move towards the Marianas via the Caroline Islands. The navy and army did continue to disagree on where their forces were to link up, with Nimitz and King advocating an invasion of Formosa, and MacArthur supporting a recapture of the Philippines. The general was driven largely by personal sentiments, and a strong desire to avenge the humiliation he suffered when his troops failed to defend the archipelago against the Japanese during the opening stages of the war. Nevertheless, by late 1943, inter-service cooperation enabled the Americans to lay out a clearer direction of their war effort.

The integration of strategy within the Allied command was in stark contrast to the situation within its Japanese counterpart, where the leaders of the Imperial forces ended up fighting completely separate campaigns. Although the navy continued to focus on the Pacific areas, it followed a strictly defensive strategy, where its carriers and capital ships remained at their main base at Truk and in home waters. Admiral Koga, who succeeded Yamamoto as commander of the Combined Fleet after the latter's plane was fatally shot down while on a tour of the southwest Pacific, refrained from interfering with US operations against outlying areas such as Rabaul, out of fears that further losses could negate the prospects of prevailing in the final showdown.[20] As a result, land garrisons were not adequately covered. During the US landing on Biak in June 1944, the navy's aircraft were committed to the Marianas, and the army high command was appalled at the lack of cooperation.[21] However, the army played its own part in preventing Japan from making good use of its military strength. Because the main concentration was the Asiatic mainland, commanders were reluctant to satisfy the navy's demands that the Pacific islands be reinforced. As a result, US forces faced a much more manageable level of opposition. It was not until the very late stages of the conflict, when the Allies were poised to invade the home islands, that the Imperial army started redeploying its divisions to island garrisons such as Okinawa and Iwojima. Inter-service rivalry thus played a key role in speeding up Japan's demise.

IMPORTANCE OF GOOD PLANNING

The final feature which gave the United States and its allies a strong advantage was that they conducted their war effort while carefully assessing the challenges they were likely to face, as well as the most efficient means to overcome them. The Japanese, on the other hand, hesitated to concede that their prospects of winning the war were becoming negligible in the face of the overwhelming military strength which the Allies were bringing to bear, and consequently formulated their strategy in a haphazard manner.

In planning their operations, the Americans and the British made a conscientious effort to ensure that they had sufficient resources to achieve their objectives. During 1943, when US forces were inadequate for actions against Japanese strongholds in the Pacific, the JCS sensibly decided to adhere to a strategy of conducting minor attacks against areas in the fringes of Japan's empire, such as New Guinea and the Solomons, where enemy defenses were known to be relatively weak. The British were equally wary not to discount the effort required to defeat the Japanese. Throughout 1943, the cabinet's joint intelligence committee warned that Japan possessed ample resources for defending its territories in Southeast Asia.[22] Churchill and his defense chiefs refrained from attempting to reconquer Burma and Malaya until their forces were strong enough to take the initiative. At the theater level, General William Slim, commanding the Fourteenth Army, along with Claude Auchinleck, the commander-in-chief of the British forces in India, both ordered strenuous measures to improve the road communications to the Burma frontier so that adequate supplies and equipment could be transported to the front lines.[23]

The Allies commenced their effort to dismantle Japan's empire in earnest only after early 1944, when they had developed adequate strengths for large scale operations. Even then, military planners carefully decided to avoid moves which were likely to commit their forces to a long and costly venture. For example, the US Army Air Forces' plan for establishing bases in China for a strategic bombing campaign against Japan was scaled back, once it became clear that the move entailed formidable logistical difficulties. Maintaining and supplying bases in mainland China required fuel and ammunition to be airlifted from India over the Himalaya mountain chain, and the Allies could not provide sufficient planes without depleting their air strength in the Pacific theater.

The US navy in particular realized that the most effective way to strike at the heart of Japan's empire was by advancing via the central Pacific and capturing islands such as the Marianas. The Army Air Forces also supported the strategy when their plan to set up bases in China started to appear less feasible. The Americans were also apt to improvise their strategy in accordance with the situation which their forces had to contend with. In November 1943, US forces invaded the island of Tarawa in the Gilbert Islands. Despite days of heavy bombardment by warships and carrier-based planes, Japanese defenses were still largely intact when the landing commenced, and the American marines suffered up to 30 percent casualties as they attempted to neutralize enemy resistance. Although the operations in the Marshall Islands during January 1944 encountered less opposition, US planners concluded that taking each individual bastion was most likely to result in unnecessary delays. The JCS, along with Nimitz's staff, thus adopted a strategy of "leap-frogging," or bypassing areas such as the Carolines, and heading straight for the Marianas. In order to prevent the enemy from staging attacks on US task forces, the main bases of the Japanese navy and its air arm, including Truk, were to be neutralized through sustained bombardment. Admiral King also believed that an early attack on areas within closer proximity to Japan's home islands was likely to compel the Imperial navy to seek an engagement in order to defend key strategic points, and thus offer an opportunity to destroy the enemy fleet. In March 1944, the JCS issued a new directive for the capture of the Marianas. The tendency to avoid risky ventures was demonstrated again in June, when the navy's plans for recapturing Formosa were also placed aside in favor or MacArthur's strategy for establishing a base in the Philippines, on the grounds that the latter were less heavily defended.

At the operational level, US commanders were cautious to not to combat the Imperial fleet in disadvantageous conditions. In one of the most notable examples, during the invasion of Saipan, Admiral Spruance received word that Ozawa's carriers were approaching the vicinity. Although Spruance was presented with a good opportunity to destroy a large portion of the Combined Fleet, he decided not to do so, on the grounds that protecting the amphibious forces was a higher priority. Moreover, the admiral was wary about initiating a battle without having a clear knowledge of the composition and strength of the enemy armada.[24] Naturally, Spruance's decision was opposed by a number of commanders, including Marc Mitscher, who was in charge of the fast carrier force. Mitscher insisted that Task Force Fifty-Eight move further west, where its planes could be positioned within range to interdict the enemy carriers. Instead, US aircraft were launched to take out the approaching air force, and what followed was an epic aerial battle where Japanese losses were so high that American aviators nicknamed it the "Great Marianas Turkey Shoot." On the following morning, Spruance ordered the task force to pursue the Japanese. The carriers *Shokaku*, *Taiho* and *Hiyo* were sunk, but the rest of the fleet escaped, and US pilots did not have enough fuel for further attacks. Although Spruance's delay in attacking the Combined Fleet was cited as the main reason for the lost chance, the decision was nonetheless driven by a prudent assessment of the risks he would have taken by seeking an early engagement. The overriding concern was to avoid excessive losses that could diminish the US navy's ability to prevail.

British war planning was also based on a sober calculation of strategic realities. Offensive actions against Japan were launched only in summer 1944, when sufficient resources were allocated for the Allied invasion of northwest Europe, and surplus forces for the Far East became available. Operations in Southeast Asia were also undertaken on the understanding that staying inactive could only enable the Japanese to bolster their defenses and pose additional obstacles. British operations were to focus on recapturing Burma, where the IJA's capabilities for resistance had significantly deteriorated after its reverses at Imphal and Kohima. Hence, the COS agreed to the proposal put forward by Mountbatten, that the momentum of the Fourteenth Army's advance towards the central plains and Rangoon be maintained.[25] Yet, costs were kept at a minimum, and US forces were to bear the brunt of the effort against Japan's main forces in the Pacific. The strategy was logical in view of Britain's resource shortages. War plans were formulated after weighing a range of factors, including the strength of the opposing forces, the feasibility of various operations, and the importance of the Far East in Britain's global strategy.

Japan's strategy, by contrast, can be best described as uncoordinated, and based on fanciful expectations. The military leadership in Tokyo remained unable to comprehend the size of the forces ranged against them, in spite of the ever-increasing scale of the Allied counter-offensives and the repeated pledges by the US and Britain that they demanded the unconditional surrender of Japan. While the army adhered to its policy of holding onto its conquered territories at all costs, the Imperial navy command judged that it needed to neutralize the Americans before they captured bases for an attack against the home islands. The failure to halt the US assault on Saipan in June 1944 led the navy to adopt the *Sho* (victory) plan, which envisaged a showdown along the Ryukyus–Formosa–Philippines island chain. Yet, the plan was devised without a full comprehension of how the Japanese had minimal prospects of emerging victoriously, given the overwhelmingly superior number of ships and aircraft that the Americans were able to deploy. Military authorities continued to discount Allied fighting capabilities until the closing stages of the conflict. In a post-war memoir, Colonel Matsutani, head of the army general staff for war guidance, stated, "it is embarrassing to have to admit that there was almost no consideration of Britain and the United States," at least until spring 1945, when Germany had collapsed and Japan needed to consider how it was to single-handedly face the Allies.[26] In an organization which maintained an unquestioned faith in victory, few people were likely to pay attention to their enemy's prowess until defeat became unavoidable. Only when the atomic bombs were dropped on Hiroshima and Nagasaki in August 1945, did Japan's leaders begin to consider the option of surrendering. Even then, the military representatives in the cabinet insisted the army and navy be given the opportunity to stage one final showdown against the Allied invasion of the home islands. Indeed, Emperor Hirohito's intervention, and his decision to concede defeat, played a crucial role in saving Japan from further carnage.

CONCLUSION

The main strength of Allied strategy during the Pacific war was not only their ability to deploy larger forces than their Japanese counterpart. Careful planning played a vital role in helping the United States and its coalition partners prevail. In many ways, the Western powers were in a more favorable position to formulate an effective war plan than the Japanese were, largely because their strategic thinking called for a coordinated course of action. The Imperial forces, on the other hand, preferred to conduct their campaigns on the hope that persistence, coupled with good fortune, would guarantee an eventual victory.

The Allies had a clear vision their objectives and the means to achieve them. From the early stages of the conflict, the US and British political leadership vowed that they would continue prosecuting their campaigns until they had secured the unconditional surrender of the Axis powers. Defense planners were therefore able to identify the measures they needed to undertake. The US navy in particular understood that in order to defeat Japan, it was necessary to carry out an extended campaign with the aim of securing control over the vast expanses of the Pacific region. Such actions offered the most effective way to emasculate the Imperial forces' hold on their conquests, as well as to secure bases that could be used to stage a sustained attack on the enemy's home territory. The Japanese high command had a much less coherent plan. The fundamental problem was that the failed to comprehend how the Allies were determined to bring about the total destruction of Japan's military capabilities. The armed forces continued to base their strategy on the expectation that they could inflict a series of defeats that would eventually compel their opponents to offer some type of compromise peace. To worsen the situation, the army and navy never developed a clear vision of how their objectives were to be attained.

Political leaders, along with defense planners within the Allied camp, also devised a coordinated strategy, in spite of the numerous differences of opinion that arose between them. This was mainly because both the Americans and the British understood that in order to carry out a complex campaign such as the Pacific war, cooperation was essential. For example, within the US military establishment, the navy and army commands were divided on where the main thrust of their advance should be focused. In the end, the defense chiefs decided to give priority to the central Pacific, which provided the quickest avenue for advancing towards the heart of Japan's empire, with the army's island-hopping campaign in the southwest Pacific being a subsidiary operation. Likewise, the British leadership, in particular Prime Minister Churchill, was keen to reconquer the territories in Southeast Asia which had been lost to Japan during the early part of the war. The US, on the other hand, was lukewarm towards Britain's plans to reestablish its colonial rule in the Far East. However, in order to maintain the integrity of the alliance, Churchill and his defense staffs decided to join forces with America's campaign in the Pacific theater. Disputes were thus placed aside in the interest of enabling the Allies to defeat Japan in the most efficient manner. Japan's system for strategic planning, however, was hindered by persistent inter-service rivalry, which in turn prevented the navy and army from combining their strengths in a way that allowed them to counter their foes more efficiently.

The third, and final key advantage which the Allies enjoyed was their tendency to make a judicious assessment of their own capabilities as well as those of their enemies. Large scale offensives against the Japanese were not carried out unless friendly forces had adequate resources to overcome their opponents. Likewise, operations against areas where the Imperial forces were known to have substantial defenses were avoided, on the grounds that such actions could result in delays and setbacks. The decision to abandon plans for using China as a base for bombing operations against the Japanese mainland, and to instead develop bases in the Marianas, where logistical requirements posed significantly fewer problems, was a key example of how the Allies conducted their war effort while paying due attention to the strategic realities they had to contend with. Japan's leaders became less cautious in planning their strategy as the war progressed, and by the closing stages, the Imperial forces staged a number of operations that resulted in an unnecessary expenditure of their dwindling strengths, with the attempt to interdict the US task force the Leyte being a notable case in point. While a more effective strategy could not reverse Japan's misfortunes, the decision to continue fighting against the overwhelming forces of the Allied coalition did signify an inability to comprehend how defeat had become virtually inevitable.

7

Tactics and Technology

The tactical level of warfare deals with the methods which an armed force chooses to employ in order to secure its battlefield objectives, and it comprises some of the most detailed features of military activities.[1] Among the critical choices which commanders must make when formulating their tactics is the way they maneuver their forces before they engage the enemy, as well as during the actual fighting. Technological factors are also closely intertwined with tactics. Officers need to determine how their units are going to deliver the firepower needed to neutralize their targets and pave the way for further advances, while at the same time defending themselves against enemy attacks. Success at the tactical level thus requires armed forces to deploy the appropriate types of ships, aircraft and guns to overcome opposition. Of equal importance is to establish a set of procedures whereby the weapons are applied in an efficient manner, and to establish a training program that prepares combat personnel to properly carry out their assigned tasks.

As was the case with strategy and operations, the Allies performed noticeably better than their Japanese opponents in the realm of tactics and technology. The US and its coalition partners, including Great Britain, certainly deployed a superior quantity of advanced armaments, but a number of factors aside from material superiority enabled the Western forces to achieve their ascendancy. Tactical effectiveness on the battlefield hinges on a number of intellectual qualities, among the most important of which is to understand the elements which need to be faced in combat, as well as to determine the weapons and techniques that are required to deal with the obstacles which the enemy is able to put up. Military actions in the Pacific theaters posed a number of unique challenges. The large stretches of ocean which the opposing sides had to traverse in order to engage their foes meant that naval and air forces had to find more innovative ways to project their strength. On land, armies had to cope with the problems arising from the rugged terrain and dense jungle, along with the fact that road communications were largely underdeveloped in the sparsely populated islands of the Pacific region and in most of Southeast Asia. Both features hindered the extensive use of mechanized transport and heavy equipment. For this reason, the proper employment of infantry units, accompanied by a moderate quantity of modern weapons, such as tanks and artillery, was an utmost necessity. Although the Japanese proved adept during the opening stages of the war, when they faced relatively weak opposition, they were not prepared to encounter enemies who were properly equipped and trained. When the tide of the war turned against Japan's forces after 1943, they proved to have neither the resources nor know-how to innovate their procedures. The Allies, on the other hand, prevailed largely because they adjusted their tactics and armaments in accordance with the elements they faced when fighting the Japanese in all areas, including naval, air and ground warfare.

NAVAL WARFARE

Naval actions in the Pacific theaters required the use of vessels which possessed the endurance to move across long distances and remain capable of inflicting destruction on the enemy fleet once the latter had been located. Modern naval weapons, including maritime aviation and the submarine, were often decisive in determining the outcome of the war at sea. The US and Japanese navies both endeavored to develop the relevant weapons as well as the methods of their use. The main weakness of the IJN, however, was that it did not formulate the appropriate tactics and equipment to fight the Allies in a prolonged confrontation.

In regard to fleet aviation, even before the outbreak of war, the Americans and the Japanese realized how aircraft could play a crucial role in a conflict fought in the Pacific Ocean. Carrier-based planes, as well as aircraft operating from island bases, were expected to execute a wide range of tasks, including the escort of convoys and locating enemy forces, as well as to conduct attacks against enemy fleets while at the same time protecting friendly vessels. However, neither navy entered the Pacific war with a clear idea on the exact role which air power was to carry out. Fleet commanders considered aircraft to be an auxiliary arm that were to deal a blow at the onset of the battle, and continued to believe that the final outcome would be determined by a duel fought out between the "big-gun" surface vessels, including battleships. In the US, as late as 1939, the navy claimed that the development of air power did not provide any compelling reasons to modify existing battle procedures.[2] Likewise, the Japanese devoted a substantial amount of their resources towards constructing the super-battleships *Yamato* and *Musashi*.

Once the war broke out, there was a noticeable contrast in how the US and Japanese navies learned from their combat experiences. After Midway and Guadalcanal, the Americans devised more efficient ways of using their weaponry. The Japanese, on the other hand, reverted to a policy of withholding their fleet close to the home islands after suffering their defeats at the hands of the US navy. While the move worked to help the IJN avoid further casualties, commanders were deprived of battle lessons that could help them improvise their tactics. Equally damaging was the fact that Japan did not possess the industrial and technical resources to produce better equipment. Nor could the navy establish a training program to replace the skilled pilots it had lost during the latter part of 1942. As a result, by 1944, the capabilities of the Japanese navy air arm fell significantly behind its US counterpart.

The US navy's fleet aviation doctrine relied heavily on material and technological prowess, so as to enable the air arm to fight an intensified campaign. The ultimate aim was to secure control of the skies in the areas where the navy operated. Although the Japanese had started to withdraw the bulk of their aircraft to their rear bases at Truk and Rabaul, they still retained a good number of planes in the forward areas, and were thus capable of inflicting considerable damage on American task forces. During the invasion of Tarawa, for example, land-based torpedo bombers launched a surprise attack, and several vessels came dangerously close to being hit. To provide an effective defense, carrier groups had to deploy a large number of fighters with sufficient endurance and firepower to take down enemy planes. By late 1943, the Americans were able to carry out a multitude of tasks. The introduction of the *Essex*-class carriers, with their increased aircraft complements, significantly bolstered the navy's striking power. The construction of light carriers (CVLs) in large numbers added to the air power based on fleet carriers. CVLs were primarily assigned to cover task forces, while larger vessels sent their planes against land targets for bombing and strafing missions. Task groups were also equipped with larger numbers of advanced aircraft such as the F6F Hellcat, which had three .50-caliber machine guns fixed on each wing and fired over 1,000 rounds per minute, thus giving it a vastly superior destructive power over the Japanese Zero. The F4U Corsair had a similar performance, and was equal to the Zero in terms of maneuverability. In addition to high performance planes, carrier groups needed a sizeable cohort of qualified aircrews. At the US navy's advanced flight schools at Pensacola, Florida and Corpus Christi, Texas, pilots received nearly 500 hours of practice before qualifying for combat duty.[3] Aircrews were trained to seek opportunities to shoot down enemy planes, by initiating attacks and engaging their opponents at close range. Fighter doctrine also emphasized teamwork, and stipulated that pilots coordinate their maneuvers to defend against enemy interceptors. Emphasis was placed on flying in formation, and providing bomber aircraft with adequate cover.

To effect a better control over the movements of air groups, the Pacific Fleet made steady advances towards creating a fighter direction system. The Americans drew upon the lessons learned from the Solomons campaign of late 1942, when the haphazard deployment of fighters often meant that enemy bombers were able to raid task forces without facing difficult opposition. The main aim of fighter control was to locate the position of incoming planes, so that interceptors could counter them in a timely manner. By early 1944, all ships were supplied with at least one fighter direction officer, whose job was to coordinate the movement of planes within the immediate vicinity. Their work was aided by SC and SK radars, which were used for aerial searches, while surface-level SG radar detected low-flying targets. Radar operators were provided with extensive instruction on how to identify enemy raids, as well as to distinguish friendly and enemy aircraft through the use of identification-friend-and-foe (IFF) equipment. The information obtained through search devices was integrated with a system that could process the material and thereafter dissem-inate it to air units, in the form of a Combat Information Center (CIC). By the time of the Marianas operation of June 1944, the US navy's fighter direction capabilities were markedly enhanced, mainly because personnel understood the countermeasures which they needed to carry out against their opponent. When the Japanese launched their carrier-based bombers against Spruance's task force, radar operators were able to pinpoint the location of enemy forma-tions. Fighter directors were provided with prompt information, and as a result, aircrews managed to intercept virtually all of planes that attempted to sink the American fleet. The carrier *Hornet's* action report described the coordination between the CIC and pilots as "well-nigh perfect," with interceptions carried out "like clockwork."[4]

In addition to defending task forces against air attacks, carrier-based planes also carried out preemptive strikes against land bases, in order to destroy enemy planes before they could be brought into action. Air squadrons also prepared the ground for amphibious assaults against key islands by neutralizing enemy beach installations, so as to reduce the opposition which the landing parties had to encounter. Naval air power also played an important role in severing Japan's oceanic supply lines. As a matter of fact, around 32 percent of Japanese merchant shipping losses were caused by air raids.[5]

The IJN's air service, on the other hand, simply could not match the material strength of its opponents, nor did it have the resources to introduce new types of equipment. Aircraft carriers such as the *Shokaku* and *Zuikaku*, while equal to their US counterparts in terms of durability and striking power, were too few in number to provide the Imperial fleet with a decent prospect of achieving any meaningful victories. Japan's capacity to produce high performance aircraft was also significantly lower than that of its enemies. Newly introduced models of the Zero, while equipped with armor, were still thinly protected, which rendered them vulnerable to the heavy gunfire delivered by the Corsair and Hellcat. Engineers were not accustomed to building machines with large amounts of armor plating and firepower, since the navy's design philosophy had emphasized lightweight construction, in order to allow maneuverability.[6] Furthermore, the development of aircraft engines was a generation behind the West, and the Japanese were confined to using less efficient power units. Under the circumstances, planes could not afford the additional weight needed for bulletproofing and high caliber guns.

Improvements were also held back by the high command's mistaken perceptions which maintained that tactical skill could overcome any advantages the Allies enjoyed. One navy ace recalled how pilots were constantly told that their tactics would defeat the supposedly "lazy" Americans.[7] Military traditions had glorified less well-armed warriors overcoming more powerful opponents through skilful maneuvering. Pilots adhered to the credo, and considered defensive armor to be unnecessary.[8] As a result, navy air officers did not press manufacturers to construct more durable machines. The performance of Japanese planes was further handicapped because the majority were not fitted with radar, and pilots thus faced difficulties in carrying out accurate attacks against shipping targets. The navy did not make a serious effort to develop more advanced search instruments until after the conflict broke out, by which time it was too late to achieve anything close to the standards which the Americans had attained. The development of fighter direction systems was similarly held back by the shortage of radar devices.

In addition to poor equipment, the navy air arm suffered from a dwindling supply of manpower. The Japanese had not foreseen the need to build a large reserve of pilots that could sustain the casualties that were likely to be incurred in the event of a prolonged conflict. The instruction program was designed so that only a select few top quality airmen could enter the service. After Midway, a less rigorous training scheme was set up to compensate for the losses.[9] The new breed sometimes entered battle with less than 100 hours of flying experience. By 1944, the bulk of the remaining skilled aviators had been lost either in combat or plane crashes, and the air service was largely manned by inexperienced personnel. Many units ended up providing no more than a few months of training for their replacement pilots. During the Saipan operation, the Japanese proved incapable of coordinating their tactics. Raids consisted mainly of small and widely separated formations which US task forces found easy to counter. When the Americans launched their invasion of Leyte, the naval air forces could no longer provide effective opposition by relying on conventional tactics, and thus had to resort to suicide (*kamikaze*) raids, in a desperate attempt to hold up the Allied advance towards the home islands. The demise of Japanese fleet aviation was therefore the combined result of inadequate resources, as well as a failure to prepare for an intensified war of attrition.

One additional participant of the Pacific war which devoted a sizeable effort to develop carrier aviation was Great Britain; however, the Royal Navy's progress in this area was markedly behind its US and Japanese counterparts. Britain's strategic circumstances were not entirely conducive to enable the navy to concentrate on air power.[10] On one hand, Great Britain was an imperial nation with possessions in the Far East, which required protection against the Japanese. On the other hand, it was also a Europe-based power. Naval actions in the region did not have to be carried out over large stretches of ocean, and the navy could thus rely upon land-based air cover. The Royal Navy did make notable advances in the use of carrier-based aviation. In fact, the US navy obtained many of its ideas regarding fighter control from the British, who had pioneered the development of radar and the establishment of a system for vectoring friendly fighters against enemy planes. Experiences during the Battle of Britain in the summer of 1940 brought home how aircraft could play a key role in protecting naval vessels. The main problem was that Britain's industrial base did not permit the production of a large number of carrier-based planes and anti-aircraft equipment. The destruction of the *Prince of Wales* and *Repulse* during the opening stages of the Pacific war clearly demonstrated that aircraft had become a highly effective weapon. However, resource shortages continued to hinder carrier construction. The Royal Navy's vessels were also built for operations in the narrow waters that prevailed in Europe where land-based raids were a constant threat. The installation of heavier armor placed extra delays on completion.

Consequently, British naval air power was limited. After the Eastern Fleet was stripped of its carriers in spring 1943 owing to more pressing commitments in the Mediterranean and Atlantic theaters, no reinforcements were dispatched to the Indian Ocean until early 1944. When the British Pacific Fleet commenced its operations, it had inadequate equipment as well as a lack of prior experience. The Royal Navy's main encounter with the Japanese was at Okinawa in spring 1945. Carriers could only hold less than half of the complement carried onboard their US counterparts. Fighters such as the Seafire, which composed a fifth of the aircraft strength, were designed mainly for land-based operations. That the Fleet did not suffer greater damage was due to two factors. First, the armored decks onboard British carriers significantly reduced the damage that could be inflicted. Second, and more important, however, were the improvements that were made in the use of the available anti-aircraft guns and carrier-based aircraft. As was the case with the US navy, wartime experiences compelled the British to develop a more effective method for using its air power, albeit at a late stage.

The campaigns in the Pacific war also saw considerable developments in underwater naval warfare. Again, the Americans and the Japanese both recognized how submarines provided an innovative weapon for attacking enemy ships, owing to their ability to travel long distances without being detected. However, both fleets held differing operational concepts, which in turn had a profound impact on the development of their tactics. For the US navy, the main objective was to interdict enemy supply lines. Underwater vessels were designed for long-range missions into the far reaches of the Pacific, where refueling and resupply facilities were bound to come at a premium.[11] Nevertheless, the performance of US submarines was hindered because they were not equipped with effective torpedoes. During the interwar period, financial constraints held back experimentation, and in an effort to preserve the limited supply of ordnance, exercises were conducted without having the torpedoes detonate. As a result, there were few opportunities to discover and remedy existing faults, and when the US submarine fleet embarked on its initial operations during 1942, a large proportion of the ordnance turned out to explode either prematurely or not at all. Submarine captains pressed the navy to supply better weapons that could carry larger warheads and fire at shallower depths. Tactical doctrine also showed room for improvement. Commanders insisted that surface-level attacks exposed submarines to detection. Submarines thus remained submerged, often waiting for targets to appear, instead of seeking them out. At Guadalcanal, submarine captains were castigated for awaiting Japanese transports and warships to enter the littoral waters, instead of attempting to interdict them in the open sea.[12] Urgent calls were raised to develop aggressive combat methods that were more suitable for conducting large scale attacks. Therefore, while the US navy had a clear vision of what it wished to achieve with its submarine fleet, it did not have the necessary weapons or tactical skill.

By late 1943, however, American forces had gained a decisive edge. Submarine captains adopted the wolf pack tactics which the Germans were employing in the Atlantic, where groups of underwater vessels awaited in areas where merchant ships and transports were known to be traversing. When combined with the introduction of more efficient torpedoes, the tactic enabled the US navy to sink an ever-increasing amount of shipping. By 1944, the Americans had sunk over half of Japan's merchant fleet. The shipping route between Southeast Asia and the home islands became disrupted to the point where a convoy took up to 6 months to make a return journey, with numerous delays caused by having to take circuitous routes and seeking cover at shore when submarine attacks became too intense. The successes achieved by the US navy's underwater fleet were made possible because commanders strove to bring about the technological as well as tactical improvements that were necessary to achieve their operational and strategic objectives.

The IJN, on the other hand, rarely used its submarines for sustained attacks on convoys, mainly because the high command failed to realize that such actions could hinder the buildup of US forces in the far-flung garrisons of the Pacific theater.[13] In terms of equipment, the Japanese received substantial assistance from German technicians and engineers. By the start of the conflict, the submarine fleet was among the most advanced in the world. Underwater vessels had a fuel and engine capacity that gave them extended ranges. The Type 97 long-lance torpedo had a greater destructive power than any of its Western counterparts for the duration of the war, owing to its ability to strike at faraway targets. The oxygen propulsion mechanism also made it difficult for Allied ship crews to detect the torpedoes until they were within close range. However, because the Imperial navy was fixated with battle fleet actions, little effort was devoted towards concocting tactics geared to interdict merchant vessels and troop transports.[14] From 1943 onwards, submarines were dispatched to the waters surrounding Australia, in an attempt to harass convoys. Although several ships were sunk, the impact on the Allied war effort was inconsequential.

Japanese methods for defending convoys against submarines were equally hampered by the naval command's obsession with fleet actions. Most admirals tended to gloss over the prospect that Japan's supply lines would be highly vulnerable in the event of a war, even though they had observed how Britain, a fellow island power, came dangerously close to economic strangulation during both world wars. Instead, the Japanese concluded that enemy submarines operating in the far reaches of the Pacific, beyond the range of shore-based air cover, were more likely to face destruction. Naval policy remained fixated on offensive operations against the enemy's battle fleet, and destroyers were exclusively assigned to protect capital ships. The first escort squadron was not created until April 1942. As late as 1944, when US submarines staged regular attacks on Japanese shipping, destroyers were too slow for effective patrols, and were armed only with the most rudimentary types of depth charges and sonar. The IJN's inadequacies in the area of submarine warfare were largely the result of a failure to foresee how attacks on supply lines could have devastating effects on Japan's war effort as well as its enemies.

Although modern innovations such as the aircraft carrier and submarine played an important role in the naval campaigns of the Pacific war, the more traditional types of surface vessels, including the battleship, continued to form a valuable component of the opposing sides' fleets. In certain conditions, such as nighttime battles, aircraft could not be relied upon to deliver accurate attacks, owing to low visibility. Task forces thus had to utilize their battleships. The US navy's performance was significantly aided by the use of radar to pinpoint targets so that accurate fire could be delivered. The Japanese, on the other hand, were not adept at developing modern search devices, and this was a key factor which led the surface fleet to lose its edge over its opponents.

American tactical doctrine envisaged surface vessels approaching within ranges that permitted them to place the enemy under the maximum amount of fire, and overwhelming the latter with superior numbers. At the same time, commanders in the Pacific Fleet endeavored to deploy their vessels in a more efficient manner, and drew upon the lessons they had learned at Guadalcanal, namely that radar-guided fire control provided a valuable instrument for destroying Japanese ships before the latter could counter-attack, and without expending excessive amounts of ammunition. The idea was to take the opposing fleet by surprise.

The Imperial navy, by contrast, made minimal progress in the area of fire control. While Japan's industries were not able to produce large quantities of modern armaments, the poor results also arose from the naval establishment's habit of believing that its forces were invincible. Subsequently, the importance of technological resources when engaging the US navy was not fully comprehended.[15] The lack of efficient radar devices meant that the Japanese saw their relative capabilities vis-à-vis the Allies undergo a steady decline. Gunnery methods called for battery and fire direction crews to continuously follow their target by using their own vision and optical devices, thereby causing fatigue.[16]

Although the US navy was unable to test the effectiveness of its ships for a large part of the intervening period between the end of the 1942 Solomons campaign and the invasion of the Philippines in October 1944, owing to the inactivity of the Japanese fleet, the advances in radar and fire control were clearly visible at the Battle of Leyte Gulf. Gunnery fire was reported to have hit enemy ships with "devastating accuracy," and in light of the relatively small amount of ammunition expended, naval guns were considered "highly effective."[17] Japanese battery crews relied on a more primitive system, where they placed colored dye in their shells to mark the fall of each shot.[18] Once the shells exploded, spot checkers were ordered to distinguish the salvoes from their own ship, and relay their estimates of necessary corrections in range, bearing and deflection to fire control personnel. The Pacific Fleet's ascendancy in surface actions was not only due to its superior numbers of ships, but equally important was that officers made good use of the advanced technology at their disposal.

AERIAL WARFARE

As was the case with naval forces, aircraft played a central role in the Pacific theater because they provided a valuable means to mobilize one's military strength over extended distances. The development of maritime aviation was one of several different ways in which air power was applied. Tactical support and strategic bombing were important aspects. Tactical aviation entails aiding the battlefield operations of ground forces by bombarding enemy defenses, supply depots, and lines of communication. Strategic bombing, by contrast, constitutes raids against the opponent's home territory. The aim is to destroy the economic fabric which holds together the war effort, by attacking its industrial and economic assets, while at the same time demoralizing both the civilian population and political leadership by inflicting mass damage on the main cities. In order to conduct a successful campaign in the Pacific, air forces had to meet a number of requirements. Aircraft had to be built in sufficient numbers. Planes had to be constructed with endurance and firepower, so that they could fly long ranges and carry substantial loads of bombs and ammunition, while at the same time withstanding enemy opposition. A large cohort of qualified pilots also had to be trained, so that air units could carry out a number of complex operations over a theater covering an extensive geographic area. On all of the above counts, the Allies ended up outpacing the Japanese. This was largely because Japan's industries were incapable of matching the output of their Western counterparts, in particular that of the United States. Two additional factors played a key role in shaping the outcome of the air war. First, the Americans had a better idea of what their air forces required in a large scale conflict. Second, and closely related, the US air services were able to work closely with the industrial and scientific communities to bring about improvements in aircraft performance.

The US Army Air Forces (USAAF) had a clear lead over any of the Pacific war belligerents in developing the capacity to carry out tactical air support missions; however, the British Royal Air Force (RAF) also made good use of its aircraft to facilitate the movement of the Fourteenth Army in the India-Burma theater. Neither air service entered the conflict with a significant capability to provide close support for ground forces. During the years prior to the outbreak of the Second World War, the USAAF and RAF were both fixated on the concept of defeating the enemy via strategic bombing operations. Although their respective armies relied heavily on modern weaponry to neutralize enemy positions, they were not successful at forming cooperative links with the air services. As a result, the development of tactical aviation made relatively little progress. However, wartime experiences, in particular the British expeditionary force's encounters with German forces in Western Europe, and later, the Allied the campaigns in North Africa, highlighted how air cover was valuable in enhancing the momentum of the army's advance. Efforts were made to develop aircraft that could fly at low altitudes and speeds so that aircrews could locate their targets. Equally important was to establish a system of communications so that air units could be called upon whenever ground units were held up by enemy opposition. Many of the lessons were applied in the war against the Japanese, often to good effect.

In the southwest Pacific theater, where the bulk of the US army's land campaigns took place, the North American aircraft manufacturing company's

B-25 Mitchell was the standard plane used for tactical support. The most signif-icant problem arose not from Japanese opposition, but topographic features. The dense jungles often made enemy defenses hard to identify, and the Japanese proved adept at using tree cover to hide their positions. During the New Guinea campaign, between early 1943 and the middle of 1944, air power was more frequently used for pre-emptive strikes against aerodromes and interdicting troop convoys at sea, rather than raiding enemy defenses.[19] Aircraft also tended to cause damage to friendly forces, and was efficient only when the army and air force managed to establish adequate liaison. Air squadrons also needed accurate intelligence on their targets. Reconnaissance units were set up, whose task was to carry out preliminary fly-over missions in order to collect photographic data. The material was thereafter processed by personnel who were trained to identify enemy positions by detecting man-made features amidst the thick vegetation. By the late stages of the war, the USAAF had introduced considerable improve-ments. Preliminary raids against the island of Biak off the western coast of New Guinea destroyed approximately 90 percent of the Japanese supply dumps, and compelled the defending forces to withdraw to the interior, thereby allowing the US forces to land without facing opposition.[20] During the Philippines campaign of early 1945, American troops again faced minimal resistance when recapturing the island of Corregidor, which controlled the entrance to Manila Bay, because heavy bombs had destroyed the artillery and machine gun positions.[21] General Walter Krueger, commanding the Sixth Army during the Luzon operation, commended the Fifth Air Force for providing "superb" tactical support, and observed how it helped ground forces both in taking their objectives and defending themselves against counter-attacks.[22]

In the India-Burma theater, the British contended with similar difficulties arising from jungle cover. Nevertheless, airdrop supply missions played a vital role in helping the Fourteenth Army hold its ground during the Japanese attack against the Arakan and Manipur border regions during in 1944. When the advance of General William Slim's forces reached the central plains of Burma in the autumn, battlefield conditions were ideal for tactical aviation. In open country, the Japanese were hard-pressed to find natural features that could conceal their troop concentrations. The USAAF and RAF were able to dramati-cally expand their tactical support capabilities mainly because their respective armies understood how the extensive use of modern weapons was important in overcoming enemy forces. Furthermore, Allied forces utilized the lessons they learned in wartime, and were willing to modify their procedures in order to enhance their own efficiency.

The air services of both the IJN and IJA proved adept during the opening stages of the conflict, and carried out a number of tasks, including the destruction of Allied beach defenses and lines of communication. The US

army's military intelligence service noted how the establishment of air superiority was as one of the key reasons for Japan's successful conquest of Southeast
Asia and the western Pacific regions.[23] However, Japan's industries were unable
to produce enough aircraft to protect the overstretched empire against the
Allied counter-offensive. To make matters worse, the Japanese army did not
attach a high value to providing its units with firepower, and the use of aircraft
received scant attention in comparison to what it did within the US and British
armed forces. In the Burma and China theaters, the high command gave air
operations a low priority, and the Allies eventually secured command of the
skies "almost by default."[24] In the Pacific, the creation of a tactical support
force was made difficult because the military leadership miscalculated the
effort required to hold onto its island positions, and did not anticipate having
to provide defensive air cover for forward units. Nor did the Japanese foresee
fighting a prolonged campaign where they needed to maintain a consistent flow
of supplies to the outlying territories. As a result, air units received inadequate
munitions and spare parts. When the balance of strength turned in favor of
the US forces after 1943, the Japanese had to confine themselves to sporadic
attacks against areas where their opponent's anti-aircraft defenses and fighter
forces were relatively weak, in order to conserve their limited reserve of planes.
Army units also started to realize that they faced formidable difficulties in
protecting their positions against the large-scale air raids which the Americans
were bringing to bear.[25] When commanders in the battlefront realized that their
resources were inadequate, the situation was well-nigh irreversible.

The disparity in the development of strategic bombing also owed itself largely
to the fact that the USAAF had a larger pool of resources to draw upon that its
Japanese counterpart. The Japanese never built an air force that could carry out
extensive strategic bombing operations, because the shortage of raw materials
and industrial plant precluded the construction of planes that could carry large
payloads over the long distances which separated the outer reaches of Japan's
empire from its opponents' main bases in Australia and the continental United
States. At the same time, Japanese military thinking played its part in holding
back innovations. The high command entered the war on the expectation of
achieving a quick victory against the Allies through a series of victories on the
battlefront. Air commanders were thus fixated on supporting the army and
navy, and did not contemplate the idea of conducting sustained raids on areas
that were removed from the main theater of operations, where the enemy's
economic assets and transportation facilities were located.

The Americans, on the other hand, had made extensive preparations to carry
out large-scale air attacks against their enemies' home territories. Throughout
the interwar period, the Air Corps Tactical School's instruction program
concentrated almost exclusively on training airmen to execute strategic air

missions, and dictated that destroying the enemy's industrial infrastructure provided the key to victory in any future conflict. Bombing raids were initially carried out by the B-17 Flying Fortress, but the extended distances which planes had to fly before reaching their targets in the Pacific theaters required a more durable plane. Even before the Pacific war commenced, the top-ranking officials within the air corps decided to commission an advanced bomber type with a longer range and greater payload than any of its predecessors. The impetus did not originate from the threat posed by the Japanese, but instead, from the growing danger that Britain could fall, in which case the US would be deprived of bases from which its aircraft could carry out attacks against Nazi Germany. The air corps thus contracted Boeing to construct a bomber that could be based within the continental United States, and still carry out attacks against the Axis powers' home territories. In September 1942, the B-29 Superfortress flew its first test flight. Once US forces captured the Marianas islands in late 1944, and acquired bases within striking distance of Japan, the B-29 spearheaded the carpet bombing campaign against Japan's cities. The US air force's success in developing a strategic bombing capability therefore resulted from a combination of military planners having a clear vision of what they wanted to achieve, coupled with their possessing the resources needed to produce the weapons needed to attain their objectives.

LAND WARFARE

In the ground campaigns, the Allies prevailed mainly because they were able to deploy a larger quantity of heavy weaponry, including tanks, artillery and machine guns than their Japanese counterparts, and also because they devised a set of tactics that were suitable for fighting in the mountainous terrain and dense jungles which were common in the Asia-Pacific theater. The IJA, on the other hand, while successful during the opening stages of the conflict, rapidly lost its lead after 1943, mainly because it did not have the resources or skill to defeat opponents who were equipped with large quantities of modern weapons.

In addition to the fighting on land, amphibious assaults were a key feature of the campaigns in the Pacific. Owing to the large number of coastlines and island objectives, the participants needed to devise an efficient way to move their troops to distant locations and provide them with sufficient equipment to launch surprise attacks against enemy beachheads. The United States Marine Corps (USMC) was the most successful armed service in executing amphibious actions. In contrast to their Japanese counterparts, the Americans established an independent marine corps which had full control over how its troops, ships and aircraft were to be deployed, and this enabled them to overcome the problems which frequently arose from inter-service rivalry between the navy and army.[26] The USMC also stood alone in developing a capability to conduct landings against defended beaches.

After the Allied counter-offensive in the Central Pacific commenced in the autumn of 1943, the Marine Corps achieved a high level of efficiency. Enemy coastal fortifications were neutralized through preliminary naval and aerial bombardment. Transport ships were designed to carry heavy equipment, and fitted with hinged doors and ramps so that mechanized vehicles could be quickly unloaded and deployed ashore. US forces also improvised their procedures in accordance with the types of resistance they were likely to encounter. During the invasion of Tarawa in the Gilbert Islands, the landing force was held up by an elaborate system of offshore obstacles. Once on land, the marines discovered that the beach defenses had held up against heavy bombardment. The main lesson derived from encounter was that amphibious parties needed to prepare for a variety of circumstances. Operations were planned with a view to ensuring that the attackers would not incur excessive casualties. Aerial reconnaissance missions were carried out consistently in order to ascertain the state of Japanese defenses. Naval and aerial bombardment had to be conducted at a sufficient volume and with enough accuracy so that enemy defenses could be neutralized.[27] Marines were equipped with a variety of weapons, including tanks, flamethrowers and grenades, so that they could overcome the defending troops. Training had to be carried out to enable marines to work in teams and coordinate their maneuvers. The lessons learned at Tarawa were applied in future operations, with good results. A good knowledge of the enemy's methods, along with the development of a proper level of tactical skill, often played a crucial role in enabling the USMC to prevail.

In the land campaigns, the main problem was that the mountainous terrain and dense jungle which prevailed in the Pacific islands and in Burma did not permit the easy movement of mechanized vehicles and heavy artillery. Army units needed to fight a combined arms battle, where enemy positions were initially bombarded from a distance with tanks and artillery. Infantry units then conducted the final advance to occupy the ground and eliminate the remnants of enemy opposition. When the Allied forces launched their first counteroffen-sives in late 1942, they learned that Japanese defenses were not easy to break. The fighting abilities which the IJA displayed in defending its positions at Buna led General Robert Eichelberger, then commanding the First Army Corps, SWPA, to set up a training program geared to enable US troops carry out the appropriate moves for overcoming enemy positions. While the use of heavy weapons to wear down enemy forces was drilled into combat personnel, equally important was to train infantry troops to approach their targets at close range, and thereafter destroy Japanese bunkers by using a combination of small arms, including mortars, flamethrowers and grenades.

The British Fourteenth Army, under the leadership of William Slim, similarly reformed its tactics. India Command lengthened the periods of training which troops had to undergo before they could be deployed to the front line. Emphasis was placed on carrying out patrols of the jungle in order to determine the location of Japanese forces. The British also made use of the lessons learned by their Australian counterparts, who had extensive combat experience against the Japanese in the jungles of New Guinea. Officers from the Australian Imperial Force provided instruction on how head-on assaults against Japanese positions often resulted in high casualties for the attackers, and that a more effective method was to encircle the defenders and thus prevent them from receiving any reinforcements or supplies.[28] Upon discovering that they were surrounded, enemy troops often attempted to break out by launching a desperate counter-attack, thereby giving Allied forces the chance to kill them *en masse*.

The successes achieved in overcoming the Japanese defenses in the Pacific islands and Burma after late 1943 did not owe themselves solely to material superiority. Allied commanders also made an arduous effort to draw upon the lessons of combat experience, and developed tactics which enabled their forces to avoid excessive losses. Battlefield encounters were consistently analyzed in order to discover what had gone wrong or right. While air support, naval gunfire, and artillery were used to the fullest, bombardment often worked to merely set up the correct conditions for advancing against the Japanese. Enemy forces were not completely destroyed, and in order to neutralize the surviving elements, close-in assaults, conducted by infantrymen were necessary. Thus, as Walter Krueger, commander of the US Sixth Army, once stated, infantry units were often "the arm of final combat."[29] Field commanders learned through experience that supporting weapons were merely one of a myriad of necessities.

The IJA's main weakness stemmed again from its lack of materiel, along with the fact that its parent nation did not possess the industrial capacity to produce large amounts of hardware. However, flawed doctrine and an incompetent leadership were also at fault. Military traditions called for an unquestioned acceptance of orders from higher authority. Practices of this nature certainly gave rise to an exceptional level of dedication among troops. At the same time, the rigid command structure stifled initiative, and tactical methods reflected a corresponding level of inflexibility. Commanders held an institutionalized belief that, in spite of their deficiency in equipment, their troops would prevail in all circumstances solely by the virtue of their spiritual bravery. A key by-product of this belief was a situation where the army held onto its practice of relying upon infantrymen as its primary weapon, and failed to match Western standards in the use of supporting arms. Staff officers lacked an ability to objectively assess their enemies, nor could they admit their own methods were questionable. The army's rigid mindset was encapsulated by a seminar held at the army war college in Tokyo in August 1943. The commandant announced that a new course would be introduced to meet the growing need to counter US tactics. He then paused, and continued, "if anyone can teach this course, go ahead because frankly, I don't know a damn thing about it."[30] Japanese doctrine for defensive operations forbade withdrawals even when its positions became untenable. This practice was based on the belief that by inflicting high levels of attrition, its troops could compel the Allies to abandon their operations. As a result, at virtually every land battle, beleaguered troops conducted last-ditch suicide attacks. When employed against Allied armies who possessed superior firepower and tactical skill, such measures resulted in the annihilation of entire units. Even then, the mounting setbacks did not appear to affect tactical doctrine. A field manual captured in the Philippines during early 1945 stated that, while inferior equipment was a distinct obstacle to winning, in the final analysis, "a well-trained army, with a firm belief in victory ... [could] overcome material superiority and attain a swift victory."[31] So long as the army establishment believed that the tenacity of their troops could assure eventual success, it saw no strong reasons to investigate ways to reform its tactics.

CONCLUSION

The successes which the Western forces achieved at the tactical level owed themselves largely to their ability to deploy a greater quantity of ships, aircraft and guns than their Japanese counterpart. Nevertheless, the development of effective combat methods proved to be of prime importance. The Americans had a tactical doctrine that was particularly well suited for fighting an intensified campaign. Even before the conflict broke out, the armed forces maintained that victory on the battlefront required them to use a large quantity of techno-logically advanced armaments that could deliver overwhelming firepower. Once hostilities with Japan commenced, officers sought to draw lessons from their encounters with enemy forces so that they could modify their procedures in a way that worked to counter the unique challenges which the Imperial forces were able to put up. The British were guided by similar principles which emphasized the use of modern weapons. Although their navy did not have the resources to become extensively involved in the war against Japan until a late stage, their army and air force had ample opportunities to test their fighting skills in the Far Eastern theater, and did manage to significantly improve their tactical methods.

The Imperial navy and army, by contrast, were stifled by a military culture which discouraged any questioning of their own ability to prevail. Officers believed that they could compensate for their inability to deploy the same quantity of hardware as the Allies by relying on tactical finesse. While Japan's forces proved adept during the opening stages of the conflict, they failed to prepare for encounters with stronger enemies. By 1943, when the tide of the conflict had turned against the Japanese, military officials had neither the resources nor the know-how to improve the capabilities of their forces. Clausewitz contended that intellectual inadequacy usually results in indifferent achievement.[32] The Japanese performance at the tactical level during the Pacific war clearly proved the hypothesis. Innovations were held back because officers did not comprehend how they were engaging in a type of warfare where the widespread and efficient use of modern weapons played a decisive role in determining the outcome of the battle. Consequently, the Imperial forces failed to develop the appropriate weapons and tactics. The Allies, on the other hand, prevailed not only because they had the necessary military strength, but they also understood the procedures they needed to undertake in order to defeat the Japanese and were willing to undertake the necessary adjustments in order to improve the performance of their own forces.

8

Morale and Combat Motivation

In the same manner that military organizations need to properly plan their strategy and operations, maintaining morale and combat motivation among troops constitutes a fundamental task in conducting a successful war effort. Both factors have been recognized as important facets since ancient times. At around the sixth century B.C., the Chinese theorist Sun Tzu argued that the most successful generals were those who defeated their opponents without even engaging them on the battlefield. The idea was to win by making the enemy lose its will to initiate hostilities, either through an open display of one's military strength, or otherwise convincing the other side that fighting was not in its best interest.[1]

Morale forms a central part in any study of the Pacific war, for two key reasons. First, for the Japanese, and the army in particular, their fighting spirit formed the main weapon for waging a battle against the numerically and technologically superior Allied forces. Military leaders explicitly stated that staying power provided the only way to circumvent the disadvantages that arose from Japan's incapacity to match its opponents' industrial and military potential. The armed forces were expected to prolong the conflict to the point where the Western powers started to suffer from war-weariness, and thereafter offered the negotiated peace which the Japanese much sought. Conversely, Western forces often found that the Imperial army's will to continue fighting at all costs was one of the most formidable obstacles to achieving battlefield victories.

Secondly, in recent decades, the subject of combat motivation during the Pacific war has become a topic of scholarly debate. John Dower's seminal thesis has argued that racial hatred was the chief instrument which the Japanese and the Allies used to maintain morale among their troops.[2] The animosity, in turn, gave rise to a level of violence which was not visible in many other theaters. However, Dower and his proponents have tended to present a one-sided argument that seems to reject any suggestion that other aspects played an important role.[3] The most significant reexamination of the race issue has been put forward by Allison Gilmore. Her work on psychological warfare operations explained how the Japanese were prone to become demoralized when faced with adversities on the battlefield, and that US military officials recognized how the characteristic provided an ideal opportunity for lowering the enemy's fighting spirit through the use of propaganda and psychological warfare.[4] The conclusion suggests that the Allies did attempt to defeat the Japanese by means aside from mass annihilation, and their motivation to wage the Pacific war was not entirely shaped by a blind hatred of the enemy.

Indeed, to state that cultural antagonisms were the only, or even foremost, factor which maintained battlefield morale is an exaggeration. No matter how extensively troops were indoctrinated, they were still vulnerable to so-called "human weaknesses" such as the fear of being killed. In order to overcome this difficulty, soldiers needed to be provided with sufficient weapons and ammunition so that they could feel confident in their prospects of surviving combat. Equally important was to ensure that soldiers were guarded against elements such as starvation and disease. In this regard, the Japanese were not able to keep their front line units properly supplied, and consequently, their fighting spirit underwent a noticeable decline as the conflict progressed. On the other hand, the Allies succeeded in encouraging their troops to persist, in spite of the hardships which they faced, largely because they provided adequate materiel for their soldiers, and thus help them develop a sense of reassurance that they could eventually prevail.

ROLE OF RACIAL HATRED AND IDEOLOGY IN MAINTAINING MORALE: THE DOWER THESIS REVISITED

John Dower's argument, namely that racial and ideological views on both the Allied and Japanese side led the campaigns in the Pacific to be fought with a certain magnitude of brutality, is valid to a certain extent. The belligerent forces did extensively use fear of the enemy as an instrument for encouraging troops to risk their lives in defense of their country. For example, the Allies frequently portrayed the Japanese as a manifestation of what Dower has described as the "yellow peril," or a hostile Asiatic race that was determined to undermine the safety of the Western world. The hatred can be largely explained by the shock which arose from the unexpected level of success with which the Imperial forces ousted the Americans and the European colonial powers from Southeast Asia during the opening stages of the war. Prior to the outbreak of hostilities, Westerners, including the Americans, British and Australians tended to denigrate Japanese martial qualities. The opinion was in line with a preconception that had been held by intellectual circles for centuries, namely that Asian people had traditions that were at such variance with their

Western counterparts, that they could not achieve the same level of scientific or technological advancement.[5] Japan's intellectual development was not guided by the same "logic" in the Western sense, and its mindset was described as "pre-Hellenic, pre-rational and pre-scientific." After the supposedly inferior Japanese army defeated the Allies, the West developed another stereotype, and the enemy was portrayed as a superman, "possessed of uncanny discipline and fighting spirit." The US army's weekly magazine, *Yank*, for example, referred to the Japanese soldier as "a born and natural jungle fighter."

The rank and file of the IJA held a similar contempt towards their Western opponents. A cornerstone of military training was to uphold the idea of *Yamato damashii*, which professed that the Japanese race had descended from the gods, and thus had both a preordained right as well as a sacred duty to become the leader of the Asiatic people. Soldiers were regularly indoctrinated with this belief. For example, a pamphlet titled *Read this and the War is Won* (*kore dake yomeba ware wa kateru*), which was issued to troops heading to Malaya, clearly stated that the army's task was to end European domination in Asia. The Imperial army also set up a training program that enabled it to build up a high level of dedication among troops. A large number of the military's practices stemmed from long-standing traditions that had been ingrained in its parent society.[6] When the modern Japanese military was established during the late nineteenth century, its leaders needed to create an adequate level of solidarity. To achieve this, they sought to inculcate traditional values, including the concept of the "way of the warrior" (*bushido*), which demanded that troops possess a number of virtues, including courage, bravery, and self-sacrifice.[7] The process of forging unity was further facilitated by the way in which the upbringing and education of youths within Japanese society had been carried out with a view to instructing them to comply with orders from their superiors. The people were conditioned to be part of a hierarchical social structure, and this feature rendered them susceptible to thought control.[8] Upon entering service, the soldier was taught that the "proper attitude" to have was a willingness to "lay down his life" to fulfill his duty towards the nation.[9] Institutional cohesion was further strengthened by establishing the Emperor as the commander-in-chief of the armed forces, with the Imperial throne used as the entity which symbolized Japan's expansionist pursuits. Soldiers in the field were required pay homage in the direction of the Imperial Palace every day. The *Imperial Rescript to Soldiers and Sailors* (*gunjin chokuyu*), introduced in 1882, ordered troops, "singularly devote yourself to your most important obligation to the emperor, and realize that the obligation is heavier than the mountains and death is lighter than a feather."[10]

The practice of indoctrination created a number of benefits, in that it gave troops a clear idea of the cause which they were fighting for. The Imperial army instilled an institutionalized credo which dictated that Japan was embarking on a divine mission to secure control over the Asia-Pacific region. Military traditions stipulated that the greatest honor for a soldier was to die in battle and have his remains interred at the Yasukuni Shrine in Tokyo, which was the burial ground of Japan's war heroes. The regimentation created an exceptional fighting spirit, as evidenced by soldiers' writings. One captured diary read, "I am glad to participate in this great mission ... the dawn of Greater East Asia is near. I shall never give in until the enemy is destroyed ... I am a son of God, hence I shall fear nobody."[11]

For the Western powers, because the ultimate war aim was to rid the world of fascist and militarist regimes, troops were led to believe that they were defending valued ideals such as political freedom. In the US, a propaganda film produced shortly after the war broke out, titled *Prelude to War*, portrayed the Axis powers as symbols of barbarism and oppression. The Australians were also successful in convincing troops that fighting the Japanese was a worthy act, mainly because their home territory had been threatened with an invasion during the opening stages of the conflict. One belligerent power which faced unique difficulties in building up combat motivation was Great Britain. This was mainly because the British did not contend with the possibility of Japanese attacks on their home territory, and soldiers tended to perceive the Germans as a more immediate threat. In a notable case, during June 1943, General Wavell met the war cabinet, and voiced concerns that a large portion of servicemen were apathetic about the war against Japan.[12] Under the circumstances, the willingness to prosecute the Far Eastern conflict was likely to dissipate once Germany had been defeated. Furthermore, because the majority of the British army in Asia consisted of Indian and African troops, propagating views which suggested that the Western powers were seeking to reconquer their colonies from the Japanese was unlikely to be well received. On the contrary, the material could well be seen as an attempt to perpetuate European exploitation of the non-white races.

While convincing troops to harbor sentiments of xenophobia created a good level of fighting spirit, it also had some negative consequences. Racist outlooks frequently created misperceptions of the enemy. For the Americans in particular, while the Germans were seen as unfortunate victims of the Nazi dictatorship, the Japanese were portrayed as a categorically inhumane race. The belief that the West was fighting an alien and barbaric enemy appeared to be confirmed by the "national character" studies that were undertaken in the US. The studies were commissioned by the State Department's office of war information, and undertaken mainly by social anthropologists and psychologists. One of the key conclusions to emerge was that Japan's culture tended to be shaped by a combination of an inferiority complex vis-à-vis the West, and a craving for conquest. While many of the hypotheses were correct, they were also shaped by ethnocentric notions which praised the values held by the US, including democracy and individual freedom, while denigrating Japanese ideas such as authoritarian rule. The studies have been criticized for reinforcing racist attitudes. A number of scholars have explained how the problem stemmed from a lack of knowledge about Japanese culture.[13] Because there were only a small number of Japan experts within the US, the investigations were often conducted by individuals who had little empathy for the enemy. As a result, the Americans tended to think that the unique traits of the Japanese people indicated some type of abnormality.

Servicemen on the battlefield who had been taught that the Japanese were a grave threat often found such views to be correct, as evidenced by the enemy's insistence on fighting to the finish and inflicting high casualties on Allied forces. Japanese troops were frequently dehumanized, and treated with revulsion. For example, Charles Lindbergh's diary often referred to the Japanese as animals and "yellow sons of bitches." One veteran from the New Guinea campaign recalled, "I never thought in my own mind that I killed another human being."[14] In a passage that had to be sanitized in post-war editions of his book, Colonel Scott, a US army pilot described his joy at strafing enemy troops, and recalled, "I just laughed in my heart when I knew that I had killed another black-widow spider or scorpion."[15] In one of his first reports from the Pacific, war correspondent Ernie Pyle explained how the Japanese were "looked down upon as something subhuman or repulsive; the same way some people feel about cockroaches or mice." At Iwojima, many marines went into battle with the words "rodent exterminator" stenciled into their helmets.

Australian troops held equally hostile views. Racist attitudes had been widespread even before the war broke out, largely owing to the influx of Asian immigrants, which was perceived as a barrier to the government's effort to create a "white Australia." The majority of army personnel ended up being deployed in the Pacific theater, and more Australians were killed by the IJA than by the Germans and Italians combined.[16] In a similar manner to their US counterparts prior to the conflict, Australia's servicemen judged that the Japanese were not an enemy to be feared, only to be faced with a rude awakening when a large portion of their comrades in arms fell into captivity when the IJA occupied areas such as Singapore and the East Indies. Throughout the war, Australian troops went into battle with the conviction that they were exacting retribution on an enemy for whom they had a deep-seated and long-standing hatred. Soldiers used derogatory terms when describing their foes, such as "clever animals with certain human characteristics."[17] Observations of enemy tactics, such as carrying out suicide charges against advancing Allied armies, also gave rise to the belief that the Japanese did not value their own lives in the same manner that Westerners did. Many Australians expressed bewilderment. One lieutenant wrote home, "I have not worked out yet whether the Nip is fanatically brave or idiotically stupid."

Conversely, within the Japanese army, there was a widespread contempt regarding the white races, which in turn led military personnel to disparage their foes. Western soldiers were accused of depending excessively on technological resources, and lacking the stamina to withstand the adversities that had to be faced in combat. For example, the main lesson drawn from the encounter at Salamaua in New Guinea was that American forces were weak in hand-to-hand fighting; consequently they were "not worthy of fear."[18]

The practice of indoctrinating troops to hate their enemy and fight for their nation's cause also gave rise to a situation where both sides inevitably developed a "kill or be killed" mentality. A manifestation of this mindset was the Imperial army's frequent practice of fighting to the last man and round. The Western image of the Japanese soldier's tenacity, along with his unwillingness to surrender even when faced with certain defeat, was grounded in reality. Several factors gave rise to this tendency. Insofar as cultural influences were concerned, soldiers were taught to unquestioningly accept their duty to devote their life for the cause of their emperor and nation, as well as to abide by orders from higher authority. The precepts of the *bushido* code also stipulated that surrender was the most treasonous act which a warrior could commit. During the Meiji era, thanks to universal conscription, the attitude permeated the troops who were drawn from rural communities, and eventually became an accepted norm.[19] The field service code (*senjinkun*) of 1941, which decreed that it was impermissible for Japanese soldiers to be captured, was in many ways a mere articulation of notions which the rank and file had traditionally held. Captured diaries showed how troops considered the act of committing mass suicide in support of their nation's cause, or *gyokusai*, as the highest honor.[20] A corporal whose diary was retrieved at Cape Gloucester wrote, "smilingly, I shall return to my native land and take my place in the Yasukuni shrine."[21] At the same time, not all Japanese troops were driven by ideology. Interrogations of servicemen who fell into Allied captivity usually revealed that that their greatest deterrence was a practical concern, namely, the fear for their own safety. Because the Japanese had a limited knowledge of Western cultures except for what they had learned through military propaganda, the general impression was that the Allies regularly killed or tortured their POWs, in the same manner which the Japanese treated their prisoners.

The IJA's views regarding the treatment of prisoners was another key indication of how racial hatred raised the level of violence in the Pacific theaters. Because Japan was not a signatory of the Geneva Convention, which stipulated that POWs had to be handled in a humane manner, officers were not provided with any guidelines on the issue. The Japanese were thus prone to carry out certain types of war crimes. Furthermore, because military traditions stipulated that surrender was disgraceful, captured soldiers were not perceived to be worthy of good treatment. The Japanese applied this principle with particular vigor against the Allied troops who surrendered so easily in Southeast Asia during were opening stages of the conflict. Prisoners with Aryan features, including blond hair and fair skin, were singled out to be tortured. Notably enough, the army high command never issued explicit orders to carry out such vicious acts, and the atrocities were largely perpetrated by local commanders. As one prominent historian has argued, military personnel claimed that they were simply carrying out their duty towards their nation.[22] In this sense, Japanese war crimes showed how ideas such as patriotism and military honor were frequently construed in order to justify violent behavior. Nevertheless, incidents such as the Bataan death march, along with the use of British, Dutch and Australian slave labor to build the Burma–Thailand railway, were some of the most notorious examples of how the cultural divide between the Japanese and the Allied forces created a certain level of suspicion between the belligerents, which in turn meant that the Pacific war was bound to be characterized by brutality.

Allied servicemen were imbued with the idea that they were confronting a dangerous enemy that had to be exterminated. A US army poll taken in 1943 indicated that half of all GIs believed it would be necessary to kill all Japanese before peace could be achieved. American troops in the Pacific theater often felt they had to kill their opponent like "one might exterminate a particularly intransigent pest."[23] In a post-war memoir, correspondent Robert Sherrod recalled how soldiers felt no compunction in beating the Japanese into submission.[24] General Sir Thomas Blamey, commanding the Australian forces in New Guinea, told a unit at Port Moresby in 1942, "you are fighting a shrewd, cruel, and merciless enemy. Deep down, he is a subhuman beast, who has brought warfare back to the primeval. Kill him or he will kill you." The enemy's practice of resorting to deceptive measures also bred resentment. Beleaguered troops often tricked their Allied opponents into believing they had surrendered by placing their hands up and then let the attackers approach. When the latter got close enough, the Japanese pulled out a grenade and attempted to kill as many men as they could. Such actions led one officer returning from the southwest Pacific to describe his adversary as "cagy and treacherous."[25] Under the circumstances, taking Japanese POWs was a risk which most Allied troops were not willing to take.

LIMITS OF INDOCTRINATION: SOLDIERS' VULNERABILITY TO "HUMAN WEAKNESSES"

In spite of the untiring efforts to instill animosities towards the enemy, the extent to which such measures could sustain fighting spirit among troops was limited. Written evidence, in the form of diaries and memoirs, does show that opinions of the enemy included a range of aspects aside from hatred. Many Western personnel expressed veneration for their opponent's fighting skills, and held what appeared to be a rational image of their foe. For example, General Slim's post-war account recalled, "we began by despising our Japanese enemy," after which the British "built up [their] enemy into something terrifying."[26] Both attitudes were detrimental, and according to Slim, his troops could learn how to defeat their adversary only when they were taught to take a balanced view, which dictated that the Japanese soldier was a formidable fighting man, who nevertheless had certain weaknesses. Similarly, following the New Georgia operation, the XIV Corps of the US army concluded, "our troops should realize the ability of the Japanese, but our training must give our men confidence that they are superior" in combat.[27] John Masters, who served with the Chindits, commented on how Japanese soldiers were capable of simultaneously demonstrating signs of cruelty and humanity, "they wrote beautiful poems in their diaries, and practiced bayonet work on their prisoners. Frugal and bestial, barbarous and brave, artistic and brutal, they were the dushman [enemy] ... ."[28]

Furthermore, most servicemen felt that they were simply fulfilling their professional duties, rather than fighting for a noble cause. One American soldier wrote in 1943, "nobody out here has the slightest interest in politics; they just want to get home." Lieutenant Kermit Stewart, writing from Lingayen Gulf in the Philippines, wrote to his family, "I assure you that I've done nothing heroic." The foremost concern was to avoid being killed, and do one's part to protect the lives of fellow soldiers. The majority of GIs also recalled that their morale was frequently upheld by the bonding which evolved when they shared common experiences with their comrades. The Australian army sought to forge cohesion by placing soldiers from the same town or region in the same units, thereby building up a sense of kinship. Similarly, within the Japanese army, indoctrination was only of limited use in upholding morale. Post-war studies showed that only a small proportion of troops were the hardcore fanatics who readily sacrificed their lives for their country and Emperor. The remainder consisted of a range of personalities, including a considerable portion of conscripts who saw military service simply as a mundane obligation.

Ideological fervor therefore was not widespread among soldiers as Dower has portrayed it to be. Furthermore, the will to fight tended to decline when troops faced misfortunes. Front-line units had to regularly deal with hunger and disease, which in turn caused demoralization. For this reason, it was of paramount importance for troops to receive sufficient equipment, food and medicine, so that they could survive the elements they had to contend with. Equally important was adequate training. In this respect, the Western forces were significantly more successful than their Japanese counterparts in providing what was needed to sustain morale. Nevertheless, while morale within the Imperial army did decline as the war progressed, and a larger proportion of troops either surrendered or put up a lower level of resistance, the deterioration did not reach the point where the Japanese started to lay down their arms *en masse*. The vast majority of personnel adhered to their belief that surrendering was a disgraceful act, and that soldiers had an obligation to continue fighting to the bitter end, no matter how desperate their situation was. Fighting spirit therefore went a long way in sustaining the IJA's war effort until the closing stages of the conflict.

Among the foremost causes for demoralization was the fear of being killed. The Japanese and Allied forces both entered the conflict without a clear under-standing of how their opponent fought, and in the initial phases, the lack of familiarity frequently created trepidation. During the New Guinea campaign, American GIs often panicked when confronted by Japanese soldiers who suddenly emerged from their camouflaged positions. The 162nd infantry regiment recalled how its men hesitated to move out on patrols and maintain outposts at any distance from the main positions, because they had heard numerous stories of how the Japanese were skilled at ambushing their attackers. Major-General Griswold, in charge of the XIV Corps, noted that he saw far too much "war neurosis" in certain units, with troops being overtaken by fear when the Japanese infiltrated their positions.[29] The British-Indian army faced similar problems. During the 1942–43 offensive against the Arakan region of Burma, troops lost the stamina to carry on with the advance when they were found out that enemy bunkers were able to withstand prolonged bombardment. General Slim recalled how one of the most formidable tasks was to restore morale within an army which could "only look back on a long line of unbroken defeats."[30] The rank and file had developed an image which suggested that the IJA was invincible, and the myth had to be dismantled before an offensive spirit could be fully created.

Soldiers who had been enthusiastic about their cause quickly lost their determination as trials and tribulations started to mount. Desertions were rare, mainly because in most areas of the Asia-Pacific theater, there were practically no cities or population centers that could provide refuge. The only option was to escape into the wilderness, where troops were more likely to die of starvation and heat exhaustion. The Allied forces were able to solve the problem not only by providing their units with proper equipment. Training was conducted with a view to ensuring that troops were able to overcome their enemy. In order to secure their positions against Japanese infiltration movements, the defending forces needed to construct a perimeter consisting of mutually supporting foxholes. Tactics were also modified in accordance with the conditions that had to be faced when fighting in densely wooded environments. The limited visibility made it difficult to locate approaching forces until they were in close range. For this reason, the defenders had to become acquainted with their surroundings by conducting regular patrols. Infantry units also needed to thoroughly reconnoiter their environs in offensive operations, so they could avoid falling victim to surprise counter-attacks. By the closing stages of the conflict, the effort started to pay handsome dividends, as evidenced by the large number of troops in both the Burma and Southwest Pacific regions who expressed confidence in their ability to counter the Japanese.

For the Japanese, the Allied onslaught brought home the difficulties of fighting enemies who had superior weapons. The IJA's program of indoctrination created a number of unique disadvantages. The majority of troops held an infallible confidence in their own potential because they were inculcated with the belief that divine intervention guaranteed victory. War was not a contest of armaments, but more a matter of believing that spiritual bravery guaranteed success. When the course of the battle turned against the Japanese soldier and casualties mounted, he "reacted according to his initial expectations."[31] The higher the initial faith in victory, the greater the sense of betrayal when defeat loomed. As the war progressed, and the army became less able to keep its combat units properly equipped, soldiers regularly expressed their despondency. A lieutenant whose unit was constantly bombarded by enemy aircraft lamented in his diary, "[we] were the target for a mammoth raid for the second time since landing in New Guinea. [We] were boiling over with rage and resentment but there was nothing [we] could do about it."[32] During the US invasion of Lingayen Gulf in late 1944, one soldier conceded, "the artillery shelling and bombing was terrific. We do not know from where the enemy observes, but his shelling is truly accurate."[33] Captured diaries revealed that beleaguered soldiers often began to question the wisdom of fighting to the finish.

Japanese units which suffered continuous defeats also suffered a breakdown in cohesion. Servicemen inevitably blamed their officers for making poor decisions, and relations among the ranks became strained. At Salamaua, officers had a difficult time commanding their troops, owing to the heavy casualties they had suffered.[34] A private whose unit was being driven out of its position by Australian troops complained, "due to the ignorant platoon leader, men and NCOs do all of the suffering."[35] The diary continued a few days later, "had an argument with the platoon leader. Why must I be attached to a confounded, conceited, ignorant fool like him?" Therefore, Japanese soldiers proved to be humans who became demoralized when faced with adversities and setbacks. Nevertheless, the declining enthusiasm rarely gave rise to mass surrenders, and discipline within the Imperial army remained adequate, in spite of the mounting setbacks which its troops suffered.

Food shortages and disease were further obstacles to sustaining combat motivation. In tropical climates, a range of ailments, including malaria and dengue fever were commonplace. At Guadalcanal, the US army's Twenty-Fifth Infantry Division reported that almost half of its men had succumbed to malaria. The disease was so widespread, and the emergency services were stretched to their limit, to the point standing orders had to be issued, stating that a soldier was not to be evacuated until his body temperature was over 104 degrees Fahrenheit (40 degrees Celsius). The Japanese likewise fell victim. To make matters even worse, the army was poorly equipped to deal with tropical illnesses because it did not have an adequate logistical network through which front line units could receive medical supplies. On occasions when Allied forces captured enemy positions which had a field hospital attached to them, observers were appalled by the standard of treatment. Diseases of insanitation such as dysentery were also prevalent. During the Wau operations, the majority of troops succumbed to stomach ailments, and one soldier wrote, "it is impossible to carry out most of the duties of the battalion."[36]

The conditions in the Pacific theater were also not conducive for providing food in the forward areas. Logistical factors were an impediment, and the humid climate made it difficult to properly preserve the supplies which combat units were able to receive. Conditions in the Japanese army were particularly distressing. During the opening phases of the war, supply requirements were simplified because troops lived off the country and hoarded supplies from the indigenous population. Especially in Southeast Asia, local agriculture was developed, and conquering armies could find plenty of rice fields and farms. However, conditions were not as favorable in the islands of the Pacific, where the undeveloped nature of the country meant there was little to plunder. At Guadalcanal and New Guinea, where Allied air and submarine attacks had prevented the Japanese from obtaining supplies, morale had declined, and this was an important cause for their failure to hold out. At Bougainville, one soldier wrote, "through shortage of rations, grass grown in rivers and sprouts of trees are being eaten," and even officers were living on a meager diet of rice gruel.[37] The Allies faced similar problems. On New Georgia, according to the unit captain, "men lived on cold rations for days at a time. Inadequate, rancid and monotonous food was the staple of the ordinary soldier." Nor did the uncomfortable temperatures help one's appetite. A company diary of the 9th Royal Essex Regiment in Burma recorded, "the rain filled the mess tins so fast that however quickly the chaps ate it, it always remained filled. Everything got soaked, including the bacon, the beans, everything."

The Allies were well placed to solve the problem, since they produced enough transports, and thus could allocate a larger quantity of their shipping and aircraft to carry supplies to the front lines. The Americans in particular managed to keep their troops properly fed by the closing stages of the conflict. The average daily intake for army personnel was 4,000 calories, well above the recommended allowance. In fact, most GIs did not complain about poor nourishment, but lamented that the food did not always satisfy their palates. The availability of daily necessities was therefore a crucial factor in sustaining morale, no matter how extensively armies endeavored to encourage troops to engage in a noble cause and kill off their enemies. Fighting men in both the Allied and Japanese armed forces could not maintain an adequate fighting spirit unless their material requirements were satisfied.

MANIPULATION OF HUMAN WEAKNESSES VIA PSYCHOLOGICAL WARFARE

The efforts which the both Allies and Japanese undertook to erode their opponent's fighting capabilities, by using psychological warfare and propaganda as weapons for attacking their morale, provide further reasons to reconsider Dower's thesis that the conduct of the Pacific war was driven primarily by an implacable desire to annihilate the adversary. The Western powers were far more successful, mainly because they preferred to base their propaganda on facts, by highlighting the difficulties which the Imperial forces were suffering. The material convinced many enemy troops that their fortunes were on the decline, and thereby compelled them to put up lower levels of resistance. The Japanese, on the other hand, tended to spread lies. Among the most notorious cases was the work conducted by Iva Ikuko d'Aquino, more popularly known as "Tokyo Rose." A Japanese born in America, D'Aquino happened to be visiting a relative in Japan when the war broke out. She later volunteered to broadcast propaganda aimed at US forces. The material consisted of exaggerated claims regarding the casualties which the Allied had suffered, as well as stories about preparations for an impending invasion of the US mainland. Owing to their obviously ludicrous nature, the daily broadcasts became popular entertainment among American servicemen.

The Allies were more shrewd in carrying out their psychological warfare (psywar) operations. Propaganda was used to show enemy troops how they were fighting a lost cause. The results also revealed that many personnel in the Imperial army did not sustain their determination to fight to the finish.

As defeats mounted, soldiers started to become receptive to propaganda which highlighted their beleaguered situation, and the incidence of surrenders increased significantly. In the Pacific theater, the main organization responsible for planning and executing psywar operations was the Far Eastern Liaison Organization (FELO). The organization was established in July 1942 under a directive from General MacArthur's headquarters, and staffed by a mixture of personnel from the US and Australia. In June 1944, as a preparatory measure for the upcoming invasion of the Philippines, Douglas MacArthur established a special psywar unit, the Psychological Warfare Branch (PWB), with Brigadier-General Bonner Fellers placed in charge. The British-Indian army had a similar apparatus, in the form of the Psychological Warfare Division, which operated under the supervision of General Slim's headquarters.

By the middle stages of the conflict, inspections of soldiers' diaries which had been retrieved when Allied forces had captured Japanese positions, along with interrogations of POWs, showed that the rank and file of the Imperial army had started to become dispirited in the face of their ever-growing spate of defeats. The evidence provided convincing reasons to believe that propaganda could further diminish the enemy's will to fight. However, in order to be successful, psywar operations had to be undertaken with a sound knowledge of the features which enabled the enemy to maintain his morale, as well as the conditions which caused his combat motivation to decline. Propaganda also had to be tailored in accordance with the particular features of the audience, and was divided into several different themes, each used for different circumstances.[38] For example, promises of food and medical care appealed to troops who were overtaken by starvation and disease. In cases where enemy positions became untenable in the face of the Allied offensive, propaganda was used to highlight Japan's declining fortunes, and the mounting misery which troops suffered as a result of their continued defeats and shortage of supplies. According to Allison Gilmore, the efforts which Allied military personnel undertook to plan their propaganda campaigns was a telltale sign that they actually viewed the Japanese as human beings, and strove to understand their strengths and weaknesses in combat.

Psywar operations in both the Pacific theater and in Southeast Asia started to achieve noticeable results. Whereas during the initial stages of the Allied counter-offensive, only a handful of enemy troops being taken prisoner, the total number captured during the winter 1944 Philippines campaign rose to well over 10,000.[39] The increase in the number of voluntary surrenders was not the only significant development. In the India-Burma theater, where operations were carried out on a land mass, the Japanese had the option of withdrawing to rear positions, and cases where troops laid down their arms were few and far between. However, the post-war memoir prepared by Slim's headquarters concluded, "there is good reason to believe that the cumulative effect of this intense propaganda bombardment was not inconsiderable."[40] In many cases, enemy soldiers became saddened after reading leaflets or listening to broadcasts, and subsequently put up a weaker fight.

Field commanders, along with their subordinates, also began to see the benefits of carrying out psywar campaigns, and this was another strong indication that the Allies did endeavor to defeat their enemies by means aside from mass extermination. Army officials introduced a program to orient troops on how propaganda could induce a larger number of Japanese to surrender, and thereby help avoid the need to carry out prolonged and costly operations to eliminate enemy resistance. During the Luzon campaign, one of the most notable features was the "keen interest" which the Sixth Army's lower echelons showed in using propaganda.[41] All of the corps and many of the divisions requested special leaflets for particular situations, and troops were willing to cooperate in taking prisoners.

Nevertheless, in spite of the results achieved by propaganda, the proportion of enemy soldiers who were captured remained low. The majority of troops, even under the most trying conditions, continued to fight until they were killed. Propagandists succeeded in eroding enemy morale; nonetheless, they failed, for the most part, to convince the Japanese to reject the "fundamental tenets of their military indoctrination."[42] Psywar operations thus were carried out while paying due heed to a key feature of the Imperial army's cultural characteristics, namely, the extent to which its troops were imbued with what often proved to be an implacable aversion to surrender. Under the circumstances, propaganda could only convince a small, albeit increasing, percentage of them to capitulate. For this reason, Western forces had to devise tactics which worked to eliminate enemy resistance. The measures undertaken to annihilate Japanese units were often formulated in order to achieve the Allies' objective of securing battlefield victories in the most efficient manner. Combat methods were developed primarily out of concerns for military necessities, and were not purely driven by a passionate hatred of the enemy.

CONCLUSION

Morale played a pivotal role in enabling both the Allied and Japanese armed forces to carry out their battlefield operations during the Pacific war. Sustaining an adequate level of enthusiasm was essential to motivate troops to put their lives at risk for the sake of their respective nation's interests. John Dower's hypothesis, which suggested that the belligerents extensively used ideological fervor and racial hatred as a way to build up fighting spirit, is a credible one. A large proportion of Western military personnel became convinced that Japanese soldiers were a barbaric adversary who needed to be killed off *en masse*, if their own lives were to be safeguarded. Within the IJA, the rank and file frequently expressed a contempt for their Allied opponents. Many troops also firmly believed that Japan was undertaking a sacred mission to achieve domination over Asia, and eliminate Western influence in the region.

However, animosity towards the enemy and its importance in upholding morale needs to be placed in its proper context. Despite the arduous efforts which army commanders made to indoctrinate their subordinates, such measures were of limited value in upholding enthusiasm. This was largely because fighting spirit most often deteriorated when troops faced adversities while in combat. Servicemen were overtaken by the fear of being killed by their opponents, and a lack of confidence in their ability to fight effectively. Food shortages and disease, coupled with the uncomfortable climatic conditions that prevailed in the Asia-Pacific theater, caused further debilitation. Front line units therefore had to be provided with sufficient quantities of weapons and supplies, so that personnel could feel confident in their prospect of defending themselves against the elements they had to contend with. The Western forces were significantly more successful than their Japanese counterparts in this respect, since they had the resources and logistical network to keep their troops properly supplied. Allied armies also undertook to learn lessons through their experiences in fighting the Japanese, and taught their soldiers the tactics they needed to use in order to overcome their foes. The Imperial army command was in a less favorable position to provide the materiel which its soldiers needed in order to sustain their morale, largely because its generals underestimated the resources that its units required in a large scale confrontation against the Allied and thus failed to establish adequate supply lines. At the same time, one must not ignore the fact that indoctrination did go a long way in sustaining the Japanese soldier's martial spirit. In spite of the mounting setbacks and declining fortunes which the rank and file faced as the war progressed, and the corresponding decline in morale which resulted, the majority of servicemen staunchly abided by their practice of fighting to the finish. This was largely because troops had been imbued with the idea that surrender entailed an act of treason, and those who fell into captivity were condemned to be disgraced in the eyes of their family and peers. The fear of being tortured and mistreated by the Allies also acted as a powerful motivator to avoid being taken prisoner. Under the circumstances, no matter how arduously Western forces attempted to convince their enemies to surrender, either via propaganda or an open display of overwhelming firepower, the proportion of Japanese troops laying down their arms was bound to remain low. The Imperial army's morale thus played a crucial role in enabling the Japanese to sustain their war effort for the extended period that they did. Likewise, in order to develop the capacity to defeat their opponents, the Allies had to build up an adequate level of combat motivation among their troops. Thus while material resources were important in determining the outcome of the Pacific war, psychological factors such as fighting spirit proved to be crucial in sustaining the war efforts of the belligerent forces.

9

The Intelligence War

The previous chapters have illustrated how the armed forces fighting in the Pacific theater needed material resources, including weapons and supplies, in order to defeat their opponents. At the same time, proper planning was often of paramount importance in allowing them to achieve victories without incurring unnecessary delays and casualties. The following chapter will examine how intelligence and knowledge of the enemy played a central role in helping the Allies deploy their available military strength against the Japanese in an efficient manner. During the opening stages of the conflict, the Western powers were overwhelmed by the successes which the Imperial navy and army achieved, such as the destruction of a large part of the US fleet at Pearl Harbor, as well as the conquest of Britain's Far Eastern bastion at Singapore. This was largely because Japanese fighting capabilities had been underestimated, and the miscalculation was one of the greatest blunders committed by the Allied intelligence services. Yet, by the later stages of the conflict, as Japan's hold on its conquered territories crumbled under the weight of the Allied counter-offensive, the Imperial armed forces proved to be even more misinformed about their enemies, and this was one of the key factors which speeded up the collapse of their war effort.

The intelligence dimension of the Pacific war has not been extensively explored until recent decades, for two main reasons. First, the use of intelligence in warfare became common only at the turn of the twentieth century, and until then, scholars of military affairs, along with practitioners, made only minimal references to the subject. Secondly, intelligence activities have always been carried out with exceptional secrecy, and governments thus prefer to conceal the work of their intelligence organizations whether they are successful or otherwise. For example, it was not until the 1980s that freedom of information acts allowed the public to consult archival materials related to US and British intelligence operations during the Second World War. Since then, with the increasing availability of evidence, scholars have put forward a number of works which have explained the intelligence efforts of both the Allied and Axis powers.[1] Much of the literature has focused on signals intelligence, and the way in which the Western services succeeded in decoding the communications of the German and Japanese armed forces. The material provided commanders with information that was vital for carrying out their operations. An equally important aspect was the quest to obtain "qualitative" intelligence on the enemy's combat methods. The material proved useful in helping military officials understand their opponent's operational, tactical and technological capabilities.

In both aspects of the intelligence war, the Allies were significantly more proficient than their Japanese counterparts. The achievement was due to the strategic thinking which prevailed within the US and British defense establishments. Both powers had a long-standing practice in scrutinizing the policies and war-making potential of their foreign rivals, as well as planning for large-scale conflicts which required a careful analysis of the military situation. Because Allied defense officials placed a high importance on developing a realistic image of their adversaries, they developed an intelligence apparatus that could collect and analyze information on the Japanese, and thereafter disseminate the material to military personnel. Japan's experience in these fields, by contrast, was rudimentary, and its information-handling capabilities lagged accordingly.

DEVELOPMENT OF ALLIED AND JAPANESE INTELLIGENCE PRIOR TO THE PACIFIC WAR

The main feature which facilitated the Western powers' intelligence activities during the Pacific war was that their leaders held an accepted view which dictated that an accurate knowledge of the outside world was essential for safeguarding their national interests. The habit stemmed from their historical legacies. Great Britain was an imperial nation which had been maintaining overseas territories and spheres of influence throughout the globe for over two centuries, and for this reason, it had a tradition of keeping a lookout on potential enemies. By 1900, the British had developed a network of human agents and communication listening posts within their empire, and were able to acquire a range of information on the political and military situation in their worldwide colonies. Nevertheless, the experiences of the 1914–18 Great War clearly showed how Britain was not fully capable of gauging the military potential of its rivals on the European continent. Drawing upon this lesson, the service departments undertook an earnest drive to further develop their intelligence apparatus during the interwar years.

Although the United States had pursued a policy of avoiding military action outside the Western hemisphere, by the early part of the twentieth century, the Americans developed a significant presence in the Pacific rim area, the protection of which required a vigilant watch on enemy incursions. The Navy and War departments both established their own intelligence branches during the late 1800s, and steadily expanded their capacity to monitor the strategic situation in the Far East. Of equal importance, British and US war planning was geared for an extended campaign fought on a multitude of fronts. Intelligence assessment was subsequently conducted with a view to helping the armed forces develop a course of action which could help them prevail in the long run.

Japanese leaders, on the other hand, held intelligence in low regard. As an insular nation which had purposely secluded itself until 1854, Japan was inexperienced in key intelligence tasks such as gauging the capabilities and policies of foreign powers. To complicate matters, a combination of historical factors, including a centuries' old belief in self-superiority, coupled with a conviction which dictated that Japan was earmarked to dominate Asia, gave rise to a situation whereby the rank and file of the military tended to ignore evidence which suggested that they could face problems in defeating their opponents.[2] The army leadership in particular lacked experience in tackling the critical questions of Allied industrial output and their capacity to wage a protracted war.

Because the Western powers attached high importance to improving their intelligence, the interwar years saw significant progress. In the US and Britain, the machinery was designed to provide officials with information needed to conduct a war effort at all levels: strategic, operational and tactical. The British established an array of bodies that were dedicated to handling information on their potential enemies, the most menacing of whom was Germany. The intelligence directorates of the service departments monitored the development of foreign armed forces, while the Government Codes and Cyphers School (GCCS) was established to decode the communications of Britain's rivals, and to gain an insight into their foreign policy objectives. Attachés in overseas diplomatic offices regularly provided reports on the political, military and economic trends in the country they were assigned to. The outbreak of the Second World War provided the impetus needed for a dramatic strengthening of the intelligence community. Churchill's government began to allocate generous funds to develop systems that could gauge Germany's forces, who were posing a direct threat to the home islands and Britain's oceanic lifelines.

For the Americans, the main organizations responsible for handling foreign intelligence were the War Department's military intelligence division (MID) and the Navy Department's Office of Naval Intelligence (ONI). Although financial shortages and Congressional cuts in defense expenditure constrained their activities, the ONI and MID undertook a sizeable effort to collect and evaluate information on the Japanese. Naval intelligence policy explicitly stated, "all preparation for war must be premised on the best available information."[3] Likewise, after 1918, when the MID was reconstituted as a separate division of the War Department's general staff, one of its assigned tasks was to estimate military threats that affected US interests.[4] Service attachés based in Japan and across the Far East provided extensive reports on the performance of the IJA and IJN in their operations in China. In the area of signals intelligence, although the State Department curtailed America's capabilities when it dismantled its black chamber in 1929, the War and Navy departments managed to significantly enhance their codebreaking facilities in the Pacific regions, and subsequently, became more able to read Japanese communications.

By the time hostilities against Japan commenced in December 1941, the Allied powers had acquired the know-how to conduct a competent intelligence operation. The main problem with their pre-war intelligence efforts was the shortage of reliable information. The secrecy with which Tokyo formulated its strategy prevented the US and Britain from predicting the moves Japan was likely to undertake. Furthermore, the Japanese authorities successfully concealed the progress of their rearmament program, to the point where Western observers were unable to obtain accurate intelligence on the types of military action which the Imperial forces were able to carry out. Under the circumstances, it was natural for Allied officials to base their opinions on preconceptions which dictated that, as a second-rate power, Japan did not have the aptitude or technological capability to challenge the West.

The development of Japanese intelligence, by contrast, made minimal progress. The main problem was that the defense establishment thought that formulating a calibrated appraisal of its opponents was a tedious task. Assessments of potential adversaries reflected a widespread belief that the Imperial forces were superior to all others. The army's views of the Anglo-Saxon powers were particularly denigrating. In spite of its economic power, the US was considered too pacifist to instill a sufficient level of martial spirit among its populace. Most officers tended to base their opinions on snap judgments, rather than hard evidence. One general, whose writings received widespread attention, alleged that in terms of training and discipline, "the Americans are the worst of all nationalities."[5] The reason cited was that, whereas the Japanese army was drawn from a homogeneous population, the US army comprised a large number of ethnic minorities, and thus could not develop the cohesion needed to fight a drawn-out war.

Because the Japanese did not attach a high value to intelligence, their activities covered a narrow domain. In contrast to their Western counterparts, who were tasked to handle information on a wide range of matters, the Imperial army and navy focused more on collecting and utilizing battlefield intelligence, or short-term information needed for planning and executing operations. The track record prior to 1941 suggests that there was good progress in certain areas. The accomplishment stemmed from a tradition handed down from the *samurai* warlords. For centuries, Japan was a war-torn feudal society where spies, information-gatherers and "purveyors of secrets" were in demand.[6] The US military intelligence service once described Japanese espionage as "superior," because it played a vital role in facilitating operational planning in China.[7] Likewise, the post-war study conducted by the Strategic Bombing Survey noted how prior to the conflict, the government had developed a "vast organization throughout the world" for collecting intelligence, by relying on its overseas diplomatic and military representatives, together with a large network of spies.[8] The success which human agents achieved in ascertaining the layout of Allied bases and the position of enemy ships was a key factor which enabled the navy and its arm to inflict crippling losses on their opponents during the opening months of the Pacific war.

Yet, when one looks at the broader picture, the Imperial forces did not pay much attention to long-term intelligence concerning their enemies' war potential. The oversight played an important role in leading the high command to commence a war effort in which Japan was poorly equipped to prevail. Strategic thinking was based on the notion that all wars could be won by dealing a knockout blow at the onset, and waiting for its enemies to offer peace, in the same way the conflicts against China and Russia at the turn of the twentieth century had transpired. Military officials thus assumed that everything hinged on the initial operations, and did not give much thought to what might happen thereafter. When Japan's leaders were finalizing their decision for the southward advance during autumn 1941, the war ministry's second (intelligence) division was not asked to assess the quality of the US and British armies. Only after the decision for war had been made, was the division ordered to collect information to help the army execute its operational plans. Naval intelligence was also relegated to providing operational planners with a limited range of information. The functions of the navy's main intelligence organs, the third (intelligence) division and the fourth (communications) division, were confined to informing the operations division on current enemy dispositions. Military authorities made only a haphazard effort to investigate wider issues, including the Allied nations' potential to fight a protracted war, where superiority in weapons production and deployment played a critical role in determining the outcome.[9] Even the navy command, whose officers had been educated in the US and Britain, tended to hold a misinformed view. Much of the material which intelligence staffs collected on matters such as America's industrial capacity was brushed aside. In March 1941, the naval attaché in Washington, who had fostered close ties with Rear-Admiral Richmond Turner, the Navy Department's director of war plans, warned his superiors in Tokyo that caution needed to be exercised before embarking on a war on the America.[10] The warning apparently went unheeded, and consequently, the navy seriously underestimated America's capacity to recuperate after the Pearl Harbor attack.

WARTIME ACHIEVEMENTS

After the Pacific war commenced, the contrasts in Allied and Japanese intelligence capabilities grew wider. Whereas the setbacks in Southeast Asia during early 1942 encouraged the US and British defense establishments to dramatically improve their information-handling capabilities, the Japanese record of unbroken victories enhanced the widespread attitude of disdain within the military command.

In terms of organization, Allied intelligence benefited from centralized management. In Britain, at the apex of the military hierarchy, the cabinet was served by the Joint Intelligence Committee (JIC). The committee consisted of representatives from the government offices, including the service ministries and the Foreign Office, who exchanged their views through round-table discussions in order to produce detailed assessments of the war situation. Churchill and his chiefs of staff were assured constant access to informed opinions that were not overly tainted by the biases of individual organizations. The American defense chiefs also created a joint intelligence committee, along the lines of their British counterparts. When the JCS was established in February 1942, a charter was issued, stating that the committee was the main body responsible for handling information used by US defense staffs. In order to ensure thorough representation by the service departments, the committee was composed of the director of naval intelligence, along with the head of the War Department's military intelligence division, and head of Air Force intelligence, as well as representatives from civilian organizations such as the State Department and Board of Economic Warfare.

The Japanese, on the other hand, never established a centralized intelligence body. The navy and army operated their own arms, with few channels available for communication. The general staffs based their conclusions mostly on information provided by their respective operations bureaus. Neither the opposing services nor civilian members of the cabinet were consulted until a very late stage, and the system did not permit a balanced estimate of Japan's adversaries.

At the lower levels of the intelligence machinery, the Allies also established an apparatus which provided their forces with an accurate image of the Japanese, so that further setbacks could be avoided. Signals intelligence organizations received the largest share of the available funding, and a painstaking effort was made to decode the communications signals of the Imperial navy and army. Using a system dubbed *ULTRA*, the Americans and the British managed to make significant inroads. The Pacific Fleet's main sigint unit was located at Pearl Harbor. In the southwest Pacific, Allied forces were served by Fleet Radio Unit, Melbourne (FRUMEL), which functioned as a joint US-Australian unit. In addition to naval sigint, FRUMEL was also responsible for providing the central bureau at General MacArthur's headquarters with decrypts of Japanese army communications. The British made similar progress. The Wireless Experimental Centre (WEC) in New Delhi, with a staff of over 1,000 as well as a number of outstations, managed to decipher the majority of the signals which the Japanese transmitted in the India-Burma theater. The Royal Navy relied mainly on the Far Eastern Combined Bureau, based at Colombo.

Allied intelligence also benefited from cooperation among the coalition members. The sharing of information on Japanese communications had already begun before the war broke out, and as early as January 1942, Nimitz authorized an arrangement where task force commanders could forward intelligence directly to their Australian and New Zealand counterparts without routing everything through their respective headquarters.[11] In October of the same year, collaboration with Great Britain was strengthened. At an Anglo-American meeting in Washington, naval representatives of both countries agreed that the British sigint headquarters at Bletchley Park was to work on the Imperial navy's general cipher, and pass all decoded messages to its American counterpart.[12] Coordination between the two powers was sealed with the signing of the May 1943 BRUSA agreement, which demarcated a clear division of labor where the US was to focus on Japan, with the British working primarily on German code systems.

Signals decrypts often offered invaluable information on the dispositions and movements of Japanese units. The material enabled the Allies to make optimal use of their military strength by deploying it their forces at the correct time and location. Prior to the Battle of Midway, the US navy's success in breaking the Imperial fleet's JN-25 code provided the Pacific Fleet with an ideal opportunity to dispatch its carriers to counter the approach of Admiral Nagumo's task force. In a breakthrough that allowed the Americans to significantly speed up their efforts to strangulate Japan's oceanic supply lines, naval intelligence deciphered the water code, which revealed data not only on the movements of enemy merchant ships, but also the details of their cargoes along with the destination of the convoy. The distribution of information was facilitated when the submarine force operations officer was designated a combat intelligence officer, and given access to all communications decrypts. Operations officers were authorized to furnish the material to all individual force commanders and submarine captains through an encrypted line.[13] As a result, submarines could be stationed at selected points along the key Japanese shipping lanes and wait for enemy vessels to appear, rather than sail aimlessly in search of targets around the far reaches of the western Pacific.

In the ground campaigns, the use of communications intelligence proved to be more difficult than it was against the Japanese navy. This was mainly because IJA commanders usually transmitted their messages over landlines or short-range low-powered radio, thereby making them more difficult to intercept. However, a number of notable breakthroughs were achieved. For example during the Japanese attack on the British bases at Imphal and Kohima on the India-Burma frontier, signals intelligence revealed how General Mutaguchi's Fifteenth Army was running desperately short of supplies. The information provided William Slim with concrete proof that his forces could go onto the counter-offensive without facing formidable opposition. In the southwest Pacific, General MacArthur's headquarters also used sigint, with good results. During early 1944, when MacArthur was drawing up plans for a pincer movement along the north coast of New Guinea, *ULTRA* provided a comprehensive picture of the Japanese Eighteenth Army, including information on the arrival of reinforcements. Signals decrypts also revealed that enemy commanders expected the Allies to land in areas closer to their front lines such as Madang or Awar. The Japanese were thus not preparing to oppose a leap-frogging attack against their rear bases at Hollandia and Wewak. Subsequently, the majority of the combat units were moved to the forward areas, with the Hollandia garrison consisting mainly of non-combat troops, including construction workers and supply depot personnel.[14] In order to prevent the Japanese from reinforcing the rear bases, MacArthur approved a deception plan that called for intensive air raids to be carried out against the Madang-Awar sector, with the aim of convincing the enemy that a landing in the area was imminent. As a result, when MacArthur's troops landed at Hollandia in April, they encountered a much more manageable level of opposition. In both the naval and land campaigns, the good use of intelligence enabled the Allies to formulate battle plans whereby their forces could exploit enemy weaknesses, while at the same time circumventing the challenges which the Japanese were able to pose. In short, the material helped commanders minimize their costs, both in terms of resources and human lives.

The Allies also used intelligence to develop a better understanding of Japanese combat methods and weapons technologies. In this area, captured documents and prisoners of war offered valuable information. In the US, the ONI and MID both set up their own language-training programs so that intelligence officers could learn how to interpret the information they gathered through captured material and personnel. Japanese military practices enabled the Allies to obtain ample data through such sources. POWs showed an unusual desire to cooperate with their interrogators. The phenomenon stemmed from the way in which the Japanese were indoctrinated into believing that when they fell into enemy hands, they lost all ties with their country. Prisoners thus did everything possible to win favor with their vanquishers, and divulged military secrets without hesitation. Enemy documents were also useful. The rank and file of the Imperial forces depended heavily on the written word, and tended to record every aspect of their activities in detail. The situation was further helped by the high command's faith that the complexities of the Japanese language precluded translation. When coupled with the institutionalized notion that Japan's forces were invincible, a situation arose where the most basic precautionary measures were overlooked. Troops often went into battle carrying sensitive material, and when their positions were overrun, Allied forces were able to retrieve a copious collection of papers.

The army commands operating in the Pacific theaters and in Southeast Asia front succeeded in gaining a deeper insight into the principles and doctrines that governed the way in which Japanese forces fought. Specialized organizations were established to facilitate the processing of intelligence obtained through captured sources. In the central Pacific theater, the Joint Intelligence Center, Pacific Ocean Areas (JICPOA), was designated as an inter-service group that was responsible for a range of activities, including document translation. The British had a similar body in the India-Burma theater, in the form of the Southeast Asia Translation and Interrogation Centre (SEATIC). However, the Allied Translation and Interrogation Service (ATIS), which operated in the southwest Pacific, was the most active group in processing written materials and POWs. ATIS was an inter-allied outfit, staffed by officers from both the United States and Australia. Enemy documents offered a detailed blueprint of the Imperial army's operational and tactical concepts. By the end of the war, ATIS secured over 350,000 items, of which 18,000 were translated.[15] POWs were not as useful, mainly because most of the soldiers who ended up in Allied captivity represented the lower ranks, and had a limited knowledge of the doctrines which their army followed. Interrogations proved more valuable for securing data on matters such as military morale. ATIS managed to produce almost 800 interrogation reports, based on information obtained from over 10,000 prisoners. With a wide collection of data to draw upon, the service also conducted a series of investigations into the crucial subject of cultural factors and how they affected the way Japanese troops performed in battle. Research reports put forward an introspective description of the IJA's mindset, and pointed out that, while Japanese soldiers possessed a strong discipline which enabled them to persevere under trying conditions, one of their main weaknesses was that they were unable to alter their methods when faced with setbacks, owing to the high level of regimentation which characterized their training program.[16] The information did on occasions help Allied commanders develop the appropriate tactics for overcoming the Imperial army. More importantly, the intelligence which pointed to the weaknesses in the Japanese soldier's morale provided useful material for planning psychological warfare and propaganda campaigns that were aimed at diminishing his fighting spirit.[17]

Naval intelligence was less able to secure information on the matter, mainly because the Imperial fleet kept the bulk of the relevant material, including tactical publications, onboard ships, which were most often sunk in battle before the contents could be retrieved. Moreover, because Japanese defense strategy for the outlying territories called for using small detachments of auxiliary vessels, and withholding the main fleet until the inner zones of the empire were attacked, Allied intelligence started to find out how the enemy deployed its capital ships and carriers only at the late stages of the conflict.

Last but not least, the Allies frequently relied on combat action reports prepared by naval, air and army officers. The material was treated as a vital source of information on the fighting methods and weapons used by the Imperial armed forces. As early as 1942, commanders who led the initial operations in New Guinea asserted that all units needed to make good use of accounts on enemy tactics, so that training could take place with a realistic knowledge of the elements which troops had to face on the battlefield.[18] The US army's intelligence network in the Pacific theaters evolved into an elaborate and coherent structure, with a clear division of responsibility. Each zone of command, including the central, South, and southwest Pacific had its own central organization. The individual army groups, including the Sixth and Tenth, along with the XIV and XXIV Corps, also had their own intelligence section, designated G-2. Action reports prepared by army units from the divisional level upwards were most often followed by a lengthy series of appendices, including the G-2 intelligence reports. In order to help army commanders develop a more informed tactical doctrine for fighting the IJA, the intelligence services performed a number of crucial tasks. First, the G-2 sections of the various army units forwarded their findings on Japanese combat methods and weapons to their respective commanders, as well as to the operations section. The lessons learned from battle experiences were passed up the chain of command, so that the army and corps headquarters could establish a more coherent set of procedures. To facilitate the sharing of information between the army groups, the War Department set up a combat analysis section that evaluated the salient features of the key engagements which American forces conducted. Secondly, the military intelligence service in Washington disseminated information on the Japanese army throughout the units operating at the battlefield level. The G-2 regional file contained a wealth of information related to lessons learned through battle experience and it constituted the main reference source which military intelligence drew upon for producing information bulletins and technical manuals.

Intelligence publications, which included monthly summaries, as well as *Tactical and Technical Trends*, and *Military Reports of the United Nations*, not only provided descriptions of Japanese tactical methods. As the conflict progressed, army intelligence began to propagate suggestions put forward by field commanders, concerning the moves which were most effective for countering the IJA. For example, following the New Georgia campaign, a military intelligence bulletin included a recommendation by the commanding general of the Forty-Third Infantry Division.[19] The encounter reemphasized how, when fighting in the jungle, where visibility was restricted by thick vegetation, enemy forces were able to bypass even the narrowest stretches of undefended ground. Under the circumstances, US troops had to maintain lookout posts within close range of each other and provide mutual cover so that they could avoid becoming isolated from their units.

The rank and file of the British-Indian army also understood that a balanced understanding of the IJA's combat methods was crucial in order to develop an effective tactical doctrine. India Command was the focal point for handling material on the Japanese army's tactics. When Southeast Asia Command (SEAC) was established, the intelligence directorates at Allied Land Forces Southeast Asia (ALFSEA) and GHQ India took joint control. British army intelligence activities also benefited because it capitalized on personnel who had an expertise on Japanese military practices. A center headed by Colonel Wards, the former military attaché in Tokyo, was set up in India and staffed by officers who had served attachments and exchanges with Japanese army units during the interwar period.

Naval intelligence also went through significant growth. By late 1943, the Pacific Fleet was making extensive use of intelligence on its Japanese counterpart in order to develop the tactics that were necessary to combat the Imperial navy and its air arm. Under the initiative of the Bureau of Aeronautics, intelligence officers were attached to all naval units, and their task was to interrogate pilots returning from missions and prepare action reports, and thereafter communicate the findings to the Pacific Fleet. The office of the Commander-in-Chief Pacific Fleet (CINCPAC) and Commander Air Force Pacific areas (COMAIRPAC) were assigned to oversee the activities of the various bodies. The main channels for disseminating data were the CINCPAC bulletin and the Pacific Fleet's weekly summary. By the end of the war, up to 14,000 copies of each issue were produced. One task force commander noted how personnel received what was a "prodigious quantity of periodicals, monographs and papers."[20] An equally important breakthrough was the establishment of the Technical Air Intelligence Center. Formed under the direction of the Navy Department, it coordinated the activities of the various services that were handling information on the Japanese air services, including the War Department, the Army Air Forces, and the Royal Air Force. Naval intelligence bulletins contained an extensive collection of reports based on a range of sources, including captured equipment, as well as observations made by ship crews and pilots, on how the Imperial fleet and the air arm conducted their operations. The intelligence services also acted as a channel for propagating battle lessons and tactical procedures that worked to neutralize the enemy. For example, fighter squadrons emphasized how maintaining close formations was important in order to deter the Japanese from carrying out interceptions.[21] When pursuing Zeros, the most effective approaches were from the below and aft sections, where enemy pilots could not detect their attackers.[22] The intelligence division of the office of the chief of naval operations periodically issued summaries on subjects such as anti-aircraft defense and fighter cover. The establishment of an effective intelligence network meant that Allied personnel were well informed on their opponent's strengths and shortcomings. Knowledge of the enemy provided a crucial asset which facilitated efforts to develop the proper ways of defeating the Japanese without incurring excessive casualties.

Japan's ability to gauge its opponents, on the other hand, remained static as the Pacific war progressed, and in many cases, the intelligence machinery suffered a deterioration. The swift triumphs achieved against the Allies convinced both the navy and army that they had no need to enhance their understanding of the supposedly ineffective Western forces. As a result, the military invested a minimal effort in intelligence. Between 1941 and 1945, expenditure for such activities amounted to no more than 0.5 percent of the defense budget.[23] Within the IJA and IJN alike, most intelligence positions were filled by unskilled personnel, thereby reflecting the general lack of appreciation regarding the potentialities of information-gathering.[24] Nor did the military ever develop a dedicated training program, and there were no special courses on the subject at the war colleges. Officers assigned to intelligence tasks were expected to learn while on the job.

With its intelligence organization in a desultory state, the army was severely handicapped in its ability to anticipate Allied counter-offensives. A post-war study by the US military intelligence service noted how the Japanese were "consistently unable to determine the forces opposing them" before actual contact had been made.[25] Except for information compiled from combat operations, the Japanese rarely produced a substantially accurate order of battle list for Allied forces in any theater. Predictions of enemy strategy were wide off the mark, mainly because the Japanese were not successful in reading any high-grade US or British cyphers. The only sources of information were signals traffic analysis and observations of the general operational situation. The Solomon Islands detachment commander described the Guadalcanal operation as a "surprise landing," and the American marines were able to land almost unopposed.[26] The IJA's intelligence on the British fared little better. During the attack against the Imphal-Kohima area during spring 1944, officers in the

Fifteenth Army, had no information on the area of operations, apart from a 1:125,000 map which detailed the local topography.[27]

Naval intelligence was hindered by similar problems. As the war progressed, task forces faced increasing difficulties in conducting aerial reconnaissance and submarine patrol missions, owing to the danger of being interdicted by the Americans. As a result, the Imperial fleet had little knowledge regarding the scale of opposition it was facing. By the time of the Leyte operation, the navy's supply of aircraft was depleted to the point where it could only conduct sporadic searches of its environs. Vice-Admiral Fukudome, commanding the Second Air Fleet, recalled that his planes reported sighting an Allied force of three carriers and possibly a battleship, but nothing larger.[28] Owing to the lack of information on the strength and location of Halsey's task force, the Combined Fleet was not ordered to commence battle until reports were received from coast-watchers that the Americans had arrived at Leyte. To worsen the situation, ship-borne commanders and air squadron leaders consistently exaggerated the losses they had inflicted, thereby hindering an accurate estimate of Allied numerical strength.

The intelligence machinery was further hindered by the failure to establish organizations that could systematically analyze data and thereafter distribute their conclusions throughout the various levels of the command. Assessments were most often produced by operational planners, and the role of intelligence departments was simply to provide data to their superiors on demand. Neither the intelligence nor communications divisions played a significant role in advising commanders on matters regarding strategy and policy. One officer in the naval intelligence division recalled how his section exercised "very little influence" on other bureaus in the naval general staff, and lamented that naval authorities tended to treat the work produced by his peers in a "perfunctory" manner.[29] Intelligence bodies also had to operate with an undermanned staff, and thus struggled to perform their assigned functions.[30] Within army, the intelligence branch had to cope with a persistent shortage of manpower. Although the bureau chief made numerous efforts to increase the number of officers assigned to his division, it was not until the closing phases of the conflict that the army command supplied new recruits. The IJN coped with similar problems. The third division employed a lone officer to compile material on Allied air forces, including technical, statistical, and order of battle data. Faulty information therefore compounded the Imperial forces' difficulties. The navy and army were already disadvantaged because they did not have adequate materiel to defeat their Allied opponents. Poor knowledge of the enemy prevented the Japanese from making better use of their limited resources, and speeded up their downfall.

CONCLUSION

Neither the Allies nor the Japanese entered the Pacific war with a clear idea of the opponents they had to face. However, the armed forces of the US and its coalition partners were in a more favorable position to familiarize themselves, because their parent defense establishments followed a long-standing habit of endeavoring to make a realistic assessment of the challenges confronting them. Furthermore, in the aftermath of the defeats which the Western powers suffered at the hands of the Japanese during the opening stages of the conflict, measures were promoted to formulate an accurate image of the war situation. Allied efforts towards intelligence reform were helped because their armed forces had a tradition of coping with foreign adversaries. As a result, military officials were accustomed to formulating detailed calculations regarding the full range of matters related to strategy, operations and tactics. Good intelligence helped the Allies wage a successful war effort, by allowing them to develop a realistic understanding of their opponents which in turn, enabled the armed forces to exploit their enemy's shortcomings while at the same time neutralizing their strengths.

Japan's intelligence capabilities, by contrast, were held back because the defense establishment did not place a high importance to developing a good knowledge of the enemy. Officials within the Imperial army and navy alike were imbued with a long-standing idea that their own forces were superior, and this precluded the construction of an effective machinery for collecting and processing information on Allied military capabilities. To make matters worse, the Japanese refused to acknowledge their own shortcomings, even when wartime experiences proved beyond doubt that their fighting methods were not adequate. A combination of embedded traditions, including a tendency to denigrate foreign cultures and to downplay the fighting capabilities of foreign rivals, created a situation where the armed forces tended to intelligence as a feature which made little or no difference. As a result, Japan's leaders rarely scrutinized the war situation in a calibrated manner, and misconceptions of their Western opponents led the military to embark on war that in the end brought them nothing but a total defeat.

10

Economies at War

The following chapters will examine a number of economic and political features that were removed from developments on the battlefield, but nonetheless had a significant impact on the conduct and outcome of the conflict. In a total war, such as the one fought in the Pacific theater, economic power constituted a crucial instrument. Success depended on how effectively nations mobilized their resources, and used their supplies of raw materials along with industrial plant to produce enough weapons to prevail in a prolonged series of campaigns. No matter how bravely or skillfully the troops fought, they needed to be properly equipped if they were to have a realistic prospect of defeating their enemy in battle. For this reason, victory most often went to the side with the higher productive capability.

Economic assets formed the backbone of the Allied war effort. The Americans in particular had the resources to manufacture a vastly superior quantity of ships, planes, and guns over their Japanese opponents, and this was one of the key factors which enabled the Western powers to prevail. Likewise, the fundamental cause for Japan's demise was that it could not match the industrial output of its opponents, and its armed forces were thus most often outnumbered.

However, the availability of resources was not the only prerequisite for success. Two further factors were crucial, the first of which was to secure the money needed to fund the war effort. Secondly, governments had to manage their means of production by ensuring that the resources were properly distributed, so that industries could maintain their production. Equally important was to ascertain that arms manufacturers were putting out the right types of weapons. On both counts, the Allied powers undertook significant measures to organize their war economies, and achieved a decisively higher level of efficiency than the than the Japanese managed to do.

ACQUISITION OF RESOURCES

When carrying out any type of war, one of the foremost tasks which nations must undertake is to acquire the financial resources to purchase large quantities of weapons and provide the armed forces with sufficient hardware to operate on the battlefront. Governments which fail to raise adequate money, on the other hand, often accumulate large deficits, and the depletion of capital means that the military becomes hard-pressed to prosecute its campaigns. Securing the raw materials required to produce armaments as well as fuel resources to support the activities of combat units is arguably even more crucial, since without them, no matter how much money a nation has at its disposal, it cannot develop the military power to overcome its enemies. Engaging in an armed conflict also requires the various war industries to be provided with a large amount of human resources in the form of skilled laborers, managers and technicians. The United States and its allies prevailed not only because they had a larger pool of financial capital to draw upon. They were also able to utilize a generous reserve of natural resources and labor, both within their home territory as well as the lands under their spheres of influence. The result was the construction of a military machine which was overwhelmingly bigger than the forces which the Japanese managed to deploy.

A comparison of the US and Japanese gross national products (GNP) illustrates how the Allies were in a better position to fund their military operations. Between 1939 and 1945, America's GNP rose from just over $80 billion, to nearly $260 billion, which meant that it more than tripled within the space of only 6 years.[1] As a result, the government could increase its revenues without calling upon taxpayers to make burdensome sacrifices. In fact, the government was careful not to charge high taxes, since they could adversely affect the livelihood of its citizens and eventually turn public opinion against the war effort. Instead, the minimum threshold for paying income taxes was lowered, thereby bringing nearly all working American citizens within the federal tax system.[2] Rates were also set in a progressive manner, and individuals with higher incomes paid a larger proportion in taxes, thereby saving lower income workers from financial hardship. Few Americans paid more than 20 percent of their wages in taxes. Yet, almost half of the US war effort was funded through taxation, and the amount which the government borrowed from private investors was low in comparison to the other belligerent nations. Furthermore, while the rising demand for finished products in wartime inevitably created inflation, the rationing of civilian goods helped to keep price hikes under control. Living costs went up by around 20 percent, but workers' wages grew by almost 70 percent. Because the US was generating a high level of capital, the government could raise its military expenditures without damaging the economy. The proportion of defense spending in relation to national income never exceeded 40 percent, whereas America's allies, along with the Axis powers, laid out more than half of their total incomes. Yet, in absolute terms, the American government spent overwhelmingly more money than what its foreign counterparts allocated for their war efforts. The US was not only able to fund its own campaign, but also supported its allies, including Great Britain, whose national economies were less robust. The Lend-Lease program, as well as the large sums of cash which US bankers lent to the British government, went a long way in enabling the Royal Navy, RAF and Britain's army to conduct operations in several theaters across the world simultaneously.

Japan's GNP, on the other hand, remained stagnant during the war, and by the closing years, it declined as the submarine attacks on its trade routes, followed by the bombing raids on its industrial centers, both dramatically curtailed industrial output. As a result, defense spending could not be increased without extracting significant amounts of capital away from the private sector. By 1944, war expenditure was estimated to have accounted for 76 percent of the national income. In an effort to raise extra funds, the government resorted to measures such as printing money. However, the measure ended up creating rampant inflation, and made it even more difficult for the navy and army to purchase the armaments that they needed.

The disparity in financial wealth was vividly illustrated by the quantity of hardware which the belligerent nations produced. As early as 1941, even before America entered the war, its industries were manufacturing $4.5 worth of weapons, while Japan's output was barely $2 billion.[3] Two years later, the gap grew even wider, with the US outbuilding the Japanese by a ratio of almost 9:1. Although Great Britain's industrial productivity was noticeably lower than that of its ally, it almost tripled Japan's output. The Allies had the money to build a large arsenal, whereas the Japanese simply did not.

In addition to financing the war economy, the belligerent powers also needed to secure adequate supplies of raw materials. The acquisition of vital resources, including oil, coal, and strategic metals such as iron and aluminum under wartime conditions becomes complicated. Oftentimes, nations end up fighting the same countries which had provided most of their supplies in peacetime, and subsequently, they need to find alternative sources. For example, prior to December 1941, Japan purchased its oil from the United States, but once hostilities commenced, the trade links were severed.

The Allies held a decisive advantage, in that they had immediate access to an abundant supply of natural resources, among the most important of which were fossil fuels, including oil. Without fuel, armed forces were immobile. The Western powers never faced a shortage. American companies such as Exxon produced two-thirds of the world's petroleum, while Britain was able to draw upon the supplies of the Middle East. In terms of output, the US alone pumped over 6.5 billion barrels between 1942 and 1945, which amounted to more than 200 times what Japan produced during the same period.[4] Although the Japanese could secure oil from the East Indies, while coal was available in areas such as

Manchuria, the quantity was nowhere near what the Allies had at their disposal. The Western powers also enjoyed a vast lead in the output of key strategic metals, including iron ore and aluminum. The latter, owing to its light weight, was vital for manufacturing aircraft components. US steel production outpaced its Japanese counterpart by a ratio of 13:1, while aluminum production amounted to over 2 million metric tons during the course of the conflict. With their vast resources, Allied industries produced more weapons than the entire Axis coalition put together. In 1942, the US, Britain and Russia together were assembling almost four times more aircraft that their enemies, and the ratio climbed to almost 5:1 by the end of the war.[5] Even the British industrial sector, which had struggled to produce sufficient materiel for the armed forces during the opening stages of the conflict, saw its output increase by over fivefold by 1945, thanks to the government's concerted effort to divert resources away from the civilian sector and channel them to the war-related industries.[6] The Americans and the British between them ended up achieving a phenomenal superiority over the Imperial armed forces. US warship production was 16 times that of its Japanese counterpart.[7] Although a significant portion of the output had to be deployed to the Atlantic and European theater, by 1944, the Pacific Fleet was able to operate with a comfortable margin of superiority in their operations against Japan. When focusing on balance in the Pacific theater alone, some of the statistics were astounding. The Japanese production of mortars and small arms ammunition in 1944 was no more than 7 percent of the American total.[8]

Inferior economic output was not the only weakness which plagued Japan's war effort. Production was further handicapped because the merchant marine did not have enough shipping to transport the resources of the southern regions back to the home islands, where the bulk of the industrial facilities were located. Prior to the war, the Japanese had anticipated how hostilities with the US were bound to cut off their main source of imports, and subsequently built up a considerable stockpile of essential materials, including oil. However, because neither the government nor armed services expected a prolonged conflict, they accumulated a limited reserve, and Japan continued to depend on supplies from abroad. To worsen the situation, shipyards did not have the capacity to build a tanker fleet that was large enough to absorb the losses which were to be incurred as a result of Allied interdiction moves. Oil imports constituted the most critical shortfall.[9] In peacetime, the bulk of Japan's supplies had been carried in foreign-owned vessels, and in December 1941, shipping space was insufficient to meet the navy's demands. Construction was accelerated from early 1942 onwards, and at the end of 1943, the tonnage of the tanker fleet reached its peak. However, in the following year, when the US navy intensified its attacks on Japanese shipping, losses started to outnumber production. Stockpiles were also running out, to the point where the IJN did not have sufficient fuel to carry out large scale operations in areas far removed from the home waters. By the closing stages of the war, the Americans were sinking over four times the tonnage of vessels which Japan could launch. The destruction of the tanker fleet gave rise to a situation where the flow of oil supplies for the armed forces came to a virtual halt.[10]

In regard to the merchant fleet as a whole, the total size started to decline from the early stages of the war.[11] Although planned output was increased by over 250 percent in 1942, the Japanese grossly underestimated their potential losses. The amount of cargo space available for transporting raw materials was reduced when the military requisitioned a large portion of the fleet to transport troops and equipment to battle areas in the outer reaches of the empire. As a result, only 37 percent of the existing fleet was available for industrial purposes. By 1944, the depletion of Japan's merchant navy reached a critical point. The Americans had sunk over 6 million tons of shipping, and shipyards could only replenish less than half of the total losses. With a fleet whittled down to 40 percent of its pre-war size, the Japanese had to prioritize on which raw materials were to be transported back to the home islands. Steel and aluminum production fell from their 1943 peak by almost a quarter.[12] Under the circumstances, a drop in the production of certain categories of weapons was unavoidable. Although the aircraft industry managed to maintain its output, thanks to generous government support, warship construction suffered. The carriers *Aso*, *Ikoma* and *Kasagi* were never completed, owing to shortages of raw materials and industrial plant.[13] While vessels originally laid down as battleships and cruisers, including the *Unryu*, *Amagi* and *Katsuragi* were eventually completed as carriers, none of them held enough planes to engage in large scale fleet actions. By the time of the Marianas operation of June 1944, a large part of Mobile Fleet's vessels had either been sunk, or were reaching a state of obsolescence, to the point where it was in "sad need of rebuilding."[14] Yet, Japan's limited productive capacity precluded any hope of launching new ships. By summer 1945, the prolonged submarine attacks on Japan's merchant fleet worked to deny its industries of vital raw materials, to the point where armaments production came come to a standstill.[15]

Two additional categories of resources formed a crucial component of the belligerent powers' war economies, the first of which was labor, the second being industrial plant. In regard to the former, the Allies were in a good position to out-produce the Japanese because they had a larger work force to draw upon. In America, the effects of the 1929–33 Great Depression had been visible on the eve of the war, and a large percentage of the population remained unemployed. However, the situation proved advantageous, since factories could draw upon the pool of under-utilized workers. Wartime conditions also meant that a large number of young adult males joined the armed forces, thus further increasing the demand for workers on the home front. The US workforce grew by 14 million, and with an abundant supply of labor, industries were able to correspondingly accelerate their output. Prior to the war, the average factory operated on a 40-hour week, but the number grew to 90 at the closing stages.[16] Interestingly enough, the dramatic rise in the production of war-related goods did not significantly burden the civilian sector, largely because the populace was large enough to absorb the diversion of labor. In fact, only 15 percent of the workforce participated either in the armed forces or in industries that were specifically assigned to support the war effort. The US government was also careful not to infringe on the daily life of its citizens by demanding an excessive decrease in the output of consumer goods. Conditions in Britain were less favorable, since the pool of workers was not as large as its US equivalent. More than half of the population served either in the armed forces or in essential industrial of agricultural jobs. Nevertheless, the labor supply proved sufficient to keep Britain's forces functioning.

Japan's economy, by contrast, faced a labor shortage. The army in particular demanded a disproportionate amount of manpower, mainly because it relied heavily on infantry units, whose activities were far more labor-intensive than those of mechanized forces. In 1944, when the government started to introduce measures for increasing production, the workforce was stretched to the limit. In order to provide more personnel, children and the elderly were recruited to work on the production lines. By the end of the war, many factories relied entirely on untrained workers, which in turn had an adverse effect on the quality of the weapons being manufactured.

Insofar as productive facilities were concerned, the Allies likewise had a significantly larger capacity to expand their output by building new factories. The US had entered the war with a clear lead over Japan, and in 1941, it produced more steel, aircraft and motor vehicles than the combined output of all the World War Two participants.[17] The main problem was that the bulk of the industrial plant had been used to manufacture consumer goods, and the Americans did not have a long-standing tradition of gearing their production for military purposes. On the eve of the conflict, while the US had one of the largest navies in the world, the army lagged far behind its foreign rivals. Its numerical size was akin to the medium-ranking European powers such as Portugal and Belgium. The air force had fewer than 1,700 planes, most of which were obsolete. However, by the end of the conflict, US industries provided almost two-thirds of the military equipment used by the Allies. The production of machine tools trebled in just 3 years. New factories were built from scratch. One of the most notable achievements was the "Willow Run" project, just outside of Detroit.[18] In a bid to promote its methods of mass production, the Ford motor company offered to construct a factory where entire planes could be assembled in a single purpose-built plant. The army accepted the plan, and Ford set up an assembly line that spanned over 60 acres. Aircraft which required over a million parts to be welded together were completed every hour, and by 1944, the plant put out over 5,000 new bombers annually. For each airplane that a Japanese aircraft plant worker could put together, the average American laborer assembled up to four, thanks to the streamlined process. In total, the investment in new plants and assembly lines increased US productive capacity by an estimated 50 percent.

Japan faced the opposite problem, namely that it was attempting to maintain a war economy without an adequate productive base. Industrialization had begun late in comparison with the West, and factories had yet to match the efficiency of their US and European counterparts. Among the most serious shortcomings, insofar as manufacturing capabilities were concerned, was that the Japanese imported the bulk of their machine tools from abroad. During the interwar period, Western observers frequently noted how locally made designs were inadequate for producing high quality aircraft, since they lacked the precision required to cut metals, and had poor durability. Once the war broke out and Japan could not longer purchase equipment from the west, industries faced an arduous task of increasing their output of specialized tools. Aircraft producers suffered from a distinct handicap both in terms of the quantity and quality of weapons they could assemble.

The situation was further complicated because the Japanese did not attempt to develop a more centralized system for constructing their planes. Whereas in America, manufacturers such as Boeing assigned their subcontractors to produce a set number of components, such as engines, landing gears, and flight instruments, in order to ensure that the planes could be completed in an orderly manner, the Japanese continued to rely on a haphazard system where quotas were never established. Sub-contractors worked at their own pace, and transported the finished product to the main factory whenever they were completed. As a result, aircraft manufacturers often faced either a shortage or over-supply of key parts, and the set-up inevitably created bottlenecks. Despite the seemingly formidable obstacles, as the war progressed, the Japanese did manage to significantly raise their production of planes. This was made possible by intensive government efforts to divert resources away from the civilian sector and ensure that war industries received priority. The main beneficiaries were aircraft firms, whose output peaked during 1944.[19] The US Strategic Bombing Survey concluded that the achievement was "not inconsiderable in view of the essential limitations within which the Japanese economy had to operate."[20] However, by 1945, the sustained bombing raids on the home islands and resulting destruction of factories brought about a dramatic decline, down to 50 percent below the high point reached in 1944.[21] No matter how painstakingly

Japan's industries attempted to overcome their weaknesses, the fact of the matter was that they had neither the facilities nor methods of production to achieve anything close to the results accomplished by their US counterparts.

MANAGING THE MEANS OF PRODUCTION

In a total conflict like the Pacific war, where a significant demand was made on the war industries, the belligerents needed to make optimum use of their national resources. Productivity often depended on how efficiently the limited supply of money, raw materials and labor was channeled towards the manufacturers who were putting out war-related goods. In addition, governments needed to effect a good degree of collaboration between the armed services and the manufacturers in order to make sure that the correct types of weapons were being assembled. However, a number of obstacles inevitably arose, among the foremost of which was competition between the various branches of the military, including the navy, air force and army. Governments also contended with opposition from the civilian sector, which was averse to making excessive sacrifices. Equally important was to control prices so that the armed services could purchase weapons and supplies at an affordable cost, while at the same time, allowing the industries to generate sufficient revenue. Both the Allies and the Japanese faced problems in all areas. However, one can argue that the United States, owing to its vast pool of resources, never faced an urgent need to manage its economy, and thus could afford a certain degree of wastage.

As Richard Overy has pointed out, America's industrial productive capacity made an Allied victory possible, but it did not in any sense guarantee the outcome of the conflict.[22] In order to supply the armed forces with the most efficient equipment, the government needed to set up a planning agency to manage the activities of the key industries. No such organization had existed in peacetime, and it was only in 1942, with the creation of the War Production Board, that the US introduced centralized control. Even then, the board had limited powers. For example, in regard to the distribution of raw materials, the ordnance bureaus of both the Navy and War departments were still able to procure resources as they wished, without consulting outside bodies. The dilemma did not cause a serious strain only because America was operating with a surplus economy, and could afford to allow the various organizations to compete for their share of what was a much more generous supply than the other belligerent powers could draw upon.

A more challenging difficulty stemmed from the fact that the US had traditionally been a free market economy, and most industrial magnates were not receptive to the idea of the government dictating their business activities.

Manufacturers could not easily be coerced to stop producing consumer goods and switch over to making planes, tanks and warships. Imposing a state-run economy was most likely to alienate big businesses, whose support was essential for the Americans to carry out a successful war effort. Instead, President Roosevelt created a system which gave industrial leaders the opportunity to use their entrepreneurial skills, and encouraged them to come up with new armaments designs and develop more efficient ways of assembling them. In January 1942, William Knudsen, an automobile industrialist, was appointed to run the Office of Production Management. Knudsen called together a group of leading business leaders, and they were presented with a list of key military weapons, and asked to devise ways of mass-producing them. The setup presented the business community with numerous potential benefits. Companies started to scramble for contracts, and offered to manufacture high-quality weapons at a lower cost then their competitors. Contracts were awarded to the most efficient producers. The General Motors corporation alone provided up to 10 percent of America's war production.

The introduction of new aircraft types, including the B-29 Superfortress, was also made possible by close collaboration between the industrial sector and the military. In 1940, approximately a year before the US entered the war, the army air corps received congressional approval to develop a new super-bomber.[23] After sending requests to all of the major aircraft producers, the air corps decided that Boeing offered the best design, and in May 1941, General Hap Arnold, the chief of the air force, placed a production order. Boeing drew up plans to modify one of its prototype bombers, and aimed to construct a test plane which had twice the weight and payload capacity as the existing B-17 Flying Fortress. The experimental plane was originally designated the XB-29. Aeronautical engineers worked around the clock to determine what types of components the bomber had to be fitted with in order to achieve its expected standard of performance. To provide better protection from interceptors and anti-aircraft fire, the XB-29 was fitted with bigger guns and heavy armor plating, as well as self-sealing fuel tanks. The larger payload inevitably required a correspondingly higher fuel capacity. Subsequently, the plane had to be designed with a much longer fuselage and wingspan than any of its predecessors. By the end of 1942, the USAAF had committed over three billion dollars into developing the B-29 and constructing the factories needed for the bomber to be mass-produced. Twenty million dollars alone were allocated to expand the Boeing plants at Wichita, Kansas and Renton, Washington, while General Motors was awarded a $40-million deal to supply over 6,000 of the B-29's propellers. The development of the US war economy was driven by traditions which had underpinned its industrial community, namely a widespread experience with mass production methods, coupled with the ethos of promoting competition between firms. Both characteristics ensured that the government and armed services could motivate businesses to devise mass quantities of weapons that were both effective and affordable.

In Japan, the government did not attempt to introduce centralized control over the economy until a late stage. The ministries of the navy and army, along with finance, functioned independently of each other, and the cabinet preferred not to get involved in the inter-departmental conflicts, on the grounds that resolving the disputes was too complicated. In January 1943, Tojo introduced proposals to give himself quasi-dictatorial powers.[24] He was allowed to make all priority decisions concerning the five main war industries, including shipbuilding, aircraft, coal, iron and steel, and non-ferrous metals. Imperial approval for the scheme was granted in March of the same year, but the prime minister's prerogatives were still limited. This was largely because Japan's cartel of industrial magnates, also known as the *Zaibatsu*, insisted on retaining control over the war economy. Tojo was therefore obliged to exercise his powers in collaboration with an advisory council composed of leading members from the large industrial trusts.

The *Zaibatsu* continued to implement decisions over the allocation of raw materials, and even managed the production of most weapons, including aircraft. In a further attempt to facilitate the allocation of resources, the government set up a munitions ministry in November 1943, assigned to administer matters such as the control of labor and distribution of raw materials. Although Tojo took charge of the new ministry, the measure by no means guaranteed that his decisions would be carried out. It simply meant that certain areas of production which did not receive high priority could no longer compete for allocations. Without effective government management, the army and navy wrangled over access to the limited supply of resources until the very end of the conflict. Contracts often went to the highest bidder, which meant that war materials were not always sold to those who needed them most urgently. The system also lacked any mechanisms for price control, and as a result, inflation ran rampant, making it even more difficult for the armed services to purchase the weapons they required.

Nor did the government ever try to administer the details regarding the types of weapons being produced. The problem was particularly acute within the aircraft industry. The main manufacturers, including Nakajima, Mitsubishi and Kawasaki, were independent of government supervision. The armed services thus had direct access to them, and could place demands as they wished. In accordance with their desire to strive for quality over quantity, the navy and army frequently requested the construction of new designs. By the end of the war, the Japanese built over 100 different prototypes, as opposed to the Allies, who tended to focus on developing a handful of high performance bomber and fighter designs. Each new model required new parts to be assembled, which placed a strain on the manufacturers, as factories had to temporarily cut back on production while their assembly machines were reconfigured. The system had some visible effects on output. For example, the numerous demands imposed on the Nagoya works, the main plant for assembling naval planes, gave rise to a situation where its monthly construction figures often lagged behind its army rivals.[25] Yet, in spite of the flaws, the armed services continued to insist that plants be kept under their control. Oftentimes, manufacturers were ordered to achieve targets that were up to four times beyond their productive capacity. Japan's aircraft industry avoided a collapse only because the political leadership eventually decided to allocate it a greater share of resources. However, government efforts to manage the quantity and types of planes being produced were largely unsuccessful, and the situation did not enable Japan to make the best use of its scarce resources.

Facilitating the production of appropriate weapons also required governments to provide adequate support for research and development. In the United States, the Office of Scientific Research and Development was established in May 1941 to coordinate the activities of universities and industrial laboratories. One of the most significant innovations which the Allies achieved was radar, which proved vital not only for detecting enemy aircraft, but also to help anti-aircraft fire and fighter planes to be directed at precise locations so that the targets could be neutralized. The British made the initial advances in this area. During the late 1930s, even before hostilities in Europe broke out, the Air Ministry appointed Sir Henry Tizard, a former director of research for the RAF, to preside over a committee to explore possible means of detecting enemy aircraft before they reached the airspace over the home islands.[26] The committee received generous financial support, and by 1939, the British had developed the technological and material capabilities to construct a chain of radar stations along their coastline. The US eventually benefited, thanks to a close liaison with its ally. The Naval Research Laboratory already had made progress in developing ship-borne aerial search devices. During the autumn of 1940, Tizard headed a special mission to North America, in an effort to secure information on technical developments that were taking place on the other side of the Atlantic. American naval officers saw how radar could go a long way in easing the task of locating enemy planes in the open sea, and obtained details on how the Royal Navy had used radar for tasks such as anti-aircraft fire control and fighter direction during the Battle of Britain. By 1943, the navy's research labs produced an array of devices that could be used for different purposes, including the detection of enemy planes at low altitudes. Computers were installed in order to enable officers to calculate the speed and trajectory of incoming aircraft.[27]

The development of radar also enabled the US navy to develop its night-fighting capabilities. In addition to providing ship crews with data on the location of Japanese ships and thereby facilitate the delivery of accurate gunfire, search devices also helped pilots detect enemy planes under the cover of darkness. During the opening months of the conflict, the navy set up a dedicated program to train fighter pilots in the use of airborne radar sets. When Rear-Admiral John S. McCain, who commanded the naval air campaign in the Solomons, became chief of the Bureau of Aeronautics in October, he initiated an investigation into ways to deal with Japanese night fighters. The Grumman corporation was commissioned to develop the XF-7F Tigercat, and the first production model flew in December of the following year. Indeed, radar was a crucial innovation which allowed the Allies to ease the burden of having to locate fast-moving enemy planes, so that pilots could put up countermeasures in a timely manner. The development of modern search devices was made possible not only because the Western powers had the industrial and technological resources. More importantly, their governments encouraged the scientific community to invent high performance instruments that could be produced on a large scale, and enable the armed forces to operate more efficiently.

The generous levels of funding allocated for research and development gave rise to the introduction of a number of additional useful technologies, the most notable of which was nuclear fission. In 1941, a team of scientists approached Vannevar Bush, the head of the Office of Scientific Research, to discuss the possibility of developing an atomic weapon. The War Department had a great deal of confidence in Bush, and endorsed his demands for the manpower, raw materials and money needed to undertake the project. In 1943, after experiments at Columbia University and at the University of Chicago showed that uranium atoms could be harnessed to produce massive explosions on an unprecedented scale, the Manhattan Project was commissioned under a secret presidential order. Although the US provided the money, materiel and facilities, the project also relied on help from British scientists. The exact role which the dropping of the atomic bombs played in compelling Japan to surrender in August 1945 and subsequently bringing about the end of the Pacific war is open to debate. Nevertheless, the fact remains that out of all the belligerent powers, the US was the only one with the resources to devote over two billion dollars towards developing a previously untested weapons technology, even when there was no guarantee that the project would bear fruit.

Japan's research and development, by contrast, never reached the same level of dynamism as its Western counterparts. This was largely due to the lack of financial and technological resources; however, progress was also stifled by the military leadership's mindset which dictated that the Imperial forces were capable of circumventing whatever challenges they faced. Prior to the war, both the navy and army had imported most of their weapons from abroad, and proved adept at copying foreign technologies and thereafter adapting them to suit their own methods of fighting. At the same time, scientists were not encouraged to make new discoveries, and they received minimal funding. Once the war began, and the Imperial forces achieved numerous successes, military leaders saw no incentive for bringing about technical improvements.

Efforts towards innovation most often lacked coordination between the military establishment and the industrial community. For example, Japanese officials realized that their radar was inferior to the West's, and starting in 1940, they managed to secure help from the Germans, who offered samples of their devices. However, the help came too late to permit mass production, and when the war broke out, and trade links between the two nations was curtailed as a result of the Allied blockade, Japanese technicians and scientists had to rely on their own expertise. In 1942, the military attempted to organize the development of radar by setting up a scientific council, consisting of scientists and engineers from the armed forces. While the quality of the research was sometimes of a high order, the council did not maintain a consistent liaison with manufacturers, and consequently, the devices that were developed turned out to be types which Japanese industries could not produce on a large scale. Consequently, Japan was perpetually outclassed by the Allies. Carriers were not equipped with radar until after the disastrous battle of Midway. Even then, the devices were "mediocre," and could detect formations at only at short distances.[28] The super-battleship *Yamato*, which received priority for being fitted with the latest electronic equipment, did not have modernized types of surface and air search radar installed until September 1943.

The limited funds that were available for developing new weapons were also squandered into projects that were of little use for the armed forces. The Imperial army did operate a specialized research laboratory in Manchuria, known as Unit 731, and the unit carried out some notorious experiments with biological and chemical weapons. However, the equipment never progressed beyond the experimental stage. The amount of resources allocated towards the development of tanks and artillery pieces, which served more practical purposes, remained minimal.

CONCLUSION

Although the Allied coalition's war effort was certainly aided by its possession of a vastly superior quantity of resources over the Japanese, the exact role which material factors played in determining the outcome of the Pacific campaigns still needs to be placed in its proper context. John Ellis and Paul Kennedy have contended that the US and its allies prevailed primarily because of their indus-trial predominance, which in turn enabled them to build an enormous supply of military hardware. Economic prowess certainly enabled the Allies to produce a far greater number of ships, aircraft, guns and munitions over their Japanese counterpart. At sea, the US navy was able to achieve supremacy over the Pacific Ocean with its armada of warships and supply vessels. The submarine force managed to reduce the Japanese merchant fleet to a fraction of its pre-war size. In the air, US forces outnumbered their opponent by a ratio of almost 3:1 by the start of 1944, and the superiority rose to almost 4:1 by the following year.[29] US air squadrons frequently turned the Imperial army's defenses into rubble, and bombed Japan's main cities until they were burnt to their foundations. The armies of the US and the British empire used their firepower to blast out Japanese fortifications and kill their occupants. In short, material superiority constituted the foundation of the Allied war effort, by providing the weapons needed to secure battlefront victories. Without it, the Western powers could not hold any realistic hopes of winning.

Yet, while brute force was certainly a vital requisite, and economic power was needed in order to build a strong fighting force, such assets still had to be channeled in an efficient manner. Richard Overy has gone as far as to argue that an equally important advantage which the Allies enjoyed was their ability to properly manage their materiel. In the same way that strategy, operations and tactics had to be planned in a way that allowed the armed forces to overcome the challenges they had to contend with, the running of the war economy required national leaders to understand what types of hardware had to be produced, and figure out how the armed forces were going to be supplied with the goods that they needed. The US and its coalition partners not only had more money, raw materials and productive plant at their disposal. Their governments intervened to ensure that the resources were allocated efficiently, so that the war industries could manufacture the weapons that were appropriate for defeating the enemy. Likewise, inferior economic output was not the only weakness that hindered Japan's conduct of the war. Its demise was speeded up because the leadership did not make an earnest effort to coordinate the activities of the industrial community. Nor did the government act quickly enough to encourage manufacturers to produce hardware which the armed forces needed the most, with the failure to construct an adequate merchant fleet being a prime example of this shortcoming.

The most credible argument is that economic resources provided the Allies with the hardware they needed in order to defeat the Japanese. Likewise, the fundamental reason why Japan's war effort collapsed in 1945 was that it could not produce the weapons needed to hold out against its enemies. The only question remaining was how the Western forces were going to harness their materiel to defeat the Japanese and compel them to surrender. To achieve this end, good planning was of the utmost importance. The US and its coalition partners therefore won because they not only had the necessary assets, but also because they made good use of what they had.

11

A War of Coalitions

Among the key factors which characterized the Pacific war was that it consti-tuted a conflict fought not only by individual nations. The belligerent powers were invariably tied to coalitions which included countries with differing political goals and cultural backgrounds. Conducting an effective war effort often hinged upon forming a cooperative relationship with one's partners, and thereafter developing a coordinated course of action against a common enemy. In this respect, good diplomacy enabled the US and its allies to merge their resources and military strengths in a manner that worked to defeat Japan more expeditiously than would have been the case had they acted alone. The achievement was made possible because the Allied powers made a conscien-tious effort to pursue a shared cause of eradicating the threat posed by the Axis powers, including Japan, Germany and Italy, as well as to establish an interna-tional system in which military aggression was discouraged, if not outlawed. The US and its coalition partners did start off with a number of differences in opinion which obstructed their ability to collaborate. Nevertheless, as the war progressed, political leaders, along with their military staffs, realized that the disputes had to be set aside if the Allies wished to forge the cohesion that was necessary to execute a successful campaign.

Within the Allied camp, the main component was the Anglo-American relationship. At the same time, there was an array of other members who played a valuable role in the Pacific conflict. The dominions of the British empire, including Australia and New Zealand, not only provided bases from which Allied forces carried out their offensives against Japan's empire, but also supplied a considerable amount of troops and equipment. India made a similar contribution to Britain's war effort. Nationalist China was the first nation to become involved in hostilities with Japan, and its armies could be credited for fighting a larger proportion of enemy forces than any other participant. More than two-thirds of the IJA's divisions were committed to mainland Asia, and by simply remaining in the war on the Allied side, the Chinese prevented Japan from redeploying its strengths to fight the British and the Americans. Although the Soviet Union entered the war against Japan at a late stage, the Western powers saw the Red Army, with its large supply of manpower, as a useful addition to the forces which the Allies planned to put up for their invasion of the home islands.

The Axis coalition included Japan, Germany and Italy. Bound by the Tripartite Pact of 27 September 1940, the common aim was to deter the United States from entering the global conflict. Once America declared war, the objective was to overstretch the Allied forces so that they could not fight simultaneously in both Europe and the Pacific. However, the Axis Powers failed to articulate the means by which they were to work in partnership in order to achieve their war aims. In fact, cooperation between Japan and Germany was minimal, to the point where their coalition was more an alliance in name rather than in practice.

DIPLOMACY OF THE ALLIED COALITION: THE US AND THE BRITISH EMPIRE

The main powers responsible for upholding the solidarity of the Allied coalition were the United States and Great Britain. Throughout the conflict, both nations proclaimed that they were united by a common aim to rid the world of fascist dictatorships and militaristic regimes. The Atlantic Charter, signed in August 1941, declared that the main objective of the Allied powers was to create a post-war order in which the people of the world were granted the right to choose their own form of government. The United Nations was to be established as an international organization which could both uphold and enforce the principles of national self-determination and collective security. Once the US entered the global conflict, the Allies agreed to continue fighting until the Axis powers' war-making potential was completely destroyed. Germany, Italy and Japan were to be subjected to a prolonged post-war occupation, the purpose of which was to eliminate their ability to pursue a policy of aggressive expansion. The political leaders of America and Britain, namely President Franklin Roosevelt and Prime Minister Winston Churchill, played a key role in fostering the cooperative relationship. However, individuals at the lower echelons were often important actors. Diplomats from the British Foreign Office and the US State Department, for example, managed the day-to-day liaison between the two powers. Likewise, the defense chiefs, along with commanders at the theater level, were instrumental in resolving the question of how their armed forces were to coordinate their operations. Finally, in order to uphold the Anglo-American alliance, the respective governments needed to generate a sufficient amount of public support, so that their policies could be legitimized among their citizens.

At the same time, while the US and Great Britain showed a good level of cohesion, there were a number of differences which strained their relationship. After all, both nations were sovereign states who held their own interests. For this reason, the interaction was frequently characterized by an uneasy mix of mutual cooperation along with competition, whereby both powers vied to have their say as to how the alliance was going to function.[1] Yet, in the long run, leaders from both nations realized that in order to accomplish the objectives which they sought, a certain level of compromise was necessary.

The US and Britain did not see each other not as equal partners. On the contrary, as the war progressed and America's economic power grew significantly larger than that of its ally, Washington's political clout was correspondingly enhanced. Yet British statesmen were reluctant to accept their nation's diminished standing in international affairs. Churchill in particular held a vision for a post-war world to be led by "Anglo-America." Both nations were to become the world's moral and political leaders. Their people were to have a common citizenship, and be unified by a shared language and cultural background. Such proclamations of plans to uphold Britain's position as a superpower invariably created negative images among the Americans, who started to view their allies as old-school imperialists who were losing their grip on power, but still trying to perpetuate an order whereby Asia and the other "non-white" regions of the globe remained an underling of Western colonialism. For example, John Davies, who served as a political advisor to General Stilwell, once warned that Churchill possessed "the power and influence to force through ... a policy of nineteenth-century imperialism and power politics."[2] Henry Stimson, the Secretary of War, went as far as to opine that the "virile, energetic, initiative-loving and inventive" Americans were likely to play the key role in winning the war, rather than the "decadent" British.[3]

The war years also saw Britain becoming increasingly dependent on US economic support, and subsequently less able to dictate the terms of the Anglo-American alliance. From the early stages of the conflict, Britain's war effort relied heavily on Lend-Lease supplies. In July 1944, Sir John Anderson, the Chancellor of the Exchequer, presented to the war cabinet a memorandum prepared by the economist John Maynard Keynes, which estimated that Britain was likely to suffer a trade deficit of over one billion pounds once hostilities drew to a close. In addition, the nation needed to secure from the US up to two billion pounds worth of Lend-Lease, plus an equal amount in interest-free cash loans, just to keep its own economy afloat.[4] Within the administration of President Roosevelt, many leaders noticed how their transatlantic partner showed ever-growing signs of needing outside support. However, instead of accepting its reduced power, Britain appeared to be seeking US help in upholding its hegemonic position. Secretary of State Cordell Hull, along with the defense chiefs such as Admiral Ernest King, suspected that Churchill's government was seeking to lure the US into following strategies and policies that favored Britain's imperial interests. For example, at the Anglo-American summits, the British representatives constantly insisted that Allied strategy focus on areas where Britain had a significant presence, namely North Africa, the Mediterranean and Indian Ocean areas.

Likewise, British leaders resented Washington's attempts to gain the upper hand in the alliance. Statesmen in London perceived the US as a nation which had the resources to exert their influence, but one whose policies demonstrated a large degree of inexperience, naivety and a lack of knowledge regarding world affairs. Within Whitehall, there was a large and influential body of opinion that could not comprehend why Britain was obliged to play the role of a junior partner. Many leaders accused the US of attempting to use its military and economic power to impose its own ideas on strategic and political issues, without taking into account the opinions of its allies. For example, the American government's insistence that Lend-Lease be ceased in peacetime, after which loans would incur interest charges, caused antipathy among British politicians. Another notable case where the US was perceived to be snubbing its ally arose over the atomic bomb project. At the 1943 Quebec conference, a deal was signed which required both powers to secure mutual consent on any decisions to use nuclear weapons. The atomic resources of Britain and America were also to be pooled and made openly available to both powers. However, as the war progressed, the Americans slowly eased themselves out of the commitment. Shortly after the atomic bombs were dropped on Hiroshima and Nagasaki in 1945, the US openly refused to share any of its expertise or technology with the British. Similarly, on the issue regarding the post-war occupation of Japan, the US declared itself as the main arbiter. General Douglas MacArthur, who headed the Allied administration, gained full control over matters related to reconstruction, government reforms, and the dismantling of the Imperial armed forces. The British made repeated calls for inter-allied cooperation, but Washington continued to limit the participation of its allies by restricting their representation at MacArthur's general headquarters.

Because the US and Britain were independent powers, they were bound to hold opposing views on how Asia was to reconstructed after the Japanese had been defeated. Indeed, differences over the post-war settlement were the root cause for friction within the alliance. Whereas the Americans fought their campaigns against Japan with the purpose of securing its unconditional surrender, and creating a new world order where the peoples liberated from Axis rule were granted the opportunity to build their own sovereign nations, Britain not only wanted to defeat its enemies, but also strove to reestablish its global empire. Both nations, incidentally, interpreted the Atlantic Charter in divergent ways. US leaders insisted that the principles of national self-determination and freely elected governments had to be applied throughout the world. The British, on the other hand, argued that the terms were relevant only to the European nations under the control of Nazi Germany and Fascist Italy.[5] British government officials and the public alike started to believe that the US was attempting to use the charter as a way to dismantle the empire. Likewise, Roosevelt and his political advisors often expressed reservations on how far Britain was likely to go in pursuing the stated ideals. There were also strong doubts whether London was willing to cooperate with Washington's moves to establish a worldwide system of free trade, and abolish the long-standing practice of imperial preference and offering special economic privileges to the subject nations of the British empire.

One of the most notable examples of US disapproval for British imperialism could be seen over the question on Indian independence. By the start of the Pacific war, India's independence movement had reached an advanced stage. Already in 1939, the All-India Congress committee resolved that the nation be declared independent, and demanded that a new constitution be drawn up by a locally elected constituent assembly. When the European war broke out, the Indian people showed considerably less enthusism about supporting Britain than they had been during the First World War. Because Britain needed to concentrate on the task of defeating Germany, the government in London could only reply that all major constitutional changes were to be finalized when the war was over. Still, India demanded immediate independence. Nationalist leaders such as Mohandas Ghandi initiated a civil disobedience campaign. The more radical independence supporters, such as Subdas Chandra Bose, called for India to align itself with the Axis powers. The unrest threatened Britain's hold over a colony which was vital for its war effort. In response, the British dispatched a special mission, headed by Sir Stafford Cripps, during the early part of 1942, to work out an agreement with the pro-independence parties. The Cripps mission offered Dominion status, which meant that India was to be granted autonomy on all matters, including foreign policy, but still remain a subject of the empire, in the same manner as the former white colonies, including Canada, Australia and New Zealand. The Indians, however, insisted on a complete break from the empire, and the negotiations reached a deadlock. The situation took another turn for the worse in the autumn, when mass uprisings broke out in the eastern provinces, including the populous Bengal region. Large sections of the public launched the "Quit India" movement, which called for the immediate withdrawal of British forces from the subcontinent. Under the circumstances, the British saw few choices apart from promising full post-war independence. During the entire episode, the US State Department made it abundantly clear that America was not willing to help Britain solve its differences with the Indian government. On issues related to European colonies in other parts of Asia, including the question of extending support for French and Dutch efforts to reestablish control over Indochina and the East Indies, the Americans turned down British requests to support the reconstitution of imperial rule.

The disagreements which Allied leaders held in regard to the post-war settlement gave rise to a marked discrepancy in US and British strategy. A distinctive feature of Anglo-American relations in the Asia-Pacific theater was the absence of common objectives aside from bringing about the enemy's defeat. In their crusade against Germany, the coalition partners held a binding interest to protect the Atlantic sea lanes and the British isles. Furthermore, neither power had any territorial claims at stake in Europe, and the Allies fully agreed that all nations liberated from German rule were to be granted autonomy.[6] By contrast, the fight against Japan saw both powers focusing on separate geographic areas, with few compelling motives to carry out a joint effort. The Americans focused on the Pacific, and their aim was to clear away Japanese forces from the region, and thereafter develop bases from which attacks could be launched against the home islands. Within the British political leadership, on the other hand, a large number of influential politicians insisted that a paramount objective was to reestablish Britain's status as the leading imperial power in Southeast Asia. Churchill himself once stated, "I have not become the King's first minister in order to preside over the liquidation of the British Empire."[7] Hence, British strategy tended to concentrate on liberating areas such as Burma and Malaya from Japanese rule, and using the Indian subcontinent as the main base for operations.

By 1943, when the tide of the war had turned against the Axis powers, and the Allies were in a position to draw up a concrete plan on how they were going to dismantle Japan's empire, the differences in strategy became clearly visible. At the January 1943 Casablanca conference, the US and British defense chiefs agreed to step up the momentum of their campaign in the Asia-Pacific theater. The Americans committed themselves to an amphibious drive through the southwest and central Pacific, while simultaneously the British were to launch their invasion of Burma (code-named *Anakim*). However, during the following months, Churchill and his chiefs of staff decided that commitments in Europe and the Mediterranean continued to hold up the diversion of large forces to the Far East. When the Allied leaders met at Washington in May, the British delegates reneged on their commitments in the Far East, and informed their US counterparts that operation *Anakim* was impracticable unless America provided material support, including aircraft and landing vessels. Such acts of vacillation led many US officials, including Admiral King and General Marshall, to suspect that Britain was not fully committed to the war effort against Japan, and was more concerned about liberating its former colonies of Malaya and Singapore.

Further strains arose when the British expressed their reluctance to join in General Stillwell's effort to reopen the supply route to China via the Burma Road. The lack of cohesion stemmed from the two powers' conflicting views regarding the importance of China in world affairs. While the US leadership was determined to ensure that China stayed in the war and became a key ally of the West in the post-war era, Churchill and his chiefs of staff did not see any merit in using their precious resources to aid Chiang Kai Shek's regime, which was notorious for its corruption and unpopularity among the Chinese people. At the November 1943 Cairo conference, Chiang was invited to discuss Allied strategy in the Far East with his US and British counterparts. When Roosevelt pledged to step up the campaign in the China-Burma-India theater (CBI) and increase the flow of supplies to the Nationalists' base at Chungking, Churchill made it clear that he was skeptical about the operation, and viewed the plan as a product of America's obsession with China.[8] Britain's apparent hesitation to play a cooperative role in the Asia-Pacific theater inevitably led the Americans to lose faith in their ally.

Nevertheless, despite the ever-present disagreements, in the end, Britain's leaders realized that they needed to significantly enhance their involvement in the Asia-Pacific theater, and synchronize their strategy with their US counterparts if they wished to maintain an effective working relationship. At a gathering of the Commonwealth prime ministers in May 1944, Churchill stated that in the war against Japan, Britain had to accept the role as America's underdog. Even if the Pacific strategy was disagreeable, the British could not do anything to alter US decisions.[9] The understanding drove British leaders to develop a concrete strategy. At the August 1943 Quebec conference, Churchill and his advisors vowed to commence offensive operations in Southeast Asia by mid 1944 at the very latest. A year later, when the Allied leaders met again at Quebec, the defense chiefs offered to dispatch a contingent of Royal Navy vessels to fight alongside the US Pacific Fleet, as well as to contribute ground troops for an invasion of Japan's home islands. Concerns arising from maintaining the integrity of the Allied coalition, along with securing US support for the restoration of Britain's empire in the Far East, thus acted as the prime impetus for cooperation. Likewise, Roosevelt's acceptance of the offer was largely driven by political motivations, namely concerns over US public opinion.[10] If American forces continued to take on the bulk of the fighting in the Pacific theater, the populace was likely to raise questions as to why their nation was battling the Japanese single-handedly, and become infuriated over any word that US officials had rejected a British proposal for joint action. The ambassador to London, John Winant, went as far as to recommend to the president's advisor, Harry Hopkins, that British soldiers be transported via the Atlantic and US mainland on their way to the Pacific, in order to show the public that their ally was fully committed to the campaign against Japan.

The British offer to contribute ground troops for an invasion of the home islands was also driven by a desire to maintain the integrity of the Anglo-American alliance. During the Yalta summit in February 1945, Churchill and his advisors were excluded from the negotiations concerning the USSR's entry into the Pacific war. The British feared that they were being left out of major decisions in the Far East, and were determined to participate in the US-led operations against Japan's mainland.[11] On 4 July, Churchill and his chiefs of staff endorsed a plan whereby Britain Commonwealth land forces were to fight under MacArthur's command, and the CCS accepted the proposal at the Potsdam conference on 17 July. Likewise, the decision to contribute ground forces for the final assault on the Tokyo region (code-named *Coronet*), in spite the stiff resistance likely to be encountered, was based on the understanding that Britain could not risk criticisms from the US and the Dominions for abandoning its commitments in Asia.[12]

America and Britain therefore smoothed over their differences to bring about an adequate level of mutual support, so that the Allies could achieve their goals. US leaders understood that, even though their nation had greater economic and military clout than their ally, Washington could not afford to alienate London. Such actions were most likely to create a scenario where the US had to work alone to attain its wartime objectives and create the post-war order which it sought, without much help from influential friends. Of all the nations within the coalition, Great Britain did have more experience in conducting political affairs on the global stage, and thus wielded a considerable amount of credibility, both among the European powers as well as the dominions of its empire. For this reason, America took care not to offend the sensibilities of the British and their subject nations. For example, when US forces took responsibility for defending the southwest Pacific, Washington made sure not to meddle in the political affairs of Britain's dominions or in the latter's relations with London. Following the fall of Singapore, Britain's reputation within Australia and New Zealand had been severely tarnished. The Australians in particular accused their mother nation of neglecting to defend its subjects, and Prime Minister Curtin openly stated that his country had to depend on the US for protection against the Japanese threat.[13] At the same time, Curtin's government was concerned about growing American influence in the Pacific region, and feared that the trend could result in a loosening of Canberra's ties with the British Commonwealth.

In light of the precarious state of Britain's relations with its dominions, US officials refrained from luring Australia and New Zealand into any agreements which committed America to safeguard their security in the post-war world. The Americans were also cautious not to breed bad feelings by exercising unilateral control over Australia's military activities. When the Allies excluded Australia from their major summit meetings, and did not allow its delegates to have any voice over matters on strategic planning, Canberra became disaffected. However, General MacArthur was aware that a large proportion of the troops fighting under his southwest Pacific command originated from Australia, and for this reason, he regularly consulted the Canberra government over decisions regarding operational planning and troop deployment.

Likewise, while Churchill and his cabinet ministers resented being treated as a junior partner, they accepted the fact that cooperating with America offered one of the few ways by which Britain could hope to retain its status as a world power. London therefore avoided over-pressing the issue of re-establishing British colonial rule in Asia, on the grounds that such moves could well cause a breach with the US.

Effective diplomacy within the Anglo-American alliance thus enabled both partners to fight the war on a global scale. American aid, in the form of Lend-Lease, as well as participation in the theaters where British forces were engaged, allowed the latter to fight a two-hemisphere war. Likewise, Britain's support for US policies worked to legitimize the latter's war aims, both in the eyes of the Dominions, as well as within the American public.

The uneasy mix of competition and cooperation in Anglo-American relations was also present in areas beyond the realm of high politics. At the theater level, Southeast Asia Command had a unique power structure, where the British appointed the supreme commander, but a number of US officials held key positions and were thus in a position to influence strategic decisions. This was in stark contrast to the Pacific areas, where US commanders, including General MacArthur and Admiral Nimitz, along with their subordinates, had a virtual monopoly of control. Mountbatten was served by a deputy chief of staff, Major-General Albert Wedemeyer, who had been a member of the army's planning staff in Washington, along with Stratemeyer, who commanded the US air force units in the theater. Wedemeyer did concede that, at the start of his appointment, he faced difficulties in dealing with the British, and was most often inclined to oppose Mountbatten on matters related to planning. Both commanders adamantly defended their respective nation's strategic concepts, with Mountbatten advocating a push towards Singapore, and Wedemeyer pressing for an advance against southern China. In the end, the British and the Americans conceded that their interests lay in separate areas, and that their forces were better off carrying out independent campaigns, rather than relying on each other's support. Nevertheless, the Allies did continue offering mutual assistance. The US extended to the British a large amount of material aid, in the form of aircraft and landing vessels. Likewise, American forces in Burma were allowed to use the road and rail network in India for logistical purposes. A certain level of success was also achieved in integrating Allied operations. For example, Mountbatten eventually obtained an agreement whereby Stratemeyer's air units were to be combined with the RAF to form a single force.

In the area of intelligence cooperation, interactions between the allies also reflected the extent to which their interests did not always coincide. At a conference held in October 1942, an agreement was reached where the US navy's sigint unit conducted the main effort against Japanese cyphers, and then passed the decrypted signals to the headquarters of the British code-breaking network at Bletchley Park, from which the material was to be forwarded to the intelligence branch of Admiral Somerville's Eastern Fleet.[14] Yet the sharing of information was made difficult because British and American operations covered separated areas, owing to geostrategic factors. While US intelligence organizations concentrated on the Pacific, their counterparts were primarily interested in Japanese traffic directed to the Indian Ocean areas. Although Britain needed to establish a coordinated system whereby its services operating at the theater level could communicate directly with the Americans, the latter were reluctant to set up such an apparatus, out of fears that a decentralized chain of communication could compromise security. In September 1944, the situation was improved when the US navy's director of communications offered to install two teletype channels between Colombo and the Pacific Fleet's intelligence center at Pearl Harbor, via Guam. Thus, while bureaucratic and political obstacles did hinder Anglo-American collaboration until the late stages of the conflict, in the end, both powers realized that sharing information could significantly aid their military operations.

In developing the tactics and weapons for fighting the Japanese, the British and the Americans managed to offer each other considerable assistance. The initial steps were taken in London. In June 1943, the chiefs of staff decided to dispatch a mission headed by Brigadier John Lethbridge, the purpose of which was to obtain a firsthand account of US and Australian operations against the IJA in the Pacific theatres. The main concern was that British forces in Southeast Asia had not received much information on how their counterparts had developed the appropriate methods in key areas, including operations in jungle terrain and amphibious landings. The Lethbridge mission conducted an extensive tour of the Asia-Pacific theater, and learned a plethora of important lessons on how Britain's army could fight the Japanese more efficiently. The Americans also allowed British observers to be attached to naval and air units in the Pacific theater, thereby further facilitating the development of combat methods and weaponry. Likewise, British commanders in the India-Burma theater shared their knowledge on tactical matters with their US counterparts. Publications by the War and Navy departments frequently included useful material prepared by officials from the armed forces allied to America. The diplomatic relations forged between the US on one hand, and Great Britain and her overseas dependencies on the other, allowed them to cooperate in the area of military operations. As a result, they were able to pool their resources and expertise, thereby creating mutual benefits for the coalition members.

RELATIONS WITH THE NON-WESTERN ALLIES: CHINA AND THE SOVIET UNION

The Anglo-American members of the allied coalition also needed to develop a dialogue with nations whose political systems and cultures were considerably at variance with their own, the most important of whom were China and the Soviet Union. The USSR had pursued a policy of propagating its Marxist-Leninist ideals around the world, to varying degrees, ever since its creation in 1917. The Nationalist regime in China, meanwhile, had been fighting a prolonged power struggle with its Communist opponents for over two decades. In many ways, one can argue that the foundations of the Cold War in East Asia, and the ideological conflict between Western democracy versus Communism, had already been laid down even when the Allied powers were preoccupied with the task of defeating Japan. However, in the same way that the US and Great Britain avoided disputes over post-war settlements, the Western allies did not fight the Pacific war to curb Communist expansion, but instead sought to enlist the support of the USSR and China. The US in particular maintained that the support of both nations was essential to accomplish a quick and economical defeat of the Axis coalition.

In regard to China, while the British remained lukewarm towards Chiang Kai Shek's regime, American post-war plans called for bestowing it with the role of protecting Asia from Communist incursions, and raising the nation to the status of a great power. During the war, many leaders within the Roosevelt administration, along with State Department officials, hoped that Nationalist China would emerge as one of the "big four" policemen of the new world order, along with the US, Great Britain and France. At the 1943 Cairo conference, and again in September 1944 at Dumbarton Oaks, a proposal was raised, whereby in return for its cooperation with the Allies, China was to be assigned a permanent seat on the security council of the new post-war world organization. However, as the war against Japan progressed, the possibility of a take-over by Mao Tse-Tung and his Communist party had to be duly acknowledged. The latter had gained a considerable level of popular support, while the Nationalist regime in Chungking began to falter as a result of its failure to reverse the economic problems which had been brought about by the prolonged fight against the invading Japanese forces. Instead of attempting to contain the rise of Mao, US officials attempted to broker a settlement whereby they shared power with the Nationalists. In 1944, the Americans dispatched their "Dixie Mission" to observe the situation in the province of Yenan, where Mao's Communists had been based. After a round of talks with Mao, the mission returned with the conclusion that a coalition government was more likely to prove amenable to US interests in China than one dominated by the Nationalists.

Soviet aspirations for territorial gains in the Far East also became a distinct threat. As early as the Teheran conference of November 1943, Premier Josef Stalin hinted that the USSR wished to regain the lands that Russia had lost to Japan during the 1904–5 war, including the southern portion of Sakhalin and the Kuriles archipelago. US and British leaders were aware that the Soviets could become a potential rival. Between 1944–45, the American joint chiefs of staff produced a number of memorandums which predicted that following the defeat of Japan, Asia was most likely to be wracked by Nationalist rebellions, which the Soviets would seek to exploit. Indeed, revisionist historians have argued that the atomic bomb was used to deter Moscow from exerting its power and influence in Asia. The contention is supported by the fact that the Soviets were denied a zone of control in post-war Japan, and were not allowed to participate in any of the Allied councils responsible for administering the occupation.

However, a closer look at the facts does reveal that the Allies fought the war with a view to securing Soviet participation. In September 1943, the US defense chiefs produced a summary on the importance of Soviet military support, and concluded that the Red Army's substantial strength provided a valuable addition to the forces which the Western powers could muster for an invasion of the Japanese home islands. At the Teheran conference, when Stalin declared that Russia would join the Far Eastern war shortly after Germany's defeat, US military planners expressed satisfaction that, with the Red Army's help, Japan could be defeated more quickly. At the Yalta conference of February 1945, in an effort to secure a Soviet pledge of support for in the Pacific war, Roosevelt promised Stalin that the USSR would be granted the right to reoccupy the territories it had lost in the 1904–5 war, including Sakhalin and the Kuriles. Russia was also to gain a warm-water naval base at Port Arthur, along with railway concessions in Manchuria that could provide a direct link with Siberia. The demarcation of post-war spheres of influence was also drawn up. The US was to bear responsibility for the Pacific area, with Britain taking care of Southeast Asia. The USSR was specifically designated as the protector of northeast Asia, including the Chinese province of Manchuria. The agreement has been cited by one prominent Cold War historian as "a classic example of Roosevelt's failure to coordinate military strategy with his post-war political objectives."[15] The president agreed to the terms for Soviet entry into the war against Japan without consulting his civilian advisors in the State Department, and simply followed the recommendations put forward by the joint chiefs, who insisted that that Moscow's support had to be secured at all costs.

However, the US leadership's dealings with Stalin do demonstrate how it was more concerned about defeating the Axis powers, and was not prepared to risk a row with the Soviets over territorial issues, at least until the ongoing war drew to a close. Defense planners agreed that the USSR's participation was necessary in order to defeat Japan. At a meeting held on 18 June with the JCS and service secretaries, the president asked for an assessment of how necessary it was to have Russia enter the war. All agreed that an invasion of the home islands, coupled with Soviet entry, were essential to force the Japanese to capitulate.[16] During the Allied conference held at Potsdam in July, President Harry Truman made yet another concerted effort to secure Stalin's promise that the Red Army would commence its invasion of Manchuria at the earliest opportunity. The US was thus eager to secure Soviet participation, and willing to make certain concessions to secure Stalin's cooperation. Although political leaders were aware that the USSR was pursuing goals that ran contrary to the interests of the Western powers, their suspicions were placed aside for the benefit of the war effort against the Axis powers.

THE AXIS COALITION: AN ALLIANCE ONLY BY NAME?

In contrast to the cooperation achieved by the Allied coalition, the Axis powers of Japan, Germany and Italy failed to forge a meaningful level of coordination, at least in the Asia-Pacific theater. The three nations were united by a common goal to wear out the Allied war effort. The Axis powers also shared an ideological affinity. Their governments were shaped along the ideals of fascism, and they held similar aspirations which called for reconstructing the world order by diminishing the power of the established states, namely the US and Great Britain. However, the way in which Germany and Japan were to collaborate was never clarified, and one can contend that the Axis pact was an alliance only by name.

Even before the Pacific war broke out, Japan's leaders showed a reluctance to align their policies with their partners. In early June 1941, 3 weeks prior to Germany's invasion of the Soviet Union, Hitler informed the Japanese ambassador in Berlin, Oshima Hiroshi, of the impending operation. In Tokyo, the German embassy made a number of approaches to the *Gaimusho*, to secure an agreement that the IJA would join forces with the *Wehrmacht* and conduct a simultaneous invasion of Siberia. Japan's leaders found the news of their ally's decision to be most unsettling. Foreign Minister Matsuoka argued that his diplomatic moves since the conclusion of the Axis Pact, including the signing of the

April 1941 neutrality agreement with Moscow, had been geared to prepare the armed forces for an invasion of Southeast Asia, and an eventual confrontation with the US and Britain.[17] The southern regions provided the resources which Japan needed to sustain its military operations, whereas Siberia did not offer any tangible rewards. After Germany launched *Barbarossa*, Tokyo vacillated over the issue of supporting Germany. On one hand, a policy conference held in July ruled that intervention remained a possibility, and the army needed to be kept on hold along the Manchuria-Siberia frontier. However, in the end, the leadership decided that the future course of Japan's strategy depended first and foremost on how the China venture and the situation in the southern regions transpired, rather than any obligations which it owed under the terms of the Axis pact. Any decision to declare war against Russia was to be made independently, without paying too much heed to pressure emanating from Berlin.

When Japan became embroiled in hostilities with the US and Britain, dialogue with Germany remained minimal. The geographic distance which separated the Axis powers precluded any moves to synchronize their military operations. Further obstacles arose from the scornful views which the Nazis held towards their Japanese allies. Following the signing of the Axis pact, the German government did take measures to remove references to the so-called "yellow peril" from popular literature and official statements. Nevertheless, for the Fuhrer, the Japanese remained an inferior people, possessing no affinities with the Germans.[18] The alliance therefore did not have any strong basis for mutual trust. Nor did the Axis leaders, including Tojo and Hitler, hold any face-to-face meetings in the same manner that their Allied counterparts did.

The failure to coordinate Axis strategy in India clearly illustrated the lack of common goals. Berlin and Tokyo did harbor plans to bring the subcontinent under their sphere of influence, by inciting a revolution against the British colonial administration. Under an agreement drawn up between the two powers in January 1942, the Imperial forces were to take responsibility for all areas that lay east of 70 degrees longitude, which included India. At an Imperial liaison conference, Japan's leaders issued a document stating, "the government has no hesitation in making wholehearted efforts to help the independence movement, irrespective of whether inside or outside India."[19] The main problem was that the Japanese government did not have any direct contacts with Indian political parties, and was reluctant to support independence movements unless its Axis partners promised to simultaneously send forces to the region. Because neither Germany nor Italy wanted to undertake operations east of the Suez Canal, a concrete strategy was never drawn up. Poor liaison between the Axis powers therefore prevented them from taking advantage of a favorable opportunity to achieve a significant inroad against the British empire, and subsequently inflict a further blow on the Allied coalition. The strategic priorities of Japan and

Germany covered separate areas, with the former focusing on the Asia-Pacific region, and the latter concentrating on Europe. Under the circumstances, the prospects of coordinated military action against the Allies were bound to remain slim.

Any acts of cooperation which the Germans and Japanese carried out had a minimal impact on their war effort. For example, the ambassador to Berlin, General Oshima, managed to forge close ties with Hitler and his top advisors. As a result, Oshima gained privileged access to a range of secret information on the German military, including the dispositions of the *Luftwaffe*, the state of progress in constructing the Atlantic wall, and the *Wehrmacht's* order of battle. The material was regularly transmitted back to the foreign ministry in Tokyo. However, it was the Allies who ended up profiting from the exchange. US cryptanalysts, who were able to read virtually all pieces of communication sent by Japan's diplomats abroad, passed on the decoded messages to the military. Consequently, the Americans were able either to secure valuable information which they could not obtain by decoding German signals or, in other cases, the intelligence confirmed the data that had been extracted by reading the *Wehrmacht's* communications.

The Japanese also secured a good deal of technical assistance from their German ally. Between 1943 and 1945, in return for deliveries of raw materials from Southeast Asia, U-boats transported numerous samples of the latest weapons which the Nazis had to offer, including jet aircraft and flying bombs, along with licenses for Japanese companies to construct copies of the equipment.[20] In some areas, most notably radar, the Imperial forces were able to significantly enhance their capabilities, thanks to the exchange. However, the assistance came too late to permit the Japanese to significantly close their technological gap vis-à-vis the Allies. Industrial facilities were also not sufficient to produce advanced equipment on a large scale. In the end, the Axis powers ended up pursuing their own independent war efforts, and were unable to achieve any type of collaboration that allowed them to combine their military strength in a more effective manner.

CONCLUSION

Effective diplomacy and the proper coordination of wartime strategy were among the key factors which enabled the US and its allies to prevail in the Pacific theater. The Allies did hold a number of differences of opinion that could potentially hamper their campaign against Japan. In particular, disagreements over the post-war settlement in Asia were the key cause of tensions within the Western alliance. Whereas the US wished to bring about an end to colonialism and encourage the European powers to dismantle their overseas empires, Great Britain, under the leadership of Prime Minister Winston Churchill, wished to reestablish its empire in the Far East, once the Japanese had been defeated. For this reason, the British were reluctant to join forces with America's operations in the Pacific, and preferred to focus their attention on recapturing areas such as Singapore. The lack of synchronization with US strategy, in turn, led many American leaders to develop mistrust towards their partner. However, by the closing stages of the conflict, the British realized that any moves towards reconstituting their empire depended on US support. In order to uphold the integrity of the alliance, and enable the coalition to achieve its aim of bringing about the total defeat of the Axis powers, Britain needed to show a satisfactory level of cooperation. Likewise, the leadership in Washington realized that, in spite of their nation's growing economic and military power vis-à-vis its allies, British support was essential if America wished to implement the goals laid out in the Atlantic Charter, namely to create a post-war order in which dictatorships and militaristic regimes were abolished. The Allies therefore managed to place their differences aside in the interest of achieving their common objective of defeating their adversaries.

America's handling of its relations with China and the USSR also demonstrated the extent to which its leaders carried out their war effort with a view to forging a global coalition against the Axis powers, even if it meant having to make certain concessions. The administration of President Roosevelt, along with his successor Harry Truman, saw Russian support as a vital instrument for defeating Japan. Subsequently, US officials took all necessary measures to ensure that the Red Army participated in the Pacific campaign, by promising Stalin that in return for his cooperation, the Soviets would be allowed to acquire territories in the Far East. Fears over Soviet expansion in Asia and the spread of Communism were thus shelved in order to ensure that the Allies achieved their wartime goals. Indeed, the coordination of efforts among the coalition members enabled them to pool their economic, military and political power in a way that enabled them to defeat the Axis powers in an expeditious manner.

The Axis powers, including Germany and Japan, by contrast, achieved minimal cooperation for the duration of the Pacific war. Their interests covered widely separated areas, with the Germans concentrating on Europe, while the Imperial forces were preoccupied with Asia. Nor did the two powers share any meaningful common objectives, aside from wearing out the Allies' ability to fight. However, the Axis nations never clarified the means by which they were to achieve their aims. In the end, Nazi Germany and Imperial Japan ended up waging separate war efforts against the Allies, and never managed to pool their resources. The lack of coordination, in turn, speeded up the collapse of the Axis war machine.

12

War and the Home Fronts

In a total war effort that requires a full mobilization of national resources, the populace inevitably gets involved. Whether civilians are conscripted to serve in the armed services, or called upon to work in the factories and farms which are producing the goods needed by the military, wartime conditions tend to bring significant changes to their daily lives. Further repercussions are felt when citizens have to make financial sacrifices by paying higher taxes to support the war effort. The diversion of resources towards military activities, and away from the civilian sector, also means that the government is compelled to impose austerity measures, which include the rationing of everyday necessities such as food, clothing and fuel. Subsequently, the living standards of ordinary people are affected. Last but not least, the population becomes subjected to attack, either in the form of aerial bombardment or economic blockade. Enemy forces tend to follow the rationale that citizens form a crucial component of any nation's war effort, since they provide the labor for the war industries, as well as the political support which the government needs in order to carry out its policies. For this reason, non-combatants are considered a legitimate target. In short, total wars have a weighty impact on civilians, and for this reason, the home front becomes a theater of prime importance.

For both the Allied powers and the Japanese, generating public support was a crucial component of their war effort. The foremost task was to educate the citizens on the reasons why their nation was undertaking such a demanding endeavor to fight an enemy in a faraway land. In addition, families who had one of their members serving on the front lines needed to know the causes for which they were putting their lives at risk. Governments often addressed the issue by using propaganda, either in the form of television and radio broadcasts, official publications, or political cartoons, to show how the enemy posed a direct danger to the lives of the populace. In the nations belonging to the Allied coalition, particularly the US and Australia, the Japanese were depicted as barbarians who were determined to achieve world domination and impose an Asiatic-style dictatorship on the Western democracies. Likewise, in Japan, towards the closing stages of the war, when an invasion of the home islands became a likely scenario, the people were told to do everything in their power to save the nation from destruction by the American imperialists.

The Japanese were successful at indoctrinating their population, as evidenced by the fact that the people made minimal efforts to coerce their leaders to cease hostilities, in spite of the deprivations arising from increased military expenditures, as well as the destruction caused by the Allied bombing raids on Japan's cities at the closing stages of the conflict. The phenomenon stemmed largely from the way in which the society had been conditioned to accept orders from higher authorities. The home fronts of the Allied nations, on the other hand, did not have their resolve put to the same test. Although faced by rations and higher taxation, the livelihood of ordinary citizens did not significantly decline. The most pressing concern was to maintain a sufficient level of enthusiasm, and thereby alleviate any opposition that could arise from mounting casualties on the battlefront.

PUBLIC OPINION AND THE WAR

In order to mobilize public support for the war effort, the governments of Japan and the Western nations promoted feelings of hatred and fear of the enemy, in the same way that such sentiments were instilled to build up morale among troops on the battlefront. Within the Japanese public, radio broadcasts and newspapers regularly disseminated propaganda which aimed to imbue a sense of racial superiority. Emphasis was placed on traditional beliefs, including the notion that the Japanese were a purebred race who had descended from the gods. Furthermore, the people held a the sense of polity (*kokutai*), which bestowed them a number of unique virtues, including loyalty towards their nation, as well as a propensity to make sacrifices for the benefit of the wider community.[1] Societies with such merits were more likely to unite for a common cause and wage a successful war effort than the self-centered Americans or British. During the initial stages of the conflict, when the Imperial forces dismantled the Allies' hold on Southeast Asia within a matter of months, the government could propagate the view that the Western powers were incapable of putting up a strong fight, with a good level of credibility. Even after the Japanese began to face declining fortunes, following their defeats at Midway and Guadalcanal, the home islands remained unaffected by enemy attacks, and the military prowess of the Allies could easily be downplayed.

The Western nations were frequently portrayed to be lacking any moral values, and the attribute allegedly hindered their fighting abilities. For example, Roosevelt and Churchill were not only represented as tyrants who sought to retain their dominance over world affairs and thereby prevent Japan from securing its rightful position as the leader of Asia. Both leaders were also depicted as decadent gangsters, who were more interested in daily pleasures such as eating, drinking and debauchery. The negative images were also applied to society in general. The Americans in particular were absorbed by the pursuit of materialistic gain, and thus could not withstand the hardships brought about by wartime conditions. One newspaper article read, "money making is the one aim in life of Americans. The men make money to live luxuriously and over-educate their wives ... Sex relations have deteriorated with the development of motor cars, and divorce is rife."[2] In spite of its strong points, including scientific and economic development, America was considered an inherently corrupt and decadent nation. Similarly, an editorial in the *Asahi Shimbun* suggested that, because America was a rich country, it was a common characteristic to feel that there was no point in fighting to risk one's life. The attitude was an inherent weakness of the democratic system, which placed the individual's interests above those of state and society.

When the tide of the war started to turn against Japan after 1943, the government had to deal with the task of hiding the setbacks which the Imperial forces had suffered. Yet, until the Allies were in a position to carry out large scale operations against the home islands, the populace could not comprehend the vulnerable situation which their nation faced. The government had a further advantage, in that it exercised a complete monopoly of control over the press and the media through its information bureau, and was thus able to follow a wide variety of propaganda lines so as to prevent the rise of public anxieties.[3] The extent of the reverses suffered in the southwest Pacific areas was largely concealed. After the Guadalcanal campaign, for example, the *Domei* news agency reported that even though a number of the Imperial fleets vessels had been sunk, the Americans had lost the bulk of their aircraft carriers, and that for every Japanese aircraft shot down, up to nine Allied aircraft had been destroyed. When the public began to express apprehensions in regard to US industrial capacity and its ability to produce larger quantities of aircraft, propaganda statements made fanciful boasts that the Japanese could easily out-build their opponents, so long as factory workers put in extra hours.[4] Civilian morale could thus be maintained, as long as the populace was prevented from learning the facts.

News of defeats could also be presented with an accompanying statement to the effect that Japan's forces could eventually secure a decisive victory. In this respect, historical memories limited the prospects of a collapse in public support. Whereas for Germany, military defeats could potentially recreate the humiliation suffered at the end of the Great War and thereby destroy confidence in the nation's ability to continue fighting, in Japan, there was no equivalent of a "1918 syndrome."[5] Setbacks were more likely to conjure up recollections of 1905, when the gains of a year's fighting stood to be lost by the approach of the Russian fleet, only to be saved by a decisive battle in the home waters. Territorial losses in the Pacific, such as the evacuation of the Aleutian Islands, could easily be presented as tactical withdrawals designed to shorten Japan's outer lines of defense while luring the Allies closer to the proverbial lion's den. In the same manner that naval staffs became convinced that the fleet could annihilate the American armada as it approached mainland Japan, and repeat its success at Tsushima four decades earlier, the wishful line of thinking was sold to the public. Propaganda also purported that the Japanese people's will to avoid surrender was bound to result in victory, whereas the Allies were more likely to falter as a result of war-weariness. The government's efforts to reassure its citizens that Japan would eventually prevail over its enemies did prove effective in containing the rise of popular opposition until the closing stages of the conflict.

In the West, the people were inundated with propaganda which depicted the Japanese as a vicious adversary. Public opinion tended to fully support the nation's effort to curb the Imperial forces' quest to impose their dominance on the rest of the world. A notable exception was Great Britain. Its home territory was geographically removed from the Asia-Pacific theater, and the populace was fixated on fighting the Germans, the latter whom constituted the archenemy. Aside from families who had members fighting in the Far East, most civilians perceived the war against Japan as a distant event that had little or no effect on their lives. One officer returning from Southeast Asia on home leave described his dismay at the "dreadful ignorance" which the British people showed about the Fourteenth Army and the Burma campaign.[6] In the US and Australia, on the other hand, a Japanese invasion was treated as a real and present danger, at least during the opening phases of the conflict. The public outcry over the sneak attack on Pearl Harbor and the expulsion of Western forces from Southeast Asia never died away. Further indignation arose when the atrocities which the Japanese carried out against Allied POWs became public knowledge. While the government played its part in propagating hostile opinions, the press and media, neither of which were state-controlled, frequently used racist and bellicose slogans to describe the Japanese. In Australia, an article in the *Sydney Morning Herald*, written shortly after the fall of Singapore, read "the enemy's immediate object ... is our total destruction."[7] Popular songs were also composed to denigrate the adversary. One that was written shortly after Pearl Harbor contained the lyrics, "there will be no more yellow 'Japs' to fear". In political cartoons that related to the Germans or Italians, faces of national leaders such as Hitler or Mussolini appeared most frequently, thereby suggesting that the fight was against the dictatorships of enemy nations, rather than the people. However, posters depicting the Japanese invariably included caricatures of the masses, where they embodied a number of stereotyped features, including short stature, rimmed glasses, and facial expressions which suggested an ignorance of the outside world.

In other cases, the Japanese were illustrated as sub-human beasts. The front cover of an issue of *Time* magazine contained a cartoon with Japanese soldiers resembling chimpanzees, wearing helmets and carrying guns, while swinging from tree to tree. The British embassy in Washington once noted in a weekly report, "the Americans perceived the Japanese as a 'nameless mass of vermin'". In many cities, signs appeared in shop windows declaring "open season on the Japs," with many retailers selling "Jap hunting licenses" as novelty souvenirs. Towards the closing stages of the war, the press sold the idea of dropping of atomic bomb on the Japanese, as the most effective way of subduing an atrocious people. Shortly after the bombing of Hiroshima in August 1945, one Australian newspaper wrote, "the use of the bomb against a race which trained their soldiers so thoroughly to lust arms and killing ... is fully justified ... while it refuses to accept defeat." Historians such as Dower have suggested that the US leadership's decision to use such destructive weapons was partly driven by public pressure to mete out retribution on the much-hated Japanese.[8] A closer analysis of the events leading to Hiroshima and Nagasaki does show that the Truman administration's overarching concern was to end the Pacific war as quickly as possible, without having to incur the high casualties that could arise from an invasion of the home islands. Racial hatred thus played a minimal role in influencing policy decisions, including the use of the atomic bomb.

However, enmity towards the Japanese did lead the US administration to undertake questionable actions, the most disturbing of which was the internment of Japanese-Americans who resided in the west coast states. In February 1942, President Roosevelt signed Executive Order 9066, which authorized the army to commence its relocation of over 100,000 Americans of Japanese ancestry from California, Oregon and Washington. The evacuees were placed in detention centers which had been established in the hinterland, where they remained incarcerated until war's end. The move arose from widespread suspicions that with the outbreak of hostilities, Japanese-Americans were likely to carry out fifth-column activities that involved sabotage and espionage activities against key defense installations, in an effort to pave the way for an impending invasion.[9] Japanese immigrants living on the west coast were susceptible to becoming scapegoats even before the war started. A large portion had not fully integrated with their local communities, owing to discriminatory measures which made them wary of American society. The Immigration Act of 1924 had prohibited further immigration from Japan while at the same time making up to 47,000 first-generation (*Issei*) Japanese immigrants ineligible for naturalization. In many states, laws had also been passed to forbid Japanese-Americans from voting in local elections or owning land. Treated as second-class citizens, many of the immigrants retained their old traditions. Families as old as the second generation (*Nisei*) continued to send their children to schools where education was conducted in the Japanese language, and married according to arrangements made by Japanese intermediaries. The failure to assimilate, in turn, created suspicions that their loyalty to the US was questionable.

The decision to intern the Japanese community was not based on any credible evidence that they posed a security threat. On the contrary, the Federal Bureau of Investigation reported to the president on a number of occasions that there were no indications of plans for subversive activities. Nevertheless, Roosevelt was under pressure from politicians representing the west coast states, whose constituents held implacable suspicions of what the Japanese could do in the aftermath of Pearl Harbor. The president, along with key members of the White House staff, also held racial prejudices, which in turn led them to concede to mounting public pressure. The incarceration was carried out with a complete disregard for the fact that many of the internees were US citizens, and legally protected by the constitution. Property was seized without due compensation, and the rights of *habeas corpus* were revoked, which meant that the Japanese could be held without being formally charged for specific crimes. Nor did government authorities need to present any legal evidence to justify detainment. Although both the Justice Department and the Supreme Court explicitly voiced their objections, the internment was carried forward.

Yet despite the racial animosity which pervaded certain sections of the populace, a large part of the civilian population in the Western nations remained indifferent about a conflict that did not have any visible effects on their livelihood. For example, a Gallup poll showed in September 1942 that 40 percent of the American public could not identify the reasons why their nation was at war, nor could they explain the objectives which their leaders were seeking.[10] Most US citizens admitted that they could not locate Japan, or any of the key battle areas such as New Guinea, on a map. Such indications of apathy do bring into question the extent to which civilian morale and support for the war effort were maintained by instilling a sense of hatred towards the enemy. In order to keep public opinion on their side, governments needed to care for the well-being of their citizens, and ensure that they were still able to obtain adequate amounts of food and daily necessities, in spite of the large portion of resources being diverted to the military. Failing that, national leaders had to justify the hardships that befell their nations in wartime.

WAR AND ITS EFFECT ON CIVILIAN LIFE

The civilian populations of both the Allied nations and Japan had to deal with common adversities, such as lowered living standards resulting from the increased consumption by the armed forces. Rationing became necessary in all of the belligerent nations, albeit to varying degrees. Furthermore, in a total war such as the one fought in the Pacific theater, the civilian population faced the prospect of an enemy attack on their home territory.

Although wartime conditions demanded sacrifices from people across the globe, the Japanese faced a significantly more difficult challenge. Despite measures towards rationing and limiting consumer spending, the US and Australian public still enjoyed comfortable living conditions. In both nations, fears of an invasion were at their peak during 1942, when the Imperial forces appeared to reign supreme, but the scare dissipated quickly by the following year, as the Allies started to push their opponents onto the defensive. For the Americans in particular, the war was an event taking place in regions that were far removed from their homeland.[11] While most of Asia had been occupied, and the Japanese ended up facing a blockade along with constant bombing attacks against their main islands, the populace living within the continental United States never had first-hand experience with the death and destruction that the conflict unleashed on their overseas counterparts. In Japan, the war brought about a severe disruption of everyday civilian life. The US navy's blockade of the home islands, which curtailed the flow of imports from abroad, compounded the problems which had been created by the military's requisitioning of goods. By the closing stages of the war, the shortage of basic necessities such as food became acute. Further problems arose after the Americans intensified their bombing attacks against Japanese cities in early 1945, which destroyed a large part of the infrastructure, including workplaces, transportation networks and public utilities. For most of the urban populace, the tribulations of being dislocated from their homes became a norm. Nevertheless, in spite of the mounting hardships, the government managed to avert a public uprising, largely because it effectively used repression and thought control to prevent the people from subverting the war effort.

Because the Western nations, and the United States in particular, were able to fight the war with a surplus economy, the livelihoods of the population remained relatively untouched. On the contrary, World War II produced numerous benefits for the Americans. It helped bring into employment the millions of workers who had been put out of work as a result of the Great Depression. A total of 17 million new jobs were created between 1939–45, almost half of which were in the industrial sector. For most citizens, the war brought secure jobs, a larger income, and economic wealth.[12] The rationing of food and clothing was more of a gesture on the government's behalf, to show the people that the nation was carrying out a campaign that required a substantial commitment of resources. Living conditions actually improved as the conflict progressed. Average family incomes in most major cities, including New York and Los Angeles, rose by 50 percent, while in Washington, DC it more than doubled. Consumer purchases rose by 12 percent.[13] Corporate profits after taxes, which stood at $6.4 billion in 1940, jumped to $10.8 billion by 1944. The automobile industry, whose production of cars had been cut back, in fact prospered. Its plants employed over a million workers, and produced over a billion dollars worth of armaments each month.[14] Aware of the prosperity which had been borne by the war, the government used the trend as an instrument for generating popular support. A propaganda film titled "Is This Worth Fighting For?", depicted the luxuries which Americans were able to enjoy as a result of the economic boom brought about by increased wartime productivity. A column in the Saturday Evening Post once boasted that, whereas the Japanese were enduring deprivations to fight a losing battle, the US was fighting for "a glorious future of mass employment, mass production, and mass distribution and ownership."

Similar developments took place in the other Allied nations. On one hand, Australia's economy was not as productive as its US counterpart. Wartime demands placed a strain on the workforce, since a large portion of the young male population joined the armed services, thus creating a shortage of laborers for the industrial and agricultural sectors. The large influx of American personnel who arrived in Australia after spring 1942 also created problems. Wages for US sailors and soldiers were considerably higher than what the average local earned, and their lavish spending habits drove up the prices of most commodities and services. However, on the whole, Australia's economy did benefit. The output of metals and machines more than doubled, and the war brought about "a large and decisive shift" towards industrialization.[15] In a similar manner to their American counterparts, the civilian population reaped the profits of economic growth, which included greater employment oppor-tunities. As long as casualties were kept to a minimum, public enthusiasm for the war effort was easy to maintain, and never became an immediate problem. Only towards the closing stages, when Germany had been defeated, did Allied political leaders begin to express anxieties about the public dissatisfaction that could arise if the war in the Pacific theater continued without showing any signs of coming to a successful finish.

Wartime conditions also brought about significant social changes. In the US, the need for a larger workforce meant that industries were compelled to draw upon the sectors of which had previously been marginalized in the workplace, including women. By July 1944, the workforce included 19 million females, which was nearly a 50 percent increase from the start of the war. The proportion of American women working away from home jumped from a quarter to over one-third. Most of them were employed either on the factory floor, or in clerical positions in the federal government. Unfortunately, the development did not bring about gender equality. Wages for women remained considerably lower than their male counterparts, and after the demand for war materials declined after hostilities terminated in 1945, the majority were made redundant. Nevertheless, the changes brought about by World War II did, in time, force the American public to "reconsider the roles of both men and women in family, work and national life."[16]

Minority ethnic groups also enjoyed new opportunities. The onset of the conflict saw 700,000 African-Americans migrating from the southern states to cities in the Great Lakes region. The majority resettled in Detroit, to take up jobs at the multitude of factories that had been constructed to produce motor vehicles and aircraft. By the end of the war, the proportion of black Americans in the workforce almost tripled. An equal number served in the armed forces. Again, however, the black community still did not gain equal rights under the law. The right to vote was still denied, and racial discrimination remained rife. Yet, at the same time, the removal of key hurdles, resulting from the entry of African-Americans into the industrial sector and the armed services, was the first step towards the eventual passing of legislation which granted them recognition as full members of society.

In Japan, the main obstacle to maintaining public morale was that the nation had to operate on a shortage economy, and therefore could not provide for the military without making a sizeable demand on the civilian sector. In order to convince the people to endure Spartan conditions, the government waged a campaign to highlight the fact that the nation was fighting a war in which its survival was at stake. Morale was maintained largely through coercion and repression. For example, the Imperial Rule Assistance Association (IRAA) was established as an instrument of social control in October 1940, when Japan was already at war with China. Its administrative work was assisted by neighborhood associations (*tonari-gumi*) that were set up in each individual precinct, whose task was to report on any indications of seditious behavior.[17] When the associations were initially set up, the idea was to prepare the population for a protracted war, by generating a sense of communal spirit. Councils were expected to "organize and unify the people who live in cities, towns and villages" with a view to building neighborhood solidarity, as well as to provide "spiritual and moral training" for local citizens. The system also offered a medium to carry out more practical tasks, such as the rationing of everyday necessities and setting up civil defense measures against air raids. As the war progressed, and Japan's ventures required a greater contribution from the populace, the associations took on the role of acting as a "thought police" force and cracking down on suspected dissidents. However, neither the IRAA nor the *tonari-gumi* succeeded in attracting the mass following which characterized the Fascist parties of Germany and Italy.[18] The press frequently voiced opposition to government policies and criticized the mismanagement of resources, as well as the failure to control inflation.[19] Post-war studies have also shown that the Japanese were susceptible to becoming despondent in the face of deprivations.[20] Nor did the people hold onto their unquestioned belief that their nation could defeat the Allies. The US Strategic Bombing Survey revealed that by 1945, 68 percent of the public believed that Japan had lost the war.[21]

The closing stages of the war brought about a wide range of hardships. The production of consumer goods fell to just 17 percent of the total national income.[22] Food shortages reached serious proportions. A staff report prepared for the top government leadership in August 1944 realistically predicted that with the exception of rice, the supply of all foodstuffs was bound to decline in the following year.[23] Indeed, by 1945, the average daily calorie intake per citizen fell to less than 1,800, which was well under the level required to sustain nutrition. Even in rural areas, where food was produced, rice consumption fell by one-fifth below the previous year.

The Allied bombing raids against urban areas placed an enormous strain on public life, and brought home the magnitude of their Japan's plight. Japanese cities were particularly vulnerable because they were constructed of wood, which meant that incendiary bombs could set fire to entire neighborhoods. To complicate matters, precautionary measures were rudimentary. Bomb shelters could house only a small proportion of the population. The water supply system was inadequate to deal with large scale fires. Citizens often carried out fire drills by forming human chains to pass along buckets of water and pour them manually to put out flames. The most devastating raid was the one against Tokyo on the night of 9–10 March 1945. Sixteen square miles of the city's commercial, industrial and residential sections were reduced to ashes. The conflagrations burned out of control, to the point where the metropolitan fire chief later conceded that his crews could no longer follow any set procedures within 30 minutes after the raid commenced. Most of the deaths were caused by suffocation because the flames ended up consuming all of the available oxygen. In other cases, panicked residents tried to escape the inferno by jumping into swimming pools at local schools or into the canals, only to be scalded to death as temperatures reached horrific levels. Thousands more congregated along the banks of the Sumida River and the spanning bridges to seek refuge from the firestorm. Their fate was sealed when a northerly wind started to blow a wave of gigantic flames downstream, burning everyone who stood in its path. Those who jumped into the river either drowned, or were so badly burnt that they could not swim ashore. On the following morning, the Sumida was described by surviving residents as a sea of charred bodies. At one bridge, the Kototoi-bashi, hundreds of blackened corpses piled on top of each other, showing how the hopes of surviving were slim. In total, over 267,000 buildings were destroyed, with more than a million people made homeless. The official death toll amounted to 83,000, with an additional 40,000 wounded. In most neighbor-hoods, the damage was so extensive that the survivors could not even identify the streets where their homes and businesses once stood. During the following months, similar levels of destruction were inflicted on other major cities, including Osaka, Kobe, Nagoya and Yokohama. Fears over the effects of further raids caused a mass exodus, with city-dwellers migrating to the countryside, where bombing targets were fewer and further between. By summer 1945, the populations of the main urban areas fell to 40 percent of their pre-war figures.[24] Daily routines, such as commuting to work, became virtually impossible with the public transport networks in ruins. Absenteeism sky-rocketed, causing a further decline in factory production.

Public opinion also began to turn against the war effort. The special high police reported to the home ministry that subversive opinions had flourished to an alarming magnitude. Although prohibited during the war, the Japanese had a pastime of reciting seditious poems and riddles while in the company of their family and close friends. Denied the opportunity to express dissent in public, the people found solace at social gatherings, where they engaged in gossip and rumor. The thought police also collected from the walls of public places and private homes a collection of graffiti which suggested, among other actions, "kill the rich. Carry out a red revolution. Stand up, proletariat. Destroy the bourgeoisie. Long reign anarchism. Kill the emperor. Bury the politicians. Unite and overthrow Japanese imperialism."

However, in contrast to its Axis partners, Japan managed to avoid an attempted overthrow of its regime, either by the public or elements within the armed forces and government. Despite arduous efforts by post-war historians to uncover evidence of a Japanese "resistance" movement along the lines of those which operated in Hitler's Germany, extensive research has shown that there were neither underground organizations which actively fought the regime, nor any noteworthy instances of open defiance.[25] The populace had been imbued with the belief that surrender entailed the extinction of their nation, and the indoctrination, in turn precluded a scenario whereby the military dictatorship could be coerced into accepting a premature termination of hostilities. Even after the Allies had established bases in the Marianas and Okinawa, and the home islands were exposed to an invasion, the public held an unfaltering willingness to contribute to the military's efforts to defend their nation. Civilian youth were recruited to take up arms against the invading enemies. After the surrender, one high-ranking army official recalled that the air attacks had "strengthened the people's enmity towards the United States and the will to carry the war through to a successful conclusion."[26] The military police, or *Kempeitai*, also managed to suppress dissent through the wholesale arrest and internment of those who expressed anti-war sentiments, including the Communists, pacifists, and anarchists. Publications which showed even the slightest threat of promoting subversion were censored, or banned, under the peace preservation laws.[27] The Japanese nation's war effort thus remained functional in spite of the growing discontent.[28] Most importantly, the people were accustomed to accepting government policies without raising serious questions. The populace was told that the military dictatorship had earned its right to rule through a mandate passed on from the Emperor's supreme authority, and this feature acted as the key reassurance against any popular efforts to force the government to accept a premature surrender.[29] The successful efforts towards maintaining civilian morale, in turn, was one of the key factors that enabled Japan's leaders to follow through with their venture, in spite of the ever-declining fortunes which the nation suffered. By the same token, when Emperor Hirohito announced the surrender in August 1945, the Japanese proved to be "passive recipients" to the termination of hostilities that their ruling elite had decreed.[30]

WAR AND THE PEOPLES OF JAPANESE-OCCUPIED ASIA

The book has thus far focused on how the war was conducted by the major powers, namely the Western nations and Japan, without paying attention to the experiences of those nations which fell victim to the Japanese occupation. Indeed, a large portion of the literature on the Pacific war has tended to portray the countries of Asia as mere pawns in the wider conflict that was fought out between the Great Powers.[31] For the vast majority of the civilian population in China and Southeast Asia, the war brought economic deprivations and a drastic curtailment of political freedom, rather than the co-prosperity and liberation which the conquerors had claimed to be bringing.

Japanese occupation policies in areas such as Korea, Formosa and China, which had been part of the empire even before the outbreak of the Pacific war, provided the basis for the treatment which was to be dealt to the subject people of the southern regions. In all but a few rare cases, the local populations ended up being exploited to serve the political, economic and strategic needs of their Japanese masters.[32] Korea and Formosa, which were colonized in the early part of the twentieth century, constituted a vital source of food, as well as labor for Japan's growing industries. In both areas, Tokyo never even considered granting autonomy. Minimal efforts were made to create local governments, and virtually all important positions were reserved for Japanese officials. In an effort to assimilate Korea with metropolitan Japan, schools were required to conduct their curriculum in Japanese, with students forced to recite the oath to the Emperor. Similar measures were undertaken in Formosa, where Chinese-language columns were prohibited in local newspapers. Citizens also had to endure disadvantageous living conditions. In Korea, for example, average salaries for locals were less than one-third of what Japanese expatriates earned. Factory workers were forced to live in accommodation that was often unsanitary, and death rates from contagious diseases such as tuberculosis were more than double the figure for their Japanese counterparts.

When the IJA occupied Manchuria, and later on China, during the 1930s, the Japanese again used oppression to secure control over their new subjects. In the puppet state of Manchukuo, the commander of the Kwangtung army held the role of governor-general, with all matters related to domestic law and order placed under Japanese control. The economy was systematically plundered to provide the occupiers with the materials needed to develop their war machine. Factories and mines were administered by Japanese companies, and peasants' lands were seized to create living space for settlers. After 1937, mainland China suffered a similar fate. The Japanese did establish local administrations, such as the reorganized Nationalist government in 1940, headed by Wang-Ching-Wei, but they were merely instruments of the occupying forces. Looting was commonplace, with the violence carried out against the residents of Nanking in December 1938 being one of the most notorious Japanese wartime atrocities.

In planning the occupation of Southeast Asia during the autumn of 1941, the Japanese expressed conflicting goals. On one hand, policymakers did suggest that the aim was to win the support of the local populations by bringing better living conditions and greater political freedoms. At the liaison conference of 20 November 1941, the "Principles for Administration of Southern Areas" was ratified. The document stated, "existing political organizations shall be utilized as much as possible, with due respect for native practices," thereby suggesting that the Japanese intended to show sympathy towards the local populations.[33] However, the overriding priority was to extract the resources which Japan required to prosecute its war effort against the Allies. Under the circumstances, the possibility of having to resort to exploitive actions was acknowledged. Military governments were to be established, and the hierarchical positions of the conquerors were clearly delineated. In short, the natives were to "cooperate in the establishment of the co-prosperity sphere under the leadership of the [Japanese] empire." Any economic hardships imposed upon the natives were to be endured, with pacification measures against the natives undertaken to attain the stated objectives.

Therefore, despite claims that Japan was creating a "co-prosperity sphere" for the Asians, in reality, a system was being established whereby the Japanese manipulated the locals for their own benefit. Decree Number 1, issued by the Sixteenth Army in Java, did proclaim that the Japanese and Javanese were members of one race, and the class divisions which had been imposed by the Dutch colonizers were a thing of the past.[34] At the Greater East Asia Conference of 1943, convened by Prime Minister Tojo, one of the main aims set out was to "abolish the systems of racial discrimination" which the European colonial powers had imposed on their subjects, and to "plan the economic development of Asia."[35] Relations between the nations under Japanese influence were to be based on the ideas of "coexistence and co-prosperity." The idea propagated by the Japanese, of the Asiatic nations joining forces to eradicate Western colonial rule, was indeed embraced by a number of influential leaders, including Sukarno of the East Indies, and Ba Maw of Burma.

However, the fact remains that the Japanese carried out their conquest of Southeast Asia without seriously considering the question of how they were going to set up governments that were amenable to the local population. In most areas, there was a lack of cooperation between the various bureaucratic organizations and the military. Nor did the local authorities maintain an effective dialogue with Tokyo on how to administer the occupied territories and promote independence movements among the populace. Most importantly, extracting the raw materials to support the Japanese war effort became the first and foremost priority. The general concept dictated that Japan assumed leadership in all aspects of life, including the military, political, economic and cultural realms.[36] All members of the so-called "co-prosperity sphere" were to look towards Japan as their sovereign, whose ways were to be imitated.

The policy of exploitation had a number of damaging effects. Because local economies were geared towards producing war-related materials, the output of civilian goods, including food, declined dramatically. Imports from Europe and America, both of which had been valuable trading partners prior to the occupation, were cut off. Further disruption arose after 1944, when the submarine attacks against Japanese shipping routes meant that the conquerors were unable to make use of the raw materials which Southeast Asia had to offer. The livelihood of the populace was adversely affected. The occupying forces introduced their own currency, and troops were issued with paper notes to pay for goods and services. Money was printed with few restrictions placed by the Tokyo government. The result was hyperinflation, and daily necessities became unaffordable. Malnutrition was widespread, as the rations allotted to the natives fell to less than half the amount handed to the Japanese.

The occupation also brought about a drastic curtailment of civil liberties, as the subjugators brutalized their subjects in an effort to secure loyalty. Anyone even suspected of plotting against the Japanese was detained by the *Kempeitai*. In Singapore, 70,000 Chinese residents accused of subversive activities were arrested, with many of them slaughtered in a vengeful massacre. The natives of Southeast Asia who initially saw the Japanese as liberators came to believe that they were even more oppressive than their European predecessors. One Malayan lamented "the pompous English were replaced by the rough, vulgar Japanese." Antisocial behavior was a common occurrence. Japanese soldiers regularly got drunk in public, and carried out random assaults on the locals. In many cases, the populace had fewer political rights than they had under Dutch and British rule. In the East Indies, all group meetings were banned, with a prohibition placed on any speeches, writings and activities that were related to politics. Independence was often granted only in name. For example, the Burmese Nationalist leader, Ba Maw, was treated as a vassal even after he was permitted to declare independence, and had to consult the Japanese when making any type of policy decision. Nor did the Burma National Army ever become an autonomous force. Although the Japanese successfully propagated the idea of seeking liberation from white colonialism, they were unable to convince the Asian people that Japan offered a viable solution. On the contrary, towards the closing stages of the war, opinion started to turn decisively against Japan's influence. In Thailand, the pro-Japanese government of Luang Pibul fell in 1944, when it became clear that the partnership with Tokyo had caused mounting economic hardships. The wartime experiences of the Asian people thus shows that Japan's concept of creating a "co-prosperity sphere," and a harmonious grouping of Asiatic nations, remained at best a distant pipedream, and in the worst of cases, a mere propaganda tool to cover up the true objectives of the military, namely to exploit the conquered regions for its own interests.

CONCLUSION

The civilian populations of the belligerent nations played a key role in the conduct of the Pacific war, and the home front thus constituted a vital theater for all of the countries involved. For both the Allied powers and Japan, generating public enthusiasm for the war effort was crucial. Without popular support, governments could not realistically expect citizens to make a sufficient contribution. Whether the people were being asked to make economic sacrifices and accept lowered living standards as a result of increased military spending, or to tolerate the casualties which the armed forces were incurring on the battlefront, the political leadership needed to offer an acceptable explanation as to why the nation was involved in a war that demanded such a substantial commitment. In this respect, the Japanese faced a more arduous challenge than their Allied counterparts, mainly because the Western powers were able to conduct the war with a surplus economy and thereby circumvent the need to impose burdensome demands on the civilian populace. In the US and Australia, the increased demand for finished goods in wartime brought about better employment opportunities and higher wages for the average citizen, and with it, improved living conditions. Austerity measures were kept to a minimum, and the government's main concern was to avoid a situation where the war became prolonged and the armed forces started to incur an excessive loss of lives.

Japan, by contrast, had to operate with a shortage economy, and the diversion of resources towards the military had some adverse effect on civilian life. After 1943, when the tide of the war turned against the Imperial forces, the government also had to find ways of hiding the nation's declining fortunes from the public. Towards the closing stages, when the home islands were subjected to a devastating blockade and bombing attacks, and food shortages became acute, the morale of the home front faced a most trying test. Yet public discontent never reached the point where the regime faced the danger of being overthrown. The majority of the populace was inclined to support the war effort, in spite of the hardships they had to live with. The phenomenon stemmed largely from the mentality of Japanese people, who held a long-standing tradition of complying with orders from higher authority. The leadership also undertook to educate the people on the reasons why the war was being carried out, and successfully used propaganda to convince them that surrendering to the Allies entailed the complete destruction of the nation. Under the circumstances, opposition to the war effort was unlikely to the type that could compel the government to alter its policies.

For the people of Japanese-occupied Asia, wartime conditions mainly brought economic hardships and political oppression, in spite of boastful claims to the effect that Japan was providing prosperity and a liberation from European colonial rule. Occupation policies in all areas invariably stated that the territories were to be administered with a view to enabling the Japanese acquire the resources needed for their war effort. The subject people were thus treated as servants to their conqueror's cause, rather than equals in a community of Asiatics.

The Pacific war had a profound and far-reaching impact on the civilian populations of the nations involved. In the US, the war offered the long-awaited panacea to the economic downturn of the Great Depression, and reversed the problems arising from widespread unemployment and poverty. The deprivations which the populace suffered in wartime Japan created an aversion to involvement in military conflicts which has lasted to the present day. Finally for the people of occupied Asia, while Japanese rule was frequently characterized by exploitation, the wartime developments did bring a long-term benefit. By expelling the colonial overlords, the Japanese discredited the West's ability to maintain its hold on Asia, and encouraged the growth of independence movements. Indeed, when the European powers attempted to re-establish their rule in Malaya, Indochina and the East Indies after the Japanese surrender, they most often received a cold reception. World War II in Asia was therefore a total conflict, not only in the sense that it involved the participation of the masses. Perhaps of equal importance, it was a defining event for the citizens of the nations who fought it, with the effects of the conflict felt long after it finished.

13

The Endgame, Autumn 1944 to Summer 1945

After mid 1944, when US forces captured the Marianas islands, Japan's war effort began to rapidly deteriorate as the Allies breached the inner perimeter of its empire and established bases within striking distance of the home islands. By the start of 1945, the Philippines were recaptured, and although the southern regions, including Malaya and the East Indies remained under Japanese control, the sea communications were severed. Consequently, the war industries could no longer receive supplies of raw materials from the occupied territories. By spring, the maritime transport links with China were disrupted, and even when traveling within the home islands, merchant ships faced a high risk of being sunk. Further destruction was inflicted when the US Army Air Forces commenced their daily bombing attacks against Japanese cities, which laid waste the majority of the industrial plants and transportation networks. The island of Iwojima was captured in March. In May, Okinawa fell, and Allied forces started to draw up plans to invade the main islands of Kyushu and Honshu. Yet, as late as July 1945, the leadership in Tokyo refused to acknowledge the fact that neither the Imperial navy nor army could defend Japan against the military might which its opponents were bringing to bear, and that defeat was only a matter of time. On the contrary, the government continued with its effort to secure a negotiated peace, while the high command prepared a last-ditch effort to repel an Allied invasion.

ALLIED STRATEGY FOCUSES ON BRINGING THE PACIFIC WAR TO A FINISH

The main aims of Allied strategy, namely to secure the unconditional surrender of Japan and to concentrate on defeating Germany before seeking a victory in the Pacific theater, remained unchanged until the closing stages of the war. However, whereas during the initial phase of their counter-offensive, the US and its coalition partners had been primarily concerned with choosing their route of advance towards Japan's home territories, by 1944, their plans called for specific measures that were geared to destroy the enemy's war machine in the most efficient and expeditious manner. The Allies deployed their forces to achieve three key objectives, the first of which was to dismantle Japan's hold on its conquests. From the political standpoint, the US and Britain wished to avenge the defeats they suffered during the start of the conflict by liberating the territories which the Imperial forces had acquired, including the Philippines, Burma and Malaya. In strategic terms, occupying areas such as China and Southeast Asia enabled the Allies to establish bases that could be used for an assault on mainland Japan. The second, and more significant, component of Allied strategy was to destroy the Japanese war economy by a combination of blockade and bombardment. By early 1945, the submarine campaign was extended to the home waters, and US aircraft began mining the main shipping routes, including the Inland Sea. As a result, maritime traffic came to a virtual standstill. The economic infrastructure suffered a further blow when the Americans intensified their aerial bombing attacks, and destroyed the majority of industrial plants. Third, and most importantly, Allied defense officials realized that in order to defeat Japan, their armed forces had to physically occupy its home territory, and for this reason, they started to assemble plans for an invasion of the southern island of Kyushu, to be followed by a final assault on the Tokyo region, which was the political and economic heart of the Japanese nation.

For the US and Britain alike, their conduct of the Pacific war was to a certain extent shaped by a desire to reconquer the colonies they had lost to the Japanese earlier in the conflict, and thereby rebuild their prestige and credibility among the people of Asia. General MacArthur's plan for liberating the Philippines was among the key manifestations of this sentimentality. By May 1944, US forces, with the help of the Australians, had completed their conquest of New Guinea, and the Philippines were exposed to an invasion. The JCS had already ordered MacArthur to prepare for an operation against the southern island of Mindanao, and on 15 June, the general called for an invasion to take place in October, followed by a landing at Leyte. Yet the commander of the Allied forces in the southwest Pacific continued to face an oftentimes insurmountable dispute with his counterpart in the central Pacific, Admiral Nimitz, along with the defense chiefs back in Washington.[1] Both parties insisted that the main effort be concentrated on Formosa, which, owing to its geographic proximity to Japan, provided a favorable base for launching an attack on the home islands. The island also commanded the sea communications to Southeast Asia, and its capture was most likely to facilitate the navy's effort to strangulate the trade route. However, MacArthur pushed for his plan to liberate the Philippines archipelago, including the main island of Luzon. The strategy was largely borne from his personal desire to vindicate the humiliation which the Japanese inflicted when they ejected his forces from the archipelago in early 1942. The general vowed to uphold the statement he made to the Filipino people just before he escaped to Australia, namely, "I shall return!"

The JCS eventually decided to approve an invasion of the Philippines, largely as a result of heavy politicking by MacArthur. Nevertheless, strategic considerations also played an important role. Defense planners realized that US forces did not have sufficient strength to conquer a large and well-defended island such as Formosa. In July 1944, the joint chiefs formally rejected MacArthur's plan, on the grounds that it would delay the invasion of Formosa. Instead, the Americans were to capture the islands of Leyte and Mindanao in order to protect the southern flank of the Allied thrust into the western Pacific. The general agreed with the plan, since it allowed him to at least secure a foothold in the Philippines and prepare the ground for a possible invasion of Luzon. The Leyte operation was scheduled to take place by the end of the year, and the Pacific Fleet was to cooperate by invading the island of Palau, which lay roughly halfway between the Marianas and Philippines. The aim was to provide a fleet base as well as land-based air cover for the Leyte invasion force.

However, events in Europe had a far-reaching effect on the Formosa operation. By September, the failure of Operation *Market Garden* in Arnhem meant that the Allies could not hope to defeat Germany by the start of 1945, and the hold-up precluded any large diversion of troops to the Pacific. Defense officials in Washington also discovered that an invasion of Formosa required considerably more manpower than they had estimated. The island had been occupied by the Japanese since 1895, and its defenses were thus far more developed than any area which the Allies had conquered so far. Nimitz calculated that up to 200,000 troops were needed, and in order to build up such strengths, the Americans needed to wait until the fighting in Europe was finished. In October, the JCS, including Admiral King, conceded that the Formosa operation was impracticable, and decided that, following Leyte, Luzon was the next objective.

The continued efforts which the Americans made to help Nationalist China expel the Japanese invaders were a further example of how their strategy was geared to secure bases within closer proximity to the enemy's homeland, while at the same time seeking to win the goodwill of potential allies in the region. In autumn 1944, Albert Wedemeyer, a protégé of George Marshall, was placed in command of the China theater. Lend-Lease supplies flowed in increased quantities via the air route over the Himalayas, also known as the Hump. However, the channel could handle only a limited amount of traffic, and an overland passage did not become available until the Ledo road via Burma was opened in January 1945. Wedemeyer had hoped that with more equipment, the Chinese army could join forces with the Americans in liberating

Japanese-occupied territory. Allied forces were to land on the east coast of China, and form a link with Chiang Kai Shek's Nationalists. The plan faltered, once again, owing to delays that arose in the European theater, which hindered the provision of the necessary troops. US commanders therefore could only partially fulfill their the aim of using China as a base for operations against Japan, and the theater ended up being of secondary importance in relation to the Pacific.

Meanwhile, in Southeast Asia, the British and Australian forces went ahead with their plans to liberate Japan's territories. In Burma, the tide of the campaign turned decisively in favor of General Slim's Fourteenth Army after the Japanese launched their failed attacks on Imphal and Kohima in spring 1944. General Mutaguchi decided to withdraw his forces to the central plains after they suffered extensive casualties and depleted their supplies. The British-Indian army, on the other hand, had developed the strength and logistical capacity to conduct an offensive against the Irrawaddy valley (code-named *Capital*), with a diversionary pincer movement along the Arakan coast (code-named *Romulus*). When the monsoon season lifted in September, the British were poised to advance into the central plains. In March 1945, the Imperial army's stronghold at Mandalay was captured, and the capital city of Rangoon was retaken in May. The Japanese, with their lines of communication broken and their divisions scattered in small parties, could only put up sporadic pockets of resistance. As British forces established themselves in Burma, they prepared to reconquer areas further afield, including Malaya. Operation *Zipper*, which called for an amphibious landing in the Malacca Straits, followed by an advance towards Singapore, was planned for August 1945. Fortunately, Japan surrendered just a few days prior to the scheduled launching of the operation, and Malaya ended up being liberated without any opposition. The island of Borneo, which was an important source of oil, also became an Allied objective. In May, the Australian 7th Division, joined by a contingent of Dutch troops, landed at Tarakan, off the northeast coast of the island, after US naval and air forces conducted an extensive preliminary bombardment attack to clear the ground. On the following month, Australian troops captured Brunei, and on 1 July, they took the oilfields of Balikpapan on the east coast. The landings were carried out at a time when Japan's maritime supply lines from the southern regions had been severed, and the capture of Borneo did not bring any significant strategic benefits for the Allies. Nevertheless, the operations did serve a political purpose, in that they enabled British Commonwealth and Dutch forces to reconquer their own colonial possessions.

While Japan's hold on its conquered territories was dismantled, the Allies started to turn their attention towards undertaking an intensified blockade and bombing campaign against the enemy's mainland, with a view to crippling its war economy. The submarine attacks against Japan's shipping routes continued, and by 1944, the total size of the merchant fleet had been reduced to 2.5 million tons. During the following year, the tonnage dropped even further to a mere 1.2 million, which amounted to less than one-fifth of the tonnage available at the commencement of the war. The US navy managed to strangle the flow of oil from the East Indies. Equally destructive was the mining of the home waters. In October 1944, Hap Arnold authorized B-29 squadrons to attack key shipping routes in and around Japan proper.[2] The 313th Wing was tasked with the operation, and in January 1945, Major-General Curtis LeMay, commanding the Twenty-First Bomber Command, ordered a four-stage program that was to begin with a partial blockade, and gradually grow into a complete stoppage of sea traffic to and from the Japanese mainland. By March, two-thirds of the regular convoy routes became unusable. Even the shorter-haul trade routes to China and Manchuria via the Shimonoseki straits became difficult to navigate. Finally, in June, all ports facing the Pacific had to close down for the remainder of the war, and the movement of merchant vessels around the coastal areas and the main shipping routes, including the Inland Sea, fell to less than 10 percent of where it stood a few months previously.

Attacks on Japan's economic infrastructure were also extended beyond maritime commerce, and industrial plants became a prime target. In April 1944, the JCS approved Operation *Matterhorn*, which called for the China-based B-29 Superfortresses, operating under the Fifty-Eighth bomber wing, to raid the home islands. The first mission took place in June, against the Yawata steel works on the southern island of Kyushu, followed by a series of raids launched during the summer and autumn. However, on most missions, the number of aircraft deployed was too small to cause significant damage. The problem continued to stem from logistics, and the formidable obstacles involved in airlifting fuel, ammunition and spare parts across the Hump.[3] As late as November, the Americans could fly no more than three missions per month. When it became clear that China did not provide an adequate base for large squadrons of B-29s, Hap Arnold scrapped *Matterhorn*, and decided to shift the weight of the campaign to the Twenty-First Bomber Command, based in the Marianas islands of Saipan, Tinian and Guam.

Defense planners were also aware that the blockade and bombardment were unlikely to be sufficient to compel Japan to surrender, and that an invasion of the home islands might become necessary. Measures were therefore taken to secure islands that provided suitable bases. Within the JCS, Admiral King persisted with his proposal that Formosa needed to be captured as a staging post, and in October 1944, he met with representatives from the Central Pacific Command in order to sell his plan. However, Nimitz rejected the idea, on the grounds that the US and its coalition partners had yet to divert sufficient strength to the Pacific. For this reason, any effort to take an island as large as Formosa was considered likely to end in failure. The admiral suggested that smaller islands such as Iwojima and Okinawa offered a viable alternative, since they were not only easier to conquer, but also located closer to Japan. When King returned to Washington, the JCS endorsed the plan, and ordered preparations to execute the invasions of Iwojima and Okinawa during the following spring.

JAPAN'S OPTIONS

By 1944, Japan's options were limited to either surrendering or reinforcing its outlying garrisons for a last-ditch effort to forestall the Allied counter-offensive. The idea of ceasing hostilities remained an anathema for the leadership. After Tojo resigned his post as prime minister following the fall of the Marianas, the successor government vowed to continue prosecuting the war effort. Although the high command acknowledged that the conquered territories were untenable, it adhered to the belief that carrying on with the conflict was worthwhile, as long as the Imperial navy and army remained operational. The Japanese understood that no single defeat could destroy the enemy's capacity to advance towards the home islands. Instead, the aim was to inflict the maximum level of casualties on the Allies in each operation that they executed, in the hope that the armed forces could wear out the Americans and their coalition partners.

The final stages of the conflict saw the Japanese developing several new courses of action in an effort to mete out attrition on their opponents. The first of these was the *Sho* (victory) operations. In July 1944, IGHQ ordered the Combined Fleet to prepare for an all-out strike against the US navy as it approached the western Pacific.[4] The location of the decisive engagement hinged entirely on where the enemy armada appeared. The first variation, *Sho-1*, envisaged the battle taking place in the Philippines, while the second and third variations called for the Japanese to forestall an invasion of Okinawa, and the home islands, respectively. The *Sho* plan in fact formed the blueprint for the IJN's attempt to halt the US amphibious landing at Leyte in October 1944, which ended with the sinking of a large portion of Japan's remaining capital ships and aircraft carriers.

Japan's forces also started to resort to suicide tactics. The first *kamikaze* air units were deployed at the Battle of Leyte Gulf, and by the time of the Okinawa operation, the Japanese had recruited hundreds of volunteers to carry out crash dives against Allied warships. On one hand, *kamikaze* attacks entailed a reckless expenditure of dwindling resources, and they were largely a product of the naval command's desperate effort to change the course of the conflict when

Japan's defeat was only a matter of time.[5] The 201st Air Corps of the First Air Fleet was assigned to execute the operation to defend Leyte, and staff officers were told, "the situation is so grave that the fate of the empire depends" on the outcome of the operation. Commanders judged that, given their shortage of aircraft, conventional methods were unlikely to achieve results. Yet suicide dives often missed their targets, and could not sink a large proportion of enemy vessels. Moreover, the initial sorties were often flown by experienced pilots, since novice airmen were considered incapable of striking ships in the open sea. The result was a further diminution of what little remained in Japan's pool of qualified aviators. As the navy air arm's supply of planes and crews began to dwindle, it had to enlist the help of army aviators, as well as volunteers, neither of whom had the skill to carry out accurate attacks. Towards the end of the Okinawa operation, Japanese forces were running so short of fuel, aircraft and pilots that IGHQ ordered the majority of suicide planes to be withdrawn to the home islands and held in readiness to meet the expected invasion.[6]

However, in terms of their ability to harm task forces in the short term, *kamikaze* attacks provided a relatively economical weapon, since pilots could achieve a higher ratio of hits than in conventional raids. Tactics were also planned in detail, with approaches made either at extremely high or low altitudes, in order to evade radar detection. Against carriers, the best points of aim were the deck elevators, since their destruction ensured that the vessel would be disabled from launching its aircraft. The training of *kamikaze* units was also relatively easy. Japanese military traditions demanded a constant show of valor, and volunteers signed up in large numbers. Many of the personnel in the special attack forces (*tokkotai*) stoically accepted suicide, owing to deep-seated sentiments of patriotism. The primary motivation was to die in what was viewed as the most glorious act of sacrifice. Nevertheless, most pilots claimed to be driven by more practical concerns, and the belief that one needed to forego his own life in order to safeguard his nation.[7]

The final move which the Japanese high command undertook to prepare for the endgame was to commence preparations to counter an Allied invasion of the home islands. As early as July 1944, orders were issued to each military district, with a view to strengthening their defensive posture.[8] During spring 1945, when an enemy landing appeared imminent, measures were undertaken to consolidate the homeland defense forces. Each of the major cities was placed under a special commander, whose job was to mobilize the population for a last-ditch struggle. Elite divisions were also activated, along with a number of tank brigades. The idea was to interdict the invasion force while it was at sea, and to annihilate the remainder once the Allies started disembarking on the beaches. *Kamikaze* squadrons were to be launched against troop convoys and warships. On land, the army was to reinforce the coastal defenses in areas where the enemy was expected to land. IGHQ predicted that Kyushu would be initially captured as a staging area, after which the Americans were most likely to head for the Kanto region. The overriding idea was to inflict casualties that were so high as to compel the Allies to abandon their attempt to occupy the home islands, and instead seek an end to the war by offering Japan a negotiated peace.

In addition to military measures, the Japanese sought diplomatic means to secure a favorable end to the conflict. During the early part of 1945, the *Gaimusho* ordered its ambassador in Moscow to obtain a promise from the Soviet Union to adhere to the 1941 neutrality pact. The aim was to persuade the USSR to side with Japan in brokering a peace settlement with the Western Allies. Although the Kremlin announced in May its intention to abrogate the neutrality pact within a year, and Ambassador Kato received a cold shoulder on every occasion that he approached the Soviets, the Japanese continued to seek a deal until the closing stages of the conflict.

IMPLEMENTATION OF ALLIED STRATEGY, OCTOBER 1944 TO JUNE 1945

The period following autumn 1944 saw the US-led coalition implementing its strategy to isolate Japan from its conquered territories, and thereafter establish bases within striking range of the home islands. As was the case throughout the course of the conflict, the Allied victories stemmed largely from their ability to deploy an overwhelmingly superior number of ships, aircraft and weapons against their Japanese opponents. The numerical gap, which was already considerable at the early stages of the conflict, was growing ever wider as the Pacific counter-offensive approached the nerve center of Japan's empire. At the same time, good planning and the efficient use of resources played an important role in determining the outcome of many of the key battles. The armed forces of the US and its partners continued to modify their strategy with a view to avoiding unnecessary delays and casualties. At the battlefield level, commanders adjusted their tactics in accordance with the challenges posed by the enemy, and used the lessons learned from their encounters with the Japanese to develop better ways of deploying their equipment.

The first step towards dismantling Japan's inner empire was to liberate the Philippines. As a preparatory move, the Americans captured the Palau islands, in order to bring land-based planes within range of their main target, thereby enabling the invasion force to be provided with regular air cover. The island of Peleliu, with its airfield was the main target. The First Marine Division, under Major-General William Rupertus, had little information on the island's fortifications and terrain features, aside from a few aerial photos. The Japanese had constructed an elaborate system of cave defenses, and the preliminary bombardment caused little damage. The bloodiest fighting took place after the marines secured the airfield and moved into the interior, where they had to clear the defending troops from each individual cave. Artillery and air support were of little use, since they could not score direct hits. In order to blast the Japanese out of their positions, the marines had to use flame throwers, demolition charges and grenades. In the end, the operation cost the US marines over 1,000 killed and another 5,000 wounded.

With Peleliu captured, the Americans moved to their objective at Leyte. The preliminary air raids on the Philippines destroyed a large portion of Japan's air strength. Emboldened by reports received from aerial reconnaissance teams, to the effect that the Japanese did not have sufficient aircraft to put up large-scale opposition, Admiral Halsey decided to push the date of the landings forward from December to October 1944.[9] The admiral was in charge of the Third and Fifth fleets, comprising a total of 300 vessels which were centered on over half-a-dozen fleet carriers. The armada was backed by a logistical force that included oilers, as well as ships transporting ammunition and aviation fuel. Escort carriers were used to bring in replacement aircraft. The ground forces, under the command of General MacArthur, numbered over 160,000 troops. The Sixth Army, under General Walter Krueger, was to land on the east coast of Leyte, while the Third Fleet, along with the Seventh Fleet, commanded by Admiral Thomas Kinkaid, provided naval and air support.

Meanwhile, the Fifth Fleet was to patrol the surrounding areas and intercept any Japanese task force that attempted to interfere with the operation. The landings took place on 24 October without facing any substantial resistance. The main battle took place between the navies. Admiral Toyoda, commander of the Combined Fleet, believed that the opportunity for a decisive fleet engagement was to be sought in the Philippines. For the navy, the archipelago had to be defended at all costs, since its loss entailed the severance of the sea communications with Southeast Asia. The battle plan was to allow the fleet to optimize is single-remaining asset, namely the firepower of its battle-ships and heavy cruisers. When the navy high command learned that the US task force was heading towards Leyte, the carriers *Zuikaku*, *Chitose*, *Chiyoda* and *Zuiho* were sent southward from the home islands to draw Halsey's fleet away from the invasion area. Meanwhile, a second strike force, composed of surface vessels, sailed from Brunei to rendezvous with the carriers. The decision to seek a main fleet engagement was also based on a miscalculation regarding the size of the US armada. Earlier in the same month, Halsey's carriers had raided Formosa in order to destroy enemy aircraft and prevent them from being used to reinforce the Philippines. The Japanese counter-attacked, and estimated that they had sunk a large portion of the American fleet. Vice-Admiral Kurita's task force thus entered the Battle of Leyte Gulf without a clear idea of its opponent's strength.

On the Allied side, intelligence on the location and composition of the Combined Fleet was equally unclear. American code-breakers monitored the IJN's communications, but could only ascertain that most of the enemy's heavy ships were in the Singapore area. Neither Halsey nor Kinkaid expected the Japanese to make a fight for Leyte. Seventh Fleet headquarters concluded that the major elements of the fleet would not be deployed, and that the opposition would be limited to an assortment of cruisers, destroyers and submarines.[10] Only on 18 October, less than a week prior to the scheduled landing, did radio intelligence disclose that Kurita had sailed from Singapore, with a task force composed of several heavy battleships.[11] Even then, Halsey remained unsure as to where the Japanese carriers were sailing, and the only way to secure accurate information was to thoroughly reconnoiter the surrounding waters. When the admiral received word that Japanese carriers were approaching his northern flank, he decided to divert his ships to interdict the enemy fleet and in doing so, he left the landing area unguarded against Kurita's surface vessels. Halsey judged that a pre-emptive strike was necessary to prevent the carrier-based aircraft from shuttle-bombing the amphibious force.[12] The admiral also wanted to avoid the criticisms that had been leveled against Spruance following the Marianas encounter, for allowing the enemy carriers to escape. During the ensuing battle the Japanese lost the bulk of their fleet, including the carriers, along with three battleships, including the *Musashi*. The remaining vessels were compelled to withdraw in the face of the US navy's overwhelming fire power. Following its defeat at Leyte, the IJN was to never again to take the initiative.

Meanwhile, on land, despite the ease with which the landings took place, MacArthur's forces had to contend with difficult opposition when his troops moved to the interior. At the Ormoc Valley, the Japanese built defenses at such high altitudes on the ridges that artillery and mortar fire could not reach them.[13] Machine gun posts were also well-camouflaged, and troops had to "approach within spitting distance" before they could locate the weapons.[14] The performance of US forces also continued to show room for improvement. Advancing units frequently fell back and called for supporting fire if they met anything more than minor resistance. General Krueger insisted that infantry units needed to fight more aggressively, and be prepared to close in immediately after artillery fire had ceased.

American naval and ground forces alike also had to contend with heavy air raids. Japanese aircraft strengths in the Philippines had been underestimated, and most US commanders, including George Kenney, who served as MacArthur's chief of air staff, concluded that the enemy could not put up a substantial defense of the archipelago. However, the Imperial forces brought in a large reserve of planes from areas such as Formosa and mainland China, and US reconnaissance crews had not detected the buildup. The scale of opposition which the Japanese were able to put up did not become clear until the invasion of Leyte commenced, and even after the island was secured, air attacks complicated MacArthur's effort to break out of his foothold. Kenney conceded that he did not have sufficient planes to achieve control over the areas where the Americans were operating, and he started to raise questions about whether the advance towards Luzon could be carried out successfully. Enemy forces appeared to have sufficient aircraft to stop an expedition against most areas, including the Lingayen Gulf, which offered the easiest route of access to the capital city of Manila. US forces thus had to adjust their operational plans in accordance with unexpected circumstances. The island of Leyte did not provide the airfields which MacArthur had hoped to secure in order to cover his ground forces, and constructing new bases required more engineers and equipment than anticipated. The nearby island of Mindoro offered the only suitable site. The landing on Mindoro took place in December, and despite the air attacks which the amphibious forces encountered, the general ordered that the push towards Manila be carried out according to schedule. Finally, on 8 January, the Americans established a beachhead at Lingayen Gulf.

The Pacific Fleet faced similar troubles. On 30 October, *kamikaze* raids struck three US aircraft carriers, causing damage so severe that they had to withdraw temporarily for repairs. Despite the navy's arduous efforts to perfect its fighter direction systems, the available radar equipment proved inadequate for tracking the swift and evasive approaches which the Japanese carried out. As a result, fighter squadrons could not be positioned to conduct timely interceptions. In order to provide a more effective defense, task force commanders ordered fighter squadrons to patrol at greater distances away from the main vessels, so that incoming planes could be shot down at an early stage. Japanese airfields were also subjected to constant bombing and strafing attacks by carrier-based planes, so that *kamikaze* squadrons could be prevented from getting airborne. Modifications in enemy tactics compelled the Americans to devise new countermeasures until the closing stages of the conflict.

Back on land, MacArthur's troops broke out of their beachhead at Lingayen, and the Japanese had drawn up a plan to inflict as many casualties as possible by building strongpoints at key areas, including Manila. The battle for the capital turned into a bloody street-by-street struggle. Thousands of civilians were killed before the city was liberated, and Manila ended up suffering more destruction than any Allied city in World War II. The island of Corregidor, which commanded the entrance to the harbor, was recaptured after bitter fighting in the caves. Yamashita's forces on Luzon withdrew to the surrounding mountains, and the subsequent months were spent routing out the remnants of opposition, which often proved difficult to break. In the Baguio region, for example, the defenders established a system of mutually supporting machine gun emplacements to "control every twist" on the trail and "every fold in the ground."[15] US infantry units often cleared enemy troops from one side of a ridge, only to find them relocated to the other side. With a relatively small force, the Japanese were able fight a drawn-out battle.

While the navy and army were busy reconquering the Philippines, the USAAF commenced its strategic bombing campaign against the home islands. The first raid by the Twenty-First Bomber Command, based in the Marianas, was launched in November, against aircraft-assembly plants that were located in the outskirts of Tokyo. However, most of the attacks continued to cause little damage, since bombardiers had yet to overcome the difficulties of locating targets from high altitudes. The layout of Japan's industrial infrastructure was a key obstacle. Unlike in Germany, where production plants were concentrated in certain sections of the cities, the Japanese tended to disperse their facilities, with numerous subcontractors building the various components. Factories and workshops tended to be spread out, and a large area had to be destroyed in order to have a significant effect on overall output. Meteorological factors also hindered the USAAF's operations. The high winds created by the jet stream meant that bombs frequently missed their target. Enemy opposition caused further problems. B-29 pilots had to take a circuitous route, owing to the fighter defenses which the Japanese put up from their base at Iwojima, which commanded the air route from the Marianas to the home islands. The presence of a radar station on Iwojima also enabled the Japanese to receive advanced warnings, and send up their interceptors. By the time the bombers reached Japan, they were often running low on fuel, and had to contend with enemy fighters. Unable to spend an extended length of time in search of targets, the crews ended up dropping their ordnance randomly.

The situation improved dramatically after December 1944, when Hap Arnold relieved Haywood Hansell from the Twenty-First Bomber Command, and replaced him with Major-General Curtis LeMay, who vowed to solve the problems facing US bomber squadrons. The interference caused by Japanese fighters based at Iwojima was eliminated in March, when US marines occupied the island. LeMay addressed the problems involved in hitting targets by ordering attacks to be carried out at lower altitudes, and using incendiary bombs.[16] The tactic proved highly effective, since Japan's cities consisted largely of wooden structures. Fire-bombing could set off large conflagrations which eventually engulfed and destroyed the industrial plants and other centers of war production. The first incendiary bombing attack took place on 4 February, against the port city of Kobe. The results were encouraging, with 5 of the 12 principal factories, along with one of the largest shipyards in Japan, suffering serious damage.

Under Hap Arnold's directive, incendiary attacks against the main cities were given second priority after aircraft-engine factories.[17] The most devastating raid took place on the night of 9 March, against Tokyo. LeMay ordered the B-29s to attack at altitudes between 5,000 and 8,000 feet, so that the crews could achieve accurate hits. To maximize the damage, incendiaries were dropped over an area covering 16 square miles of the industrial, commercial and residential sections of the city, which were estimated to be among the most densely populated urban districts in the world. Buildings covered up to 50 percent of the surface area, in comparison to 10 percent in the average American city, thus creating ideal conditions for creating uncontrollable fires. When the bombers reached mainland Japan, weather conditions were clear, and almost 90 percent of the planes located their targets. Over 1,600 tons of bombs were dropped within 3 hours. Aircrews recalled the inferno lighting up the night sky to a bright shade of orange. Some claimed that on the return journey, they could clearly see the blaze from 100 miles away. Subsequent raids on Osaka, Yokohama, Nagoya and Kobe set up to 70 percent of all buildings ablaze.

Only Hiroshima, Nagasaki and Kyoto remained unscathed. Overall, the bombing attacks achieved notable results, in that they inflicted mass destruction on Japanese cities and civilians, with minimal casualties for the USAAF. At the same time, the effect on industrial production was questionable, since most factories had been made idle by the lack of raw materials.[18] Nevertheless, the raids did have an important psychological effect. Even though the Japanese leadership was not compelled to surrender, the bombing campaign did demonstrate how the nation could not hold out against the Americans.

US forces also commenced their preparations for invading the home islands. In order to provide the Allies with bases that were within closer range, as well as to deny the Japanese any staging posts from which they could interfere with the attacking forces, Iwojima and Okinawa were captured during spring 1945. The battles for both islands turned into some of the most brutal encounters of the Pacific war. The defense of Iwojima was entrusted to General Kurabayashi Tadamichi. His force was 21,000 strong, and included a crack infantry regiment. The general abandoned the original defense plan which called for engaging the invaders at the beaches, and he ordered his troops to prepare for a prolonged fight in the island's interior. The defenders constructed an elaborate system of caves, tunnels and underground bunkers. Kurabayashi's forces also made good use of the volcanic ash on Iwojima. When mixed with cement, the material could be converted into an almost unbreakable form of concrete. Over 300 artillery pieces, dozens of mortars and naval guns, along with large-caliber anti-aircraft guns were placed in reinforced blockhouses. Aircraft, submarines and high-speed motorboats were to wear out the amphibious forces prior to landing.

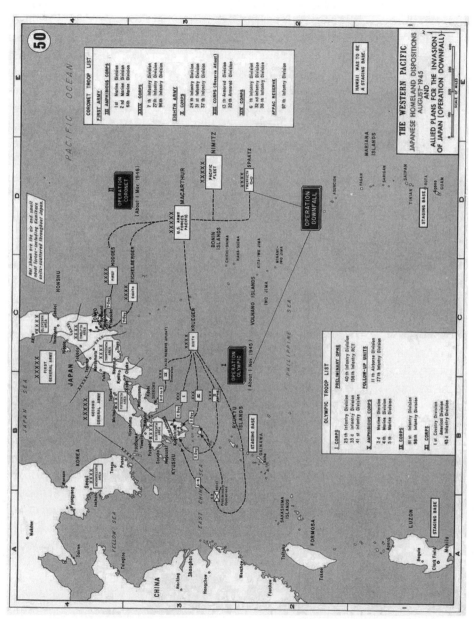

Map 5: Allied Plans for the Invasion of Japan's Home Islands, 1945

When the marines landed on Iwojima in February 1945, they did not know the full extent of the defensive effort, but they had enough information to make the commanders feel uneasy.

The Third, Fourth and Fifth Marine Divisions were organized into a single amphibious corps, under the command of Major-General Harry Schmidt. In spite of the heavy preliminary bombardment, the navy's ship-launched shells simply could not penetrate the complex of caves and tunnels which the Japanese had prepared. Their troops remained unscathed, and managed to put up fierce resistance. When the marines landed, they found that enemy defenses were hidden behind a shield of volcanic rock. By the afternoon, the entire beachhead was being bombarded by artillery fire. The advance was further complicated by the ash, which hampered the movement of vehicles. As a result, the marines had to advance to the interior by foot, without relying on tank cover. Indeed, when the marines captured Mt. Suribachi, it was a moment that was to be immortalized by the Pulitzer prize-winning photo. US forces had incurred nearly 7,000 killed and close to 20,000 wounded.

At Okinawa, the carnage began even before the Tenth Army landed. The amphibious force was supported by a fleet of more than 40 carriers, 18 battleships and 200 destroyers. Kamikaze planes launched an all-out attack against the task force, despite the months of preliminary bombardment missions. In anticipation of intensified Japanese resistance, task force commanders ordered a series of sustained air raids against all enemy airfields within striking distance of Okinawa, including those in Formosa and Kyushu. The USAAF diverted some of the B-29s that had been used for strategic bombing attacks against Japan's cities for missions against airdromes where the Japanese were known to have assembled a large proportion of their suicide squadrons. Unfortunately, the preemptive strikes did not completely destroy Japanese air power, and kamikaze squadrons appeared in record numbers when the Allies commenced their attack on Okinawa. The US navy continued to face difficulties in defending its vessels. The Japanese proved adept at avoiding detection, by flying at low altitudes where radar was unable to track their movements. To remedy the situation, destroyer units were placed at the outer perimeter of the task force to provide an early warning system. Personnel were ordered to keep a constant lookout by relying on their own vision, rather than on search devices. Fighter squadrons were also placed at various sectors and altitudes, so that they could provide an all-round defense of the carriers and battleships. Nevertheless, the kamikaze units managed to inflict a level of casualties which alarmed most US commanders. In total, 64 ships from the Fifth Fleet were sunk during the campaign, with scores more damaged. Close to 5,000 sailors were killed.

The land battle was equally ferocious. The invasion was launched on 1 April by a force consisting of more than 180,000. The First Marine Division, along with soldiers from the Tenth Army, established a beachhead on the southwest coast of the island. On the Japanese side, the defense of Okinawa was entrusted to Lieutenant-General Ushijima's Thirty-Second Army, comprising two infantry divisions drawn from China and Manchuria, as well as an armored regiment. The plan was to set up a system of defenses in the interior, and draw the Americans into the central hills to fight a prolonged battle of mutual annihilation. Ushijima concentrated his effort in the Shuri sector, a mountainous area in the center of the island, where he constructed a series of concentric positions with caves, emplacements, blockhouses and pillboxes built into the hills, all connected by an elaborate labyrinth of underground tunnels. Cave entrances were covered by machine gun and mortar fire, with weapons sited to provide mutual support. US troops landed almost unopposed, but most commanders sensed that the situation could not last. Indeed, within a week, when the army reached the outermost ring in Ushijima's defenses, the Japanese launched a massive counter-attack. US forces had to conduct a slow and painstaking advance, by using a combination of artillery and air bombardment to force the defenders to retire to the inner recesses of their caves.[19] When the bombardment was lifted, infantry units advanced within close range of the defenses, and used a combination of hand grenades and flamethrowers to keep the Japanese back in the tunnels. In the final phase, the entrances to each position were systematically sealed, with the occupants left to suffocate. It was not until 21 June that the Americans managed to crush all pockets of organized resistance; 7,000 US soldiers and marines had lost their lives, and another 70,000 Japanese, along with 80,000 native Okinawans, were killed in the fighting.

Experiences at Okinawa compelled US strategists to reconsider whether their forces were prepared for an invasion of Japan's home islands, where enemy opposition was likely to be far stronger than what the Allies had encountered in any of their previous engagements. Operation *Downfall* called for a two-stage assault, the first of which was to occupy the southernmost island of Kyushu (code-named *Olympic*), with the aim of further tightening the blockade, and exposing the main island of Honshu to an intensified bombing campaign.

In the second, and final phase (code-named *Coronet*), Allied forces were to land in the Kanto region, and advance towards Tokyo, thereby emasculating the economic and political nerve center of the Japanese empire. Estimated casualties ran into the hundreds of thousands, with the Japanese incurring up to 20 million dead, including civilians.

The question arises as to what kept Japan's war effort afloat, even when their home territory were exposed to a full scale Allied invasion that was bound to result in nothing but widespread carnage. The main factor was the prevailing belief, both within the government and the military high command, that surrendering entailed the total destruction of the nation's sovereignty. This was a fate which no Japanese leader could accept. Furthermore, the armed forces remained operational, and had the capacity to resist an enemy landing in the home islands. The Imperial army possessed substantial divisions, including some armored ones, while the air services had a reserve of over 4,000 kamikaze planes. Although the industries could not produce armaments, there were still stockpiles hidden away in supply centers away from the main cities. As long as Japan possessed active forces, its leaders believed that the nation could repel an invasion of the home islands, and under the circumstances, a decision to surrender was unlikely to emerge. Indeed, the atomic bomb played an important role in convincing the ruling elite that Japan could not defeat the forces ranged against it.

CONCLUSION

The manner in which the Allied powers and the Japanese carried out their military operations during the final stages of the Pacific war, and the outcome of the key engagements, highlighted a number of key features that had characterized the conflict from the very beginning. Firstly, effective planning was often equally important as material superiority in enabling the Americans and their coalition powers to succeed. As late as the Battle of Leyte Gulf, combat experience showed that the Allied forces had to devise their strategies in accordance with the changing circumstances, with tactics adjusted to counter the particular challenges which the Japanese were able to put up. Secondly, and perhaps more importantly, the capacity of the Imperial Japanese forces to fight prolonged battles of attrition, and their tendency to fight to the last man, could not alter the fact that they were destined to lose the war, but nevertheless, such practices did go a long way in prolonging the conflict. The casualties which US forces suffered in their attempts to capture the islands of Iwojima and Okinawa raise the question as to whether an invasion of the home islands could ever have succeeded, and whether the Americans would have been willing to continue fighting, even after they had incurred the high level of casualties that had been anticipated. The answers to these profound questions will never been known. As the final chapter will demonstrate, the dropping of the atomic bombs on Hiroshima and Nagasaki in August 1945, which was promptly followed by Japan's surrender to the Allied powers, negated the need for an invasion of the home islands.

14

The Atomic Bomb and the End of the Pacific war

On 26 July 1945, the Allied leaders, who had gathered for a summit meeting at Potsdam, issued their final ultimatum to Japan, which called for the government to surrender unconditionally without delay, or face the prompt and complete destruction of the nation. The Japanese leadership, upon receiving the communiqué, decided to ignore the demands, and the administration of US President Harry Truman took the failure to respond as a rejection. In a move to fulfill the promises of the Potsdam proclamation, on the morning of 6 August, the B-29 bomber *Enola Gay*, piloted by Colonel Paul Tibbets, took off from the island of Tinian in the Marianas archipelago, laden with an atomic bomb christened "Little Boy." Shortly after 8:00 a.m., the *Enola Gay* appeared over the city of Hiroshima, and dropped the first atomic device that was ever used in combat. A massive mushroom cloud and firestorm engulfed the city, and the final death toll is estimated to have reached 140,000 people. The Japanese continued to vacillate over their decision to surrender, and in the absence of an explicit acceptance of Allied demands, the US leadership executed its plan to stage further atomic attacks against the home islands until Tokyo acquiesced. On 9 August, the second bomb was dropped on Nagasaki. Concurrently, the Imperial government commenced its deliberations on the peace terms which it wished to secure from the Allies, and on the following day, the Japanese announced that they would agree to surrender, on the condition that the safety of Emperor Hirohito and the Imperial polity was guaranteed. Although the reply was ambiguous, and did not amount to an unconditional surrender, on 11 August, the US Secretary of State James Byrnes issued a note which stipulated that the power of the Imperial throne was to be regulated by the supreme commander of the Allied occupation force. Following the surrender, the post-war system of government was to be established through the "freely expressed will of the Japanese people." On 14 August, after days of wrangling among cabinet ministers, and Emperor Hirohito making a final deliberation, Japan accepted the Byrnes note. Finally, on 15 August, the Allies acknowledged Japan's surrender, and the Pacific war drew to a close.

The dropping of the atomic bomb and the role it played in bringing about the end of the Pacific war has generated what has often been a heated and controversial debate among scholars. This is mainly because the use of nuclear weapons not only marked the end of the conflict against Japan, but it also portended the dawn of a new age in modern warfare. In the nuclear age, large scale conflicts not only entailed the loss of troops or damage to one's cities. They involved the risk of mass annihilation to entire societies and nations. Never in the history of human civilization had the stakes been so high. Therefore the use of the atomic bombs in August 1945 has raised questions as to whether the United States needed to resort to such weapons of mass destruction in order to compel Japan to surrender. The Truman administration's motives have also been scrutinized, with some scholars alleging that the bomb was used primarily to intimidate the Soviet Union, at a stage when Japan's defeat was a foregone conclusion. In this sense, the US has been accused of provoking Russia, and laying the grounds for the nuclear arms race that the superpowers fought out for the next few decades of the Cold War.

MOTIVATIONS FOR USING THE ATOMIC BOMB

The key historiographic debates as to why the US leadership decided to deploy atomic weapons against Japan can be divided into three main schools of thought, namely the traditionalists, the revisionists, and post-revisionists. The traditionalists, including Leon Sigal, maintain that Truman's actions were primarily shaped by his desire to end the war against Japan at the earliest opportunity.[1] On the other hand, the revisionists, among the most notable of whom is Gar Alperovitz, contend that by summer 1945, American officials believed that the Japanese were on the verge of surrendering. Yet, the bomb was used to coerce the Soviets to loosen their control over the territories which they had liberated from Nazi Germany, including Poland and the Balkans.[2] Recent works by Barton Bernstein have shown how the polarization between the two arguments is not entirely necessary.[3] A more realistic hypothesis is that the dropping of the atomic bombs was intended, first and foremost, to weaken Japan's war effort prior to the scheduled Allied invasion of the home islands in November 1945. The Truman administration hoped to compel the Japanese to surrender and thereby terminate the Pacific war, but did not expect to achieve such decisive results. The idea of influencing Stalin's behavior, similarly, was a secondary concern, but was not the key factor which motivated the US leadership's strategy.

By the closing months of the war, the Truman administration's overriding objective was to defeat Japan without incurring unnecessary delays and casualties. The decision to use the atomic bomb was driven by a number of underlying political and strategic considerations, as well as immediate concerns which the US leadership had to deal with during the summer of 1945. The most important long-term factor was that the Allies had fought Japan with the ultimate aim of securing its unconditional surrender, and American strategy was geared to take all possible measures to achieve this objective. When Harry Truman took office following the death of Franklin Roosevelt in April 1945, he was determined to uphold his predecessor's policies. In his first address to Congress, the newly sworn-in president vowed, "our demand has been, and it remains unconditional surrender. I want the entire world to know that this direction must and will remain, unchanged and unhampered."[4] Congress and the public were also firmly in favor of continuing the war effort until Japan was totally defeated. Under the circumstances, Truman could alter US war aims only with the greatest difficulty. Public opinion showed a burning desire to punish the Japanese. A poll carried out in June showed that nine out of ten Americans favored prosecuting the campaign in the Pacific, even if it meant increased casualties.[5] The desire to avenge the sneak attack on Pearl Harbor remained at the forefront of most people's minds, and the political climate was such that anybody who suggested a modification of the peace terms for Japan was likely to face criticism, or even become castigated as a traitor.

However, America's adherence to the policy of securing Japan's unconditional surrender was not purely driven by public opinion or a burning hatred for the enemy. Strategic concerns played the most important role. The United States and its allies needed to ensure that the Japanese could not reemerge as a threat to world peace. In June 1945, the JCS had predicted that Japan was likely to seek a termination of hostilities on any terms, provided that the Allies would not occupy the home islands. In order to preempt any such initiatives, the joint chiefs recommended that a strong demand for unconditional surrender be reiterated. Truman's determination to adhere to his policies was clearly revealed by the way in which he handled the proposals put forward by the State Department, for modifying the peace terms. Joseph Grew, the Under-secretary of State, and ambassador to Tokyo before the outbreak of war, argued that it was important to forge friendly relations and most possibly an alliance with Japan in the post-war era, so that Soviet influence in the Far East could be contained. Grew recommended a plan where the integrity of the Imperial throne and the national polity, or what the Japanese called the *kokutai*, was guaranteed. Such offers could compel the more moderate elements in the government to accept surrender, and make it easier for the Allies to administer the post-war occupation.[6] In early May, Grew met the secretaries of state, the navy and army, to discuss the question of how stringently the US needed to pursue its policy of seeking the total defeat of Japan. The main point of contention was whether the Soviet Union's participation was desirable, given that such scenarios could enhance its position in Asia at the expense of the Western powers. James Forrestal, the Secretary of the Navy, supported Grew's idea of modifying the war aims in order to reach an accommodation before Soviet intervention became necessary. With support from the navy, Grew approached Truman later in the month, but in the end, the president did not take onboard any of the suggestions for showing leniency. The president's Memorial Day message repeated the promise that Japan would face the same ruin that had been dealt to Germany if it did not surrender promptly.

The adherence to the unconditional surrender policy was therefore driven by the fear that any deviation would entail the risk of compromising Allied war aims, namely to ensure the total destruction of the Axis powers' war-making capabilities. Furthermore, to many American leaders, Hirohito was the leader of Japan's war effort and a commitment to retain him on the throne appeared risky, since it could pose obstacles to the Western powers' effort to eradicate Japanese militarism. Nevertheless, policies were shaped largely by political and strategic concerns. For example, when the issue of safeguarding the Imperial throne was raised during the Potsdam conference, Allied leaders voiced objections, on the grounds that such moves ran contrary to their long-standing aim of coercing Japan to surrender unconditionally. An intelligence estimate prepared for the CCS suggested that, "for a surrender to be acceptable to the Japanese army it would be necessary for the military leaders to believe that it would ... permit the ultimate resurgence of a military in Japan." Sir Alanbrooke, speaking for the British defense chiefs, suggested that there could be benefits arising from an attempt to explain to the Japanese that unconditional surrender did not entail the destruction of the Imperial institution. The JCS then discussed the issue, and General Marshall stated that nothing should be done to indicate that the Allied powers intended to remove Hirohito. However, the Allies had a limited scope for offering concessions. In the end, the Potsdam proclamation promised that the Allied occupation forces were to be withdrawn as soon as they had implemented the necessary political reforms, and the Japanese had "established in accordance with the freely expressed will" of their people, a "peacefully inclined and responsible government." The language allowed some room for the Japanese to retain their emperor, but an explicit guarantee was removed by Byrnes, with Truman's approval, on the grounds that such clauses could encourage the Japanese to seek additional concessions and thus prolong the conflict.[7] The decision to use the atomic bomb therefore cannot be properly understood without examining the importance which the American leadership attached to securing its wartime objectives. The weapon was perceived as a possible means to hasten the collapse of Japan's war effort. Inflicting mass destruction on the enemy's home territory offered a way to weaken its capacity to wage war. Of equal importance, it could convince the Japanese leadership that their nation had minimal prospects of emerging victoriously from the conflict, and thereby eventually compel them to cease hostilities.

The second long-term consideration that influenced US strategy against Japan was the fact that, since its inception, the atomic bomb project had been geared to produce a weapon which America could use in combat. For this reason, once the bomb became available, most officials within the Truman administration readily accepted the idea of deploying it against any nation which the US was currently engaged in hostilities. The development of atomic weapons had been in progress since 1939, even before America entered the Second World War. A large number of European nuclear scientists, many of whom were of Jewish descent, escaped persecution under the Nazi regime, and emigrated to the United States, which was one of the few countries which had the resources to sponsor their research. The émigrés included some of the most famous names of modern physics, such as Niels Bohr. Other scientists, including Robert Oppenheimer and Ernest Rutherford, had already been living in either Britain or in America. In 1939, the scientists enlisted Albert Einstein to warn Roosevelt of the possibility that Germany could develop nuclear weapons. In 1941, the scientists won the patronage of Vannevar Bush, the head of the new Office of Scientific Research and Development. Because the War Department had great confidence in Bush, he faced few problems in receiving the manpower, raw materials and money to support his program for the research and development of nuclear weapons. In 1943, the Manhattan Project took its final shape. Few policymakers knew about the project aside from Churchill and Roosevelt. In the War Department, George Marshall and the Secretary of War Stimson were kept updated on the progress of the project. General Leslie Groves, who administered the atomic program, took the initiative in organizing a committee to explore the possible uses of the bomb. The group examined a range of military and urban targets both in Germany and in Japan. There was no question either among the scientists or US leaders that, when it became available, the atomic bomb would be used. Thus, when Truman took office, he was surrounded by a team of advisors who had fully advocated using the bomb, and the president had few grounds for arguing to the contrary. The strongest proponent of using atomic weapons was Stimson, who recalled that at no point did he hear the president or any responsible government official suggest that atomic energy should not be used in war.[8] The secretary of war went as far as to advise the president to withhold the ultimatum to Japan until the US was ready to follow up on its threat by deploying atomic weapons.[9] To avoid using the bomb also entailed grave political risks. If the existence of atomic weapons became public knowledge, and the leadership was known to have refrained from using them, the American people were likely to raise an outcry, and demand answers as to why the military never used a piece of technology that had cost the taxpayers over two billion dollars, especially at a time when the US was seeking ways to end its war against Japan. Thus, once the bomb was developed in July 1945, few officials within the Truman administration were likely to raise serious questions, so long as it offered a prospect of speeding up the tempo of the campaign in the Pacific theater.

In regard to immediate causes, the atomic bombs became available at a time when US leaders faced the need to defeat Japan at the earliest opportunity. The fall of Germany in May 1945 gave rise to the strong possibility that the public would eventually start raising objections about prolonging the Pacific war. Furthermore, at the August 1943 Quebec conference, Roosevelt and Churchill had agreed that operations should be geared to defeat Japan no later than 12 months following Germany's capitulation. Defense planners began to doubt whether continuing the blockade and bombing campaign against the home islands could destroy Japan's war effort in an expeditious manner. American strategists acknowledged the prospect that an invasion of the Japanese mainland would be necessary in order to compel its leaders to surrender unconditionally. However, such moves entailed a considerable commitment of resources. Influential elements within the navy and the army air forces, led by Admiral King and General Hap Arnold, argued that a combination of blockade and aerial bombardment would do the job, and that a ground invasion was not necessary. Planners in the US army, meanwhile, concluded that the Japanese would surrender only when their home territory was physically occupied. Despite the ongoing debate, the consensus among the defense chiefs was that the Allies needed to at least plan for an invasion. The JCS never viewed the options of bombing, blockade and invasion as mutually exclusive, and understood that all three actions could be necessary to achieve their objectives.[10]

The issue of whether the Allies would stage an invasion of the home islands was not finally decided until June 1945. In April, the JCS had formally directed MacArthur and Nimitz to commence preparations for a landing in Kyushu. Defense planners back in Washington, including King and Admiral Leahy were reluctant to treat the invasion of Japan as a fixed decision. Finally, on 25 May, the joint chiefs issued a directive stating that Operation *Olympic*, or the invasion of Kyushu, was to commence on 1 November. Although the directive was issued, intelligence which pointed to the arrival of Japanese reinforcements in Kyushu compelled Truman and his defense chiefs to reconsider their plan. Communications transmitted by the IJA, and decrypted by the US military intelligence service through *Ultra*, showed that the Japanese were expecting an invasion, and undertaking measures to strengthen their defenses.[11] Signals intelligence revealed that transports were carrying up to 60,000 troops across the narrow stretch of water between Korea and Kyushu. By mid June, the military intelligence service estimated that there were 300,000 troops in Kyushu, an increase from 100,000 at the beginning of 1945, By November, the number was expected to rise to half a million. Intercepted communications also showed that the Japanese were preparing to carry out *kamikaze* attacks on a massive scale.

By summer 1945, the administration started to voice concerns over the casualties that could be incurred in *Olympic*. On 14 June, William Leahy sent a memorandum to the JCS, informing that the president had requested details on the military's plans for ending the Pacific war, so that he could discuss them during the upcoming Allied summit meeting at Potsdam. In particular, Truman wanted information on the size of the forces required to defeat Japan.[12] Another key concern was to preserve American lives, and on 18 June, at a meeting between the president, the navy and war secretaries, along with the joint chiefs, the discussion centered mainly on what the casualty rates were likely be. The upshot was that the Americans needed to plan their operation on the premise that losses would reach same level as Okinawa, or roughly 35 percent, or 63,000 of the 193,000 scheduled to be deployed for the operation.[13] Such figures do run considerably lower than the claims of some scholars, that US strategists predicted 500,000 casualties, and that the dropping of the bomb prevented such a scenario. Nevertheless, the fact remains that Marshall had informed the president that casualties would run high, and possibly into the six-digit figures.[14] The meeting ended with the president giving the green light for *Olympic*, but an invasion of the Tokyo plain was left for future decision. Truman did concede that the JCS, after weighing all the possibilities of the situation and considering all possible alternative plans were still of the "unanimous opinion that the Kyushu operation was the best solution under the circumstances." At the same time, he added that he hoped to avoid bloodshed such as the Americans had experienced at Okinawa, and the statement indicated the administration's reluctance to commit US forces to a costly operation.[15] Although the actions which Truman would have taken in the event that the bomb had been unavailable are largely open to conjecture, based on the course of events, one can speculate that had *Olympic* been launched in November 1945, and the Americans incurred high casualties, the invasion of Tokyo would have been postponed, with the administration seeking to end the war by other means.[16]

Under the circumstances, Truman was most likely to seek any opportunity to defeat Japan in a way that could minimize American casualties. The final decision to use the atomic bomb was made during the Potsdam conference, and the move was aimed at meting out further damage against Japan's war effort. The prospect of dealing a final blow and compelling the enemy to surrender was certainly welcomed, but US leaders did not anticipate such results. From the time that Truman set sail for Europe on 7 July, and throughout his stay at the summit, intelligence continued to reveal a steady increase in Japanese ground strength at Kyushu. By 9 July, estimates of total Japanese strength in Kyushu had reached the 350,000 total which George Marshall had predicted would be the maximum which the invasion force would face.[17] The record on how much of the intelligence the president actually read is fragmentary, mainly because official secrets laws forbade any mention of it in directives and official reports. However, Truman was kept regularly updated, and on 16 July, he received word that the atomic bomb test at Alamogordo, New Mexico had been successful. On the following day, the president met his advisors, including Byrnes, Stimson, and the joint chiefs, to ask for their opinion on whether the bomb should be used. The consensus was that the US should by all means utilize its newly available weapon, and at least attempt to end the war in a more quick and economical way.[18] Nevertheless, because nobody could foresee the psychological effects of atomic weapons, Truman and his advisors did not expect to coerce the Japanese to surrender. US forces were not ordered to prepare for a demobilization and, on the contrary, they were assigned to continue readying themselves for an invasion of the home islands. The intention was therefore to use the bomb to further reduce Japan's capacity to forestall its opponents.

The argument that Truman intended to intimidate the Soviets is largely based on circumstantial evidence. The dropping of the atomic bomb did heighten Moscow's feelings of insecurity, and was the first step towards the post-war nuclear arms race between the superpowers. Revisionist historians have argued that even during the war, the US saw the bomb as an instrument that could be used to deter Soviet aggression. The statement gains further credibility when viewed alongside the American refusal to share the secrets of their scientific research. Roosevelt and Churchill had both maintained that the bomb should be used to strengthen the military might of the Western coalition, and rejected all proposals for keeping the Soviets updated on the Manhattan Project. When Truman took office, he was surrounded by advisors who had supported his predecessor's policies, and the president was not in a position to reverse the decision to prevent the USSR from learning about America's achievements.

The decision to deploy the atomic bombs also coincided with a period of growing US–Soviet tensions over the territorial settlement in Eastern Europe, and the Truman administration was seeking ways to coerce Stalin to moderate his behavior. Using the atomic bomb against the only nation which America remained at war with appeared to offer a viable course of action. However, the opportunity to demonstrate the destructive potential of the bomb in combat appeared to fade away when, on several occasions prior to the Potsdam conference, Truman's military advisors suggested that the Japanese were close to capitulating, and that a mere Soviet declaration of war might induce them to accept unconditional surrender.[19] In such eventualities, the USSR could claim that it played the decisive role in ending the Pacific war. Revisionists have even gone as far as to contend by summer 1945, the Truman administration and its defense advisors no longer believed that an invasion of Japan was necessary, but still proceeded to use the bomb, owing to a number of Soviet-related factors.[20] First, the US no longer had to share the victory over Japan with the Russians, and once the atomic bomb was developed, American leaders ceased their efforts to secure the Red Army's participation in the Pacific war. Secondly, Byrnes in particular was reported to have expressed the view that the US possession of the bomb would make Russia "more manageable in Europe," and could also limit the USSR's encroachment on Asia. Once the atomic device became available on 16 July, plans to use it as a way to coerce Moscow gained a prominent place in the minds of American leaders. US diplomacy began to actively press for territorial changes in the Balkans, with Truman declaring that nations such as Rumania, Bulgaria and Hungary were not under any power's sphere of influence.

Yet, as much as the possession of the bomb may have emboldened the Americans, the foremost concern of the leadership was to secure Japan's unconditional surrender at the earliest opportunity, while at the same time avoiding excessive casualties. On 1 June, Byrnes submitted a set of recommendations to the president, which clearly stated that the bomb was to "compel the Japanese to recognize that instant surrender was the only way to avert ruin, if not the extinction of their nation."[21] Written evidence also suggests that keeping the Soviets out of the war against Japan was never a central concern for Truman. On 18 July, the president wrote in his diary "believe the Japanese will fold up before Russia comes in." Yet, on the same day, in a letter to his wife, he emphasized, "I have gotten what I came here for! Stalin goes to war on August 15. Think of all the boys that won't be killed."[22] The president sincerely wanted the Soviets to join the war, or at the very least, understood that the US could not prevent the Red Army from conquering large sections of Northeast Asia. After all, the Roosevelt administration had maintained that the USSR's help was vital to help the Allies carry out their final assault on Japan, and Truman did not depart from his predecessor's stand. That Stalin was not included as a signatory of the Potsdam ultimatum owed itself more to legal reasons, namely that the USSR had not yet declared war on Japan and thus was not in a position to threaten punitive action in the event of non-compliance. Nor did Truman expect the Japanese to surrender so quickly, and he merely anticipated that the combination of the atomic bombs and the Soviet entry into the war would bring about an expedited victory. Yet, the president conceded that the length of time that could elapse before Tokyo capitulated was unknown, and he was surprised when the Japanese offered a conditional surrender within days of Hiroshima.

Using the bomb to prevent the USSR from entering the conflict and making inroads in the Far East therefore did not fit in with Truman's predictions regarding the possible turn of events. Even if sending a warning to Stalin was part of the administration's plans, it was, at the very most, a secondary objective in relation to defeating Japan.

The revisionists' arguments lose further credibility when viewed in light of the fact that not all American leaders saw the bomb as a way to coerce the USSR to offer concessions. While Truman and his top advisors wished to see the US retain its monopoly over atomic technologies, they did not envisage a rapid build-up of their arsenal. The number of atomic weapons in stock was low, and the president's defense chiefs constantly warned how their use could not prevent the Soviets from deploying their conventional forces to conquer Western Europe. Ideas on how to use the bomb as a weapon of diplomacy were also muddled, and few officials had developed a coherent strategy. Key members of the White House, notably Stimson, started to believe that if atomic weapons were kept secret forever, the Soviets could be irretrievably embittered towards the United States. Others, including Byrnes, felt that the monopoly had to be maintained at all costs, in order to give America a stronger hand in its negotiations with the USSR. Opinions regarding the role of the bomb as an instrument of foreign policy were rarely uniform, and most policymakers did not have a decided view on how the weapon could be used to placate their rivals. Under the circumstances, arguments which suggest that the Truman administration's decision to use the atomic bomb against Hiroshima and Nagasaki were part of a calculated plan, aimed at deterring Soviet expansion, can be accepted only with utmost reserve.

THE ATOMIC BOMB AND JAPAN'S DECISION TO SURRENDER

Equally contentious as the Truman administration's motives for using the atomic bombs is the role which the weapons played in compelling the Japanese government to surrender in August 1945. The main question is whether the atomic bomb provided the most effective way to finish the Pacific war in accordance with the Allied demand that Japan accept a total defeat. The traditionalist view argues that Japan's leaders had no intention of surrendering prior to the attacks in Hiroshima and Nagasaki, and that the government, along with the military high command, was determined to continue fighting the war at all costs. After Tojo resigned from his post as prime minister in June 1944, following the loss of Saipan, a number of officials within the newly appointed government of Prime Minister Koiso did concede that Japan was losing the conflict, and the outcome was irreversible. Yet nobody within the leadership was prepared to sue for peace.[23] Koiso called for a strategy aimed at securing a decisive victory in either the Pacific islands or in Southeast Asia, and using it as a bargaining tool for negotiating a peace treaty with the Allied powers. In the following April, after the USSR announced its abrogation of the Neutrality Pact and affirmed that it would expire within a year's time, Suzuki, a former navy admiral, took power, and his cabinet pledged to bolster the defense of the home islands in an effort to repel the expected Allied invasion. Again in May, when Germany's collapse became imminent, the government declared that Hitler's downfall would not cause the "slightest change" in national policy.[24] Despite the mounting bombing and blockade campaign, coupled with the loss of Okinawa, the prospects of Japan accepting the Western powers' demands for an unconditional surrender appeared negligible. On 9 June, the supreme council for the direction of the war laid out its "Fundamental Policy" which declared that Japan would "prosecute the war to the bitter end in order to uphold the national polity, protect the imperial land," and "accomplish the objectives for which [it] went to war." The army and navy staffs not only expected the armed forces to be fully mobilized to counter the impending Allied invasion, but the entire civilian population was also to be conscripted. On the same day, Emperor Hirohito issued a rescript which ordered the nation to "smash the inordinate ambitions of the enemy nations."[25] The atomic bombs therefore offered the only means to convince the Japanese that they could no longer hold out against the military force which the Allies were bringing to bear against their home territory.

The revisionists, on the other hand, suggest that the ruling elite in Tokyo had already begun to consider the possibility of surrendering even before the bombs were dropped. Using weapons of mass destruction was therefore an unnecessary act of cruelty on the part of the Americans. A more moderate hypothesis has been put forward by the post-revisionists, who have claimed that Japan's declining fortunes had convinced some leaders to start considering the possibility of seeking an end to hostilities.[26] The peace faction consisted of key members from the Imperial court, along with the civilian members of the cabinet, including Prime Minister Suzuki and Foreign Minister Togo. However, while the advocates of peace were apprehensive whether continuing the fight could bring positive results, they were also aware that any decision to end the war required unanimous approval from the cabinet, which comprised several ministers representing the armed forces, the latter of whom insisted on a fight to the finish. The civilian leaders were wary about initiating a protracted debate with the militarists, and did not openly press their views. The dropping of the atomic bomb on Hiroshima persuaded Japan's top leaders, the most influential of whom was the Emperor, to speed up the process of war termination, and take active measures to prevail on the die-hards to abandon their hopes for securing a lenient set of peace terms. The second bomb on Nagasaki, on the other hand, was not necessary, since the cabinet had already commenced its discussions on surrendering when it received news of the attack. For this reason, the Japanese were most likely to have capitulated when they did, even if the US had only destroyed Hiroshima.[27]

Regardless of which view scholars choose to support, any answer must be based, to a large degree, on speculation as to how the Japanese could have behaved if the US had not used the bombs. All of the competing arguments therefore draw upon counter-factual scenarios in order to determine whether Tokyo was likely to have surrendered prior to November 1945, the scheduled date for launching *Olympic*. Nevertheless, by examining the various strategies which the Allies employed during the closing stages of the conflict, and the Japanese nation's reactions, one can find convincing evidence which suggests that the bomb offered the only realistic alternative to a costly and protracted invasion of the home islands.

The first possible option was to modify the surrender terms. Revisionist historians in particular have argued that an explicit guarantee of the Imperial institution may have convinced the moderate elements within Japan's government to prevail upon the Emperor to cease hostilities. However, the policy was unlikely to succeed, mainly because the minimum terms which the Japanese were willing to accept went considerably beyond a mere maintenance of the Emperor. For example, during June and July 1945, when the Foreign Ministry was seeking to enlist Soviet assistance in brokering a peace settlement with America and its allies, Japan's officials were unable to provide precise instructions to Ambassador Sato in Moscow regarding the terms to be sought.[28] US diplomatic missions in neutral countries, including Switzerland and Sweden, also received a number of approaches from Japanese "peace feelers" who attempted to negotiate a settlement via informal channels, but again, the peace feelers never clarified the conditions which Japan was willing to accept. This was mainly because the cabinet in Tokyo found itself divided on the issue. While the civilian leaders were ready to settle for a guarantee that the Emperor be protected, the military, and the army in particular, demanded a substantial list of additional terms, including the permission to retain Korea and Formosa, a promise of no foreign military occupation, and Japanese supervision of its own disarmament.[29] Furthermore, the militarists vehemently insisted on staging a last-ditch battle against the Allied invasion force. The army remained confident that the strategy of inflicting horrific losses on the Allies could bring a termination of hostilities on more favorable terms, even though the possibility of an ultimate victory had become unrealistic.[30] Under the circumstances, a promise to preserve the Imperial system was unlikely to elicit a surrender. Even after the bombings of Hiroshima and Nagasaki, the military leaders within the cabinet continued to call for terms which went beyond simply retaining Hirohito on the throne, including a limit on the number of occupation troops which the Allies could station in Japan.[31] Modifying the peace terms also entailed grave political risks for the Truman administration. The American public was most unlikely to accept moves which compromised the originally stated demands for unconditional surrender.

A continuation of the strategic bombing and blockade campaign offered the second possible strategy for destroying Japan's war effort. The USAAF's Strategic Bombing Survey did conclude, "certainly prior to 31 December 1945, and in all probability prior to 1 November 1945, Japan would have surrendered even if the atomic bombs had not been dropped, even if Russia had not entered the war, and even if no invasion had been planned or contemplated." The statement was based on a series of post-war interviews which the Survey conducted with top Japanese officials. However, the investigation was heavily influenced by the air force's organizational agenda, which aimed to sell its wartime achievements to the US defense community, by explaining how its strategic bombing campaign had played a decisive role in defeating Japan. The conclusions were therefore derived from a selective reading of the evidence, with the results of the interrogations construed so that they supported the USAAF's pre-set argument.[32] The contention that conventional air attacks could have compelled an early surrender becomes less convincing when one takes into the account how even after Hiroshima, the Japanese cabinet remained deadlocked on the question of war termination. Until the Emperor intervened in the cabinet discussions on 10 August, Admiral Toyoda, the chief of the naval general staff, along with representatives from the army, maintained that final defeat was not certain, and Japan still had a decent prospect of winning a decisive battle in the home islands.[33] Furthermore, after the conflict finished, many Japanese leaders testified that without the atomic bomb, the nation would have carried on fighting. Prince Konoye told the Survey that the war "probably would have lasted throughout 1945."[34] Suzuki emphasized the army's plans for staging a full-scale battle in defense of the home islands, and explained how the supreme war council did not believe that Japan could be defeated by air attacks alone, at least until the atomic bomb was dropped.[35] In short, maintaining the momentum of the bombing campaign may have destroyed Japan's infrastructure and highlighted to its leaders the negligible prospects of winning, but it was unlikely to have the same effects as a single device that could annihilate an entire city within a matter of minutes.

The US navy's strangulation of Japan's maritime supply lines was also unlikely to have compelled the Japanese to surrender. The blockade had curtailed the enemy's imports of raw materials and brought industrial production to a halt, while at the same time causing acute food shortages. By spring 1945, US navy officials argued that Japan had already been defeated.[36] William Leahy also claimed, after the war had finished, that the destruction of Japan's shipping would have caused its military machine to "fall by its own weight," and that the US army did not show an adequate understanding of this reality. Hence, George Marshall had forced upon the JCS the plan to invade the home islands, even though the navy argued that it was not necessary. Yet, in light of the fact that the Japanese were already subjected to significant deprivations, a continuation of the blockade was likely to do little aside from compel them to withstand the hardships. In fact, most Japanese leaders, including Suzuki, did not even acknowledge starvation among the populace as a key influence which shaped their decisions.[37]

The third option was to await the Soviet Union's entry into the war, in the hope that the Japanese would realize that the coalition of enemies ranged against them was too great to bear. The Red Army's invasion of Manchuria on 8 August, 2 days following Hiroshima, did come as a severe shock to the leadership in Tokyo, who had counted upon Moscow to intervene on Japan's behalf, either by negotiating a more favorable set of peace terms with the Western powers, or providing raw materials and weapons so that the Imperial forces could continue fighting. The rapid collapse of the Japanese armies on the Asiatic mainland had a decisive impact on the military, who became convinced that their forces were unlikely to perform well against a US assault on the home islands.[38] Whereas War Minister Anami, along with Umezu, the chief of army staff, had rejected all proposals for surrendering prior to the Soviet invasion, by 9 August, they both agreed to attend a special meeting of the supreme war council in order to discuss the terms which Japan was going to propose to the Allies. The vice-chief of the army staff, Kawabe Torashiro, stated that the atomic bomb actually had little effect on the military leadership, since Tokyo was not attacked. The Soviet entry, by contrast, showed the Japanese how the vast strengths of the Red Army had been turned against them.[39] However, scholars who argue that Stalin's declaration of war played the most important role in compelling Japan to surrender tend to focus on the reactions of commanders within the Imperial army, while neglecting the key policy decisions that were made by the top ministers within the cabinet during the crucial period between Hiroshima and the Soviet entry into the war. The true effects which the USSR's actions would have brought, if it happened without the atomic bomb, will never be known. Post-war testimonies by Japanese officials, nevertheless, often referred to the bomb as the decisive factor. In fact, many leaders, including Togo, doubted whether the Soviets would offer any useful support, and the Red Army's invasion came as no surprise.[40] Hiroshima, by contrast, destroyed the beliefs held by the civilian leaders, including Prime Minister Suzuki, namely that Japan could continue fighting. Most critically, Hirohito was given convincing reasons to conclude that the time had come for Japan to sue for peace.[41] If the Soviet attack on Manchuria was necessary to convince the military to accept defeat, the bomb played an essential role in coercing the civilian factions of the leadership to expedite Japan's capitulation. Whether the USSR's actions alone could have produced the same results is open to question. A surrender might have emerged before November 1945, but the scenario was by no means guaranteed.[42]

The final option was to use the atomic bomb in a non-combat capacity. In June 1945, the science panel of the interim committee, chaired by Stimson, discussed a proposal to demonstrate the devastating power of the bomb to intimidate the Japanese.[43] However, the move was deemed impractical, for a host of reasons. There was the possibility that the bomb would malfunction, in which case the Americans were likely to suffer an almost irreversible embarrassment. If an uninhabited site was to be found in the home islands, the Japanese could easily move Allied prisoners there, while a test at a remote Pacific island would have been difficult to arrange, especially since Japanese observers had to be transported there by some means. Most importantly, any moves to organize a demonstration required a level of liaison between the US and Japan which was most difficult to achieve under wartime conditions. The interim committee therefore acknowledged that a technical demonstration was unlikely to end the war, and the only acceptable option was to use the atomic bomb in a combat role, so that the Japanese could gain a first-hand view of the weapon's capacity for destruction.

Pursuing a combination of the alternative strategies was also feasible. Bernstein, for example, envisaged a three-part, counterfactual scenario that involved a Soviet entry into the war, a US guarantee of the Imperial institution, and intensifying the bombing and blockade campaign.[44] Nevertheless, while the prospects of ending the war by such means were "quite probable," a Japanese surrender was certainly less definite. The atomic bomb therefore offered the most effective way of compelling Japan to terminate hostilities, and none of the options were likely to achieve the same decisive results before the Allies launched their scheduled invasion of Kyushu in November 1945.

CONCLUSION

The US leadership's decision to deploy the atomic bombs against Hiroshima and Nagasaki in August 1945 was not the culmination of a calculated plan to compel the Japanese to surrender by inflicting mass casualties on their civilian population. Top-ranking officials within the Truman administration, along with the president's military advisors, acknowledged the possibility that, if the Allies wished to see the Pacific war end with the complete destruction of Japan's war effort, they needed to invade and occupy the home islands. Alternative courses of action, such as continuing with the blockade and bombing campaign, or enlisting the Soviet Union's entry into the conflict, were considered more likely to weaken, rather than destroy, Japan's capacity to resist. The atomic bomb offered an additional weapon which could reduce the obstacles which the armed forces of the US and its coalition forces had to deal with in their effort to conquer the Japanese mainland.

At the same time, from the moment the administration of President Franklin Roosevelt endorsed the Manhattan Project, atomic bombs were developed with a view to deploying them against the Axis powers, or against any nation which the United States was at war with. When the weapons became available in July 1945, Germany had capitulated, and US leaders had to deal with the question of how to defeat Japan, which remained as the only surviving member of the Axis coalition. Using the bomb was seen as an essential move to help the Allies achieve their ultimate objective of compelling Japan's leaders to surrender unconditionally. Of equal importance, there were compelling political motivations to use the bombs. Developing atomic technologies had cost American taxpayers over two billion dollars, and the leadership could not afford to alienate public opinion by foregoing available opportunities to end the war in a more economical and expeditious manner.

The main purpose of dropping the atomic bombs was therefore to weaken Japan's war effort and eventually compel its leaders to surrender. Coercing the Soviet Union to moderate its behavior in Eastern Europe and in Asia was treated as a potential benefit which the US could accrue, but the Truman administration did not have any clear plans on how to use the bomb as a way to influence Moscow. The contention that the Americans wished to intimidate the Soviets and prevent them from making inroads into the Far East becomes questionable when viewed alongside two key facts. First, until the closing stages of the Pacific war, US leaders made a concerted effort to ensure that the Red Army joined forces with the Allied powers' final assault against the Japanese mainland, and were aware that such scenarios could enhance Stalin's ability to establish a foothold in areas such as China. Second, Truman's advisors were divided on how to use the atomic bomb as an instrument for facilitating America's dealings with the USSR, with some key members of the White House proposing that the technologies be shared in order to secure Moscow's goodwill. At the same time, officials who advocated using the bomb as a weapon of deterrence remained unsure as to how the Soviets could react to the atomic threat.

On the question of whether the atomic bombs were necessary to compel Japan to surrender, the existing literature reveals convincing evidence that, prior to Hiroshima, the Imperial government had no intention of accepting the peace terms demanded by the Allies. The destruction inflicted by the weapons compelled the top leaders, the most influential of whom was Emperor Hirohito, to prevail upon the die-hards within the military to decide on what conditions Japan was going to offer in order to bring the conflict to an early conclusion. The Americans were unlikely to have achieved similar results by pursuing the other available options including an intensification of their blockade and bombardment of the home islands, or by waiting for the Soviet Union to declare war on Japan. Likewise, a move to modify the surrender terms and guarantee the preservation of the Imperial institution could have appealed to the moderates within the Japanese government, but the militarists were unlikely to accept a termination of hostilities without staging a last-ditch attempt to forestall the Allied invasion force. The use of the atomic bomb may not have been necessary, and the Allies could have ended the Pacific war by staging an assault on the home islands. Nevertheless, the use of the weapons was justifiable, in the sense that it offered the only realistic prospect of concluding the conflict on the terms which the US and its coalition partners wished to secure, and before the landing in Kyushu was scheduled to be launched in November 1945.

Conclusion

The Pacific war officially terminated on 2 September 1945, when Japanese dignitaries, acting on behalf of the Imperial government and the armed forces, formally submitted their surrender to the Allied powers. The ceremony took place onboard the US battleship *Missouri*, anchored at Tokyo Bay, and representing Emperor Hirohito and the government was Foreign Minister Shigemitsu Mamoru, with the army chief of staff, Umezu Yoshijiro, acting on behalf of Imperial General Headquarters. After a short speech delivered by General Douglas MacArthur, who had been appointed as the Supreme Commander of the Allied Powers (SCAP) for the post-war occupation of Japan, Shigemitsu and Umezu placed their signatures on the instrument of surrender. In the end, the surrender was accepted by delegates from virtually all of the nations who had fought with the Allied coalition, including the United States, the Republic of China, and Great Britain. The dominions of the British empire, namely Canada, Australia and New Zealand, were represented. The Soviet Union, which joined the conflict at the final stages, was also a signatory, as were France and Holland. The former's colonies in Asia had been overrun by the Japanese even before the war began, while the Dutch had lost theirs during the early months.

The multifarious grouping of nations that participated at the surrender ceremony reflected a key feature of the Pacific war, namely the manner in which it was not merely a regional conflict, but a crucial theater in what was indisputably a global war. Yet, because America's contribution was overwhelmingly larger than its coalition partners, a large part of the available literature has portrayed the conflict as one fought almost entirely between the US and Japan. Such perspectives offer a limited view of the causes and dynamics of the conflict. In order to understand why the Imperial armed forces initiated hostilities with the US in December 1941, one needs to examine how Japan's expansionist activities during the previous decade clashed with other powers who held interests in Asia. In many ways, the Pacific war was an extension of the conflict that had broken out in 1937 between Japan and China. The failure to achieve a decisive victory in the China venture led the Japanese to seek other ways of subduing their enemy, by moving into Indochina in an effort to outflank Chiang Kai Shek and the Nationalists. However, by expanding into Southeast Asia, the Imperial forces began to threaten the European nations who held colonies in the region, including Great Britain and the Netherlands. The United States also did not wish to see a hostile power gain a hegemonic position in the Asia-Pacific area, and sided with the Western powers. The freezing of Japan's overseas assets, and the oil embargos which were imposed in response to the occupation of southern Indochina in July 1941 was part of the US leadership's policy which aimed to deter the Imperial government and making Tokyo reconsider the wisdom of provoking a war. Yet, the sanctions goaded Japan into further aggressive action. The government and the high command judged that the only feasible way to secure the resources which had been denied by the embargoes was to conquer areas such as British Malaya and the Dutch East Indies. America became involved because Japan's ruling elite decided that US military power had to be eliminated before the Imperial forces could carry out their plan to occupy Southeast Asia. The outbreak of the Pacific war therefore stemmed from Japan's failure to resolve its differences with the major powers which held interests in Asia.

Once the Pacific war commenced, the military forces committed by the United States dwarfed those of its coalition partners. Nevertheless, America's ability to conduct a successful campaign depended on forging close cooperative relationship with its allies. The dominions of the British empire, including Australia and New Zealand, provided important bases for launching operations, owing to their proximity to the outer reaches of Japan's conquered territories. China continued to play a pivotal role in containing the Japanese. The bulk of the Imperial army remained tied down on mainland Asia, and by carrying on with their fight, the Chinese prevented the IJA from reinforcing its garrisons in the Pacific, where they could be used to forestall the American counter-offensive. As the war progressed, American leaders also realized that the Soviet Union's participation was desirable, given the important contribution which the vast strengths of the Red Army could make towards the final Allied assault on the home islands. Last but not least, Britain's contribution was essential for the US to secure its wartime objectives in the Pacific theater. Aside from the operations carried out by Lord Mountbatten's Southeast Asia Command and General Slim's Fourteenth Army, British political support enabled America to secure international approval for its policies towards Japan, both during the conflict, as well as its aftermath. British leaders, including Prime Minister Churchill, along with his top cabinet ministers and defense chiefs, were included in all of the major summit meetings, including Casablanca, Teheran, Yalta and Potsdam. Roosevelt and his joint chiefs of staff could not dictate the policies of the anti-Axis coalition without alienating America's closest friends. Such moves entailed the risk of facing isolation on the international political arena. Nor could the US plan its strategy without paying heed to the sensibilities of the British, the latter of whom maintained that Germany had to be defeated before the Allies could concentrate on the Pacific theater. American officials therefore needed to move cautiously in their attempts to allocate a greater portion of resources for the fight against Japan. World War II in the Asia-Pacific theater was, by every definition, a coalition war, in which several nations played their own roles in bringing about the defeat of the Japanese empire.

The previous chapters have also examined the main reasons for the Allied victory against the IJN and IJA. The performance of the American-led coalition provides a key example of how economic strength and industrial productivity often lay the foundations for success in war. Without access to their vast supply of raw materials and manufacturing facilities, the Allies could not build an arsenal that enabled them to bring about the complete destruction of Japan's military capabilities. The aphorism put forward by Voltaire during the eighteenth century, namely that "God always favors the big battalions," is certainly applicable to the Pacific war, where the outcome was determined, to a significant extent, by the ability to construct and deploy a superior quantity of weapons over one's opponents.

At the same time, while material resources provided the hardware which the armed forces needed in order to prevail, they were among a multitude of advantages which the Allies held. A metonymic adage that the "pen is mightier than the sword," and that military actions have to be planned in a calibrated manner, holds true for the conduct of the Pacific war. In order to harness their assets, the Western nations had to organize their war economies. Governments often intervened in order to ensure that the key industries were assembling equipment that was suited for the tasks which the military had to undertake. The Allied powers also invested a considerable amount of capital towards the research and development of more efficient weapons. American industries were exceptionally successful in terms of both the quantity and quality of the equipment they put out. By war's end, the US navy was able to procure over 100 aircraft carriers that could carry out a variety of missions, including the protection of task forces, and preliminary bombardment raids against island bastions. The USAAF's B-29 bombers reduced Japan's cities to ashes, and laid ruin to its industrial infrastructure. On land, the US army and marine corps had enough tanks, artillery pieces and munitions to annihilate the IJA's defenses and their occupants. The creation of such a vast military machine was made possible not only because the US had the necessary resources. The government, along with the defense establishment, endeavored to optimize the available assets in order to develop the capability to achieve their objective, namely to bring about the complete destruction of its enemy's war-making potential. The British war economy was less dynamic than its US counterpart, and the bulk of the armaments produced were deployed for the fight against Germany, with the Far East being treated as a backwater. Nevertheless, the armed forces were eventually supplied with the weapons they needed to prevail over the Japanese. Towards the closing stages of the conflict, General Slim's Fourteenth Army, along with Air Command Southeast Asia, achieved a decisive numerical superiority over their adversary, which enabled them to push Mutaguchi's armies out of Burma. Again, the achievement resulted from the moves which Britain's leadership undertook to channel the nation's limited resources to the war industries, and make good use of what was available.

In the same manner that industrial prowess gave the Allies a decisive edge, Japan's fundamental weakness was that it lacked the capacity to achieve the same output as its opponents. During the opening stages of the war, the Imperial navy and army were able to fight with a comfortable lead, particularly in regard to warships and aircraft. However, as the conflict progressed and US forces became able to deploy an ever-increasing quantity of armaments, the armed forces had to fight with a numerical inferiority so disadvantageous that they had minimal prospects of achieving any meaningful victories.

The situation was made worse because neither the government nor the military high command endeavored to ensure that Japan made good use of its limited resources. For example, the available shipping did not permit the industries to receive sufficient supplies of raw materials from the conquered territories. Nor did the navy pay attention to the danger of Allied attacks on Japanese merchant convoys, and did not undertake measures to provide protection until a late stage in the war. The shortcoming eventually led to the strangulation of Japan's imports, to a point where arms manufacturing ground to a halt by 1945. The government also never made a concerted attempt to establish centralized control over the war economy. As a result, the industries lacked the efficiency which characterized their Western counterparts. The navy and army were allowed to place production orders without securing government approval. Consequently, defense expenditures ran far higher than what the state could afford. The result was rampant inflation which made it difficult for the military to purchase weapons at an affordable cost. Poor resource management did not cause the Japan's demise, since its war effort was already handicapped by a hopelessly inferior industrial base to what its opponents had. Nevertheless, the disorganized state of the economy did speed up the nation's defeat.

Insofar as the actual fighting of the Pacific war was concerned, the Allies were likewise not only aided by their vast supply of weapons and munitions. The effective planning of their campaigns in all areas, including the strategic, operational and tactical levels, was vital. The US and British empire did suffer a number of strategic setbacks during the opening stages of the conflict. The attacks on Pearl Harbor, Singapore and the Philippines caught the Western powers by surprise. Prior to December 1941, the political leadership of the Allied nations and their defense establishments judged that the Japanese were unlikely to risk a confrontation Indeed, the conquest of Southeast Asia and the western Pacific regions during the early part of 1942 presented America and its coalition partners with an unexpected situation. Nevertheless, the US in particular was well-placed to recover from its initial defeats, largely because it had drawn up plans to deal with the emergency it faced. Defense planners had identified the Japanese as a potential adversary, and carefully calculated the strategies they would need to execute in the event of hostilities. Naval planners realized that the most effective way to neutralize Japan's forces was to secure control over the expanses of the Pacific Ocean, thereby restricting their movement, and eventually subjecting the home islands to attack. The construction of the US navy's weapons, including aircraft, surface vessels and submarines, as well as the doctrines governing their use in combat, were geared to help the Americans defeat the IJN in a protracted war effort. Although the Army and the USAAF had been more concerned about the possibility of a conflict against Nazi Germany, once Japan declared war, both services were quick to adopt the navy's line of strategic thinking. Although Great Britain's involvement in the Far Eastern theater was restricted by the demands arising from its commitments in the European theater, British strategy was similarly based on a realistic calculation of the moves that were necessary to achieve its wartime objectives. The chiefs of staff in London, along with commanders in the India-Burma theater, undertook to gradually increase the strengths they could deploy against Japan, so that they could develop the capacity to reconquer Britain's territories in Southeast Asia.

By early 1943, when Japan's offensive capabilities had been blunted, following its defeats at Midway and the Solomons, and the Allies had turned the tide against the Axis powers in all theaters, US and British strategy acquired a further degree of coherence. President Roosevelt and Prime Minister Churchill decreed that their ultimate objective was to bring about the unconditional surrender of their enemies and the complete destruction of their war-making capabilities. As a result, defense planners had a concrete goal to work towards, and were able to identify the military actions they needed to carry out. The American joint chiefs of staff ordered the navy and army to conduct a counter-offensive into the far reaches of the western Pacific, so they could secure bases for an assault on Japan's home islands. The various services disagreed on which route of advance was to be taken towards the Japanese mainland, with the navy favoring a thrust through the Central Pacific, while the Army supported an island-hopping campaign via New Guinea and the Philippines. The USAAF, meanwhile, focused on setting up bases in mainland China. Nevertheless, the differences were resolved, once the army and the air force conceded that the navy's Central Pacific strategy offered the most direct path towards the nerve center of Japan's empire. US war plans were eventually accepted by their British ally. Churchill, who had advocated a campaign to recover Britain's territories in the Malaya-Sumatra area, conceded to the views held by his military advisors, that such moves involved a protracted and costly venture that was unlikely to have a significant impact on the enemy war effort. Defense planners also acknowledged that if Britain wished to reconstitute its empire, it had to secure America's approval by supporting its partner's strategy. At the same time, the British did realize that, in order to maintain their influence in Asia, they needed to independently reconquer their lost colonies. For this reason, they decided to launch a campaign in Burma, where Japanese defenses were known to be relatively weak.

At the theater level, Allied operations were also planned with a view to achieving their objectives in an efficient manner, and enabling the armed forces to exploit their numerical superiority vis-à-vis the Japanese. The overarching principle was to defeat the enemy as quickly as possible, without incurring excessive casualties. Top-ranking US commanders, including Admiral Nimitz, conceded that they could not launch large-scale counter-offensives against Japan's empire unless the Allies deployed sufficient strength to overcome the Imperial armed forces in a prolonged series of pitched battles. The recapturing of the Solomon Islands in late 1942 was a defensive measure, to prevent the Japanese from occupying Guadalcanal and thereby threatening a vital sector of the trans-Pacific supply line. Likewise, General MacArthur ordered an advance against the IJA's positions in New Guinea, the aim being to forestall the enemy's moves to establish a base within range of the Allies' forward base at Australia. The difficulties which the Allies faced during their initial efforts to dislodge the Imperial forces reminded theater commanders how they needed to deploy enough ships, aircraft and equipment to neutralize the significant levels of resistance which the enemy was able to put up. Equally important was to set up a logistic network that covered the expanses of the Pacific Ocean, so that front-line units could be supplied.

When the United States became able to allocate more resources for the Pacific theater after 1943, thanks to its rapidly increasing industrial productivity, military commanders sought to exploit the enemy's weaknesses and hasten the collapse of its war effort. The US navy stepped up the submarine campaign against Japan's supply lines, with the aim of hampering the army's effort to reinforce its outlying garrisons, and more importantly, to prevent Japanese war industries from receiving supplies of raw materials from the conquered territories. The Americans also continued to act cautiously, and avoided situations where their forces became held up by difficult opposition. When MacArthur recommended an island-hopping campaign through the New Guinea region and eventually establish a base in the Philippines, Nimitz raised apprehensions that the move would commit US forces to a slow overland advance against a series of well-defended positions. The Central Pacific offered a more favorable area of operations, since its large expanses of water, interspersed by a small number of Japanese island bastions, enabled the Americans to make full use of their naval and air power. The area also provided a direct route of advance towards Japan's home islands. After months of endless debates, MacArthur conceded that Nimitz's push through the central Pacific was to constitute the main effort, and the campaign in New Guinea was a diversionary operation to maintain pressure on the Imperial forces. Both movements were to converge in the Philippines–Formosa area, from which the Americans and their allies planned to launch their final assault on mainland Japan.

Operations were also planned with flexibility, so that the armed forces could cope with a range of contingencies. After the marines incurred significant casualties during their invasion of the Gilberts/Marshalls archipelago, Nimitz decided to reduce the number of positions that were to be captured. Whereas the original plan called for retaking all of the islands which lay between Hawaii and the western Pacific, including the Carolines, the admiral chose to head straight for the Mariana Islands. The remaining strongholds, including the IJN's main base at Truk, were to be neutralized through bombardment, rather than occupied. The move offered the most efficient way to establish bases within striking distance of Japan's home territory. Likewise, the USAAF scrapped its plan to launch bombing attacks against Japan from mainland China, once it became clear that establishing bases posed numerous logistical difficulties. Instead, B-29 squadrons were to be based in the Marianas where they could easily receive a consistent flow of supplies from Hawaii and the US mainland. The idea of securing Formosa as a staging area for the invasion of the home islands was also abandoned when US planners realized that they did not have sufficient troops to capture the most heavily defended overseas possession in the Japanese empire. Instead, the Americans chose to take islands which were either less heavily guarded or more compact in size, such as the Philippines and Okinawa. In all cases, the ultimate aim was to optimize the overwhelming firepower which US forces were able to deploy. Operations were geared to exploit the weak points of Japan's war machine, while at the same time avoiding engagements where enemy defenses were strong.

The British were similarly judicious in planning their campaigns in Southeast Asia. The failed attempt to break through Japanese defenses in the border regions of Burma during the winter of 1942–43 served as a poignant reminder of how sufficient numerical strength, coupled with a sound logistical apparatus, were essential when fighting well-entrenched opponents. Upon taking command of the newly-created Fourteenth Army, General Slim made a concerted effort to procure enough equipment and munitions to enable his troops to reconquer Burma. The road networks in the eastern regions of India were also improved so that front-line units could receive the supplies they needed. By spring 1944, when Mutaguchi launched his offensive against the British strongholds at Imphal and Kohima, Slim's army was not only prepared to repel its attackers. The British-Indian army inflicted casualties that significantly diminished the IJA's defensive capabilities, and Slim exploited the situation by ordering a full-scale advance into Burma. Concurrently, Lord Mountbatten, the head of Southeast Asia Command, who had pressed for an operation to liberate the Malaya-Sumatra region, conceded that his plan was not feasible, since British naval forces in the Far East were not sufficient to support amphibious operations against strongly defended positions. By focusing on Burma, the British chose to fight in an area where they had better prospects of dismantling Japan's empire in the southern regions.

The prudence with which the Allies planned their strategy and operations was in stark contrast to the lack of sober judgment which frequently characterized Japan's conduct of the war. The demise of the IJN and IJA offers a telling example of how military organizations which fail to realistically assess the situation facing them most often end up incurring a decisive defeat. From the moment when Japanese leaders finalized their decision to initiate hostilities with the US and the Western powers in autumn 1941, their war plans overlooked their nation's fundamental problem, namely its inability to prevail in a total war, where victory hinged on the capacity to out-produce one's enemies. Instead, the high command placed its hopes on fighting a limited campaign where the aim was to conquer large parts of Southeast Asia, and establish an outer defense ring that included key island positions in the Pacific. Thereafter, Japan's forces were expected to inflict crippling losses on any Allied force that attempted to breach the perimeter. The Japanese could not expect to force their enemies to surrender by conquering their home territories, such as the US mainland or the British Isles. Instead, they hoped that the Allies would lose their will to continue fighting as their counter-offensive became forestalled, and eventually offer a negotiated peace whereby Japan's predominant position in Asia was recognized. There was little consideration of the possibility that that the US and its coalition partners would mobilize their economic might to construct a vastly superior force, and continue prosecuting their war effort until the Japanese nation capitulated. Even after 1943–44, when the Allied counter-offensive started to penetrate key strongholds along Japan's defense perimeter, including New Guinea, the Marianas and Burma, and the US and Great Britain made repeated demands that the Japanese surrendered unconditionally, the military high command held onto its wishful hope of arriving at a compromise peace. Thus, while resource shortages were the main handicap of Japan's war effort, flawed military thinking played a critical role in propelling the leadership to pursue a plan which was bound to end in failure.

At the tactical level, the Western powers again showed a good knowledge of the elements they had to deal with and the means to overcome them, while the Japanese tended to be less well informed. For the armed forces of the US and British empire, the overarching principle was to exploit the ample supply of technologically advanced weapons which they had at their disposal. The defeats which the Allies suffered during the opening stages of the war, along with the obstacles they faced during their initial counter-offensives in the latter part of 1942, demonstrated how had the IJN and IJA had the skill to inflict considerable levels of attrition on their opponents. Officers on the battlefront acknowledged how they needed to drastically improve the quality of their weapons as well as the standard of training among their personnel. The Americans were most successful in developing a capability to engage the Japanese in all dimension, at sea, in the air, and on land. The navy's doctrine emphasized the extensive use of modern innovations such as carrier-based aviation and radar-guided gunfire to destroy enemy fleets and secure control over the expanses of the Pacific Ocean. The Army Air Forces developed both the aircraft and techniques to carry out a range of missions, including the destruction of enemy air power to the provision of close support for ground troops, and conducting strategic bombing attacks against the enemy's economic facilities. On land, the US army and the Marine Corps devised a combination of moves to oust the Japanese from their garrisons. Heavy armaments such as tanks and artillery were deployed to reduce enemy positions, while infantry units carried out the final advance and killed off enemy troops. The British empire did not manage to build a navy that was large enough to conduct a large scale campaign against the Japanese, and for this reason, they were unable to develop the same combat effectiveness as the Americans. Nevertheless, in a manner similar to their US counterparts, the armies of Great Britain and Australia succeeded in developing a tactical doctrine that was well-suited for fighting the IJA. As was the case with the strategic and operational aspects of the conflict, Allied successes at the tactical level did not owe themselves solely to their ability to deliver overwhelming firepower. Intellectual factors, such as an ability to adjust procedures in accordance with the challenges posed by the enemy, and to comprehend the measures required to prevail in a fight against a resilient opponent, played a vital role in influencing the outcome of the conflict.

The fighting capabilities of the Imperial armed forces, on the other hand, were held back not only by their lack of weaponry. A number of deeply ingrained traditions within the military establishment, namely a tendency to downplay the qualities of enemy forces, along with a refusal to recognize the shortcomings of the Japanese navy and army, gave rise to a situation where commanders faced formidable difficulties in bringing about any types of innovations. The IJN and IJA both pursued a tactical doctrine which aimed to circumvent the problems arising from their numerical inferiority, by relying on tactical finesse. The move was unlikely to enable the Japanese to prevail in the long run, and one of their main failures was to overlook the need to prepare for engagements with properly equipped enemies. The navy did not make a serious effort to develop advanced technologies such as radars and search devices until the war broke out. The air services deployed planes which were fast and maneuverable, but lacked the armor and armament to withstand damage. Pilots were highly skilled, but too few in number, and the Japanese could not afford casualties. The army maintained that the dedication and bravery of its infantry troops guaranteed success, and did not attempt to improve its methods of using heavy weaponry. When the Japanese were forced onto the defensive after 1943, and realized that they faced enemies with better hardware and tactical skill, the armed forces were at a loss to find ways to improve their performance. By the closing stages of the war, the navy and army ended up resorting to suicide tactics, in a desperate attempt to inflict as many casualties as possible on the advancing Allied forces. While the tactical weaknesses of the IJN and IJA can be largely attributed to Japan's narrow industrial base and subsequent difficulties involved in producing large quantities of modern hardware, in the final analysis, the Japanese were defeated largely because they did not prepare for a prolonged war of attrition.

In addition to illustrating the strengths and weaknesses of the opposing sides' war efforts, and explaining the reasons for the Allied victory, the book has also attempted to address the pressing question of how racial factors shaped the conduct of the Pacific war. Owing to the distinct ethnic divide which separated Japan and the Western powers, students of the Pacific war find it almost impossible to ignore the issue of race and culture. Indeed, racial prejudices did influence the way in which the belligerents perceived each other, and the perceptions in turn had far-reaching effects on how they fought their campaigns. The Japanese held xenophobic views which dictated that the US and Britain were imperialist nations who sought to thwart the empire's ambitions. The opposition to Western colonialism, and the belief that the people of Asia were being liberated from exploitation, was one of the key aspects which the ruling elite used in order to justify their decision to declare war on America and its allies. The Japanese also viewed themselves as a superior race that had both a divine right and obligation to achieve an ascendant position in the Far East. The war crimes which the IJA carried out against the native populations of their occupied territories, as well as the use of Allied prisoners for slave labor, largely stemmed from a desire to subjugate Japan's enemies. The conviction that the Japanese were destined to dominate Asia and eliminate Western influence from the area also prevented the rank and file of the Imperial armed forces from acknowledging the problems they could face in attempting to defeat their Allied opponents.

For the Americans and their coalition partners, the war against Japan was similarly perceived in racial terms. The collapse of the Western powers' hold on Southeast Asia in the early part of 1942 gave rise to a mixed attitude of contempt and fear. The Japanese were portrayed as a vicious enemy who possessed an uncanny fighting ability along with a grandiose ambition for world conquest. Allied troops were indoctrinated to view their adversaries as a threat which had to be annihilated. The manner in which Japanese soldiers fought to the last man and carried out suicide charges against the advancing Western armies, along with the news of the atrocities which had been meted on Allied prisoners, created further hatred, and gave rise to the impression that the enemy was devoid of any human values. Such people could be defeated only by killing them off in their entirety. Racial animosities therefore laid the grounds for a magnitude of violent behavior which was not visible in many other theaters of World War II.

However, the previous chapters have also demonstrated how racist views did not significantly influence the key decisions which Western nations made on how their war efforts were to be conducted. The political leadership, along with decision-makers within the military, were motivated first and foremost by a practical concern, namely a desire to defeat the enemy as quickly as possible, while at the same time keeping casualties to a minimum. As the war progressed, the crude images, which depicted the Japanese as a backward, ruthless and inscrutable enemy, gradually gave way to a more complex assessment which acknowledged how their fighting capabilities were shaped by a number of unique traits. Among the most notable characteristics was a high level of dedication, which led both the army and navy to use bold tactics in battle. At the same time, because Japan's culture emphasized a strict adherence to set rules, there was a visible lack of initiative to devise new methods of fighting. Personnel within the Imperial forces were also seen to share some common characteristics with their Western counterparts. Soldiers tended to get demoralized when faced with setbacks, and the feature proved that the Japanese had weaknesses that hindered their fighting abilities. The development of a better knowledge regarding the underlying causes of the strengths and weaknesses of Japan's armed services, in turn, gave the Allies a strong advantage. Whereas the Japanese held onto their myopic views of the West until the closing stages of the conflict, the Western powers used their understanding of their opponent to facilitate their own war effort. By basing their judgments on pragmatism, rather than racism, the Allies managed to devise an efficient way to defeat their enemies.

The Pacific war remains an episode of considerable interest for historians of warfare and international relations because it was fought on a massive scale, and the conflict encompassed an array of facets, ranging from strategy and operations, to the development of tactics and weapons technologies, to mobilizing national economies and populations, and, last but not least, forging political relations with one's allies in order to defeat a common enemy. Of equal significance, the war marked a watershed, and gave birth to a modern East Asian order which has lasted until the present day. Among the most significant shifts was the dismantling of the European colonial empires, and the creation of sovereign states, many of which have become important regional powers. The successes which the Japanese achieved in expelling the Allies from Southeast Asia during the early part of 1942 discredited the European powers' ability to maintain their rule. Although Japan's claims to be creating a "Greater East Asia Co-prosperity Sphere" turned out to be propaganda, the local populations of Southeast Asia began to see a clearer path towards achieving independence. By the end of the war, nationalist parties developed into an advanced stage, thanks to two developments, the first of which was the moves that the Japanese undertook to promote anti-Western sentiment in their occupied territories. Secondly, the resistance movements which the people of Asia created against Japanese rule helped to forge a more coherent organization that could promote the idea of independence. Many of the post-war leaders of the newly-created nations, including Sukarno of Indonesia, and Ho Chi Minh of Vietnam, gained their popularity by either taking charge of the nationalist parties which the Japanese had established, or in other cases, by spearheading the opposition. When the British, French and Dutch attempted to re-establish their empires following Japan's surrender, they did not receive an all-too-warm reception from the populace. Within a decade, virtually all of the former colonies, including Malaya, Indochina and the East Indies, were given independence.

The demise of Imperial Japan also gave rise to a post-war government and society which has eschewed military action as a means to protect national interests, and as a result the Japanese continue to refrain from wielding a level of world power that is more commensurate with their economic clout. The post-war constitution, which was drawn up with help from MacArthur's SCAP headquarters, forbade the nation from engaging in armed conflicts. Although the growing threat of the Soviet Union and the spread of Communism in Asia during the Cold War gave rise to slight amendments that allowed the creation of a homeland defense force, the deployment of military forces beyond the confines of the home islands and adjacent waters was still prohibited. The government, along with the vast majority of the population, have whole-heartedly embraced the idea of pacifism, so much so that even in the post-Cold War world, with the United States cutting back on its overseas military commitments and pressing its allies in to take on greater responsibility for their own defense, the Japanese have remained reluctant to do so. The principles espoused by Yoshida, the first post-war prime minister, of concentrating on economic growth and keeping defense spending to a minimum, while relying on the US to provide security against external threats, continue to form the basis for Japan's foreign policy. The government is currently contemplating possible ways to play a more active role in world politics. After all, Japan is a full member of the G-8 organization of the world's richest countries, and has the potential to become a leading power, both in the Asia-Pacific region and on the international stage. Following the 11 September attacks on the United States and the subsequent declaration of the "war on terror," a legislative package gave the self-defense forces a more active non-combat role, and units were sent to operate in foreign war zones, including Afghanistan and Iraq, for the first time since 1945. The legislation raised serious questions on whether the government can continue following Article Nine of the constitution, which renounces Japan's right to participate in foreign conflicts. Although the leading political parties have endeavored to revise the restrictions, public opinion has opposed such measures, out of fear that they would lead to a resurgence of militarism. A more serious obstacle, however, is that Japan's neighbors in Asia are uneasy about the possible revival of their former enemy. The situation is complicated because East Asia is now one of the most volatile areas of the world with two of the main Communist powers in the region, namely China and North Korea, demanding territorial concessions. Both powers also possess nuclear forces which act as a destabilizing factor. While Japan certainly has the resources to develop a military force that can provide security for Asia, for most countries in the region, such scenarios still raise fears of Japanese militarism, and threaten to bring back memories of the destruction and exploitation which had been endured during the wartime occupation. The legacy of the conflict thus acts as a key hindrance to introducing measures that can resolve some of the urgent security issues which currently riddle the nations of the Far East. For this reason, the Pacific war is not simply a matter of mere historical interest, but is also of direct relevance to any study of present-day international relations.

Notes

Notes to Introduction

1   J. Costello, *The Pacific War, 1941-1945* (NY: Rawson-Wade, 1981); and R. Spector, *The Eagle Against the Sun: the American war with Japan* (NY: Vintage Books, 1985).

2   S. Hayashi, in collaboration with A. Coox, *Kogun: the Japanese Army in the Pacific War* (Quantico, VA: Marine Corps Association, 1959); and P. Dull, *A Battle History of the Imperial Japanese Navy, 1941-45* (Annapolis, MD: Naval Institute Press, 1978).

3   For the US Navy, see S. Morison, *Coral Sea, Midway and Submarine Actions, May 1942 to August 1942; The Struggle for Guadalcanal, August 1942 to February 1943; Breaking the Bismarcks Barrier, 22 July 1942 to 1 May 1944; Aleutians, Gilberts and Marshalls, June 1942 to April 1944; New Guinea and the Marianas, March 1944 to August 1944; Leyte, June 1944 to January 1945; The Liberation of the Philippines: Luzon, Mindanao, the Visayas, 1944-45; Victory in the Pacific, 1945,* in series *History of United States Naval Operations in World War II,* reprinted versions, (Boston: Little, Brown & Co.; Chicago: Illinois UP; Urbana: Illinois UP; and Edison, NJ: Castle Books, 1989-2002).
For the US Army, see J. Miller, Jr., *Cartwheel: the Reduction of Rabaul;* P. Crowl and E. Love, *Seizure of the Gilberts and Marshalls;* P. A. Crowl, *Campaign in the Marianas;* R. Smith, *The Approach to the Philippines;* M. Cannon, *Leyte: the return to the Philippines,* and *Triumph in the Philippines;* R. Appleman, *Okinawa: the last battle,* in series *The US Army in World War II: The War in the Pacific* (Washington, DC: Historical Division, Department of the Army, 1944-81).
For an account of the operations of the US Army Air Forces, see W. Craven and J. Cate (eds.), *The Army Air Forces in World War II, Vol.4, The Pacific: Guadalcanal to Saipan, August 1942 to July 1944,* and *Vol.5, The Pacific: Matterhorn to Nagasaki, June 1944 to August 1945* (Washington, DC: Office of Air Force History, 1983).

4   See A. Iriye, *The Origins of the Second World War in Asia and the Pacific* (London: Longman, 1987).

5   J. Ellis, *Brute Force: Allied strategy and tactics in the Second World War* (London: Andre Deutsch, 1990), pp. 495, 538. Similar arguments can be found in P. Kennedy, *The Rise and Fall of the Great Powers: economic change and military conflict from 1500 to 2000* (London: Harper-Collins, 1988), pp. 456, 458-9; A. Millett and W. Murray, *A War to be Won: fighting the Second World War* (Cambridge, MA: Belknap, Harvard UP, 2000), pp. 204, 337-8, 351-2, 527-45; G. Weinberg, *A World at Arms: a global history of World War II* (Cambridge: CUP, 1994), p. 338.

6   R. Overy, *Why the Allies Won* (NY: Norton, 1995), pp. 2, 5–6, 192, 318, 345.

7   J. Dower, *War Without Mercy: race and power in the Pacific War* (NY: Pantheon, 1986).

Notes on Chapter 1

1   Kennedy, 1988, pp. 265–9.

2   W. Beasley, *The Rise of Modern Japan* (NY: St. Martin's, 1990), pp. 87–8.

3   E. Norman, *Japan's Emergence as a Modern State: political and economic problems of the Meiji Period*, Reprinted version (Westport: Greenwood, 1973), pp. 121–5.

4   See W. Beasley, *Japanese Imperialism, 1894–1945* (Oxford: OUP, 1987), chapter 3; R. Benedict, *The Chrysanthemum and the Sword: patterns in Japanese culture* (Cambridge, MA: Riverside, 1946), chapter 4; C. Gluck, *Japan's Modern Myths: ideology in the late Meiji period* (Princeton: Princeton UP, 1985), especially chapters 1–2, 8 and Epilogue; C. Tsuzuki, *The Pursuit of Power in Modern Japan, 1825–1995* (Oxford: OUP, 2000), pp. 113–15.

5   R. Storry, *Japan and the Decline of the West in Asia, 1894–1943* (London: Longman's, 1979), pp. 15–17.

6   A. Iriye, *After Imperialism: the search for a New Order in the Far East, 1921–31* (Cambridge, MA: Harvard UP, 1965), p. 6.

7   E. Miller, *War Plan Orange: the US Strategy to defeat Japan, 1897–1945* (Annapolis: Naval Institute Press, 1991), pp. 19–114. "Orange" was the color code which US defense planners designated for Japan's forces.

8   See S. Asada, "From Washington to London: the Imperial Japanese Navy and the politics of naval limitation, 1921–30," and D. Armstrong, "China's Place in the New Pacific Order," in E. Goldstein and J. Maurer (eds.), *The Washington Conference, 1921–1922: naval rivalry, East Asian stability and the road to Pearl Harbor* (London, Frank Cass, 1994), pp. 156–62, 255–6.

9   L. Morton, *Strategy and Command: the first two years*, in series United States Army in World War II: *The War in the Pacific* (Washington, DC: Office of the Chief of Military History, 1962–89), p. 27.

10   T. Buckley, "The Icarus Factor: the American pursuit of myth in naval arms control, 1921–36," in Goldstein and Maurer (eds.), 1994, pp. 134–6.

11   Miller, 1991, pp. 75–6, 114.

12   S. Kirby, *Singapore: the chain of disaster* (London: Cassell, 1971), pp. 11–18.

13   Iriye, 1965, pp. 24–8.

14   Ibid., pp. 283–5.

Notes on Chapter 2

1   A. Iriye, *The Origins of the Second World War in Asia and the Pacific* (London: Longman's 1987), pp. 35–6.

2   See I. Morris (ed.), *Japan, 1931–1945 militarism, fascism, Japanism?* (NY: D. C. Heath &

Co., 1963), especially Part 2; M. Maruyama, *Thought and Behaviour in Japanese Politics*, edited by I. Morris (Oxford: OUP, 1963), chapters 2, 4–5.

3   M. Barnhart, "Japanese intelligence before the Second World War: "best case" analysis," in E. May (ed.), *Knowing One's Enemies: intelligence assessment before the two World Wars* (Princeton, NJ: Princeton UP, 1984), pp. 432–5.

4   M. Peattie, *Sunburst: the rise of Japanese naval air power, 1909–1941* (Annapolis: Naval Institute Press, 2001), pp. 109–21.

5   J. Chapman, "Japanese intelligence, 1918–1945: a suitable case for treatment," in C. Andrew and J. Noakes (eds.), *Intelligence and International Relations, 1900–1945* (Exeter: Exeter UP, 1987), pp. 168–9.

6   A. Coox, *Nomonhan: Japan against Russia, 1939* (Stanford: Stanford UP, 1985), p. 1027.

7   Barnhart, "Japanese intelligence," in May (ed.), 1984, pp. **???**.

8   L. Humphreys, *The Way of the Heavenly Sword: The Japanese Army in the 1920s* (Stanford: Stanford UP, 1995), p. 15, 79–83.

9   E. Drea, *In the Service of the Emperor: essays on the Imperial Japanese Army* (Lincoln: Nebraska UP, 1998), pp. 64–5.

10   United States National Archives and Records Administration, College Park, MD (NARA 2), RG 165, War Department, Military Intelligence Division, M-1216, General correspondence regarding conditions in Japan, 1918–1941 (hereafter M-1216), Roll 25, MID 2023–1005, Tactical Doctrine of the Japanese Army, by Captain Maxwell D. Taylor (Field Artillery), 1 April 1939.

11   Coox, 1985, pp. 1009–32.

12   Peattie, 2001, pp. 109–21.

13   See: A. Best, *British Intelligence and the Japanese Challenge in Asia, 1914–1941* (London: Macmillan, 2002); J. Ferris, "Worthy of some better enemy?: the British estimate of the Imperial Japanese Army, and the fall of Singapore, 1919–1941," in *Canadian Journal of History*, 28/2, (1993), pp. 223–56; D. Ford, "The best equipped army in Asia?: US military intelligence and the Imperial Japanese Army before the Pacific War, 1919–1941," in *International Journal of Intelligence and Counterintelligence*, 21/1, (2008), pp. 86–121; T. Mahnken, *Uncovering Ways of War: US intelligence and foreign military innovation, 1918–1941* (Ithaca: Cornell UP, 2002); A. Marder, *Old Friends, New Enemies: the Royal Navy and the Imperial Japanese Navy, 1936–45, Vol.1: Strategic illusions, 1936–41* (Oxford: OUP, 1981).

14   NARA 2, RG 165, M-1444, Roll 10, MID 2637-I-276, Reports on Military Events by Military Attaché (China), 12 January and 6 April 1938.

15   United Kingdom National Archives, London (UKNA), WO 106/2440 Appreciation by General L. V. Bond (GOC Malaya), 13 April 1940, and comments by General Staff, War Office, 5 May 1940.

16   O. Chung, *Operation Matador: Britain's war plans against the Japanese, 1918–41* (Singapore: Times Academic Press, 1997), pp. 133–41.

17   UKNA, CAB 56/4 JIC 90 Intelligence Regarding Air Warfare in Spain and China: Report No.2 – Air Cooperation with Land Forces, 10 June 1939.

18   J. Thach, "Butch O'Hare and the Thach Weave," in E. Wooldridge (ed.), *Carrier Warfare in the Pacific: an oral history collection* (Washington, DC: Smithsonian Institution, 1993),

pp. 10–12; J. Rearden, *Cracking the Zero Mystery: how the US learned to beat Japan's vaunted WWII fighter plane* (Harrisburg, PA: Stackpole, 1990), p. 17.

19   M. Okumiya and J. Horikoshi, with M. Caidin, *Zero!: the story of the Japanese Navy Air Force, 1937–1945* (London: Cassell, 1956), pp. 38–9.

Notes on Chapter 3

1   A. Iriye, *The Origins of the Second World War in Asia and the Pacific* (London: Longman's 1987), pp. 116.

2   N. Ike (ed.), *Japan's Decision for War: records of the 1941 Policy Conferences* (Stanford, CA: Stanford UP, 1967), p. 50.

3   Iriye, 1987, p. 135.

4   S. Kirby, *The War Against Japan, Vol.1* in series *History of the Second World War* (London: HMSO, 1957–70), p. 33.

5   M. Matloff and E. Snell, *Strategic Planning for Coalition Warfare*, in series *United States Army in World War II: The War Department* (Washington, DC: Office of the Chief of Military History, 1950–55), pp. 13–14.

6   L. Brune, *The Origins of American National Security Policy: sea power, air power and foreign policy, 1900–1941* (Manhattan, KA: MA/AH Publishing, 1981), p. 116.

7   O. Chung, *Operation Matador: Britain's war plans against the Japanese, 1918–41* (Singapore: Times Academic Press, 1997), pp. 142–69.

8   Imperial War Museum, London (IWM), Percival Papers, P 49 Some Personal Observations of the Malaya Campaign, 1940–2: prepared by B. H. Ashmore, 27 July 1942.

9   L. Allen, *Singapore, 1941–1942* (Newark: Delaware UP, 1977); H. Bennett, *Why Singapore Fell* (Sydney: Angus & Robertson, 1944); R. Callahan, *The Worst Disaster: the fall of Singapore* (London: Associated University Press, 1977); P. Elphick, *Singapore: the pregnable fortress* (London: Hodder & Stoughton, 1995); Kirby, 1971, passim, and 1957–70, Vol.1, passim.; A. Percival, *The War in Malaya* (London: Eyre & Spottiswoode, 1949); A. Warren, *Singapore, 1942: Britain's greatest defeat* (London: Hambledon, 2002).

10   Liddell Hart Centre for Military Archives, King's College London (LHCMA), Pownall Diaries, February 25, 1942.

11   M. Lowenthal, *Leadership and Indecision: American war planning and policy process, 1937–1942*, Vol.1 (NY: Garland, 1988), p. 398.

12   Matloff and Snell, 1950–55, p. 43.

13   Iriye, 1987, pp. 144–6; N. Shinjiro, "The drive into southern Indochina and Thailand," in J. Morley, (ed.) *The Fateful Choice: Japan's advance into Southeast Asia, 1939–41*, from translated series, *taiheiyo senso e no michi: kaisen gaiko shi* – Japan's Road to the Pacific War (NY: Columbia UP, 1980), pp. 235–7.

14   M. Barnhart, *Japan Prepares for Total War: the search for economic security, 1919–1941* (Ithaca, NY: Cornell UP, 1987), pp. 239–44; Ike, 1967, pp. 112–29; J. Morley, *The Final Confrontation: Japan's negotiations with the United States, 1941*, from translated series, *taiheiyo senso e no michi: kaisen gaiko shi* (NY: Columbia UP, 1994), pp. 163–7.

15   Ike, 1967, pp. 131–2, 135–8, 160.

16 Lowenthal, 1988, Vol.1, p. 427, and Vol.2, p. 594; R. Dallek, *Franklin D Roosevelt and American Foreign Policy, 1932–1945* (Oxford, OUP, 1995), p. 242.

17 NARA 2, RG 165, War Department, General Staff, WPD, Box 214, File 4344–2, WPD Memorandum on Oil Wells in the East Indies, 13 January 1941.

18 NARA 2, RG 165, War Department, General Staff, WPD, Box 109, File 3251–60, WPD Memorandum for the Secretary of War, on the Strategic Concept of the Philippine Islands, 3 October 1941.

19 UKNA, CAB 80/29 COS (41) 474 (Annex) Report by Joint Planning Subcommittee, 3 August 1941.

20 R. Butow, *Tojo and the Coming of War* (Stanford: Stanford UP, 1961), pp. 246–7.

21 M. Barnhart, "Japanese intelligence before the Second World War: 'best case' analysis," in E. May (ed.), *Knowing One's Enemies: intelligence assessment before the two World Wars* (Princeton, NJ: Princeton UP, 1984), p. 424.

22 D. James, "American and Japanese strategies in the Pacific War," in P. Paret et al. (eds.), *Makers of Modern Strategy: Machiavelli to the nuclear age* (Oxford: Clarendon, 1986), p. 715.

23 Ike, 1967, p. 153.

24 Ibid., p. 191; Also see Morley, *Final Confrontation*, pp. 296–7.

25 Butow, 1961, p. 317.

26 The most comprehensive secondary accounts on this aspect include: I. Cowman, "Main fleet to Singapore? Churchill, the Admiralty and Force Z," in *Journal of Strategic Studies*, 17/2, (1994), pp. 79–93; J. Pritchard, "Churchill, the military and imperial defence in East Asia," in S. Dockrill (ed.), *From Pearl Harbor to Hiroshima: the Second World War in Asia and the Pacific, 1941–45* (Basingstoke: Macmillan, 1994), pp. 26–54 and chapter 11 of S. Roskill, *Churchill and the Admirals* (London: Collins, 1977).

27 M. Watson, *Chief of Staff: Prewar Plans and Preparations*, in series *United States Army in World War II: The War Department* (Washington, DC: Office of the Chief of Military History, 1950–55), p. 439; W. Craven and J. Cate, *The Army Air Forces in World War II, Vol.1: Plans and Early Operations* (Washington, DC: Office of Air Force History, 1948), pp. 176–7, 184–5.

28 Brune, 1981, p. 119; W. Heinrichs, *Threshold of War: Franklin D Roosevelt and the American entry into World War II* (Oxford: OUP, 1988), p. 195.

29 L. Morton, *The Fall of the Philippines, and Strategy and Command: the first two years*, in series *United States Army in World War II: The War in the Pacific* (Washington, DC: Office of the Chief of Military History, 1962–1989), pp. 31–2, 64.

30 NARA 2, RG 165, War Department, General Staff, WPD, Box 109, File 3251–61, WPD Memorandum for Chief of Staff, on Command in the Philippines, 13 October 1941.

31 See J. Toland, *Infamy: Pearl Harbor and its aftermath* (Garden City, NY: Doubleday, 1982); R. Stinnett, *Day of Deceit: the truth about FDR and Pearl Harbor* (NY: Free Press, 1999).

32 J. Prados, *Combined Fleet Decoded: the secret history of American intelligence and the Japanese Navy in World War II* (Annapolis: Naval Institute Press, 1995), p. 163.

33 L. Farago, *The Broken Seal: the story of "Operation Magic" and the Pearl Harbor disaster* (NY: Random House, 1967), p. 159.

34   G. Prange, *At Dawn We Slept: the untold story of Pearl Harbor* (London: Michael Joseph, 1981), p. 355.

35   Prados, 1995, pp. 167–8.

36   In addition to the works cited in notes 31–4, above, see R. Aldrich, *Intelligence and the War against Japan: Britain, America and the politics of secret service* (Cambridge: CUP, 2000), chapter 5; Costello, 1981, pp. 670–714; R. Wohlstetter, *Pearl Harbor: Warning and Decision* (Stanford, CA: Stanford UP, 1962).

37   See K. Kotani, "Pearl Harbor: Japanese planning and command structure," in D. Marston (ed.), *The Pacific War Companion: from Pearl Harbor to Hiroshima* (NY: Osprey, 2007), pp. 31–45.

38   S. Morison, *The Rising Sun in the Pacific, 1931 – April 1942*, in series *History of United States Naval Operations in World War II*, Vol.3, reprinted version (Chicago: Illinois UP, 2001), pp. 129–31.

Notes on Chapter 4

1   P. Dull, *A Battle History of the Imperial Japanese Navy, 1941–45* (Annapolis, MD: Naval Institute Press, 1978), pp. 10–18.

2   For details, see S. Hayashi in collaboration with A. Coox, *Kogun: the Japanese Army in the Pacific War* (Quantico, VA: Marine Corps Association, 1959), pp. 36–9.

3   D. Evans and M. Peattie, *Kaigun: the strategy, tactics and technology of the Imperial Japanese Navy, 1887–1941* (Annapolis: Naval Institute Press, 1997), pp. 187–8, 194–201, 205–12, 238–9.

4   M. Tsuji, *Japan's Greatest Victory, Britain's Worst Defeat* (NY: Sarpedon, 1993), pp. 6, 24–6, 33–41.

5   P. Elphick, *Far Eastern File: the intelligence war in the Far East, 1930–45* (London: Hodder & Stoughton, 1997), pp. 3–4, 48–51, 215–18.

6   H. Jentschura et al., *Warships of the Imperial Japanese Navy, 1869–1945*, translated by A. Preston and J. Brown (Annapolis: Naval Institute Press, 1992), p. 35; A. Watts and B. Gordon, *The Imperial Japanese Navy* (NY: Doubleday, 1971), pp. 40–1, 52–8.

7   A. Yoshimura, *Zero Fighter*, translated by R. Kaiho and M. Gregson (Westport, CT: Praeger, 1996), pp. 39–49. For a firsthand account, see J. Horikoshi, *Eagles of Mitsubishi: the story of the Zero fighter*, translated by S. Shindo and H. Wantiez (London: Orbis, 1981), pp. 3–8, 32–64.

8   M. Peattie, *Sunburst: the rise of Japanese naval air power, 1909–1941* (Annapolis: Naval Institute Press, 2001), pp. 21–51.

9   W. Karig, *Battle Report: Pearl Harbor to Coral Sea* (NY: Farrar & Rinehart, 1944), p. 169.

10   LHCMA, HUTTON 2/40 Précis of Operations in Burma, Undated? late 1942.

11   LHCMA, Pownall Diaries, Note by Lieutenant-Colonel Phillips (formerly GSO1(O) Malaya Command), Undated? March 1942.

12   US Army Military History Institute, Carlisle, PA (MHI), *Infantry Journal*, "Lessons of Bataan," by Colonel Milton A. Hill, October 1942.

13   LHCMA, Pownall Diaries, "Causes of Failure," 5 March 1942.

14   K. Akagi, "Leadership in Japan's planning for war against Britain," in B. Bond and K. Tachikawa (eds.), *British and Japanese Military Leadership in the Far Eastern War, 1941–1945* (Abingdon: Frank Cass, 2004), pp. 57–8.

15   H. Willmott, *Empires in the Balance: Japanese and Allied Pacific strategies to April 1942* (Annapolis: Naval Institute Press, 1982), p. 437.

16   R. Tobe, "Tojo Hideki as war leader," in Bond and Tachikawa (eds.), *British and Japanese Military Leadership in the Far Eastern War, 1941–1945* (Abingdon: Frank Cass, 2004), pp. 26–7, p. 31–2.

17   P. Kennedy, "Japanese strategic decisions, 1939–45," in idem., *Strategy and Diplomacy, 1870–1945* (London: Allen & Unwin, 1983), p. 186.

18   See J. Wood, *Japanese Military Strategy in the Pacific War: was defeat inevitable?* (Lanham, MD: Rowman & Littlewood, 2007), pp. 26–8.

19   United States Strategic Bombing Survey (USSBS), *Japanese Military and Naval Intelligence Division* (Washington, DC: Government Printing Office, 1946), pp. 20–1.

20   S. Hayashi, in collaboration with A. Coox, *Kogun: the Japanese Army in the Pacific War* (Quantico, VA: Marine Corps Association, 1959), p. 45.

21   B. Shillony, *Politics and Culture in Wartime Japan* (Oxford: OUP, 1981), p. 134.

22   A. Oi, "Why Japan's anti-submarine warfare failed," in D. Evans (ed.), *The Japanese Navy in World War II: in the words of former Japanese naval officers*, 2nd edition (Annapolis: Naval Institute Press, 1986), p. 387.

23   M. Parillo, *The Japanese Merchant Marine in World War II* (Annapolis: Naval Institute Press, 1993), pp. 7–12, 14–17.

24   G. Krebs, "The Japanese air forces," in H. Boog (ed.), *The Conduct of the Air War in the Second World War: an international comparison* (Oxford: Berg Publishers, 1992), p. 230.

25   J. Parshall and A. Tully, *Shattered Sword: the untold story of the Battle of Midway* (Washington, DC: Potomac, 2005), pp. 404–6.

26   S. Kirby, *The War Against Japan*, 5 Vols. in series *History of the Second World War* (London: HMSO, 1957–70), Vol.2, p. 128.

Notes on Chapter 5

1   UKNA, CAB 79/56 COS (42) 4th Meeting (O), 21 January 1942.

2   UKNA, CAB 80/34 COS (42) 128 Far East Situation: Report by COS, February 21, 1942. Also see Kirby, 1957–70, Vol.1, pp. 296, 357–8, 424.

3   G. Hayes, *The History of the Joint Chiefs of Staff in World War II: the war against Japan* (Annapolis: Naval Institute Press, 1982), pp. 108–20.

4   E. King and W. Whitehill, *Fleet Admiral King: a naval record* (London: Eyre & Spottiswoode, 1953), p. 164.

5   C. Thorne, *Allies of a Kind: the United States, Britain, and the war against Japan, 1941–1945* (Oxford: OUP, 1978), pp. 252–9.

6   C. Barnett, *Engage the Enemy More Closely: the Royal Navy in the Second World War* (NY: Norton, 1991), p. 863.

7   S. Kirby, *The War Against Japan*, 5 Vols. in series *History of the Second World War* (London: HMSO, 1957–70), Vol. 2, pp. 127–30.

8   J. Costello, *The Pacific War, 1941–1945* (NY: Rawson-Wade, 1981), p. 249.

9   S. Roskill, *The War at Sea, Vol.2*, in series *History of the Second World War* (London: HMSO, 1954–61), p. 29; A. Marder, assisted by M. Jacobsen and J. Horsfield, *Old Friends, New Enemies: the Royal Navy and the Imperial Japanese Navy, 1936–45, Vol.2: The Pacific War, 1942–45* (Oxford: Clarendon, 1990), pp. 137–42.

10   H. Willmott, *The War With Japan: the period of balance, May 1942 – October 1943* (Wilmington, DE: Scholarly Resources, 2002), p. 90.

11   Ibid., pp. 94–5.

12   Hayes, 1982, pp. 177–86.

13   US Naval Historical Center, Washington, DC (NHC), Papers of Chester Nimitz, Series 1, World War II Command Series, Box 11, Future operations in the Solomons Sea area, 8 December 1942.

14   R. Spector, *The Eagle Against the Sun: the American war with Japan* (NY: Vintage Books, 1985), pp. 208–9.

15   D. Warner et al., *Disaster in the Pacific: new light on the battle of Savo island* (Annapolis: Naval Institute Press, 1992), pp. 215–16.

16   Morison, *Guadalcanal*, pp. 61–2.

17   E. Bergerud, *Fire in the Sky: the air war in the South Pacific* (Boulder, CO: Westview, 1999), pp. 248–62, 466.

18   J. Lundstrom, *The First Team and the Guadalcanal Campaign: naval fighter combat from August to November 1942* (Annapolis: Naval Institute Press, 1994), pp. 62–3 .

19   NARA 2, RG 38, ONI, Air Intelligence Group (Op 16-V), Serials and Publications, Box 12, Narrative of Japanese anti-shipping attacks, 1941–43, Comment by Commanding Officer, USS *Hornet*, on Battle of Santa Cruz, 26 October 1942.

20   R. Spector, *At War at Sea: sailors and naval combat in the Twentieth Century* (NY: Viking, 2001), p. 203.

21   US Air Force Historical Research Agency, Maxwell Air Base, AL, (AFHRA), Call Number 730.168, US Army Forces in Australia, Air Section, Tactical lessons from aircraft in combat, prepared for Chief of Army Air Forces, 27 March 1942.

22   NHC, Papers of Chester Nimitz, Series 1, World War II Command Series, Box 11, Future operations in the Solomons Sea area, 8 December 1942.

23   J. Lindley, *Carrier Victory: the air war in the Pacific* (NY: Elsevier-Dutton, 1978), pp. 90–1; also see J. Rearden, *Cracking the Zero Mystery: how the US learned to beat Japan's vaunted WWII fighter plane* (Harrisburg, PA: Stackpole, 1990), pp. 17–19.

24   NWC, Manuscript Collection, Papers of Edwin T. Layton, Box 30, Interview with E. B. Potter, 10 August 1972.

25   J. Luvaas, "Buna: a Leavenworth nightmare," in C. Heller and W. Stofft (eds.), *America's First Battles, 1776–1965* (Lawrence, KA: Kansas UP, 1986), pp. 188–9.

26   J. Shortal, *Forged by Fire: Robert L. Eichelberger and the Pacific War* (Columbia, SC: South Carolina UP, 1987), p. 45.

27   S. Milner, *Victory in Papua*, in series *The US Army in World War II: The War in the Pacific*

(Washington, DC: Historical Division, Department of the Army, 1949–57), pp. 245–6, 262–3.

28   M. Johnston, *Fighting the Enemy: Australian soldiers and their adversaries in World War II* (Cambridge: CUP, 2000), p. 77.

29   NARA 2, RG 127, Records of the US Marine Corps, World War II Operations, Box 39, First Marine Division, *Division Commander's Final Report on Guadalcanal Operations, Phase III: Organization of the Lunga Point Defenses, 10–21 August.*

30   Miller, *Guadalcanal*, p. 318.

31   See LHCMA, Alanbrooke papers, 6/2/6 f.8B Operation *Fantastical*: Most Secret Memorandum by Wavell for Alanbrooke, 17 September 1942.

32   UKNA, WO 203/4615 Dispatch on Operations in India Command, 1 January to 20 June 1943 by Field-Marshal Wavell.

33   Willmott, 2002, pp. 167–70.

Notes on Chapter 6

1   J. Ellis, *Brute Force: Allied strategy and tactics in the Second World War* (London: Andre Deutsch, 1990), pp. 483–4.

2   A. Millett and W. Murray, "The effectiveness of military organizations," in *International Security*, 11/1, (1986), pp. 37–71.

3   K. Greenfield, *American Strategy in World War II: a reconsideration* (Malabar, FL: Krieger, 1963), pp. 4–5, 10–12.

4   S. Ross, *American War Plans, 1941–1945* (London: Frank Cass, 1997), pp. 44–5.

5   J. Costello, *The Pacific War, 1941–1945* (NY: Rawson-Wade, 1981), pp. 418–19.

6   C. Thorne, *Allies of a Kind: the United States, Britain, and the war against Japan, 1941–1945* (Oxford: OUP, 1978), p. 364.

7   J. Barlow, "World War II: US and Japanese naval strategies," in C. Gray and R. Barnett (eds.), *Seapower and Strategy* (London: Tri-Service Press, 1989), p. 248.

8   N. Friedman, *The US Maritime Strategy* (London: Jane's 1988), pp. 213, 235.

9   G. Hayes, *The History of the Joint Chiefs of Staff in World War II: the war against Japan* (Annapolis: Naval Institute Press, 1982), p. 390.

10   K. Akagi, "Leadership in Japan's planning for war against Britain," in B. Bond and K. Tachikawa (eds.), *British and Japanese Military Leadership in the Far Eastern War, 1941–1945* (Abingdon: Frank Cass, 2004), pp. 61–2.

11   P. Dull, *A Battle History of the Imperial Japanese Navy, 1941–45* (Annapolis, MD: Naval Institute Press, 1978), pp. 494, 515.

12   K. Ikeda, "Japanese strategy in the Pacific War, 1941–1945," in I. Nish (ed.), *Anglo-Japanese Alienation, 1919–52: papers of the Anglo-Japanese Conference on the history of the Second World War* (Cambridge: CUP, 1982), pp. 125–46.

13   M. Chihaya, "An intimate look at the Japanese navy," in D. Goldstein and K. Dillon (eds.), *The Pearl Harbor Papers: inside the Japanese plans* (Dulles, VA: Brassey's, 1993), p. 319.

14   S. Hayashi, in collaboration with A. Coox, *Kogun: the Japanese Army in the Pacific War* (Quantico, VA: Marine Corps Association, 1959), pp. 72–3.

15 H. Willmott, *Grave of a Dozen Schemes: British naval planning and the war against Japan, 1943–45* (London: Airlife, 1996), *passim*.

16 A. Marder, et al., 1981–90, Vol.2, pp. 295–8; S. Kirby, *The War Against Japan*, 5 Vols. in series *History of the Second World War* (London: HMSO, 1957–70), Vol.2, p. 420.

17 N. Sarantakes, "One last crusade: the British Pacific Fleet and its impact on the British-American alliance," in *English Historical Review*, 121/491, (2006), pp. 437–40.

18 Greenfield, 1963, pp. 55–6.

19 Ross, 1997, pp. 50–2.

20 T. Wilds, "The admiral who lost his fleet," in *United States Naval Institute Proceedings*, 77 (November 1951), pp. 1175–8.

21 Hayashi, 1959, p. 107.

22 UKNA, CAB 81/114, JIC (43) 117 (O), The *Anakim* Plan: Reply to Future Planning Section Questionnaire by JIC, 16 March 1943; CAB 80/73, COS (43) 471 (O), Enclosure: js (*Quadrant*) 6, Operations in Sumatra, Report by JIC, 8 August 1943; CAB 81/117, JIC (43) 369 (O) (Revised Final), Operations Against Northern Sumatra: Report by JIC, 27 September 1943.

23 W. Slim, *Defeat into Victory* (London: Cassell, 1956), pp. 169–77.

24 E. Forrestel, *Admiral Raymond A Spruance: a study in command* (Washington, DC: Naval Historical Center, 1966), pp. 137–8; B. Tillman, *Clash of the Carriers: the true story of the Marianas Turkey Shoot of World War II* (NY: Nal Caliber, 2005), p. 100; pp. 331–2; W. Y'Blood, *Red Sun Setting: the Battle of the Philippine Sea* (Annapolis: Naval Institute Press, 1981), pp. 212–13.

25 J. Ehrman, *Grand Strategy, Vol.5*, in series *History of the Second World War* (London: HMSO, 1956–72), pp. 495–6; Kirby, 1957–70, Vol.4, p. 7.

26 A. Coox, "Flawed perception and its effect upon operational thinking: the case of the Japanese Army, 1937–41," in M. Handel (ed.), *Intelligence and Military Operations* (London: Frank Cass, 1990), pp. 242–3.

Notes on Chapter 7

1 A. Millet and W. Murray, "The effectiveness of military organizations," in *International Security*, 11/1, (1986), p. 60.

2 J. Kuehn, *Agents of Innovation: the General Board and the design of the fleet that defeated the Japanese Navy* (Annapolis: Naval Institute Press, 2008), p. 101.

3 J. Belote and W. Belote, *Titans of the Seas: the development and operations of Japanese and American carrier task forces during World War II* (NY: Harper & Row, 1975), p. 212.

4 S. Morison, *New Guinea and the Marianas*, p. 262.

5 R. Overy, *The Air War, 1939–45* (London: Europa, 1980), pp. 95–6.

6 Okumiya and Horikoshi, with M. Caidin, *Zero!: the story of the Japanese Navy Air Force, 1937–1945* (London: Cassell, 1956), pp. 293–4.

7 H. Sakaida, *Imperial Japanese Navy Aces, 1937–1945* (Oxford: Osprey, 1999), p. 63.

8   J. Horikoshi, *Eagles of Mitsubishi: the story of the Zero fighter*, translated by S. Shindo and H. Wantiez (London: Orbis, 1981), p. 144.

9   M. Peattie, *Sunburst: the rise of Japanese naval air power, 1909–1941* (Annapolis: Naval Institute Press, 2001), pp. 181–4.

10 G. Till, "Adopting the aircraft carrier: the British, American and Japanese case studies," in A. Millett and W. Murray (eds.), *Military Innovation in the Interwar Period* (Cambridge: CUP, 1996), pp. 197–203, 205–9, 218–19.

11 G. Weir, "The search for an American submarine strategy and design, 1916–1936," in *Naval War College Review*, 44, (Winter 1991), pp. 41–4.

12 C. Blair, *Silent Victory: the US submarine war against Japan* (NY: J. B. Lippincott, 1975), p. 280.

13 D. Evans and M. Peattie, *Kaigun: the strategy, tactics and technology of the Imperial Japanese Navy, 1887–1941* (Annapolis: Naval Institute Press, 1997), pp. 496–7.

14 C. Boyd and A. Yoshida, *The Japanese Submarine Force and World War II* (Annapolis: Naval Institute Press, 1995), pp. 34–5, 50–1, 124–5, 189–90.

15 Evans and Peattie, 1997, pp. 507–8.

16 J. Campbell, *Naval Weapons of World War Two* (London: Conway, 1985), p. 176.

17 Battle Experience, Leyte Gulf, 23–7 October 1944, dated 1 March 1945, accessed via www.ibiblio.org/hyperwar/USN/rep/Leyte/BatExp, on 10 February 2009, Enclosure: Carrier Task Group 77.2 Comments on Gunnery.

18 R. Cox, *The Battle off Samar: Taffy III and Leyte Gulf* (Groton, CT: Ivy Alba, 2003), p. 61.

19 J. Miller Jr., *Cartwheel: the Reduction of Rabaul*, in series *The US Army in World War II: the war in the Pacific* (Washington, DC: Historical Division, Department of the Army, 1944–81), p. 142.

20 W. Craven and J. Cate (eds.), *The Army Air Forces in World War II*, Vol.4, *The Pacific: Guadalcanal to Saipan, August 1942 to July 1944*, pp. 634–5.

21 G. Kenney, *General Kenney Reports* (NY: Duell, Sloan & Pearce, 1949), p. 520.

22 Craven and Cate, Vol.5, *The Pacific: Matterhorn to Nagasaki, June 1944 to August 1945*, p. 442.

23 NARA 2, RG 313, Records of Naval Operating Forces, JICPOA, BLUE 644, Box 6, File A8/22c, MIS Air Information Bulletin No.3, *Timely Tactical Topics II*, Undated? spring 1942.

24 R. Mikesh, *Broken Wings of the Samurai: the destruction of the Japanese air force* (Shrewsbury: Airlife, 1993), p. 22.

25 NARA 2, RG 165, War Department, "P" File, Box 542, US Pacific Fleet Weekly Intelligence Bulletin, Vol.1, No.10, 15 September 1944, Enclosure: CINCPAC-CINCPOA Item No.9083, Japanese air battle lessons from New Guinea, issued on 5 February 1944.

26 A. Millett, *Semper Fidelis: History of the Unites States Marine Corps* (NY: Free Press, 1980), pp. 402–9.

27 J. Isely and P. Crowl, *The US Marines and Amphibious War: its theory and its practice in the Pacific* (Princeton, NJ: Princeton UP, 1951), pp. 232–4, 251–2.

28 T. Moreman, *The Jungle, the Japanese and the British Commonwealth Armies at War, 1941–45* (Abingdon: Taylor & Francis, 2005), pp. 100, 124.

29   M. Cannon, *Leyte: the return to the Philippines*, and *Triumph in the Philippines*, in
     series *The US Army in World War II: the war in the Pacific* (Washington, DC: Historical
     Division, Department of the Army, 1944–81), p. 247.
30   Cited in E. Drea, *In the Service of the Emperor: essays on the Imperial Japanese Army*
     (Lincoln: Nebraska UP, 1998), p. 72.
31   NARA 2, RG 496, GHQ SWPA, Psychological Warfare Branch, Box 2726, Daily Collation
     Summary, "Challenge adequacy of spiritual force alone," 8 March 1945.
32   C. von Clausewitz, *On War*, Indexed Edition, edited and translated by M. Howard and P.
     Paret (Princeton: Princeton UP, 1984), p. 101.

Notes on Chapter 8

1   Sun Tzu, *The Art of War*, translated, with a historical introduction by R. Sawyer (Boulder,
     CO: Westview, 1994), p. 177.
2   J. Dower, *War Without Mercy: race and power in the Pacific War* (NY: Pantheon, 1986),
     passim.
3   For similar accounts, see J. Ellis, *The Sharp End of War: the fighting man in World War II*
     (London: David & Charles, 1980), and C. Laurie, "The ultimate dilemma of psychological
     warfare in the Pacific: enemies who don't surrender and GIs who don't take prisoners," in
     War and Society, 14, (1996), pp. 99–120.
4   A. Gilmore, *You Can't Fight Tanks with Bayonets: psychological warfare against the
     Japanese Army in the Southwest Pacific* (Lincoln: Nebraska UP, 1998).
5   Dower, 1986, pp. 9, 94–9.
6   E. Drea, "In the army barracks of Imperial Japan," in *Armed Forces and Society*, 15/3,
     (1989), pp. 343–4.
7   E. Drea, *In the Service of the Emperor: essays on the Imperial Japanese Army* (Lincoln:
     Nebraska UP, 1998), pp. 75–6; E. Ohnuki-Tierney, *Kamikaze, Cherry Blossoms and
     Nationalisms: the militarization of aesthetics in Japanese history* (Chicago: Chicago UP,
     2002), p. 13.
8   R. Benedict, *The Chrysanthemum and the Sword: patterns in Japanese culture* (Cambridge,
     MA: Riverside, 1946), p. 61–5; R. Mitchell, *Thought Control in Prewar Japan* (Ithaca:
     Cornell UP, 1976), pp. 20–1; T. Lebra, *Japanese Patterns of Behavior* (Honolulu: Hawaii
     UP, 1976), p. 71.
9   MacArthur Memorial Library, Norfolk, VA (MML), RG 3, Box 126, ATIS, SWPA,
     Enemy Publication No.80, "Morale Lecture," (printed booklet published by *Moto
     Group*, 51st Division), captured at Cape Dinga, July 1943, translated 29 January
     1944.
10   Ohnuki-Tierney, 2002, pp. 80–1.
11   UKNA, WO 208/1446, ATIS, SWPA, *Information about the Japanese*, 14 June 1943.
12   IOLR, L/WS/1/1357 WP (43) 232 Morale and the War against Japan: Memorandum by
     Leo Amery (Secretary of State for India), 5 June 1943.
13   See R. Minear, "Cross-cultural perception and World War II: American Japanists of
     the 1940s and their images of Japan," in *International Studies Quarterly*, 24/4, (1980),

pp. 555–80; S. Johnson, *American Attitudes towards Japan, 1941–1975* (Washington, DC: AEI / Hoover Institute, 1975), pp. 4–7.

14 P. O'Donnell, *Into the Rising Sun* (NY: Free Press, 2002), p. 127.

15 A. Coox, "The effectiveness of the Japanese military establishment in the Second World War," in A. Millett and W. Murray (eds.), *Military Effectiveness, Volume 3: the Second World War* (Boston: Allen & Unwin, 1988), p. 1.

16 M. Johnston, *Fighting the Enemy: Australian soldiers and their adversaries in World War II* (Cambridge: CUP, 2000), p. 73.

17 Ibid., p. 79.

18 NARA 2, RG 165, War Department, "P" File, Box 531, CINCPAC-CINCPOA Translations, Item No.7,216, Imperial Headquarters, Army Section, Battle Training Report #7, "Some lessons based on experiences gained in fighting American and Australian forces in eastern New Guinea," dated 25 September 1943, translated 10 March 1944.

19 I. Hata, "From consideration to contempt: the changing nature of Japanese military and popular perceptions of prisoners of war through the ages," in B. Moore and K. Fedorovich (eds.), *Prisoners of War and their Captors in World War II* (Oxford: Berg, 1996), pp. 260–2,

20 U. Straus, *The Anguish of Surrender: Japanese POWs of World War II* (Seattle: Washington UP, 2003), pp. 42–3.

21 MML, RG 3, Box 79, ATIS, SWPA, Information Bulletin, No.808, Item 1–9981: Diary belonging to Corporal Takano Ryoichiro, captured at Cape Gloucester, received at ATIS, SWPA, 28 January 1944.

22 Y. Tanaka, *Hidden Horrors: Japanese war crimes in World War II* (Boulder, CO: Westview, 1996), pp. 199–212.

23 Ellis, 1980, p. 320.

24 R. Sherrod, *On to Westward: the battles of Saipan and Iwojima* (Baltimore, MD: Nautical and Aviation Publishing, 1990), p. 27.

25 NARA 2, RG 127, Records of the US Marine Corps, General Subject File, Box 12, T. L. Chambers, Intelligence Branch, Security and Intelligence Division, *Interview with Officer from Southwest Pacific Theater*, 9 August 1944.

26 W. Slim, *Defeat into Victory* (London: Cassell, 1956), p. 539.

27 NARA 2, RG 494, US Army Forces in the Middle Pacific (MIDPAC), Box 68, Headquarters XIV Corps, *Lessons Learned from Joint Operations*, 21 January 1944.

28 J. Thompson, *The Imperial War Museum Book of the War in Burma, 1942–1945* (London: Sidgwick & Jackson, 2002), p. 9.

29 NARA 2, RG 165, War Department, G-2 Regional File, Box 2130, File 6000, Observer's Report, from Major-General O. Griswold, 29 August 1943.

30 Slim, 1956, pp. 181–9.

31 Drea, 1989, p. 343.

32 UKNA, AIR 22/80 "Sweet dreams and a nightmare" (Diary kept by Japanese Lieutenant in first half of 1943, atis Current Translation No.106, pp. 33–4), in Air Ministry Weekly Intelligence Summary No.244, 6 May 1944.

33 NARA 2, RG 165, War Department, "P" File, Box 1205, Headquarters South Pacific Base Command, Intelligence Bulletin No.25, 7 March 1945.

34   NARA 2, RG 165, War Department, "P" File, Box 323, ATIS SWPA Interrogation Report No.205, POW JA 145567, 4 December 1943.
35   UKNA, WO 208/2276 "Discipline in the Japanese army," in War Office Weekly Intelligence Review No.15, 24 November 1943.
36   MML,RG 3, Box 74, ATIS, SWPA, Information Bulletin, No.276, Item 7–2960: "Medical situation during Wau operations".
37   NARA 2, RG 165, War Department, "P" File, Box 1205, Headquarters South Pacific Base Command, Intelligence Bulletin No.14, 20 December 1944.
38   Gilmore, 1998, pp. 6–8.
39   Ibid., pp. 149–54.
40   UKNA, WO 208/147 Intelligence Notes from Burma: published by GSI (x), GHQ India, October 1945, Part I: Intelligence in Army Headquarters – Field propaganda.
41   NARA 2, RG 407, Records of the AGO, World War II Action Reports, 1940–48, Box 1955, File 106–0.3, 6th Army, *Report of the Luzon Campaign, 9 January to 30 June 1945*, G-2 Report.
42   Gilmore, 1998, p. 179.

Notes on Chapter 9

1   Among the most significant works include: D. Alvarez (ed.), *Allied and Axis Signals Intelligence in World War II* (London: Frank Cass, 1999); A. Bath, *Tracking the Axis Enemy: the triumph of Anglo-American naval intelligence* (Lawrence: Kansas UP, 1998); E. Drea, *MacArthur's ULTRA: codebreaking and the war against Japan, 1942–1945* (Lawrence: Kansas UP, 1992); F. Hinsley et al., *British Intelligence in the Second World War, 4 Volumes*, in series *History of the Second World War* (London: HMSO, 1979–90); Prados, 1995, passim.; J. Winton, *ULTRA in the Pacific: how breaking Japanese codes and cyphers affected naval operations against Japan, 1941–1945* (London: Leo Cooper, 1993).
2   D. Ford, "Strategic culture, intelligence assessment and the conduct of the Pacific War, 1941–1945: the British-Indian and Imperial Japanese armies in comparison," in *War in History*, 14/1, (2007), p. 95.
3   W. Packard, *A Century of US Naval Intelligence* (Washington, DC: Office of Naval Intelligence / Naval Historical Center, 1996), p. 16.
4   B. Bidwell, *The History of the Military Intelligence Division, Department of the Army General Staff, 1775–1941* (Frederick, MD: University Publications of America, 1986), pp. 251–2.
5   A. Coox, "Flawed Perception," in Handel, 1990, p. 251.
6   I. Nish, "Japanese intelligence, 1894–1922," in Andrew and Noakes (eds.), 1987, p. 129.
7   NARA 2, RG 165, War Department, MID Regional File, 1922–44, Box 2131, File 6000, Japanese Army Monograph, prepared by G-2, Undated,? Spring 1941.
8   USSBS, *Japanese Intelligence*, p. 1.
9   Ibid., pp. 20–1.
10   S. Asada, "The Japanese navy and the United States," in D. Borg and S. Okamoto (eds.), *Pearl Harbor as History* (NY: Columbia UP, 1973), p. 257.

11   Bath, 1998, p. 176.

12   Aldrich, 2000, pp. 238–40, 242–3.

13   E. Drea, 'The role of communication inteligence in submarine warfare in the Pacific, January 1943 to October 1943, Intelligence furnished to submarine commanders, Pacific Fleet', in R. Spector (ed.), *Listening to the Enemy: key documents on the role of communications intelligence in the war with Japan* (Wilmington, DE: Scholarly Resources, 1988), pp. 130–1, and "Comint contributions, submarine warfare in WWII, 17 June 1947: Vice-Admiral Lockwood on value of communications intelligence against the Japanese', in *Ibid.*, p. 134.

14   E. Drea, "*ULTRA* intelligence and General Douglas MacArthur's leap to Hollandia, January–April 1944," in Handel (ed.), 1990, pp. 336–40.

15   NARA 2, RG 319, Records of the Army Staff, "P" Files, Library Branch, Box 1822, GHQ Far East Command, Military Intelligence Section, *Operations of the Allied Translator and Interpreter Section, GHQ, SWPA*, 12 July 1948.

16   For examples, see NARA 2, RG 165, War Department, "P" File, Box 341, ATIS, SWPA, Research Report No.76, Part VI, *Defects Arising from the Doctrine of "Spiritual Superiority" as Factors in Japanese Military Psychology*, 10 October 1945; MML, RG 3, GHQ SWPA, Box 120, ATIS, SWPA, Research Report, No.76, *Prominent Factors in Japanese Military Psychology*, 7 February 1945.

17   See A. Gilmore, *You Can't Fight Tanks with Bayonets: psychological warfare against the Japanese Army in the Southwest Pacific* (Lincoln: Nebraska UP, 1998), chapters 3–5.

18   NARA 2, RG 127, Records of the US Marine Corps, World War II Subject File, Box 58, *Notes on Jungle Warfare, No.1*: prepared by General Jens A Doe, (US Army), 27 April 1943.

19   NARA 2, RG 165, War Department, "P" File, Box 570, Military Intelligence Service, *Combat Lessons*, No.1, "Security in the Jungle," derived from Report of Commanding General, Forty-third Division, New Georgia campaign, undated,? early 1944.

20   UKNA, ADM 199/1542, Commander Task Group 38.1, Action Report, 1 July to 15 August 1945.

21   NARA 2, RG 38, ONI, Air Intelligence Group (Op 16-V), Box 6, COMAIRPAC, Air Operations Memorandum No.32, "Tactical lessons learned in the South Pacific," 29 May 1944.

22   NARA 2, RG 313, BLUE 627, Box 80, A9, Air Intelligence Group, Fighter tactics: excerpts from aircraft action reports and battle narratives, January to April 1944.

23   L. Allen, "Japanese intelligence systems," *Journal of Contemporary History*, 22, (1987), p. 560.

24   USSBS, *Japanese Intelligence*, p. 3.

25   NWC, Manuscript Collection, Papers of Edwin T. Layton, Box 22, Military Intelligence Service, *The Japanese Intelligence System*, 4 September 1945 .

26   UKNA, WO 208/2275, "Japanese Military Intelligence," War Office Weekly Intelligence Review (WOWIR) No.2, 26 August 1943.

27   UKNA, WO 208/2280, "Japanese failures and mistakes in the attack on India," WOWIR No.69, 6 December 1944.

28   USSBS, *Japanese Intelligence*, pp. 57–8.

29   K. Kotani, *Japanese Intelligence in World War II*, translated by C. Kotani (Oxford: Osprey, 2009), pp. 107–8, 159.

30   USSBS, *Japanese Intelligence*, pp. 18–20.

Notes on Chapter 10

1   H. Rockoff, "The United States: from ploughshares to swords," in M. Harrison (ed.), *The Economics of World War II* (Cambridge: CUP, 1998), p. 83, Table 3.1. Figures are in 1940–45 prices.

2   J. Abrahamson, *The American Home Front* (Washington, DC: National Defense University, 1983), p. 140.

3   P. Kennedy, *The Rise and Fall of the Great Powers: economic change and military conflict from 1500 to 2000* (London: Harper-Collins, 1988), p. 458, Table 35.

4   J. Ellis, *Brute Force: Allied strategy and tactics in the Second World War* (London: Andre Deutsch, 1990), p. 478, Table 22.

5   Kennedy, 1988, p. 455, Table 34.

6   S. Broadberry and P. Howlett, "The United Kingdom: 'victory at all costs'," in M. Harrison (ed.), *The Economics of World War II* (Cambridge: CUP, 1998), p. 59–60.

7   R. Overy, *Why the Allies Won* (NY: Norton, 1995), p. 192.

8   Same as note 4.

9   Ellis, 1990, pp. 469–72.

10   Overy, 1995, pp. 229–30.

11   See Ellis, 1990, p. 472, Table 21.

12   See Ibid., p. 476.

13   H. Fukaya "Japan's wartime carrier construction," in *United States Naval Institute Proceedings*, 81, (September 1955), pp. 1031–7.

14   M. Ito, *The End of the Imperial Japanese Navy*, translated by A. Kuroda and R. Pineau (NY: W. W. Norton, 1956), pp. 112–13.

15   J. Cohen, *Japan's Economy in War and Reconstruction*, Volume II in series, *Japanese Economic History 1930–1960*, edited by J. Hunter (London: Routledge, 2000), pp. 58, 113–14.

16   A. Milward, *War, Economy and Society, 1939–1945* (London: Penguin, 1977), p. 65.

17   Overy, 1995, p. 190.

18   Ibid., pp. 196–7.

19   A. Hara, "Japan: guns before rice," in Harrison (ed.), 1998, pp. 247–9.

20   A. Coox, "The effectiveness of the Japanese military establishment in the Second World War," in A. Millett and W. Murray (eds.), *Military Effectiveness, Volume 3: the Second World War* (Boston: Allen & Unwin, 1988), pp. 21–2.

21   United States Strategic Bombing Survey, *Summary Report, Pacific War*, (Washington, DC: Government Printing Office, 1946), pp. 16–18.

22   Overy, 1995, p. 192.

23   J. Meulen, *Building the B-29* (Washington, DC: Smithsonian Institution, 1995), pp. 14–29.

24   Milward, 1977, pp. 118–19.

25   A. Yoshimura, *Zero Fighter*, translated by R. Kaiho and M. Gregson (Westport, CT: Praeger, 1996), pp. 165–6.

26   A. Beyerchen, "From radio to radar: interwar military adaptation to technological change in Germany, the United Kingdom and the United States," in A. Millett and W. Murray (eds.), *Military Innovation in the Interwar Period* (Cambridge: CUP, 1996), 277–87.

27   H. Guerlac, *Radar in World War II*, in series *History of Modern Physics, 1800–1950*, Vol.8 (Philadelphia: American Institute of Physics, 1987), pp. 915–16.

28   M. Stille, *Imperial Japanese Navy Aircraft Carriers, 1921–45* (Oxford: Osprey, 2005), pp. 9–21.

29   Ellis, 1990, p. 486, Table 23.

Notes on Chapter 11

1   C. Thorne, *Allies of a Kind: the United States, Britain, and the war against Japan, 1941–1945* (Oxford: OUP, 1978), pp. 699–704.

2   Ibid., p. 292.

3   Ibid., p. 392.

4   Ibid., p. 387.

5   W. Louis, *Imperialism at Bay: the United States and the decolonization of the British Empire, 1941–1945* (Oxford: OUP, 1978), pp. 123–6.

6   K. Sainsbury, *The Turning Point: the Moscow, Cairo and Teheran Conferences* (Oxford: OUP, 1986), p. 182.

7   N. Sarantakes, *Allies against the Rising Sun: the United States, the British nations and the defeat of Imperial Japan* (Lawrence, KA: Kansas UP, 2009), p. 30.

8   H. Feis, *Churchill, Roosevelt, Stalin: the war they waged and the peace they sought* (Princeton: Princeton University Press, 1957), p. 248.

9   Thorne, 1978, p. 408.

10   D. Fraser, *Alanbrooke* (NY: Atheneum, 1982), pp. 491–3.

11   Sarantakes, 2009, p. 123.

12   G. Ehrman, *Grand Strategy*, Vol. 5, in series *History of the Second World War* (London: HMSO, 1956–72), pp. 123–4.

13   C. Thorne, *The Issue of War: states, societies and the Far Eastern conflict of 1941–1945* (London, Hamish Hamilton, 1985), pp. 221–2.

14   R. Aldrich, *Intelligence and the War against Japan: Britain, America and the politics of secret service* (Cambridge: CUP, 2000), pp. 240–1.

15   J. Gaddis, *The United States and the Origins of the Cold War, 1941–1947* (NY: Columbia UP, 1972), p. 79.

16   M. Stoler, *Allies and Adversaries: the Joint Chiefs of Staff, the Grand Alliance and US strategy in World War II* (Chapel Hill: University of North Carolina Press, 2000), p. 248.

17   J. Chapman, "The Imperial Japanese Navy and the North-South dilemma," in J. Erickson and D. Dilks (eds.), *Barbarossa: the Axis and the Allies* (Edinburgh: Edinburgh UP, 1994), pp. 173–5.

18   Thorne, 1985, p. 232.

19   M. Hauner, *India in Axis Strategy: Germany, Japan and Indian Nationalists in the Second World War* (Stuttgart: Ernst Klett, 1981), pp. 392–3.
20   M. Felton, *Yanagi: the secret underwater trade between Germany and Japan, 1942–1945* (Barnsley: Pen & Sword, 2005), pp. 184–5.

Notes on Chapter 12

1   B. Shillony, *Politics and Culture in Wartime Japan* (Oxford: OUP, 1981), p. 142.
2   C. Thorne, *The Issue of War: states, societies and the Far Eastern conflict of 1941–1945* (London, Hamish Hamilton, 1985), pp. 124–5.
3   T. Havens, *Valley of Darkness: the Japanese people and World War II* (NY: Norton, 1986), pp. 63, 68; Shillony, 1981, pp. 95–7.
4   See UKNA, AIR 23/7720 "The Japanese view of air warfare" (Discussion reported in September issue of *Fuji*, translation obtained by Far Eastern Bureau of the Ministry of Information), in Air Command Southeast Asia Weekly Intelligence Summary No.5, 19 December 1943.
5   See UKNA, ADM 223/158 Political intelligence review, in Admiralty Weekly Intelligence Summary No.170, 11 June 1943.
6   Thorne, 1985, p. 121.
7   Ibid., p. 132.
8   J. Dower, *War Without Mercy: race and power in the Pacific War* (NY: Pantheon, 1986), pp. 37–8, 142.
9   For the most recent analysis, see G. Robinson, *By Order of the President: FDR and the internment of Japanese-Americans* (London: Harvard University Press, 2001).
10   Thorne, 1985, p. 122.
11   J. Blum, *"V" Was for Victory: politics and American culture during World War II* (NY: Harcourt Brace Jovanovich, 1976), p. 16.
12   Ibid., pp. 90–102.
13   Thorne, 1985, pp. 255, 261.
14   J. Abrahamson, *The American Home Front* (Washington, DC: National Defense University, 1983), p. 149.
15   Thorne, 1985, p. 251.
16   Abrahamson, 1983, p. 165.
17   Havens, 1986, pp. 74–5.
18   S. Ienaga, *The Pacific War, 1931–1945: a critical perspective of Japan's role in World War II* (New York: Pantheon Books, 1968), p. 112.
19   Shillony, 1981, p. 100.
20   Ienaga, 1968, p. 196.
21   R. Overy, *Why the Allies Won* (NY: Norton, 1995), p. 301.
22   Havens, 1986, p. 95.
23   Ibid., pp. 130–1.
24   Ibid., p. 167.
25   Shillony, 1981, pp. 126–7.

26   Havens, 1986, p. 186.
27   Shillony, 1981, pp. 120–3.
28   T. Iritani, *Group Psychology of the Japanese in Wartime* (London: Kegan & Paul, 1991),
     pp. 23, 60–1, 98; Ienaga, 1968, pp. 217, 222–3; Havens, 1986, pp. 70–1.
29   Dower 1986, p. 282 .
30   Ienaga, 1968, p. 223.
31   Exceptions include: Thorne, 1985, chapter 5; Ienaga, 1968, chapter 8.
32   Ienaga, 1968, pp. 156–71.
33   J. Lebra (ed.), *Japan's Greater East Asia Co-prosperity Sphere in World War II* (Kuala
     Lumpur: OUP, 1975), pp. 113–17.
34   Thorne, 1985, p. 145.
35   Ibid., p. 115.
36   Ibid., p. 157; Ienaga, 1968, pp. 171–80.

Notes on Chapter 13

1   S. Ross, *American War Plans, 1941–1945* (London: Frank Cass, 1997), pp. 130–4.
2   W. Craven and J. Cate (eds.), 1948–83, *Vol.5, The Pacific: Matterhorn to Nagasaki, June
     1944 to August 1945* (Washington, DC: Office of Air Force History, 1948–83), pp. 663–72.
3   K. Werrell, *Blankets of Fire: US bombers over Japan during World War II* (Washington,
     DC: Smithsonian Institution, 1996), pp. 104–6, 110–11.
4   T. Koyanagi, "The battle of Leyte Gulf," in Evans, D. (ed.), *The Japanese Navy in World
     War II: in the words of former Japanese naval officers, 2nd edition* (Annapolis: Naval
     Institute Press, 1986), pp. 357–60. Also see S. Fukudome, "The air battle off Taiwan," in
     ibid., pp. 335–6, 338–41.
5   See A. Axell and H. Kase, *Kamikaze: Japan's suicide gods* (London: Pearson, 2002); R.
     Inoguchi et al., *The Divine Wind: Japan's kamikaze force in World War II* (Annapolis: Naval
     Institute Press, 1958); R. Inoguchi and T. Nakajima, "The *Kamikaze* attack corps," in Evans
     (ed.), 1986, pp. 415–39; Y. Kuwahara and G. Allred, *Kamikaze* (NY: Ballantine, 1957);
     R. Lamont-Brown, *Kamikaze: Japan's suicide samurai* (London: Arms & Armour, 1997).
6   D. Warner et al., *The Sacred Warriors: Japan's suicide legions* (NY: Von Nostrand Reinhold,
     1982), p. 268.
7   E. Ohnuki-Tierney, E., *Kamikaze, Cherry Blossoms and Nationalisms: the militarization of
     aesthetics in Japanese history* (Chicago: Chicago UP, 2002), p. 169.
8   S. Hayashi, in collaboration with A. Coox, *Kogun: the Japanese Army in the Pacific War*
     (Quantico, VA: Marine Corps Association, 1959), pp. 114, 156–60.
9   W. Halsey and J. Bryan, *Admiral Halsey's Story* (NY: McGraw Hill, 1947), p. 199.
10   D. Robertson, *Operations Analysis: the battle for Leyte Gulf* (Newport: Naval War College,
     1993), pp. 13–14.
11   J. Winton, *ULTRA in the Pacific: how breaking Japanese codes and cyphers affected naval
     operations against Japan, 1941–1945* (London: Leo Cooper, 1993), p. 183.
12   See T. Cutler, *The Battle of Leyte Gulf, 23–26 October 1944* (NY: Harper-Collins, 1994),
     pp. 162–5, 215; S. Falk, *Decision at Leyte* (NY: W. W. Norton, 1966), pp. 152–3; W.

Halsey, "The battle for Leyte Gulf," in *United States Naval Institute Proceedings*, 78, (May 1952), 494–5; J. Merrill, *A Sailor's Admiral: a biography of William F Halsey* (NY: Thomas Y Crowell, 1976), p. 153; C. Solberg, *Decision and Dissent: with Halsey at Leyte Gulf* (Annapolis: Naval Institute Press, 1995), pp. 116–18; H. Willmott, *The Battle of Leyte Gulf: the last fleet action* (Bloomington: Indiana UP, 2005), pp. 120–5, 194; S. Morison, *Leyte, June 1944 to January 1945*, pp. 193–4.

13   R. Smith, *The Approach to the Philippines*, in series *The US Army in World War II: the war in the Pacific* (Washington, DC: Historical Division, Department of the Army, 1944–81), p. 267.

14   M. Cannon, *Leyte: the return to the Philippines*, and *Triumph in the Philippines*, in series *The US Army in World War II: the war in the Pacific* (Washington, DC: Historical Division, Department of the Army, 1944–81), p. 339.

15   R. Smith, *Triumph in the Philippines* (Office of the Chief of Military History Department of the Army, Washington, D.C., 1993), pp. 469, 497.

16   Werrell, 1996, pp. 152–4, 159–60.

17   Craven and Cate, 1948–83, Vol.5, pp. 611–16.

18   Werrell, 1996, pp. 240–1.

19   R. Appleman, *Okinawa: the last battle*, in series *The US Army in World War II: the war in the Pacific* (Washington, DC: Historical Division, Department of the Army, 1944–81), pp. 256–7; B. Frank, *Okinawa: the great island battle* (NY: Talismann, 1978), pp. 104–5.

Notes on Chapter 14

1   L. Sigal, *Fighting to a Finish: the politics of war termination in the United States and Japan, 1945* (Ithaca, NY: Cornell UP, 1988).

2   G. Alperovitz, *The Decision to Use the Atomic Bomb* (London: Fontana, 1996).

3   See B. Bernstein, "Reconsidering Truman's claim of 'half a million American lives' saved by the atomic bomb: the construction and deconstruction of a myth," in *Journal of Strategic Studies*, 22/1, (March 1999), 55–90, and "Understanding the atomic bomb and the Japanese surrender: missed opportunities, little-known near disasters and modern history," in *Diplomatic History*, 19/2 (1995), 227–73.

4   T. Allen and N. Polmar, *Codename Downfall: the secret plan to invade Japan and why Truman dropped the bomb* (NY: Simon & Schuster, 1995), p. 126.

5   Sigal, 1988, p. 95.

6   Ibid., pp. 99, 109–15.

7   G. Alperovitz et al., "Marshall, Truman and the decision to drop the bomb," in *International Security*, 16/3, (1991–92), 217, 220.

8   Sigal, 1988, pp. 175–6.

9   H. Feis, *The Atomic Bomb and the End of World War II* (Princeton: Princeton UP, 1966), p. 22.

10   R. Skates, *The Invasion of Japan: alternative to the bomb* (Columbia: South Carolina UP, 1994), p. 253.

11   D. MacEachin, *The Final Months of the War against Japan: signals intelligence, US invasion*

planning and the A-bomb decision (Washington, DC: Center for the Study of Intelligence, 1998), pp. 6–9.

12   Allen and Polmar, 1995, pp. 203–10.

13   R. Frank, *Downfall: the end of the Imperial Japanese empire* (NY: Random House, 1999), pp. 142–4.

14   Bernstein, 1999, p. 66.

15   MacEachin, 1998, p. 15.

16   Bernstein, 1999, p. 67.

17   MacEachin, 1998, pp. 17, 25–6; Frank, 1999, p. 201.

18   L. Morton, "The decision to use the atomic bomb," in K. Greenfield (ed.), *Command Decisions* (Washington, DC: Center of Military History, 1987), p. 511.

19   Alperovitz, 1996, pp. 112–13, 122–4.

20   Alperovitz et al., 1991–92, pp. 210, 244–5, 266.

21   Feis, 1966, pp. 47–8.

22   Bernstein, "Understanding the atomic bomb," pp. 245–6, 256–7.

23   Sigal, 1988, pp. 33–4.

24   R. Butow, *Japan's Decision to Surrender* (Stanford, CA: Stanford UP, 1954), pp. 79, 99–100.

25   H. Bix, "Japan's delayed surrender: a reinterpretation," in *Diplomatic History*, 19/2, (1995), 213.

26   See F. Morgan, *Compellence and the Strategic Culture of Imperial Japan: implications for coercive diplomacy in the twenty-first century* (Westport, CT: Praeger, 2003), Chapter 6.

27   Bernstein, "Understanding the atomic bomb," p. 255.

28   Ibid., pp. 238–44.

29   Feis, 1966, pp. 181–2.

30   Sigal, 1988, pp. 69–70, 229–30.

31   Butow, 1954, p. 161.

32   See Bernstein, "Compelling Japan's surrender without the A-bomb, Soviet entry, or invasion: reconsidering the US Bombing Survey's early-surrender conclusions," in *Journal of Strategic Studies*, 18/2, (1995), 101–48.

33   Butow, 1954, p. 174.

34   Bernstein, "Understanding the atomic bomb," p. 252.

35   Bernstein, "Compelling Japan's surrender," pp. 116–17.

36   Skates, 1994, p. 250.

37   Bernstein, "Compelling Japan's surrender," pp. 122–4.

38   R. Pape, "Why Japan Surrendered," in *International Security*, 18/2, (1993), pp. 156–7.

39   T. Hasegawa, Racing the Enemy: Stalin, Truman, and the surrender of Japan (Cambridge, MA: Harvard UP, 2005), pp. 197–203.

40   Bix, 1995, p. 216.

41   Sigal, 1988, p. 225.

42   Bernstein, "Understanding the atomic Bomb," p. 247.

43   Allen and Polmar, 1995, pp. 209–10.

44   B. Bernstein, "Truman and the A-bomb: targeting non-combatants, using the bomb and his defending the 'decision' ," in *Journal of Military History*, 62/3, (1998), 565.

Bibliography

PRIMARY SOURCES

The documents cited in the endnotes have been collected from the following archives:
United States National Archives and Records Administration (NARA), College Park, Maryland.
US Naval Historical Center (NHC), Washington, DC.
US Air Force Historical Research Agency (AFHRA), Maxwell Air Base, AL.
MacArthur Memorial Library (MML), Norfolk, Virginia.
United Kingdom National Archives (UKNA), London.
India Office Library and Records (IOLR), British Library, London.

In addition, private papers collections at the following repositories were consulted:
Library of Congress, Washington, DC.
US Army Military History Institute, Carlisle, Pennsylvania.
United States Naval War College, (NWC), Newport, Rhode Island.
Imperial War Museum, London.
Liddell Hart Center for Military Archives (LHCMA), King's College, London.

PUBLISHED SOURCES

BOOKS

Abrahamson, J., *The American Home Front* (Washington, DC: National Defense University, 1983).
Akagi, K., "Leadership in Japan's planning for war against Britain," in B. Bond and K. Tachikawa (eds.), *British and Japanese Military Leadership in the Far Eastern War, 1941–1945* (Abingdon: Frank Cass, 2004).
Aldrich, R., *Intelligence and the War against Japan: Britain, America and the politics of secret service* (Cambridge: CUP, 2000).
Allen, L., *Singapore, 1941–1942* (Newark: Delaware UP, 1977).
Allen, T. and N. Polmar, *Codename Downfall: the secret plan to invade Japan and why Truman dropped the bomb* (NY: Simon & Schuster, 1995).

Alperovitz, G., *The Decision to Use the Atomic Bomb* (London: Fontana, 1996).

Alvarez, D. (ed.), *Allied and Axis Signals Intelligence in World War II* (London: Frank Cass, 1999).

Andrew, C. and J. Noakes (eds.), *Intelligence and International Relations, 1900-1945* (Exeter: Exeter UP, 1987).

Appleman, R., *Okinawa: the last battle*, in series *The US Army in World War II: the war in the Pacific* (Washington, DC: Historical Division, Department of the Army, 1944-81).

Armstrong, D., "China's Place in the New Pacific Order," in E. Goldstein and J. Maurer (eds.), *The Washington Conference, 1921-1922: naval rivalry, East Asian stability and the road to Pearl Harbor* (London, Frank Cass, 1994).

Asada, S., "The Japanese navy and the United States," in D. Borg and S. Okamoto (eds.), *Pearl Harbor as History* (NY: Columbia UP, 1973).

Asada, S., 'From Washington to London: the Imperial Japanese Navy and the politics of naval limitation, 1921-30', in E. Goldstein and J. Maurer (eds.), *The Washington Conference, 1921-1922: naval rivalry, East Asian stability and the road to Pearl Harbor* (London, Frank Cass, 1994).

Axell, A. and H. Kase, *Kamikaze: Japan's suicide gods* (London: Pearson, 2002).

Barlow, J., "World War II: US and Japanese naval strategies," in C. Gray and R. Barnett (eds.), *Seapower and Strategy* (London: Tri-Service Press, 1989).

Barnett, C., *Engage the Enemy More Closely: the Royal Navy in the Second World War* (NY: Norton, 1991).

Barnhart, M., "Japanese intelligence before the Second World War: 'best case' analysis," in E. May (ed.), *Knowing One's Enemies: intelligence assessment before the two World Wars* (Princeton, NJ: Princeton UP, 1984).

—*Japan Prepares for Total War: the search for economic security, 1919-1941* (Ithaca, NY: Cornell UP, 1987).

Bath, A., *Tracking the Axis Enemy: the triumph of Anglo-American naval intelligence* (Lawrence: Kansas UP, 1998).

Beasley, W., *Japanese Imperialism, 1894-1945* (Oxford: OUP, 1987).

—*The Rise of Modern Japan* (NY: St. Martin's, 1990).

Belote, J. and W. Belote, *Titans of the Seas: the development and operations of Japanese and American carrier task forces during World War II* (NY: Harper & Row, 1975).

Benedict, R., *The Chrysanthemum and the Sword: patterns in Japanese culture* (Cambridge, MA: Riverside, 1946).

Bennett, H., *Why Singapore Fell* (Sydney: Angus & Robertson, 1944).

Bergerud, E., *Fire in the Sky: the air war in the South Pacific* (Boulder, CO: Westview, 1999).

Best, A., *British Intelligence and the Japanese Challenge in Asia, 1914-1941* (London: Macmillan, 2002).

Beyerchen, A., "From radio to radar: interwar military adaptation to technological change in Germany, the United Kingdom and the United States," in A. Millett and W. Murray (eds.), *Military Innovation in the Interwar Period* (Cambridge: CUP, 1996).

Bidwell, B., *The History of the Military Intelligence Division, Department of the Army General Staff, 1775-1941* (Frederick, MD: University Publications of America, 1986).

Blair, C., *Silent Victory: the US submarine war against Japan* (NY: J.B. Lippincott, 1975).

Blum, J., "*V*" *Was for Victory: politics and American culture during World War II* (NY: Harcourt Brace Jovanovich, 1976).

Bond, B. and K. Tachikawa (eds.), *British and Japanese Military Leadership in the Far Eastern War, 1941–1945* (Abingdon: Frank Cass, 2004).

Boog, H. (ed.), *The Conduct of the Air War in the Second World War: an international comparison* (Oxford: Berg Publishers, 1992).

Borg, D. and S. Okamoto (eds.), *Pearl Harbor as History* (NY: Columbia UP, 1973).

Boyd, C. and A. Yoshida, *The Japanese Submarine Force and World War II* (Annapolis: Naval Institute Press, 1995).

Broadberry, S. and P. Howlett, "The United Kingdom: 'victory at all costs,'" in M. Harrison (ed.), *The Economics of World War II* (Cambridge: CUP, 1998).

Brune, L., *The Origins of American National Security Policy: sea power, air power and foreign policy, 1900–1941* (Manhattan, KA: MA/AH Publishing, 1981).

Buckley, T., "The Icarus Factor: the American pursuit of myth in naval arms control, 1921–36," in Goldstein and Maurer (eds.), *The Washington Conference, 1921–1922: naval rivalry, East Asian stability and the road to Pearl Harbor* (London, Frank Cass, 1994).

Butow, R., *Japan's Decision to Surrender* (Stanford, CA: Stanford UP, 1954).

—*Tojo and the Coming of War* (Stanford: Stanford UP, 1961).

Callahan, R., *The Worst Disaster: the fall of Singapore* (London: Associated University Press, 1977).

Campbell, J., *Naval Weapons of World War Two* (London: Conway, 1985).

Cannon, M., *Leyte: the return to the Philippines*, and *Triumph in the Philippines*, in series *The US Army in World War II: the war in the Pacific* (Washington, DC: Historical Division, Department of the Army, 1944–81).

Chapman, J., "Japanese intelligence, 1918–1945: a suitable case for treatment," in C. Andrew and J. Noakes (eds.), *Intelligence and International Relations, 1900–1945* (Exeter: Exeter UP, 1987).

—"The Imperial Japanese Navy and the North-South dilemma," in J. Erickson and D. Dilks (eds.), *Barbarossa: the Axis and the Allies* (Edinburgh: Edinburgh UP, 1994).

Chihaya, M., "An intimate look at the Japanese navy," in D. Goldstein and K. Dillon (eds.), *The Pearl Harbor Papers: inside the Japanese plans* (Dulles, VA: Brassey's, 1993).

Chung, O., *Operation Matador: Britain's war plans against the Japanese, 1918–41* (Singapore: Times Academic Press, 1997).

Cohen, J., *Japan's Economy in War and Reconstruction*, Vol. 2 in series, *Japanese Economic History 1930–1960*, edited by J. Hunter (London: Routledge, 2000).

Coox, A., *Nomonhan: Japan against Russia, 1939* (Stanford: Stanford UP, 1985).

—"The effectiveness of the Japanese military establishment in the Second World War," in A. Millett and W. Murray (eds.), *Military Effectiveness, Volume 3: the Second World War* (Boston: Allen & Unwin, 1988).

—"Flawed perception and its effect upon operational thinking: the case of the Japanese Army, 1937–41," in M. Handel (ed.), *Intelligence and Military Operations* (London: Frank Cass, 1990).

Costello, J., *The Pacific War, 1941–1945* (NY: Rawson-Wade, 1981).

Cox, R., *The Battle off Samar: Taffy III and Leyte Gulf* (Groton, CT: Ivy Alba, 2003).

Craven, W. and J. Cate (eds.), *The Army Air Forces in World War II, Vol. 1: Plans and Early Operations, Vol. 4, The Pacific: Guadalcanal to Saipan, August 1942 to July 1944,* and *Vol. 5, The Pacific: Matterhorn to Nagasaki, June 1944 to August 1945* (Washington, DC: Office of Air Force History, 1948–83).

Crowl, P. and E. Love, *Seizure of the Gilberts and Marshalls,* in series *The US Army in World War II: the war in the Pacific* (Washington, DC: Historical Division, Department of the Army, 1944–81).

Crowl, P., *Campaign in the Marianas,* in series *The US Army in World War II: the war in the Pacific* (Washington, DC: Historical Division, Department of the Army, 1944–81).

Cutler, T., *The Battle of Leyte Gulf, 23–26 October 1944* (NY: Harper-Collins, 1994).

Dallek, R., *Franklin D Roosevelt and American Foreign Policy, 1932–1945* (Oxford, OUP, 1995).

Dockrill, S. (ed.), *From Pearl Harbor to Hiroshima: the Second World War in Asia and the Pacific, 1941–45* (Basingstoke: Macmillan, 1994).

Dower, J., *War Without Mercy: race and power in the Pacific War* (NY: Pantheon, 1986).

Drea, E., "*Ultra* intelligence and General Douglas MacArthur's leap to Hollandia, January-April 1944," in M. Handel (ed.), *Intelligence and Military Operations* (London: Frank Cass, 1990).

— *MacArthur's ULTRA: codebreaking and the war against Japan, 1942–1945* (Lawrence: Kansas UP, 1992).

—*In the Service of the Emperor: essays on the Imperial Japanese Army* (Lincoln: Nebraska UP, 1998).

Dull, P., *A Battle History of the Imperial Japanese Navy, 1941–45* (Annapolis, MD: Naval Institute Press, 1978).

Ehrman, J., *Grand Strategy,* Vol. 5, in series *History of the Second World War* (London: HMSO, 1956–72).

Ellis, J., *The Sharp End of War: the fighting man in World War II* (London: David & Charles, 1980).

—*Brute Force: Allied strategy and tactics in the Second World War* (London: Andre Deutsch, 1990).

Elphick, P., *Singapore: the pregnable fortress* (London: Hodder & Stoughton, 1995).

—*Far Eastern File: the intelligence war in the Far East, 1930–45* (London: Hodder & Stoughton, 1997).

Erickson, J. and D. Dilks (eds.), *Barbarossa: the Axis and the Allies* (Edinburgh: Edinburgh UP, 1994).

Evans, D. (ed.), *The Japanese Navy in World War II: in the words of former Japanese naval officers, 2nd edition* (Annapolis: Naval Institute Press, 1986).

Evans, D. and M. Peattie., *Kaigun: the strategy, tactics and technology of the Imperial Japanese Navy, 1887–1941* (Annapolis: Naval Institute Press, 1997).

Falk, S., *Decision at Leyte* (NY: W.W. Norton, 1966).

Farago, L., *The Broken Seal: the story of "Operation Magic" and the Pearl Harbor disaster* (NY: Random House, 1967).

Feis, H., *Churchill, Roosevelt, Stalin: the war they waged and the peace they sought* (Princeton: Princeton UP, 1957).

—*The Atomic Bomb and the End of World War II* (Princeton: Princeton UP, 1966).

Felton, M., *Yanagi: the secret underwater trade between Germany and Japan, 1942–1945* (Barnsley: Pen & Sword, 2005).

Ford, D., *Britain's Secret War against Japan, 1937–1945* (Abingdon, Taylor & Francis, 2006).

Forrestel, E., *Admiral Raymond A Spruance: a study in command* (Washington, DC: Naval Historical Center, 1966).

Frank, B., *Okinawa: the great island battle* (NY: Talismann, 1978)

Frank, R., *Downfall: the end of the Imperial Japanese empire* (NY: Random House, 1999).

Fraser, D., *Alanbrooke* (NY: Atheneum, 1982).

Friedman, N., *The US Maritime Strategy* (London: Jane's 1988).

Gaddis, J., *The United States and the Origins of the Cold War, 1941–1947* (NY: Columbia UP, 1972).

Gilmore, A. *You Can't Fight Tanks with Bayonets: psychological warfare against the Japanese Army in the Southwest Pacific* (Lincoln: Nebraska UP, 1998).

Gluck, C. *Japan's Modern Myths: ideology in the late Meiji period* (Princeton: Princeton UP, 1985).

Goldstein, D. and K. Dillon (eds.), *The Pearl Harbor Papers: inside the Japanese plans* (Dulles, VA: Brassey's, 1993).

Goldstein, E. and J. Maurer (eds.), *The Washington Conference, 1921–1922: naval rivalry, East Asian stability and the road to Pearl Harbor* (London, Frank Cass, 1994).

Gray, C. and R. Barnett (eds.), *Seapower and Strategy* (London: Tri-Service Press, 1989).

Greenfield, K., *American Strategy in World War II: a reconsideration* (Malabar, FL: Krieger, 1963).

—(ed.) *Command Decisions* (Washington, DC: Center of Military History, 1987).

Guerlac, H., *Radar in World War II*, in series *History of Modern Physics, 1800–1950,* Vol.8 (Philadelphia: American Institute of Physics, 1987).

Halsey, W. and J. Bryan, *Admiral Halsey's Story* (NY: McGraw Hill, 1947).

Handel, M. (ed.), *Intelligence and Military Operations* (London: Frank Cass, 1990).

Hara, A., "Japan: guns before rice," in Harrison (ed.), *The Economics of World War II* (Cambridge: CUP, 1998).

Harrison, M. (ed.), *The Economics of World War II* (Cambridge: CUP, 1998).

Hasegawa, T., *Racing the Enemy: Stalin, Truman and the Surrender of Japan* (Cambridge, MA: Harvard UP, 2005).

Hata, I., "From consideration to contempt: the changing nature of Japanese military and popular perceptions of prisoners of war through the ages," in B. Moore and K. Fedorovich (eds.), *Prisoners of War and their Captors in World War II* (Oxford: Berg, 1996).

Hauner, M., *India in Axis Strategy: Germany, Japan and Indian Nationalists in the Second World War* (Stuttgart: Ernst Klett, 1981).

Havens, T., *Valley of Darkness: the Japanese people and World War II* (NY: Norton, 1986).

Hayashi, S. in collaboration with A. Coox, *Kogun: the Japanese Army in the Pacific War* (Quantico, VA: Marine Corps Association, 1959).

Hayes, G., *The History of the Joint Chiefs of Staff in World War II: the war against Japan* (Annapolis: Naval Institute Press, 1982).

Heinrichs, W., *Threshold of War: Franklin D Roosevelt and the American entry into World War II* (Oxford: OUP, 1988).

Heller, C. and W. Stofft (eds.), *America's First Battles, 1776–1965* (Lawrence, KA: Kansas UP, 1986).

Hinsley, F. et al., *British Intelligence in the Second World War,* 4 Vols., in series *History of the Second World War* (London: HMSO, 1979–90).

Horikoshi, J., *Eagles of Mitsubishi: the story of the Zero fighter,* translated by S. Shindo and H. Wantiez (London: Orbis, 1981).

Humphreys, L., *The Way of the Heavenly Sword: the Japanese Army in the 1920s* (Stanford: Stanford UP, 1995).

Ienaga, S., *The Pacific War, 1931–1945: a critical perspective of Japan's role in World War II* (New York: Pantheon Books, 1968).

Ike, N. (ed.), *Japan's Decision for War: records of the 1941 Policy Conferences* (Stanford, CA: Stanford UP, 1967).

Ikeda, K., "Japanese strategy in the Pacific War, 1941–1945," in I. Nish (ed.), *Anglo-Japanese Alienation, 1919–52: papers of the Anglo-Japanese Conference on the history of the Second World War* (Cambridge: CUP, 1982).

Inoguchi, R. and T. Nakajima, "The *Kamikaze* attack corps," in Evans, D. (ed.), *The Japanese Navy in World War II: in the words of former Japanese naval officers, 2nd edition* (Annapolis: Naval Institute Press, 1986).

Inoguchi, R. and N. Tadashi with Roger Pineau, *The Divine Wind: Japan's kamikaze force in World War II* (Annapolis: Naval Institute Press, 1958).

Iritani, T., *Group Psychology of the Japanese in Wartime* (London: Kegan & Paul, 1991).

Iriye, A., *After Imperialism: the search for a new order in the Far East, 1921–31* (Cambridge, MA: Harvard UP, 1965).

—*The Origins of the Second World War in Asia and the Pacific* (London: Longman, 1987).

Isely, J. and P. Crowl, *The US Marines and Amphibious War: its theory and its practice in the Pacific* (Princeton, NJ: Princeton UP, 1951).

Ito, M., *The End of the Imperial Japanese Navy,* translated by A. Kuroda and R. Pineau (NY: W.W. Norton, 1956).

James, J., "American and Japanese strategies in the Pacific War," in P. Paret et al. (eds.), *Makers of Modern Strategy: Machiavelli to the nuclear age* (Oxford: Clarendon, 1986).

Jentschura, H., D. Jung, and P. Mickel, *Warships of the Imperial Japanese Navy, 1869–1945,* translated by A. Preston and J. Brown (Annapolis: Naval Institute Press, 1992).

Johnson, S., *American Attitudes towards Japan, 1941–1975* (Washington, DC: AEI / Hoover Institute, 1975).

Johnston, M., *Fighting the Enemy: Australian soldiers and their adversaries in World War II* (Cambridge: CUP, 2000).

Karig, W., *Battle Report: Pearl Harbor to Coral Sea* (NY: Farrar & Rinehart, 1944).

Kennedy, P., *Strategy and Diplomacy, 1870–1945* (London: Allen & Unwin, 1983).

—*The Rise and Fall of the Great Powers: economic change and military conflict from 1500 to 2000* (London: Harper-Collins, 1988).

Kenney, G., *General Kenney Reports* (NY: Duell, Sloan & Pearce, 1949).

King, E. and W. Whitehill, *Fleet Admiral King: a naval record* (London: Eyre & Spottiswoode, 1953).

Kirby, S., *The War Against Japan*, 5 Vols. in series *History of the Second World War* (London: HMSO, 1957–70).

—*Singapore: the chain of disaster* (London: Cassell, 1971).

Kotani, K., "Pearl Harbor: Japanese planning and command structure," in D. Marston (ed.), *The Pacific War Companion: from Pearl Harbor to Hiroshima* (NY: Osprey, 2007).

— *Japanese Intelligence in World War II*, translated by C. Kotani (Oxford: Osprey, 2009).

Koyanagi, T., "The battle of Leyte Gulf," in Evans, D. (ed.), *The Japanese Navy in World War II: in the words of former Japanese naval officers, 2nd edition* (Annapolis: Naval Institute Press, 1986).

Krebs, G., "The Japanese air forces," in H. Boog (ed.), *The Conduct of the Air War in the Second World War: an international comparison* (Oxford: Berg Publishers, 1992).

Kuehn, J., *Agents of Innovation: the General Board and the design of the fleet that defeated the Japanese Navy* (Annapolis: Naval Institute Press, 2008).

Kuwahara, Y. and G. Allred, *Kamikaze* (NY: Ballantine, 1957).

Lamont-Brown, R., *Kamikaze: Japan's suicide samurai* (London: Arms & Armour, 1997).

Lebra, J. (ed.), *Japan's Greater East Asia Co-prosperity Sphere in World War II* (Kuala Lumpur: OUP, 1975).

Lebra, T., *Japanese Patterns of Behavior* (Honolulu: Hawaii UP, 1976).

Lindley, J., *Carrier Victory: the air war in the Pacific* (NY: Elsevier-Dutton, 1978).

Louis, W., *Imperialism at Bay: the United States and the decolonization of the British Empire, 1941–1945* (Oxford: OUP, 1978).

Lowenthal, M., *Leadership and Indecision: American war planning and policy process, 1937–1942*, 2 Vols. (NY: Garland, 1988).

Lundstrom, J., *The First Team and the Guadalcanal Campaign: naval fighter combat from August to November 1942* (Annapolis: Naval Institute Press, 1994).

Luvaas, J., "Buna: a Leavenworth nightmare," in C. Heller and W. Stofft (eds.), *America's First Battles, 1776–1965* (Lawrence, KA: Kansas UP, 1986).

MacEachin, D., *The Final Months of the War against Japan: signals intelligence, US invasion planning and the A-bomb decision* (Washington, DC: Center for the Study of Intelligence, 1998).

Mahnken, T., *Uncovering Ways of War: US intelligence and foreign military innovation, 1918–1941* (Ithaca: Cornell UP, 2002).

Marder, A., *Old Friends, New Enemies: the Royal Navy and the Imperial Japanese Navy, 1936–45, Vol. 1: Strategic illusions, 1936–41*, and assisted by M. Jacobsen and J. Horsfield, *Vol. 2: The Pacific War, 1942–45* (Oxford: OUP, 1981–90).

Marston, D. (ed.), *The Pacific War Companion: from Pearl Harbor to Hiroshima* (NY: Osprey, 2007).

Maruyama, M., *Thought and Behaviour in Japanese Politics*, edited by I. Morris (Oxford: OUP, 1963).

Matloff, M. and E. Snell, *Strategic Planning for Coalition Warfare*, in series *United States Army in World War II: The War Department* (Washington, DC: Office of the Chief of Military History, 1950–55).

May, E. (ed.), *Knowing One's Enemies: intelligence assessment before the two World Wars* (Princeton, NJ: Princeton UP, 1984).

Merrill, J., *A Sailor's Admiral: a biography of William F Halsey* (NY: Thomas Y Crowell, 1976).

Meulen, J., *Building the B-29* (Washington, DC: Smithsonian Institution, 1995).

Mikesh, R., *Broken Wings of the Samurai: the destruction of the Japanese air force* (Shrewsbury: Airlife, 1993).

Miller, E., *War Plan Orange: the US Strategy to defeat Japan, 1897–1945* (Annapolis: Naval Institute Press, 1991).

Miller, J. Jr., *Cartwheel: the Reduction of Rabaul*, in series *The US Army in World War II: the war in the Pacific* (Washington, DC: Historical Division, Department of the Army, 1944–81).

Millett, A., *Semper Fidelis: History of the Unites States Marine Corps* (NY: Free Press, 1980).

Millett, A. and W. Murray (eds.), *Military Effectiveness, Vol. 3: the Second World War* (Boston: Allen & Unwin, 1988).

—(eds.) *Military Innovation in the Interwar Period* (Cambridge: CUP, 1996).

—*A War to be Won: fighting the Second World War* (Cambridge, MA: Belknap, Harvard UP, 2000).

Milner, S., *Victory in Papua*, in series *The US Army in World War II: the war in the Pacific* (Washington, DC: Historical Division, Department of the Army, 1949–57).

Milward, A., *War, Economy and Society, 1939–1945* (London: Penguin, 1977).

Mitchell, R., *Thought Control in Prewar Japan* (Ithaca: Cornell UP, 1976).

Moore, B. and K. Fedorovich (eds.), *Prisoners of War and their Captors in World War II* (Oxford: Berg, 1996).

Moreman, T., *The Jungle, the Japanese and the British Commonwealth Armies at War, 1941–45* (Abingdon: Taylor & Francis, 2005).

Morgan, F., *Compellence and the Strategic Culture of Imperial Japan: implications for coercive diplomacy in the twenty-first century* (Westport, CT: Praeger, 2003).

Morison, S., *The Rising Sun in the Pacific, 1931–April 1942*; *Coral Sea, Midway and Submarine Actions, May 1942 to August 1942*; *The Struggle for Guadalcanal, August 1942 to February 1943*; *Breaking the Bismarcks Barrier, 22 July 1942 to 1 May 1944*; *Aleutians, Gilberts and Marshalls, June 1942 to April 1944*; *New Guinea and the Marianas, March 1944 to August 1944*; *Leyte, June 1944 to January 1945*; *The Liberation of the Philippines: Luzon, Mindanao, the Visayas, 1944–45*; *Victory in the Pacific, 1945*, in series *History of United States Naval Operations in World War II*, reprinted versions, (Boston: Little, Brown & Co.; Chicago: Illinois UP; Urbana: Illinois UP; and Edison, NJ: Castle Books, 1989–2002).

Morley, J. (ed.), *The Fateful Choice: Japan's advance into Southeast Asia, 1939–41*, and *The Final Confrontation: Japan's negotiations with the United States, 1941*, from translated series, *taiheiyo senso e no michi: kaisen gaiko shi* – Japan's Road to the Pacific War (NY: Columbia UP, 1980–94).

Morris, I. (ed.), *Japan, 1931–1945 militarism, fascism, Japanism?* (NY: D.C. Heath & Co., 1963).

Morton, L., *The Fall of the Philippines*, and *Strategy and Command: the first two years*, in series *United States Army in World War II: the war in the Pacific* (Washington, DC: Office of the Chief of Military History, 1962–89).

—'The decision to use the atomic bomb', in K. Greenfield (ed.), *Command Decisions* (Washington, DC: Center of Military History, 1987).

Nish, I. (ed.), *Anglo-Japanese Alienation, 1919–52: papers of the Anglo-Japanese Conference on the history of the Second World War* (Cambridge: CUP, 1982).

—"Japanese intelligence, 1894–1922," in Andrew and Noakes (eds.), *Intelligence and International Relations, 1900–1945* (Exeter: Exeter UP, 1987).

Norman, E., *Japan's Emergence as a Modern State: political and economic problems of the Meiji Period*, Reprinted version (Westport: Greenwood, 1973).

O'Donnell, P., *Into the Rising Sun* (NY: Free Press, 2002).

Ohnuki-Tierney, E., *Kamikaze, Cherry Blossoms and Nationalisms: the militarization of aesthetics in Japanese history* (Chicago: Chicago UP, 2002).

Oi, A., "Why Japan's anti-submarine warfare failed," in D. Evans (ed.), *The Japanese Navy in World War II: in the words of former Japanese naval officers*, 2nd edition (Annapolis: Naval Institute Press, 1986).

Okumiya, M. and J. Horikoshi, with M. Caidin, *Zero!: the story of the Japanese Navy Air Force, 1937–1945* (London: Cassell, 1956).

Overy, R., *The Air War, 1939–45* (London: Europa, 1980).

—*Why the Allies Won* (NY: Norton, 1995).

Packard, W., *A Century of US Naval Intelligence* (Washington, DC: Office of Naval Intelligence / Naval Historical Center, 1996).

Paret, P. G. (ed.), with Craig and F. Gilbert, *Makers of Modern Strategy: Machiavelli to the nuclear age* (Oxford: Clarendon, 1986).

Parillo, M., *The Japanese Merchant Marine in World War II* (Annapolis: Naval Institute Press, 1993).

Parshall, J. and A. Tully, *Shattered Sword: the untold story of the Battle of Midway* (Washington, DC: Potomac, 2005).

Peattie, M., *Sunburst: the rise of Japanese naval air power, 1909–1941* (Annapolis: Naval Institute Press, 2001).

Percival, A., *The War in Malaya* (London: Eyre & Spottiswoode, 1949).

Prados, J., *Combined Fleet Decoded: the secret history of American intelligence and the Japanese Navy in World War II* (Annapolis: Naval Institute Press, 1995).

Prange, G., *At Dawn We Slept: the untold story of Pearl Harbor* (London: Michael Joseph, 1981).

Pritchard, J., "Churchill, the military and imperial defence in East Asia," in S. Dockrill (ed.), *From Pearl Harbor to Hiroshima: the Second World War in Asia and the Pacific, 1941–45* (Basingstoke: Macmillan, 1994).

Rearden, J., *Cracking the Zero Mystery: how the US learned to beat Japan's vaunted WWII fighter plane* (Harrisburg, PA: Stackpole, 1990).

Robertson, D., *Operations Analysis: the battle for Leyte Gulf* (Newport: Naval War College, 1993).

Robinson, G., *By Order of the President: FDR and the internment of Japanese-Americans* (London: Harvard UP, 2001).

Rockoff, H., "The United States: from ploughshares to swords," in M. Harrison (ed.), *The Economics of World War II* (Cambridge: CUP, 1998).

Roskill, S. *The War at Sea*, Vol. 2, in series *History of the Second World War* (London: HMSO, 1954–61).

—*Churchill and the Admirals* (London: Collins, 1977).

Ross, S., *American War Plans, 1941–1945* (London: Frank Cass, 1997).

Sainsbury, K., *The Turning Point: the Moscow, Cairo and Teheran Conferences* (Oxford: OUP, 1986).

Sakaida, H., *Imperial Japanese Navy Aces, 1937–1945* (Oxford: Osprey, 1999).

Sarantakes, N., *Allies against the Rising Sun: the United States, the British nations and the defeat of Imperial Japan* (Lawrence, KA: Kansas UP, 2009).

Sherrod, R., *On to Westward: the battles of Saipan and Iwojima* (Baltimore, MD: Nautical and Aviation Publishing, 1990).

Shillony, B., *Politics and Culture in Wartime Japan* (Oxford: OUP, 1981).

Shinjiro, N., "The drive into southern Indochina and Thailand," in J. Morley, (ed.) *The Fateful Choice: Japan's advance into Southeast Asia, 1939–41*, from translated series, *taiheiyo senso e no michi: kaisen gaiko shi* – Japan's Road to the Pacific War (NY: Columbia UP, 1980).

Shortal, J., *Forged by Fire: Robert L. Eichelberger and the Pacific War* (Columbia, SC: South Carolina UP, 1987).

Sigal, L., *Fighting to a Finish: the politics of war termination in the United States and Japan, 1945* (Ithaca, NY: Cornell UP, 1988).

Skates, R., *The Invasion of Japan: alternative to the bomb* (Columbia: South Carolina UP, 1994).

Slim, W., *Defeat into Victory* (London: Cassell, 1956).

Smith, R., *The Approach to the Philippines*, in series *The US Army in World War II: the war in the Pacific* (Washington, DC: Historical Division, Department of the Army, 1944–81).

— *Triumph in the Philippines* (Office of the Chief of Military History Department of the Army, Washington, D.C., 1993).

Solberg, C., *Decision and Dissent: with Halsey at Leyte Gulf* (Annapolis: Naval Institute Press, 1995).

Spector, R., *The Eagle Against the Sun: the American war with Japan* (NY: Vintage Books, 1985).

—(ed.) *Listening to the Enemy: key documents on the role of communications intelligence in the war with Japan* (Wilmington, DE: Scholarly Resources, 1988).

—*At War at Sea: sailors and naval combat in the Twentieth Century* (NY: Viking, 2001).

Stille, M., *Imperial Japanese Navy Aircraft Carriers, 1921–45* (Oxford: Osprey, 2005).

Stinnett, R., *Day of Deceit: the truth about FDR and Pearl Harbor* (NY: Free Press, 1999).

Stoler, M., *Allies and Adversaries: the Joint Chiefs of Staff, the Grand Alliance and US strategy in World War II* (Chapel Hill: North Carolina UP, 2000).

Storry, R., *Japan and the Decline of the West in Asia, 1894–1943* (London: Longman, 1979).

Straus, U., *The Anguish of Surrender: Japanese POWs of World War II* (Seattle: Washington UP, 2003).

Sun Tzu, *The Art of War*, translated, with a historical introduction by R. Sawyer (Boulder, CO: Westview, 1994).

Tanaka, Y., *Hidden Horrors: Japanese war crimes in World War II* (Boulder, CO: Westview, 1996).

Thach, J., "Butch O'Hare and the Thach Weave," in E. Wooldridge (ed.), *Carrier Warfare in the Pacific: an oral history collection* (Washington, DC: Smithsonian Institution, 1993).

Thompson, J., *The Imperial War Museum Book of the War in Burma, 1942–1945* (London: Sidgwick & Jackson, 2002).

Thorne, C., *Allies of a Kind: the United States, Britain, and the war against Japan, 1941–1945* (Oxford: OUP, 1978).

—*The Issue of War: states, societies and the Far Eastern conflict of 1941–1945* (London, Hamish Hamilton, 1985).

Till, G., "Adopting the aircraft carrier: the British, American and Japanese case studies," in A. Millett and W. Murray (eds.), *Military Innovation in the Interwar Period* (Cambridge: CUP, 1996).

Tillman, B., *Clash of the Carriers: the true story of the Marianas Turkey Shoot of World War II* (NY: Nal Caliber, 2005).

Tobe, R., "Tojo Hideki as war leader," in Bond and Tachikawa (eds.), *British and Japanese Military Leadership in the Far Eastern War, 1941–1945* (Abingdon: Frank Cass, 2004).

Toland, J., *Infamy: Pearl Harbor and its aftermath* (Garden City, NY: Doubleday, 1982).

Tsuji, M., *Japan's Greatest Victory, Britain's Worst Defeat* (NY: Sarpedon, 1993).

Tsuzuki, C., *The Pursuit of Power in Modern Japan, 1825–1995* (Oxford: OUP, 2000).

United States Strategic Bombing Survey (USSBS), *Japanese Military and Naval Intelligence Division* (Washington, DC: Government Printing Office, 1946).

—*Summary Report, Pacific War*, (Washington, DC: Government Printing Office, 1946).

von Clausewitz, C., *On War*, Indexed Edition, edited and translated by M. Howard and P. Paret (Princeton: Princeton UP, 1984).

Warner, D. et al., *Disaster in the Pacific: new light on the battle of Savo island* (Annapolis: Naval Institute Press, 1992).

Warner, D., P. Warner and S. Senoo, *The Sacred Warriors: Japan's suicide legions* (NY: Von Nostrand Reinhold, 1982).

Warren, A., *Singapore, 1942: Britain's greatest defeat* (London: Hambledon, 2002).

Watson, M., *Chief of Staff: Prewar Plans and Preparations*, in series *United States Army in World War II: The War Department* (Washington, DC: Office of the Chief of Military History, 1950–55).

Watts, A. and B. Gordon, *The Imperial Japanese Navy* (NY: Doubleday, 1971).

Weinberg, G., *A World at Arms: a global history of World War II* (Cambridge: CUP, 1994).

Werrell, K., *Blankets of Fire: US bombers over Japan during World War II* (Washington, DC: Smithsonian Institution, 1996).

Willmott, H., *Empires in the Balance: Japanese and Allied Pacific strategies to April 1942* (Annapolis: Naval Institute Press, 1982).

—*Grave of a Dozen Schemes: British naval planning and the war against Japan, 1943–45* (London: Airlife, 1996).

—*The War With Japan: the period of balance, May 1942 – October 1943* (Wilmington, DE: Scholarly Resources, 2002).

—*The Battle of Leyte Gulf: the last fleet action* (Bloomington: Indiana UP, 2005).

Winton, J., *ULTRA in the Pacific: how breaking Japanese codes and cyphers affected naval operations against Japan, 1941–1945* (London: Leo Cooper, 1993).

Wohlstetter, R., *Pearl Harbor: Warning and Decision* (Stanford, CA: Stanford UP, 1962).

Wood, J., *Japanese Military Strategy in the Pacific War: was defeat inevitable?* (Lanham, MD: Rowman & Littlewood, 2007).

Wooldridge, E. (ed.)., *Carrier Warfare in the Pacific: an oral history collection* (Washington, DC: Smithsonian Institution, 1993).

Y'Blood, W., *Red Sun Setting: the Battle of the Philippine Sea* (Annapolis: Naval Institute Press, 1981).

Yoshimura, A., *Zero Fighter*, translated by R. Kaiho and M. Gregson (Westport, CT: Praeger, 1996).

ARTICLES

Allen, L., "Japanese intelligence systems," *Journal of Contemporary History*, 22, (1987), 547–62.

Alperovitz, G., R. L. Messer and B. Bernstein, "Marshall, Truman and the decision to drop the bomb," in *International Security*, 16/3, (1991–92), 204–21.

Bernstein, B., "Understanding the atomic bomb and the Japanese surrender: missed opportunities, little-known near disasters and modern history," in *Diplomatic History*, 19/2 (1995), 227–73.

—"Compelling Japan's Surrender Without the A-bomb, Soviet Entry or Invasion: reconsidering the US Bombing Survey's early-surrender conclusions," in *Journal of Strategic Studies*, 18/2 (1995), 101–48.

—"Truman and the A-bomb: targeting non-combatants, using the bomb and his defending the "decision,"" in *Journal of Military History*, 62/3, (1998), 547–70.

—"Reconsidering Truman's claim of 'half a million American lives' saved by the atomic bomb: the construction and deconstruction of a myth," in *Journal of Strategic Studies*, 22/1, (March 1999), 55–90.

Bix, H., "Japan's delayed surrender: a reinterpretation," in *Diplomatic History*, 19/2, (1995), 197–225.

Cowman, I., "Main fleet to Singapore? Churchill, the Admiralty and Force Z," in *Journal of Strategic Studies*, 17/2, (1994), 79–93.

Drea, E., "In the army barracks of Imperial Japan," in *Armed Forces and Society*, 15/3, (1989), 329–48.

Ferris, J., "Worthy of some better enemy?: the British estimate of the Imperial Japanese Army, and the fall of Singapore, 1919–1941," in *Canadian Journal of History*, 28/2, (1993), 223–56.

Ford, D., "Strategic culture, intelligence assessment and the conduct of the Pacific War, 1941–1945: the British-Indian and Imperial Japanese armies in comparison," in *War in History*, 14/1, (2007), 63–95.

—"The best equipped army in Asia?: US military intelligence and the Imperial Japanese Army before the Pacific War, 1919–1941, in *International Journal of Intelligence and Counterintelligence*, 21/1, (2008), 86–121.

—"Dismantling the 'lesser men' and 'supermen' myths: US intelligence on the Imperial

Japanese Army after the fall of the Philippines, winter 1942 to spring 1943," in *Intelligence and National Security*, 24/4 (2009), 542–73.

—"Intelligence and the US Army's operations in the Pacific theatres, 1943–45: lessons learned and methods applied," in *War in History*, 16/3 (2009), 325–58.

—"Realistic caution and ambivalent optimism: US intelligence assessments and war preparations against Japan, 1918–1941, in *Diplomacy and Statecraft*, 21/2, (2010), 175–201.

—"US perceptions of military culture and the Japanese army's performance during the Pacific War," in *War and Society*, 29/1 (2010), 71–93.

Fukaya, H., "Japan's wartime carrier construction," in *United States Naval Institute Proceedings*, 81, (September 1955), 1031–6.

Fukudome S., in Evans, D. (ed.), *The Japanese Navy in World War II: in the words of former Japanese naval officers, 2nd edition* (Annapolis: Naval Institute Press, 1986).

Halsey, W., "The battle for Leyte Gulf," in *United States Naval Institute Proceedings*, 78, (May 1952), 487–95.

Laurie, C., "The ultimate dilemma of psychological warfare in the Pacific: enemies who don't surrender and GIs who don't take prisoners," in *War and Society*, 14, (1996), 99–120.

Millett, A. and W. Murray, "The effectiveness of military organizations," in *International Security*, 11/1, (1986), 37–71.

Minear, R., "Cross-cultural perception and World War II: American Japanists of the 1940s and their images of Japan," in *International Studies Quarterly*, 24/4, (1980), 555–80.

Pape, R., "Why Japan Surrendered," in *International Security*, 18/2, (1993), 154–201.

Sarantakes, N., "One last crusade: the British Pacific Fleet and its impact on the British-American alliance," in *English Historical Review*, 121/491, (2006), 429–66.

Weir, G., "The search for an American submarine strategy and design, 1916–1936," in *Naval War College Review*, 44, (Winter 1991), 34–48.

Wilds, T., "The admiral who lost his fleet," in *United States Naval Institute Proceedings*, 77 (November 1951), 1175–81.

Index